THE
LATINO
ENCYCLOPEDIA

THE
LATINO
ENCYCLOPEDIA

Volume 6

Spanish borderlands – Zeno Gandía, Manuel

Index

Editors
RICHARD CHABRÁN AND RAFAEL CHABRÁN

Marshall Cavendish
New York • London • Toronto

Published By
Marshall Cavendish Corporation
99 White Plains Road
Tarrytown, New York 10591-9001
United States of America

∞ The paper in these volumes conforms to the American National Standard for Permanence of Paper for Printed Library Materials, Z39.48-1984.

Library of Congress Cataloging-in-Publication Data

The Latino encyclopedia / editors, Richard Chabrán, and Rafael Chabrán,
     p. cm.
   Includes bibliographical references and index.
   1. Hispanic Americans—Encyclopedias. I. Chabrán, Richard II. Chabrán, Rafael
E184.S75L357 1995
973′ .0468′003—dc20   95-13144
ISBN 0-7614-0125-3 (set).   CIP
ISBN 0-7614-0131-8 (vol. 6).

First Printing

PRINTED IN THE UNITED STATES OF AMERICA

Contents

CONTENTS

THE
LATINO
ENCYCLOPEDIA

Spanish borderlands: The mid-continent region alternately described as the American Southwest and northern Mexico. Herbert E. Bolton, who is credited with coining the term, and many of his students focused on the era of Spanish exploration and settlement, thereby creating an academic historical discipline inclusive of Spain's royal authority from 1536 to 1821. Subsequent scholars have focused on the region as a borderland even after Mexico's independence in 1821, as Mexico and the United States continued to influence each other after 1821 and even after political boundaries were altered through the MEXICAN AMERICAN WAR (1846-1848). This article discusses the Spanish borderlands as the region during Spanish control. (*See* BORDER REGION AND CULTURE for information on the area after 1848.)

Sixteenth Century Exploration. Early Spanish explorations of the northern frontier did little to encourage colonization. Tales of emeralds and lost cities prompted voyages along the Pacific Coast and treks across western Texas north to what is now Kansas. The reality of adobe towns and wandering tribes, however, destroyed the images described by Álvar Núñez CABEZA DE VACA after his rescue in 1536.

In the fifty-year period beginning with Christopher Columbus' discovery of the New World in 1492 and including Francisco Vázquez de CORONADO's land expedition into the Kansas heartland beginning in 1540 as well as Juan Rodríguez CABRILLO's naval exploration of the California coast in 1542, Spain contributed to knowledge of North America on a scale and with significance hitherto unknown. Spain approached the region in two different ways in 1536. Nuño de GUZMÁN's soldiers were on a slave-hunting expedition from Nueva Galicia when they found Álvar Núñez CABEZA DE VACA, Alonso de Castillo, Andrés Dorantes, and Dorantes' Moorish slave Esteban, the four survivors from the ill-fated expedition led by Pánfilo de NARVÁEZ into Florida in 1528. Narváez had searched in horsehide boats for rescuers, making a futile attempt at following the coast to Spanish villages. Guzmán's troops were surprised to find three Spaniards and a Spanish black slave among the Indians they wished to enslave.

Spanish soldiers of the Coronado expedition. (Institute of Texan Cultures)

During the eight years that the survivors had been lost, the second *audiencia*, or system of administration and justice, had been replaced by the viceroyalty system. The first viceroy, Antonio de Mendoza, took office in 1535. It was with the viceroy that Cabeza de Vaca shared his accounts of emeralds, buffalo, and native tribes living in highly populated and well-constructed towns. His story not only supported earlier tales of wealth to the north but also encouraged Spaniards who wished to replicate the exploits of Hernán CORTÉS and Francisco PIZARRO. Cabeza de Vaca's travels probably took him through present southern Texas and Chihuahua. His account inspired Hernán Cortés to send Francisco de Ulloa to explore the Pacific Coast in 1539.

Cabeza de Vaca's accounts confirmed suspicions established by earlier explorations. Earlier claims about the Pacific Coast made by Vasco Nuñez de Balboa encouraged exploration, and Cortés had sent three vessels into the Pacific Ocean in 1527. By 1532, Cortés sent forces under Hurtado de Mendoza into northern Sinaloa. Baja California was discovered the following year. Believing that an island rather than a peninsula had been discovered, Cortés personally led a colony to La Paz, on the southern tip of the peninsula, in 1535. La Paz bears the distinction of being the first colonial effort in California, but within a short time the colony was abandoned.

Viceroy Mendoza anticipated Cortés' reaction to Cabeza de Vaca's reports. He sent a reconnaissance group north under the command of Fray Marcos de NIZA in 1538. When all four of the rescued Spaniards from the Narváez expedition declined to return to the northern wilderness, Mendoza enlisted Esteban as guide for Fray Marcos. Slowed by the burden of a caravan, Fray Marcos sent Esteban ahead with instructions to send back a crucifix as a signal of a discovery. The size of the cross would indicate the significance of the find. A cross as large as a person was the only message sent back by Esteban. As Fray Marcos hurried in anticipation of a glorious discovery, survivors brought back the story of Esteban's death at the hands of Zuni Indians.

The Search for Cíbola. The discovery of the city of CÍBOLA was reported by Fray Marcos upon his return to the viceroy. He not only described the Zuni Indian

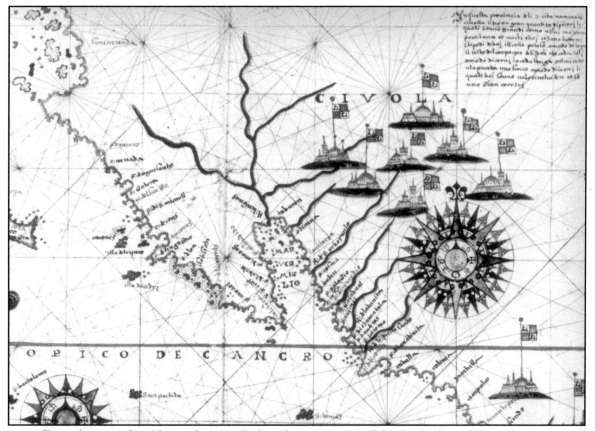

Sixteenth century Spanish map depicting the legendary seven cities of Cíbola. (Institute of Texan Cultures)

pueblo as one of seven such cities but also reported that precious stones and gold covered the Indian temples. Viewing the pueblo from a distance may have played tricks on the priest's eyes. The real trick would be played on those Spaniards who invested their fortunes in the subsequent 1540-1542 expedition led by Francisco Vázquez de Coronado.

With Fray Marcos as his guide, Coronado captured Cíbola. When the reality of adobe instead of jewels greeted Coronado's Spaniards, the commander sent the cleric south, with Coronado's soldiers threatening and cursing him. Coronado then began to send scouting parties in several directions. Pedro de Tovar went northwest and encountered the Hopi Pueblos. García López de Cárdenas went west but could not cross the Grand Canyon. Spanish scouting parties soon took Coronado to the Rio Grande, where, after excursions north to Taos and east, he established his winter camp north of present-day Albuquerque.

In the spring of 1541, Coronado began to seek the city of Quivira on the eastern plains. He had been told of Quivira by an Indian, called the Turk, whom the Spaniards met at Pecos Pueblo. The Indian promised to lead the Spaniard to the area that he called his native land. Spanish soldiers followed the Turk south on the Pecos River and, following custom, used their carts to build a bridge for hesitant sheep as they crossed the Pecos to follow the Canadian River onto the plains of western Texas.

Encountering the ravines near the Palo Duro canyon, Coronado divided his forces. The majority returned to the base camp, while Coronado followed the Turk to central Kansas. Believing that the Turk's design was to lead Spaniards to a death on the plains, the Spaniards strangled the Turk and began a return to the Rio Grande for winter camp. They probably followed the route of the SANTA FE TRAIL on their return to New Mexico. In the spring of 1542, the expedition returned to Mexico City the way it had come. The explorers returned wiser but also inspired to save souls among the pagans. Father Juan de PADILLA returned in 1542 to Kansas, where he became a Christian martyr.

Exploration of California and the Pacific. Juan Rodríguez CABRILLO sailed the California coast to the Oregon region while Ruy López de Villalobos sailed in November, 1542, to take possession of the Philippines. The viceroyalty of New Spain would include the Philippines as an administrative unit. Spain's Manila trade would necessitate ports along the California coast.

The initial era of exploration established a clear knowledge of the obstacles involved. The missionary became the initial instrument of Spanish colonial control. The second half of the sixteenth century saw little Spanish activity in the borderlands other than the work of religious and rescue parties.

From 1580 to 1640, Portugal was united with Spain. Manila became the center for commerce of the combined empires in the Pacific. With the heightening of tension between England and Spain, Spaniards moved to protect their commercial enterprises and their American lands through settlements.

In the Pacific, Francis Drake's freebooting expedition to California earned him knighthood from Queen Elizabeth in 1579. It also convinced Spaniards that to possess, one should occupy. Englishman Thomas Cavendish plundered Spanish ships off the point of California, and Spain's English competitors replaced the Portuguese in the late sixteenth century. Attacks by both sea and land alarmed Spanish authorities.

In 1595, Sebastián Vizcaíno, who had been captured by Cavendish, received authority to colonize California. This initial effort was disbanded by 1597. Additional exploring expeditions were conducted in the following years. The expeditions yielded results similar to those of Juan Rodríguez CABRILLO almost sixty years earlier.

Spaniards were concerned not only with foreign threats along the coast but also with the conversion of Indians into Catholics as well as citizens. Missionaries and explorers shouted the *requerimiento* to Indians, informing them of their new legal status as Spanish citizens.

Between 1542 and 1598, a number of Spanish expeditions entered the northern regions of New Spain (Mexico). Fray Agustín Rodríguez and Francisco Sánchez Chamuscado went in 1580 in search of New Mexican Indians to convert. In 1582, a rescue and trading expedition was led north by Fray Bernardino Beltrán and Antonio de Espejo. After learning of the deaths of the missionaries, Espejo decided to explore the area. A miner by profession, Espejo located mines in western Arizona and collected samples of minerals throughout the region.

The Espejo expedition aroused new ambitions for the New Mexico region. Applicants competed for authority to colonize while several Spaniards led unauthorized groups north. Gaspar Castaño de Sosa led Spaniards from Nuevo León to the Pecos Pueblos before his capture and arrest. Captain Francisco Leyva de Bonilla and Antonio Gutiérrez de Humaña in 1594 led a priestless and illegal expedition onto the plains of eastern Colorado. Most of the expedition was lost. An

Spaniards tried to control Indian populations by incorporating them into Spanish communities. (Arizona Historical Society)

Indian survivor told the tale of the lives lost without benefit of clergy. Through that expedition, a Colorado river gained a name, *El Río de las Animas Perdidas en Purgatorio* (The River of the Lost Souls in Purgatory).

Settlements. Three major Spanish enclaves developed on the northern frontier of the viceroyalty of New Spain in North America. New Spain's northernmost frontier included all or parts of the present-day states of Wyoming, Utah, Nevada, New Mexico, Arizona, Oklahoma, Colorado, Texas, California, and Louisiana. The upper Rio Grande region was the nucleus of the New Mexico community. The California coast and the Texas region formed the second and third major Spanish enclaves in the Spanish borderlands. The region would go through a variety of political designs during the Spanish era, with the most significant being the creation of the *provincias internas* in 1776.

The nature of the Spanish impulse to explore and colonize had been cultivated through the beliefs of Queen Isabella. When Isabella emphasized religious purity through the expulsion of the Moors and the Jews from Spain, she also established institutions to effect her beliefs. *Cofradías* (brotherhoods) would tie together the secular and the religious, and the Holy Of-

fice of the Inquisition would ensure purity of thought. The *Casa de Contratación*, the central trading house of Spain, organized in 1503, tried to guarantee that only the "worthy" would migrate to the new Spanish domain.

By 1494, Isabella had decided that the Indians of the Americas had souls and therefore should be converted to Christianity and incorporated into the political empire. Pagans, who were ignorant of Spanish religion, became the targets of conversion efforts. A Spanish notary would travel along with a priest on every official venture and inform natives that they were immediately subject to Spain. Pagans would thus be converted; heretics would feel the force of Spanish steel.

Spaniards believed that they could harness the Indian labor force through the *encomienda* (grant of land and its resident people) or the *repartimiento* (allocated labor system). Despite the efforts of defenders of the Indians such as Bartolomé DE LAS CASAS and such legislative protections as the New Laws of 1542, native peoples of the Americas suffered a demographic disaster as the Spanish colonization effort proceeded.

Attempting to control Indians through a political village structure, the Spaniards caused horrific living conditions. The Spanish colonizers attempted to incorporate Indians into the empire through an urbanization process. The process proved to be a major factor in the spread of Old World diseases to the New World. Villages, *presidios* (forts), and missions were all designed not only to convert the Indians but also to incorporate the Indians into the body politic. They even employed a Caribbean term, CACIQUE, for the Indian village leader. Detribalized Indians, called *genízaros*, were brought into Spanish families. Villages were established for the Indian populations.

The Spanish passion for religious purity and obedience often resulted in soldiers pursuing Indians who tried to escape the control of religious clerics. Presidios were often constructed near missions, with the presidio's soldiers reinforcing religious dictates and keeping the newly "converted" Indians within the geographic bounds of the religious community.

New Mexico. The contract to colonize New Mexico was granted in 1595 to Juan de OÑATE, who gained the titles of *adelantado* (governor) and captain-general. Along with those titles, he had the power to grant lands and *encomiendas*. In February, 1598, Oñate left the interior with one hundred thirty soldiers, some of their families, a band of Franciscan missionaries, and more than seven thousand stock animals. Oñate opened a more direct route, traveling north along what would become known as El CAMINO REAL.

Sending groups to explore the plains as well as to reach the Gulf of California, Oñate covered much of the same terrain as Coronado had fifty years earlier. Thirty-five colonists received *encomiendas* from Oñate. By 1608, he had lost the support of royal authorities and was replaced by another governor.

In 1609, Santa Fe was established as the new capital of the province. Santa Fe was organized into distinct barrios that originally included Tlascalan Indian allies in the Barrio de Analco. This barrio would become the home of detribalized Indians (*genízaros*) in the eighteenth century.

Although treasure and rich mines remained illusive for those early Spanish colonists, the cross had traveled with the sword, and by 1617 more than fourteen thousand natives had been baptized, and eleven churches had been built. Religious objectives thus were being met. In 1630, Fray Alonso de Benavides reported that twenty-five missions existed, serving ninety pueblos with a combined population of about sixty thousand Indians.

On August 10, 1680, New Mexican natives burdened by forced tribute payment and the suppression of their religion united in revolt under the direction of Popé, a medicine man of San Juan Pueblo. During POPÉ'S REVOLT, twenty-one missionaries became martyrs, and more than four hundred Spaniards fell in the surprise insurrection. More than two thousand Spaniards fled the region of New Mexico, many of them settling in the El Paso del Norte community, founded in 1659 at the site of present-day Ciudad Juárez.

In 1691, Diego de VARGAS Zapata Luján y Ponce de León was made governor of the area. He promised to reconquer the Pueblo Indians and establish a colonial presence. The following year, he began a campaign of resettlement. A colony of eight hundred soldiers and settlers went north to reoccupy the upper Rio Grande Valley. For the next three years, missions were reestablished, a consolidation of the pueblos was begun, and new Spanish villages were established. These efforts were accompanied by a series of battles that continued through 1696.

The reconquest was completed by 1697. Spanish settlement would continue until the independence of Mexico in 1821. Spanish New Mexico was structured into the three prefects of Rio Arriba, Rio Abajo, and Santa Fe. By 1760, almost eight thousand Spaniards were living in fourteen settlements in New Mexico; there were more than thirty-five hundred around El Paso del Norte. By the time of Mexican independence in 1821, New Mexico reportedly had nearly fifty thousand residents.

Texas. The late seventeenth century saw initial Spanish movement into other borderland regions, such as Texas. The first serious attempt to settle in Texas took place in 1690, when Domingo de Terán de los Ríos was declared governor of the province of Texas. The Texas project was abandoned after hostile Indians forced missionaries to withdraw in 1693. Spaniards were concerned with French movements in the area and sent General Alonso de LEÓN on several excursions to the region. Between 1699 and 1703, Spanish missionaries established three missions and a presidio near modern Eagle Pass, Texas. This area was a trading site for Indian tribes. Spaniards hoped that by establishing settlements there, they would find both many souls to salvage and revenues for the Spanish treasury.

The Spanish continued efforts to expand into Texas from Coahuila. A continuing French menace prompted the decision in 1715 to reoccupy Texas. An expedition under Domingo Ramon and Franciscan missionaries planted the seed from which San Antonio would grow. By the next year, missions, presidios, and towns had been established to counter the growing French influence among the Indians.

By early 1719, Spain was at war with France. The European conflict spread to North America, and border conflicts erupted from Florida to Colorado. Even though a truce was declared in 1720, the Pedro de Villazur expedition to Colorado was massacred by Indians using French arms. From Coahuila, the governor raised an army of more than five hundred men that set out, along with a band of missionaries, to take possession of Texas for Spain. Texas and Coahuila had been under the same governor, but Texas was separated, and

a capital was established at Los Adaes (present-day Robeline, Louisiana). The region's western boundary was the Medina River.

A general inspection of frontier outposts was conducted by Pedro de Rivera between the years 1724 and 1728. That inspection prompted a policy of reinforcement of troops. By 1731, additional colonists had arrived directly from the Canary Islands.

San Antonio de Béjar, the center of early Texas, contained five missions and a *presidio*. The greatest threats seemed to come from the Indians in the early eighteenth century. Despite wars and campaigns against

Early Spanish explorers in Texas. (Institute of Texan Cultures)

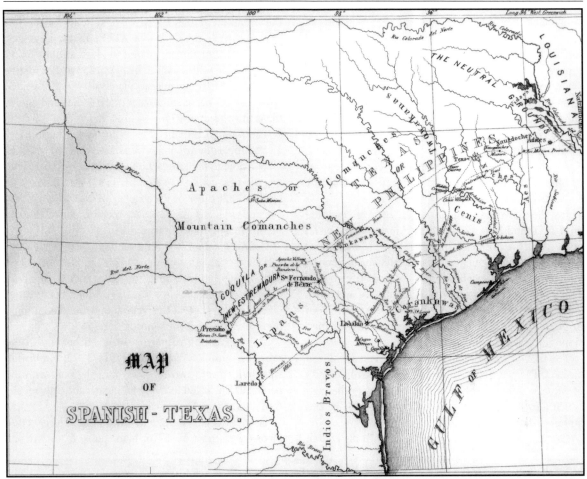

Map of Spanish Texas showing Indian tribe locations. (Institute of Texan Cultures)

Indians, the missionaries seemed to be the best answer to the repeated attacks, as military retaliation had not worked. Missionaries began to spread throughout Texas between 1745 and 1760, but it was a new war with England that encouraged new Spanish colonization on the Gulf Coast.

Political strife created Nuevo Santander, which extended from Tampico and the Pánuco River to the Medina River. It overlapped jurisdiction with Texas until 1775, when the Texas-Nuevo Santander boundary was established at the Nueces River. Conflicting claims by France and Spain to eastern Texas continued to fester until the ADAMS-ONÍS TREATY of 1819. France and Spain disputed the region from the Trinity River to the Mississippi.

Arizona. Arizona came under a variety of jurisdictions during the Spanish era. It fell variously under the political or religious jurisdictions in Sonora, New Mexico, Chihuahua, and California. It was first part of Pimería Alta, joining the interior of Mexico and the

Mexican states of Sinaloa and Sonora. The Jesuits gained a religious monopoly in Arizona and began to assert military and civil authority on the peninsula of Baja California.

Baja California had long been thought to be an island rather than a peninsula. Father Eusebio Francisco KINO's explorations of Arizona and lower California proved that Baja California was a peninsula, and in 1705 he published a map showing his results. Kino founded the mission of SAN XAVIER DEL BAC in 1700, along with several others, and established stock ranches to support missions. The most influential person in the area, Kino died in 1711.

In 1741, Jesuits were assigned to the region, and settlement was authorized to the Gila River despite Indian troubles in Sinaloa and Sonora. The Jesuits also began to establish missions in Baja California while they explored northward. In response to Indian attacks, a genocidal war was begun by Sonora's Governor Diego Parrilla. The war succeeded in suppressing Indian attacks, and two new presidios were founded.

Provincias Internas. The outcome of the French and Indian War (1689-1763) was a virtual elimination of France from North America. Spain received the Louisiana region as compensation for its losses in the war. Although the French were no longer a threat, England supplanted the French advances on the east, and Russia began to threaten Spanish sovereignty in upper California. Charles III took a series of steps to address Spain's North American empire. The Bourbon reforms resulted in a different political configuration but few substantive changes.

José de Galvéz, as *visitador general*, was entrusted with accomplishing fiscal reform. He embarked on an analysis of the northern frontier region. The marques de Rubí in 1766 began a trip from Louisiana to Sonora. He recommended establishing a chain of fifteen presidios as well as other actions, including war and abandonment of outposts. In 1767, Jesuits were ordered out of New Spain. This resulted in further shifts of missions and towns in the region.

The task of salvation of souls was granted to Franciscans. The president of the College of San Fernando of Mexico, Junípero SERRA, became a California missionary. José de Galvéz went to California in 1768 and authorized more troops and missionaries.

Galvéz's recommendations to Charles III resulted in the creation of the *intendencia* system. Under this plan, the northern region would be split into provinces, each organized under an independent military commander and with several bishoprics. An alternative scheme of creating a new viceroyalty was rejected when Galvéz became minister of the Indies and put his ideas into effect in 1776.

The internal provinces were put under the military and political control of a *comandante general* who was responsible to the king. Chihuahua became the capital, and the first *comandante* (1776-1783) was Teodoro de Croix, the brother of the viceroy of New Spain. New Mexico would send delegate Pedro Bautista Pino to the Spanish parliament in 1810.

California. In 1769, joint land and sea expeditions set out to establish missions and presidios at San Diego and Monterey; with this, the colonization of upper California began. The peninsula had long been recognized as important in the Manila trade, and additional ports were desired in the northern region.

The conversion of pagans weighed heavily in the Spanish sense of responsibility. In 1772, California was divided into two religious jurisdictions, with the peninsula entrusted to the Dominicans and upper California left to the Franciscans.

The Californias were under the political jurisdiction of one governor. By 1776, land routes from Arizona

An eighteenth century depiction of the mission at Monterey, California. (Museum of New Mexico)

had tied the provinces together, and Spaniards believed that New Mexico, along with Sonora, could be linked to California. New Mexican priests Silvestre Vélez de Escalante and Francisco Atanasio Domínguez attempted to find a land route across Colorado, Utah, and Arizona.

The following year, the capital was moved to Monterey. New communities were established in San Jose (1777), Los Angeles (1781), and Santa Barbara (1782). California found that it could not depend on overland trade with New Mexico or through Sonora. Its destiny appeared to be tied to the sea.

By the time of Junípero Serra's death in 1784, California had nine self-sufficient missions. By 1821, there were twenty missions with more than twenty thousand Indians resident.

Summary. Spain wanted to spread its faith and culture throughout the Americas. Early exploration gave the Spaniards an idea of the general dimensions of how the Spanish Empire could expand in North America. Motivated by religion, nationalism, and personal advancement, Spaniards began to colonize the northern region of the viceroyalty of New Spain in 1598. In the seventeenth century, Spanish property and claims were challenged by the French, the English, and the Russians. Survival, the basic concern of empire building, led to the expansion of Spanish settlements in Texas and California.

In 1810, a wave of republican fervor and the stirrings of revolution swept the region. In 1821, the viceroyalty of New Spain came to an end with the independence of Mexico from Spain. Although an attempt to regain the empire was attempted in 1829, the Spanish phase had come to an end. Spanish origins, in combination with Indian societies, provided the foundation for the Republic of Mexico and the American Southwest. —*David A. Sandoval*

SUGGESTED READINGS:

• Bolton, Herbert. *Bolton and the Spanish Borderlands.* Edited by John Francis Bannon. Norman: University of Oklahoma Press, 1964. An excellent introduction by a Bolton protégé is combined with six sections of selected Bolton presentations concerning the borderlands in American historical context, initial exploration, missionary and political impulses, and regional development.

• Bolton, Herbert E. *Coronado: Knight of Pueblos and Plains.* 2d ed. Albuquerque: University of New Mexico Press, 1964. Bolton's classic tale of Coronado remains the most authoritative and definitive study of this Spanish exploration in the sixteenth century.

• Bolton, Herbert E., ed. *Spanish Exploration in the Southwest, 1542-1706.* Reprint. New York: Barnes & Noble, 1967. A chronological account of several Spanish expeditions in California, New Mexico, and Texas. The original diaries and accounts are placed into context with well-written introductions.

• Bolton, Herbert E., and Thomas Maitland Marshall. *The Colonization of North America, 1492-1783.* New York: Hafner, 1971. An analysis of French, English, and Spanish colonizing efforts in North America, presented in chronological and topical forms.

• Chávez, Angelico. *My Penitente Land: Reflections on Spanish New Mexico.* Albuquerque: University of New Mexico Press, 1974. A combination of scholarly and personal insights into the culture and history of New Mexico.

• John, Elizabeth A. H. *Storms Brewed in Other Men's Worlds: The Confrontation of Indians, Spanish, and French in the Southwest, 1540-1795.* College Station: Texas A&M Press, 1975. A comprehensive and detailed analysis of Spanish and French reactions to Indian societies, with a special focus on the interrelationships of Texas, New Mexico, and Chihuahua.

• Jones, Oakah L., Jr. *Los Paisanos: Spanish Settlers on the Northern Frontier of New Spain.* Norman: University of Oklahoma Press, 1979. A cultural history of New Mexican settlements, with insight into cultural adaptation.

• Nostrand, Richard L. *The Hispano Homeland.* Norman: University of Oklahoma Press, 1992. A study of New Mexico as a *patria chica.* Addresses elements of cultural geographic dynamic fusion from Oñate to the American period.

• Simmons, Marc. *Spanish Government in New Mexico.* 2d ed. Albuquerque: University of New Mexico Press, 1990. Essential to understanding the changing complexities of Spanish political structures and their relative impact on New Mexican society.

• Spicer, Edward H. *Cycles of Conquest: The Impact of Spain, Mexico, and the United States on the Indians of the Southwest, 1533-1960.* Tucson: University of Arizona Press, 1962. A comprehensive analysis and comparison of Indian societies in the Arizona region, with detailed descriptions regarding assimilation and acculturation.

• Weber, David J. *The Spanish Frontier in North America.* New Haven, Conn.: Yale University Press, 1992. The Spanish borderlands are placed in the context of the entire Spanish empire in North America. Presents interrelationships from Florida through Louisiana and on to California.

Spanish Broadcasting System (founded 1983): Radio company. As of 1994, the Spanish Broadcasting system owned stations in the top three Latino markets: New York City (WSKQ-AM and FM), Los Angeles, California (originally KSKQ-AM and FM, changed to KLAX-FM in 1992), and Miami, Florida (WCMQ-AM and FM), in addition to a station in Key Largo, Florida (WZMQ-FM) that retransmitted the Miami station's signals.

In 1991, the combined AM and FM stations produced $23.1 million in revenue. In addition to operating its own stations, the system was the national sales representative for six stations in Texas, six in California, and three in Illinois. The company also developed revenues from promotions including concerts, sporting events, supermarket tie-ins, and on-air contests, as well as from Alarcon, the original founder's holdings in real estate. In 1990, the Spanish Broadcasting System's capital of $32.3 million made it the fifty-second largest Hispanic company in the United States.

In the Fall, 1992, Arbitron survey, KLAX-FM ranked as the top Spanish-language station in Los Angeles. The previous summer, the station had adopted a high-energy Mexican version of American "hot country" formats—a mixture of folk music popular in northern Mexico and *banda* music. The format gained a large following among Mexican Americans, the majority of the Los Angeles Hispanic population.

Spanish Conquest: Sixteenth century conquest by Spain of the AZTEC and MAYAN CIVILIZATIONS in Mexico as well as other indigenous peoples in South America and the Caribbean. The Spanish invasion of Mexico was the most spectacular event during the Hispanic conquest of the New World. Superior leadership, the devastating appearance of disease, and the negative aspects of Mesoamerican religion enabled Spain to triumph between 1519 and 1521.

Background. Aztec religion had weaknesses that enabled the Spanish conquerors to take advantage of critical miscalculations by MOCTEZUMA II, the Aztec ruler. Moctezuma was informed of a series of omens indicating negative future events. His soothsayers and interpreters mistakenly convinced Moctezuma to send gifts and invite the Spaniards to TENOCHTITLÁN, the Aztec capital. Moctezuma also became captivated by the belief that Hernán CORTÉS was QUETZALCÓATL, the benevolent god who was predicted to return at a

Engraving of a battle between Spaniards and Aztecs. (Institute of Texan Cultures)

The death of Moctezuma. (Institute of Texan Cultures)

particular time in the carefully elaborated Aztec calendar. The year 1519 happened to be a one-reed year, portending ominous events.

Spain's Military Advantages. Unlike Moctezuma, Cortés was a decisive leader. He obtained a mistress, La MALINCHE, who interpreted for and provided information to the Spanish conquerors. Without the aid of La Malinche, a noble from Coatzacoalcos, Cortés could not have communicated effectively with the indigenous tribes who joined his expedition against Moctezuma. Resentful of having to provide sacrificial victims to the god of war as well as pay high taxes to the Aztec rulers, groups such as the Tlaxcalans gave Cortés enough military support to overpower the Aztec armies.

Spain also enjoyed a military advantage over the Aztec formations sent against them. Spain had just finished the *reconquista* against the Moors, a seven-hundred-year period of intense conflict. The Spanish army was experienced and was Europe's finest. Its steel swords, horses, cannon, ships, and aggressive tactics enabled Cortés to achieve victory.

Finally, the indigenous peoples of Mexico fell to diseases Spain's conquistadores brought with them. Smallpox spread quickly with devastating consequences. Tens of thousands of native people died within a few weeks.

The Course of Battle. Although driven out of TE-NOCHTITLÁN in July, 1520, CORTÉS returned and triumphed. A diplomat of genius abilities, Cortés had encouraged more Indian allies to join him while persuading his own men not to defect. Canoes that Cortés had constructed overpowered the Aztec launches, giving the Spaniards control over the lake surrounding the island city of Tenochtitlán. The Aztec capital finally submitted on August 13, 1521.

Francisco PIZARRO, the Spanish conqueror of Peru, took advantage of a dynastic struggle after he arrived from Panama with about two hundred followers, including four brothers, a cousin, and other kin. After the death in 1535 of Huayna Capac, the Inca monarch, the court elite crowned Huayna Capac's son Huascar as king. Huayna Capac's other son, Atahualpa, responded by seizing Huascar and imprisoning him. When Atahualpa learned of the Spanish landings, he dismissed them as insignificant and assumed that he could defeat the Spanish easily.

When Pizarro realized that a civil war was taking place, he invited Atahualpa to the plains of Cajamarca, where, on November 16, 1532, the Spaniards killed several thousand indigenous soldiers. As in Mexico, the Incas hesitated to resist, in the belief that gifts of gold and silver would persuade the Spanish to leave. Although the Spanish fought among themselves constantly in Peru, the discovery of silver and mercury by 1563 drew the attention of the Spanish monarch, who finally established order under Pedro de la Gasca.

Other South American Conquests. The conquest of Chile resulted from Spanish success in Peru. In 1540, Pedro de Valdivia was given command of an expedition as a reward for his aid in capturing the Inca capital in 1538. After journeying down the coast, Valdivia in February, 1541, founded the city now known as Santiago. The imposition of labor demands provoked greater indigenous resistance than in any other South American region. The Araucanians held on to southern Chile and were undefeated until the 1880's.

Spanish occupation of Argentina resulted from a desire to find a route to Asia through the Rio de la Plata. The Spanish assumed that large quantities of precious metals awaited them in the southern cone region of South America. The cities of Asunción and Buenos Aires became permanent colonies. In the northwestern portion of Argentina, the Spanish established denser colonies. Beginning with Santiago del Estero in 1553, Mendoza in 1561, and San Juan in 1562, small Spanish colonies with a Hispanic upper class pacified the Indians and the black slaves purchased on the coast. These settlements existed primarily in order to supply the mines of Peru with food, woolens, and manufactured items. By the year 1650, Córdoba had five thousand inhabitants, Tucumán four thousand, and Buenos Aires three thousand.

The American Southwest. The first Spanish explorer to study the southwest was Alvar Núñez CABEZA DE VACA. Shipwrecked after setting out to Florida from Cuba, Cabeza de Vaca symbolized Spanish toughness by walking from the Texas coast to the gulf coast of California. The Spanish king, impressed by such heroics, named Cabeza de Vaca as governor of Paraguay. Dropped on the eastern coast of South America, Cabeza de Vaca walked inland to take up his new position.

Francisco Vázquez de CORONADO journeyed through New Mexico, Kansas, and Oklahoma in 1541 during a fruitless search for fabulous cities, the seven cities of CÍBOLA. Juan de OÑATE finally colonized New Mexico, which became the foundation of Hispanic life in the Southwest before Texas and California were effectively colonized in the early eighteenth century.

Spain put much effort toward consolidating the conquest of its American colonies. The administrators were usually able figures. The establishment of presidio fortresses and hundreds of cities anchored Hispanic life. The relentless efforts of Spanish clergymen and the energetic religious orders converted many indigenous people to Catholicism. The discovery of resource-rich mining areas lured many Spaniards to the area.

—*Douglas W. Richmond*

SUGGESTED READINGS: • Cortés, Hernán. *Letters from Mexico.* Translated and edited by A. R. Pagden. New York: Grossman, 1971. • Díaz del Castillo, Bernal. *The True History of the Conquest of New Spain.* Edited by Geraro Garcia. New York: Kraus Reprint, 1967. • León-Portilla, Miguel, ed. *The Broken Spears: The Aztec Account of the Conquest of Mexico.* Translated by Lysander Kemp. Boston: Beacon Press, 1972. • Lovett, A. W. *Early Habsburg Spain, 1517-1598.* New York: Oxford University Press, 1986. • Padden, Robert C. *The Hummingbird and the Hawk: Conquest and Sovereignty in the Valley of Mexico, 1503-1541.* New York: Harper & Row, 1970. • Vigil, Ralph H. "A Reappraisal of the Expedition of Pánfilo de Narváez to Mexico in 1520." *Revista de Historia de América,* 1974, 101-125. • White, Jon. *Cortés and the Downfall of the Aztec Empire.* New York: St. Martin's Press, 1971.

Spanish Harlem: Southern end of East Harlem, New York. Spanish Harlem, also known as "El Barrio," is the oldest Puerto Rican settlement on the U.S. mainland.

In the late 1890's, a small group of Puerto Ricans working for independence settled in New York, New York. Disappointed by the FORAKER ACT of 1900, which established U.S. dominance of the island, most returned to Puerto Rico. Their early presence, however, made New York a familiar point of reference for those who would follow.

Census data indicate that approximately one thousand Puerto Ricans were residing in New York in 1910. Among these were the founding members of the community that came to be known as "El Barrio" or Spanish Harlem.

Two factors had a direct effect on the migration of Puerto Ricans to the U.S. mainland in general and to

Puerto Rican children at play in New York City's Spanish Harlem. (Library of Congress)

Spanish Harlem in particular. First, the JONES ACT (1917) conferred U.S. citizenship upon Puerto Ricans, allowing them easy access to the mainland. Second, the United States curtailed immigration from Eastern and Southern Europe and Asia in the early 1920's. That policy and World War I resulted in U.S. labor shortages. More than fifty thousand Puerto Ricans followed the promise of economic opportunities to various stateside cities by 1930, but most were drawn to what was considered to be the Puerto Rican cultural center on the mainland, Spanish Harlem. The community was taking shape in an area of East Harlem that contained primarily Italian neighborhoods. As the number of Puerto Ricans increased, so did hostility toward them. In July, 1926, Puerto Ricans were physically attacked in what became known as the HARLEM RIOTS.

The second significant period of Puerto Rican migration to New York began during World War II and continued during the industrial growth of the 1950's. Census figures show that by 1950, Puerto Ricans accounted for 30 percent of the East Harlem population. This figure grew steadily over the next 15 years, reaching 41 percent by 1965. As it grew, the Puerto Rican community organized HERMANDADES (brotherhoods) that provided mutual aid and culturally cohesive activities. Political organizations like the Club Boriquen and La Liga Puertorriqueña also arose. Small businesses gave residents of Spanish Harlem access to familiar foods, their beloved music, and religious items. Drama and musical performances could be enjoyed at El Teatro Hispano. Culturally, the community flourished to the degree that, in 1969, El Museo del Barrio was founded to showcase Puerto Rican artists. The museum was recognized as the largest institution of its kind in the United States.

Spanish Harlem suffered the same economic decline throughout the 1970's and 1980's as the rest of New York and other urban centers in the Northeast and Midwest. An overwhelming loss of manufacturing jobs forced more people onto public assistance rolls. Housing stock deteriorated steadily, and blocks of tenements were abandoned. Despite the negative elements of urban life, there has been resilience in Spanish Harlem. Some of its residents have reclaimed empty city lots and turned them into gardens, colorful and bountiful manifestations of hope.

Spanish International Network (founded 1960): Television network. Emilio Azcárraga Vidaurreta and Reynold Anselmo created the Spanish International Network as a sister company to purchase and provide programming for their Spanish International Communications Corporation. This arrangement allowed Azcárraga, a Mexican national, to own a large share of the company. Federal Communications Commission regulations forbade issuing of licenses to non-U.S. citizens or to corporations with more than 20 percent foreign ownership but placed no such restrictions on network ownership. The television network and the Spanish International Communications Corporation were renamed Univisión in 1987 during negotiations for sale of the combined companies.

The network was the first Spanish-language network in the United States, eventually signing more than four hundred affiliate stations. By late 1986, Telemundo, a new network owned by the Reliance Capital Group, began to pose a challenge. It offered its first national broadcast in January, 1987.

The entry of Telemundo into the Spanish-language broadcast market came at a difficult time for Univisión. The company underwent a restructuring, and more than a dozen members of Univisión's news division resigned. These former Univisión employees formed Hispanic American Corporation, a news agency that produced the national news show for Telemundo. Univisión's restructuring, however, also resulted in the expansion of its news division. New ventures included the nation's first weekend Spanish-language news show and the first late-night national Spanish-language news show.

Spanish language—influence on U.S. and Canadian culture: Among human institutions, language is one of the most enduring in its effects. It is important to recognize this fact in any discussion of the influence of the Spanish language in North America.

Spanish has been extensively used on the North American continent for four centuries and continues to be the common language of almost all of Latin America. The Spanish settlement in St. Augustine, Florida, in 1565 predated the arrival of the English-speaking colonists in Roanoke, Jamestown, and Plymouth. More than three centuries ago, the area that is now New Mexico and Arizona was extensively inhabited by Spanish-speaking people.

In Florida, as well as in California, Spanish life, language, and culture are significant factors in modern society. In Texas, the intermixing of Spanish and English began early in the nineteenth century. In 1990, Spanish was spoken by approximately twenty-two million people across the United States. In many cities of the United States, including Los Angeles, California; Miami, Florida; Chicago, Illinois; and San Antonio, Texas, Spanish is spoken by a large proportion of the population. Many communities of the Southwest are almost as "Mexican" as towns in Mexico. Los Angeles is considered by some to be the second-largest "Mexican" city in the world.

Spanish is also very much alive in the literature written in the United States. Rolando HINOJOSA, Sandra María ESTEVES, Gloria ANZALDÚA, Elías Miguel Muñoz, Rosario Morales, Francisco X. Alarcón, and Dolores PRIDA are only a few of the U.S. authors who are as comfortable writing in Spanish as in English.

Place Names. One is constantly reminded of the Spanish past by place names. Hernán Cortés, the conquistador of the Aztec empire in Central Mexico, was also responsible for discovering the lower part of what the Spanish ultimately called the Californias, in reference to a place named in a Spanish novel.

Various Spanish expeditions named many of the places along their routes. The missionaries who accompanied these expeditions tended to use the names of saints as place names, choosing the saint whose day came closest to the date on which the place was reached.

Soldiers also named places, often choosing a name based on some incident or experience. Carpinteria, California, was so named because soldiers saw the natives building a boat; El Oso Flaco, California, got its name because soldiers killed a "lean bear" there.

During the colonization period, most of the important physical features in Spanish-occupied territory were given names. These include Mesa Verde and La

Veta Pass in Colorado and Río Hondo and Tierra Alta in Texas. The names of many cities and towns go back to missions, such as California's San Diego, Santa Barbara, and San Francisco. Pueblos and other California localities named by civil or ecclesiastical authorities include Monterey, Cabrillo, and Escalante.

After the American occupation, few attempts were made to change the Spanish and Indian names. Some were translated and some were garbled, but on the whole the U.S. Coast Survey, the U.S. Land Office, and other mapping agencies intentionally kept the names that were current or that were found on maps and documents.

The number of Spanish names found in the United States is enormous. California alone has more than four hundred Spanish names of cities and towns. What is more surprising is that Spanish place names can be found in almost every part of the United States. Some names recur many times. There are Mesas in at least eight states, Alamos in six, Cubas in six, Buenas Vistas in eight, Bonanzas in four, and an El Dorado in no less than thirteen. Combinations of Spanish and English words have been used to form many place names, for example, Altaville, Vacaville, Niña View, Lomita Park, and Hermosa Beach.

Adoption of Spanish Words. American English, for a variety of reasons, has adopted many Spanish words. In some cases, there existed no adequate words in English; such cases include tortilla, siesta, and cockroach.

A Spanish teacher at a U.S. high school. (James Shaffer)

Other words were taken into English for local color effects, for their richness of connotation, or for their humor or descriptive contribution. Among the words of this second type are rodeo and *mañana*. Many such words have undergone changes in spelling, pronunciation, and meaning. The word "rodeo," for example, originally meant a roundup of the livestock on a ranch but now is a staged contest emulating work done in a true rodeo.

Life on cattle ranches brought many Spanish words into the English vocabulary. Western cowboys learned the art of the lasso (including bronco busting and steer roping) from the Spanish and Mexican VAQUEROS with whom they worked. Those cowboys found it convenient and necessary to adopt Spanish names of various tools and processes.

Influences on Canada. Canada has not received as strong a Hispanic influence as has the United States. Canada's Spanish-speaking immigrants arrived primarily during the twentieth century. They can be divided in two groups, those coming from Spain or the Canary Islands, and those coming from Latin America.

The Spanish immigration is the older of the two. Economic hardship in the home country and the political cycle involving the Spanish Civil War in 1936 and the regime of Francisco Franco were decisive factors in motivating Spaniards to go to Canada.

Latin American immigration is more recent and has been more abrupt. In addition, the reasons for this immigration vary more widely. Each of the Spanish-speaking countries in Latin America has a complex history as well as its own political, social, and economic realities. Latin American immigrants to Canada seem to come from a broad range of middle classes, both urban and rural. The largest and perhaps most visible group is that of Chilean exiles.

The Spanish-speaking community in Canada is relatively small and fragmented, and its recent establishment is probably the main cause of this lack of cohesion and development. Its values lie in the human beings with creative capacity who make up that community and in their contribution to Canadian literature written in Spanish.   —*M. Cecilia Colombi*

SUGGESTED READINGS: • Beardsley, Theodore S., Jr. "Spanish in the United States." *Word* 33 (April-August, 1982): 15-27. • Bentley, Harold W. *A Dictionary of Spanish Terms in English.* New York: Octagon Books, 1973. • Cochran, Myra Bedel. *Where We Live: Our Spanish-Named Communities and Streets.* San Diego, Calif.: M. B. Cochran, 1965. • Curletti, Rosario. *Pathways to Pavements.* Santa Barbara, Calif.: County National Bank and Trust Company of Santa Barbara, 1950. • Gorden, Raymond L. *Spanish Personal Names as Barriers to Communication Between Latin Americans and North Americans.* Yellow Springs, Ohio: Antioch College, 1968. • Machalski, Andrew. *Hispanic Writers in Canada.* Ottawa, Canada: Department of the Secretary of State of Canada, 1988. • Río, Angel del. *El mundo hispánico y el mundo anglo-sajón en América.* Buenos Aires, Argentina: Asociación Argentina por la libertad de la cultura, 1960.

Spanish language—variations across Latino groups: "Latino" is a term that refers to all people in the United States of Spanish or Latin American origin. Unlike the term "HISPANIC," a label employed by the federal government in the 1970's to include all Spanish-origin subgroups, "Latino" has been used for many decades by various national-origin groups from Central and South America and the Spanish-speaking nations of the Caribbean.

LATINOS are by no means a homogeneous group: They represent a variety of national and ethnic groups. The major Latino subgroups are people of Mexican, Puerto Rican, and Cuban origin. Other smaller populations, such as people of Dominican, Nicaraguan, and Salvadoran origin, are growing rapidly. Historical evolution makes each group unique, but several factors deeply rooted in the formation of their cultural and national identities bind them together.

Foremost among these factors is Spanish, the home-country language of all the groups. Spanish was brought to the Americas by the main thrust of colonization in the sixteenth century. All people who speak Spanish understand each other, but their Spanish differs in dialect and in usage. Spanish speakers may therefore say that they speak Peruvian or Honduran rather than Spanish.

The varieties of Spanish spoken in the United States reflect the countries of origin of the Spanish-speaking communities as well as the conditions under which the language has developed in the United States. Generally, each group of people sharing common national and social origins tends to concentrate geographically. Contact with people with the same origins reinforces the use of regional features of the language.

Mexican Spanish. Spanish has been spoken in what is now the United States since the early seventeenth century, when an expedition commanded by Juan de OÑATE explored north into what is now New Mexico. Spanish-speaking people have lived in that region ever since. Mexican territory was incorporated into the

An ethnically diverse English as a Second Language class at a San Francisco community college. (Impact Visuals, Mark Ludak)

United States through the Texas revolution and the MEXICAN AMERICAN WAR (1846-1848). Various waves of Mexican immigration have also contributed to the varieties of Mexican Spanish spoken in the United States.

The oldest variety of Spanish spoken in the United States is found in New Mexico and Southern Colorado. It dates from the time of Spanish colonization in the seventeenth century. Descendants of the colonists often refer to themselves as HISPANOS. The consequences of Mexico being granted independence from Spain in 1821, followed by the Mexican American War, did not significantly change the language scenario of the Hispanos. It was only with the migration of English-speaking settlers that Spanish began to subside.

The region was relatively isolated, so that its Spanish was not much affected by changes in the Spanish used elsewhere. The variety of Spanish in the region is characterized by many features belonging to the formative period of the Spanish from Latin America. As in Caribbean Spanish, it weakens the "ess" sound at the ends of words as well as weakening the "j" and "y" sounds. Spanish speakers in this region use many words and expressions that have disappeared from varieties of Spanish used elsewhere.

In general, the Spanish spoken in the Southwest resembles Mexican Spanish of the northern provinces. Even after the MEXICAN AMERICAN WAR, large-scale movement of Mexicans into the region took place. The emigration of Mexicans to the United States accelerated during and after the Mexican Revolution (1910-1921). It is estimated that 10 percent of Mexico's population moved to the United States during and immediately after the revolution.

Urban Development. Spanish began taking a more urban development in the border region. "POCHO," a derogatory word used to refer to U.S.-born Mexicans who had lost their Mexican identity, reflects the hostile feelings that arose in Mexico toward those who left that country. Americans were referred to as *GABACHOS*, a word that Spaniards used to refer to the French.

Some Spanish terms, such as La Raza, *have taken on political connotations in the U.S. context.* (Impact Visuals, Thor Swift)

Mexicans and Mexican Americans began to use the word "Chicano," an old term that dates back to the indigenous culture of the Mexica (another name for the Aztecs). During the Civil Rights movement of the 1960's, the word "Chicano" underwent a complex evolution and took on political connotations. Terms such as *La Raza* and *Aztlán* have acquired political value when used by social activists.

Within Mexico, as in the United States, there are many regional dialects. In 1930, the U.S. government began recruiting agricultural workers from the central and southern areas of Michoacán, Guerrero, and Guanajuato. These workers spoke Spanish that was very different from that of their neighbors in the northern provinces. Groups of Mexican and Mexican American migrant farmworkers began to cross the country, following the harvest patterns of seasonal crops. Many people of this Mexican immigration settled in the midwestern cities of Chicago, Illinois; Detroit, Michigan; Milwaukee, Wisconsin; and Cleveland, Ohio.

Mexican American Spanish can be characterized according to rural versus urban lines. Pronunciation is fairly uniform, representing a broad cross section of northern and central Mexican dialects.

Some words borrowed from Amerindian languages are known throughout Spanish America. Some have traveled back to Spain and beyond. From the Nahuatl of Mexico, Spanish has taken the words chile, tequila, chicle, and chocolate, among other words for products of the region. English, in turn, has adopted many of these words. Other indigenous words are found in some varieties of Mexican American Spanish. These include *elote* (sweet corn), *camote* (sweet potato), *guajalote* (turkey), *zopilote* (vulture), *cuate* (friend), and *aguacate*, from which the English "avocado" is derived. In Mexican Spanish of the Yucatán Peninsula, as in Salvadoran Spanish, many Mayan words are used. *Cigarro*, shortened to "cigar," is perhaps the only word of Mayan origin that has become widely used outside the area occupied by Mayan speakers.

Caribbean Spanish. Although speakers of the Puerto Rican, Cuban, and Dominican varieties of Spanish can recognize their own form of Spanish as distinct, outsiders see more similarities than differences in them. Pronunciation is the most important unifying characteristic. Caribbean Spanish slurs final sounds, giving the impression that Caribbean Spanish is spoken faster than other varieties. Speakers of this type of Spanish are characterized as "swallowing" their final consonants by Spanish-speaking groups that tend to pronounce these sounds very clearly, such as

Mexicans and Central and South Americans. For example, a final "ess" may sound like an aspirated "h" or may be deleted altogether. *Mis libros* (my books) is pronounced *mih libroh* or *mi libro*. This consonant simplification is more common in colloquial speech, which is not so carefully monitored.

Another characteristic of Caribbean Spanish, and especially of the Spanish spoken by Puerto Ricans, is the change of the "r" sound to the "l" sound at the ends of words or before consonants. *Jugar* (to play) becomes "jugal"; *carta* (letter) becomes "calta." Among Cubans, this replacement of sounds is rare among the first generation of immigrants to the United States, who tended to be highly educated. It is more common among the later immigrants from rural regions and the urban working class.

Puerto Ricans, and primarily those from rural areas, pronounce a trilled "rr" like an English "h" or a French "r." *Río* (river) becomes "hio." Recently in Puerto Rico, this pronunciation came to be considered as a unique symbol of Puerto Rican cultural identity. Educated speakers may now use this pronunciation even in formal contexts.

Taino, the major Antillean indigenous language, gave Spanish many words that spread to other languages. These include *canoa* (canoe), *maíz* (maize), *cacao* (cocoa), *huracán* (hurricane), and *hamaca* (hammock). There are other words of Taino origin, such as *maní* (peanut), *ají* (hot pepper), and *caimán* (alligator), that are very common in South America as well as in the Caribbean.

Among the words that serve as ready identifiers of a person's Caribbean origin are *guagua* (bus) and *chiringa* (kite). Words that involve food and cultural practices are many times unique to a country. Puerto Ricans eat *gandules* (small greenish-brown beans), *chinas* are oranges, and *plátanos* are cooked bananas but *guineos* are the eating variety.

In Puerto Rico, the word *mahones* for blue jeans comes from the name of a town on the Spanish island of Menorca, where the canvas cloth was originally produced. Two words that have been revived are *jíbaro*, a person from the mountainous interior of the island, and *Borinquen*, the old name of the island of Puerto Rico. *Coquis*, small frogs, are indigenous to Puerto Rico, and *aguinaldos* are Christmas carols.

Cuban Spanish also contains many local words. *Guajiro*, the immortalized word of the popular song "Guantanamera" (based on a poem by José Martí), is similar to the Puerto Rican *jíbaro*. Cubans commonly address each other by using the word *chico*. It can be

Many Guatemalan immigrants such as these New Yorkers speak their own distinctive brand of Spanish. (Odette Lupis)

used even when speaking to more than one person, and the listener does not need to be male. It is equivalent to use of the word *hombre* by other speakers of Spanish or to the colloquial American English "man" that became commonplace in the 1960's. Cubans also use the diminutive "ico" suffix instead of the more general Spanish "ito." For example, a *momentico* is a small amount of time, shorter than a *momento*, or moment.

Central American Spanish. Even from Spanish colonial times, the Spanish spoken in Central America has shown striking regional differences that do not necessarily relate to geographical proximity. Guatemala and Costa Rica share more similarities with each other than with their neighboring countries, Panama (a former province of Colombia) and Nicaragua. Guatemalan Spanish is also similar to the Spanish of Mexico's Yucatán region, largely as a result of Mayan heritage. Honduran and Salvadoran Spanish resemble each other and bear striking differences from Guatemalan Spanish.

All these countries have contributed to the Spanish spoken in the United States through immigration. Latino subpopulations from various countries of Central America differ in size and relative lengths of tenure in the United States. Costa Ricans, probably as a result of their relative political stability and prosperity, have been the least numerous, followed by Hondurans. The latter group has concentrated primarily in New York, New York; Los Angeles, California; Houston, Texas; and New Orleans, Louisiana.

Civil war in Guatemala, beginning in the 1960's, forced many people to flee the country. Many of the political refugees were from the rural areas. A significant number of these spoke the Mayan language but little or no Spanish. They tended to congregate in Los Angeles, Miami, Houston, and New York.

Political instability has also been the main reason for Nicaraguan migration, which was considerable even before the Sandinista revolution in 1979. Nicaraguans have settled principally in Miami, Florida, where they have re-created the cultural structure of their homeland. Nicaraguan Americans in Miami publish their own newspaper, and local radio stations air special programs produced for and by Nicaraguans. Nicaraguan concentrations also exist in Los Angeles and San Francisco.

According to the 1990 U.S. census, Salvadorans constituted the largest Central American group in the United States. Like Guatemalans, they have settled in Los Angeles, San Francisco, Miami, Houston, and New York. The heaviest immigration of Salvadorans to the United States comes from the poorest groups, from the rural areas or from slum communities in the cities. These impoverished immigrants have little or no formal education, and their speech shows patterns of regional features. They contrast significantly with Nicaraguans, whose speech reflects characteristics of a professional middle class.

All varieties of Central American Spanish share the weak pronunciation of the "double ell" sound, which sounds like the English "y." *Amarillo* (yellow) sounds like "amario," and *lluvia* (rain) sounds like "iubia." Spanish from this region also has a weak "j" sound. For example, *trabajo* (work) sounds like "trabao." Weakening of these two sounds sets Central Americans apart from Caribbeans. In addition, Central Americans will never interchange or drop "l" or "r."

Vos is a characteristic mark of Central Americans and South Americans from the Río de la Plata. It is a pronoun used to address the second person in a familiar tone and is used instead of *tú*. It is accompanied by a different verb form, for example *tenés* instead of *tienes*, *sos* instead of *eres*, *vení* instead of *ven*, and *hacé* instead of *haz*. Most Central Americans will use *vos* when talking to one another but can quite comfortably switch to *tú* when addressing people who are not from the area. They will sometimes use *tú* among themselves when a less familiar relationship is perceived. In the United States, they may avoid using *vos* to prevent misunderstandings or so they cannot be identified by this regional mark.

Food items again demonstrate regional differences. Some Nicaraguan words are well known in the area of Miami. For example, the *pinol*, a drink made of toasted corn, has become the nickname for Nicaraguans, who refer to each other as *pinoleros*. *Gallo pinto* (red beans and rice) and *vigorón* (a type of salad) are common dishes. *Chompiche* is the name used for turkey by Nicaraguans and Salvadorans. *Pupusas* are a popular Salvadoran dish made of tortillas filled with cheese or meat.

Some Salvadoran words are not shared by Nicaraguans. These include *bolo* (drunk), *cipote* (small child), and *chero* (friend). One expression that varies from usage in other Latino regions and can cause some confusion is the preposition *hasta* (until). Salvadorans use it to refer to the beginning of an event rather than to the end. Salvadorans also commonly say *ando dinero* instead of *traigo dinero* to mean "have money."

Code Switching. Although a large proportion of Latinos are monolingual in Spanish or in English, the majority of Latinos are bilingual. For them, alternating

Businesses in Latino areas often advertise in both English and Spanish. (Library of Congress)

languages is a feature of daily speech, especially with family and friends. CODE SWITCHING is a mode of communication among bilingual speakers characterized by frequent shifts from one language to the other throughout the flow of natural conversation.

Bilingual code switching is a way of writing as well as a way of speaking. This form of Spanish-English alternation is increasingly common in literature written by bilingual Latino authors. ALURISTA, Gloria ANZALDÚA, Sandra María ESTEVES, Rolando HINOJOSA, and Rosario Morales are a few of the many writers who use different techniques of bilingual writing in their texts. These techniques constitute a unique expression of their Latino cultural identity.

English and Spanish are languages in contact in the United States. Consequently, influences of English on Spanish, especially on the lexicon, are obviously more salient than in other Spanish-speaking areas. Many of these terms may be unknown in other regions. Some idiomatic expressions and lexical borrowings would be proscribed regionalisms for many purist speakers of Spanish, though they have become common in many Spanish-speaking communities of the United States. These include *vacunar la carpeta* (vacuum the carpet), *troca* (truck), *flonquiar* (to flunk), and *sainiar* (to sign).

Spanish words were created to sound like English words.

It is important to emphasize that the fact that Spanish spoken in the United States is influenced by English does not imply that the language in question has ceased to be Spanish. The Spanish spoken is neither a mixed code nor a hybrid language, part English and part Spanish. Whether used in alternation with English or not, it is clear that all Spanish utterances used among Latino groups are undoubtedly Spanish.

Latino Unity. An uneasy ethnic solidarity exists among Latinos in the United States. Political rhetoric attempts to bring them all under one tag. The term "Hispanic" was fostered as an agent in this process.

Social relations among Latino groups in the United States defy generalization. Ties among Latino subgroups are not well developed, but similarity of religion, lifestyle, and language often draws Latinos together irrespective of their country of origin. In recent years, language has become a powerful bond that has forced Latinos into the political arena, in response to the "English-only" movement. It is ironic that at a time when the United States is emphasizing proficiency in foreign languages as a means of becoming more competitive internationally, people find threatening the ideas of bilingual education, maintenance of Spanish among Latino communities, and use of Spanish in official government documents and institutions.

In areas where they have lived together longer, as in Chicago, Mexicans and Puerto Ricans have joined in political coalitions. Other subgroups similarly have joined forces. On a more personal level, interethnic marriages necessarily result in more variation in usage of the language.

Many members of the older and larger Latino groups see themselves as Mexican Americans (Hispanos in northern New Mexico, Chicanos in the Southwest), Cuban Americans, and Puerto Ricans rather than as part of a larger national denomination. They strive to maintain their separate ethnic identities.

Furthermore, there are interethnic language prejudices, based primarily on class origin. The majority of Latinos from Mexico, Puerto Rico, and Central America are working class. Middle-class immigrants who come from Cuba, South America, or Spain often find it difficult to relate to them because of the difference in class culture. This attitude is no different from that demonstrated toward the *clases populares* in their homelands. This phenomenon is also common among upper-class Mexicans in the United States. Nevertheless, common roots exist among the Latino subgroups regardless of their national or class origin. The Spanish language functions as a cohesive force among them.

The Latino Market. The Spanish-speaking market represents a large and important share of the American economy. Entrepreneurs have opened chains of food stores called Tíanguis and Fiesta, in Los Angeles and Houston, to attract the Latino market. In San Francisco, a telephone company serving only the Spanish-speaking community has attracted a large clientele. At the local level, Spanish is used in many small businesses, such as markets, restaurants, gas stations, hairdressers, and travel agencies, that provide services to the Latino community. (*See* MARKETING AND ADVERTISING.)

Trade with Latin America is a major source of revenue for the businesses of many American cities, and financial and industrial transactions conducted in Spanish represent a large source of income. The NORTH AMERICAN FREE TRADE AGREEMENT, signed in 1993 and implemented in 1994 by Canada, Mexico, and the United States, reemphasized the importance of Spanish to the North American business community.

A Latino storefront in San Francisco. (Impact Visuals, Rick Gerharter)

Spanish Media. "Hispanidad" is a label created by three Spanish-language television networks and hundreds of radio stations that indirectly send the message of ethnic bonding into millions of Latino homes. Many entertainment programs, soap operas, and talk shows that air nationally are designed to represent the diversity of the Spanish language and to have a balanced appeal to all Spanish-speaking communities. For the most part, however, control of the Spanish sector of the airwaves and print media is in conservative hands. Print, radio, and television executives of Spanish media favor the standard language in preference to vernacular differences. The increased socioeconomic mobility of the Latino population appears to be a crucial factor weighing against official sanction of one of the socioregional dialects. (*See* BROADCAST JOURNALISM; NEWSPAPERS AND MAGAZINES.)

Since 1808, when the first newspaper written in Spanish, *El Misisipí*, appeared in New Orleans, Spanish-language newspapers have been published in all regions and in almost all large cities. In 1938, *La Prensa* of San Antonio, Texas, listed 451 papers published in Spanish in the United States.

The most important function of any newspaper is to publish local and world news. Spanish-speaking readers living in the United States also want to be informed about events taking place in the Spanish-speaking world, since they often do not get this information in the English-language press. Numerous Spanish-language newspapers have regional and even national circulation. Many Latino magazines and newspapers use Spanish; others use English or a combination of English and Spanish, sometimes with individual articles appearing in both languages. These publications serve to preserve the cultural heritage of the Latino communities as well as to stimulate a sense of identity. Most important, they have contributed to keeping the Spanish written language alive. —*M. Cecilia Colombi*

SUGGESTED READINGS:

• Amastae, Jon, and Lucía Elías Olivares, eds. *Spanish in the United States: Sociolinguistic Aspects.* Cambridge, England: Cambridge University Press, 1982. A collection of articles on the different varieties of Spanish in the United States. Analyzes the spoken Spanish of the Southwest as well as more recent varieties, such as ones developed by Cuban and Puerto Rican immigrants, from an ethnographic perspective. Includes articles on code switching, linguistic contact and change, and phonetic and morphosyntactic variants of the Spanish spoken in the United States.

• Bergen, John, ed. *Spanish in the United States: Sociolinguistic Issues.* Washington, D.C.: Georgetown University Press, 1990. Studies the Spanish used in the United States from four different perspectives: language structure and variation, language use, language pedagogy, and language policy.

• García, Ofelia, and Ricardo Otheguy. "The Language Situation of Cuban-Americans." In *Language Diversity: Problem or Resource?*, edited by S. L. McKay and S. L. Cynthia Wong. New York: Newbury House, 1988. Presents a historical view of the Cuban immigration to the United States. Describes the sociodemographic characteristics of Cuban Americans as well as their use of Spanish and English.

• Hidalgo, Margarita. "On the Question of 'Standard' versus 'Dialect': Implications for Teaching Hispanic College Students." *Hispanic Journal of Behavioral Sciences* 9, no. 4 (1987): 375-395. Discusses the theoretical distinction between standard language versus dialect and the pedagogical and societal implications of bidialectal education in several education systems. Also emphasizes the most striking structural differences between Chicano and Puerto Rican Spanish.

• Ornstein-Galicia, Jacob L., George K. Green, and Dennis J. Bixler-Márquez, eds. *Research Issues and Problems in United States Spanish.* Brownsville, Tex.: Pan American University at Brownsville and the University of Texas at El Paso, 1988. This book is divided into three major areas of study: the status of Spanish in the United States, research directions in U.S. Spanish, and issues of syntax, phonology, and the lexicon of Spanish.

• Roca, Ana, and John M. Lipski, eds. *Spanish in the United States.* New York: Mouton de Gruyter, 1993. A collection of articles on linguistics, analyzing Spanish in different areas of the United States.

• Timm, L. A. "Spanish-English Code Switching: El Porqué y How-Not-To." *Romance Philology* 28 (May, 1975): 473-482. Analyzes the linguistic constraints on switching code of bilingual talk produced by Mexican Americans living in California.

• Valdés, Guadalupe. "The Language Situation of Mexican Americans." In *Language Diversity: Problem or Resource?*, edited by S. L. McKay and S. L. Cynthia Wong. New York: Newbury House, 1988. Describes the heterogeneity and characteristics of Mexican American Spanish. Also studies the bilingual situation of Mexican American communities.

• Zamora, Juan Clemente. "Amerindian Loanwords in General and Local Varieties of American Spanish." *Word* 33 (April-August, 1982): 159-171. Discusses the distribution of Amerindian words in American Spanish.

• Zentella, Ana Celia. "The Language Situation of Puerto Ricans." In *Language Diversity: Problem or Resource?*, edited by S. L. McKay and S. L. Cynthia Wong. New York: Newbury House, 1988. Explores the language situation (the language patterns and use of English and Spanish) of Puerto Ricans in the United States and the educational implications of this situation.

Spanish-Speaking People's Division, Office of Inter-American Affairs: U.S. government agency. This agency was created on April 3, 1942, as part of the U.S. government's Office of the Coordinator of Inter-American Affairs. The division's goals were to help Spanish-speaking people participate more fully in life within the United States and to educate English speakers on the importance of ending discrimination toward Spanish speakers. The division had difficulties, including the lack of Spanish-speaking people involved in the organization and misguided appropriation of funds for activities, with cocktail parties and receptions funded while other programs were not. Some funds were used, however, for grants-in-aid to institutions in the Southwest, fellowships for Spanish-speaking students, field representatives in Austin, Texas, and Los Angeles, California, and conferences that opened dialogues on Anglo-Latino relations in the Southwest.

Spanish Speaking Unity Council: Community development corporation. Founded in 1964 in Oakland, California, the group received nonprofit status in 1967. During the early 1990's, it employed more than sixty people and had an annual budget of more than two million dollars. There is no membership in the organization. It is directed by its community constituents through representatives at large.

The organization promotes Hispanic leadership as well as programs and ventures that assist Latinos and their neighbors to help themselves within a multicultural, bilingual context. With roots in the Civil Rights movement, the organization provides social and economic development services. Organizational objectives include nurturing the development of Latino institutional and leadership capacities, promoting interagency cooperation in favor of Latinos, investigating and taking action in regard to problems that Latinos face in the community, fighting discrimination, and soliciting funds in order to help in the development of the Latino community.

One project, the Fruitvale Community Collaborative, is a consortium of fifteen organizations that promotes economic development of the community. The corporation also operates housing projects, childcare centers, and a drop-in senior center. An affiliate organization, the Bay Area Latino Nonprofit Association, was founded in 1992 for the purpose of advocating in favor of Latino-based nonprofit organizations.

Spiritism and Spiritualism: The American Spiritualist movement began in 1848 in the tiny hamlet of Hydesville, New York. Members of the Fox family often heard loud rapping noises at night that seemed to come from the walls of their isolated farmhouse. Margaret and Kate Fox, two sisters, decided to communicate with the invisible presence by snapping their fingers. The presence responded by imitating the girls, and a visiting neighbor who witnessed this phenomenon invented a code based on raps. The "spirit" identified itself as a traveling salesman who had been murdered by the previous occupant of the house. Shortly thereafter, a badly decomposed human skeleton was unearthed on the Fox homestead.

These seemingly insignificant events would eventually have global effects as "table rapping" and other parlor games aimed at communication with spirits spread across North America and Western Europe. Spiritualism, as belief in such communication was called, quickly evolved. Central to the Spiritualist philosophy was the idea that souls of the dead often remain near their living loved ones, with whom they are desperate to communicate. This communication may only be accomplished via an intermediary, or medium, whose psychic talents allow a kind of "possession" to take place, wherein the spirit may speak his or her mind.

Some mediums attained widespread fame, and their public performances eventually attracted the attention of the scientific community. Many Americans and Europeans became followers of Spiritualism, among them noted British writer Arthur Conan Doyle. Spiritualism, however, never gained the status of a major religion within the United States.

Spiritism had earlier gained a foothold in Latin America, particularly in Brazil, where it rivaled Christianity for converts. By the twentieth century, many Brazilians were both Christian and Spiritist. Spiritism of one type or another pervades Latin America and, with emigration, became established in some areas of the United States. Over time, it has blended not only with Christianity but also with beliefs brought from Africa. SANTERÍA is one example of such a blend, evolved around religious ideas imported from West Africa. Many Latinos who do not profess belief in

A Day of the Dead procession in San Francisco. (Impact Visuals, Janet Delaney)

Spiritualism nevertheless engage in various ceremonies tied to relationships with the dead, such as those practiced on El Día DE LOS MUERTOS (Day of the Dead).

Squashes: Family of American plants. Squashes, some gourds, and pumpkins all are cucurbits, a family of American plants with bulbous fruits. Many were domesticated by sixth millennium B.C.E. in Mexico and, at later dates, elsewhere in the Americas. The harder squashes and pumpkins are used in most Latin American cuisines for soups, porridges, vegetable purees, cakes, and candies. The chayote, a distinctive kind of squash, is served stuffed with various fillings throughout Latin America. The seeds of squashes and pumpkins are used to thicken *pipián* sauces in Mexico, and the flowers are used in soups and fillings for QUESADILLAS and similar dishes.

Steinbeck, John (Feb. 27, 1902, Salinas, Calif.—Dec. 20, 1968, New York, N.Y.): Writer. Steinbeck was born in and grew up in the long, narrow strip of agricultural land called the Salinas Valley. He was the third of four children, and the only son, of John Ernst Steinbeck II, manager of a flour mill and treasurer of Monterey County, and Olive Hamilton Steinbeck, a former teacher. Although his parents owned large tracts of land, the family was poor.

After graduation from Salinas High School in 1919, Steinbeck entered Stanford University, which he attended intermittently until 1925. He had to work to pay for his education and took odd jobs to earn tuition money. It was at Stanford that Steinbeck began writing fiction. His major works of fiction include *Tortilla Flat* (1935); *Of Mice and Men* (1937); *The Grapes of Wrath* (1939), which won a Pulitzer Prize; *Cannery Row* (1945); the screenplay *Viva Zapata!* (pr. 1952, pb. 1975); *East of Eden* (1952); and *The Winter of Our Discontent* (1961). He won the Nobel Prize in Literature in 1962.

Throughout his career, Steinbeck was a novelist of the people. The novels that had the most impact were about ordinary men and women, sometimes migrant workers, who battled against dehumanizing social forces or who struggled against their own inhumane tendencies and attempted to forge lives of meaning and worth.

Many of John Steinbeck's works chronicled the life of the Latino poor. (AP/Wide World Photos)

Stereotypes of Latinas: The cultures of much of Central and South America and the Caribbean region display a common heritage of language and customs, though each country has cultural elements that are unique. The Roman Catholic religion brought by the conquistadores imposed a belief system upon these countries that divided the world into good versus evil. This division between good and evil deeply affected the treatment of women in the Latin cultures of the Western Hemisphere.

The Virgin Mary is the most revered role model for women of the Catholic world. According to the Catholic model, Latinas are expected to remain virgins until they are married and then be faithful to their husbands for life. Latinas who deviate from this path are considered dishonored or "fallen" women, though that negative labeling is disappearing as Latinas change their cultural roles.

Until the middle of the twentieth century, most Latinas had only two choices open to them if they wished to avoid dishonor—marriage or the convent. Historically, the honor of the family was tied to the purity of its women, and family dishonor was punishable by death for the dishonored woman and for the man with whom she was involved. A marriage sanctified by the Catholic church was the only acceptable choice for a couple who compromised the family honor.

Latinas who became wives and mothers were expected to remain faithful to their husbands throughout their lives. The mother is the most respected figure in the family, and her sons, as well as her husband, are obligated to protect and defend her honor against physical or verbal insults. The gravest insult to a Latino is one that casts aspersions on his or her mother.

Latinas often care for large families. Early marriage, large families, and an early end to education often combine to limit the possibility of a career outside the home. Even if a Latina desires a career outside the home, her Hispanic husband is likely to believe that she, as a woman, should be at home with the children. A majority of Latinas themselves believe that men should earn most of the family's money.

The stereotypical Latina can be described as docile, compliant, accepting, faithful, maternal, and religious. These stereotypes have left many younger Latinas searching for identities. Graduation from high school

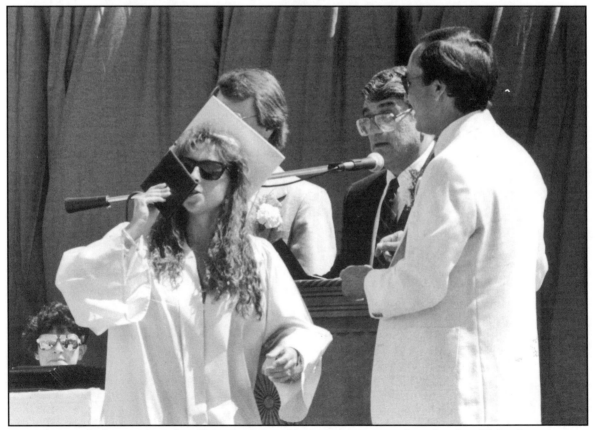

As more Latinos graduate from high school, they change stereotypes regarding education. (Elaine Querry)

is a proud achievement for a Latina and her family; however, a high school diploma marks her as more educated than most of her family and many of her peers. By attending college and working in a professional setting, a Latina finds herself interacting more with those outside her ethnic group. Her new assertiveness and financial security may make her seem less marriageable in the eyes of Latino males. Educated Latinas may therefore believe that they fit neither among Latino peers nor among young members of other ethnic groups. The rewards brought by education and assimilation, therefore, also present many challenges.

Stereotypes of Latinos: A stereotype is an oversimplified or exaggerated description of a person or thing. Stereotypes influence the perception of reality and can be positive or negative; most stereotyping is negative, or uncomplimentary and degrading. Stereotypes generally derive from prejudices. A prejudice is an opinion or feeling formed without knowledge, thought, or reason. Stereotyping can lead to discrimination, or a deliberate, conscious act based on prejudice.

In the United States, stereotypes regarding Latinos have tended to focus on people of Mexican descent. In the wake of the influx of immigrants from other Latin American countries beginning in the 1970's, stereotypes about people of other Latin American origins became more common.

The Mexican in Literature. U.S. writers have indulged in stereotyped portrayals of Mexicans and Mexicans Americans since the mid-nineteenth century. One example is John Steinbeck's *Tortilla Flat* (1935), which portrayed Mexicans as happy-go-lucky primitives. Such stereotypes are part of academic literature as well. For example, sociologist Oscar Lewis portrayed Mexicans as lacking a sense of the future and as interested primarily in immediate self-gratification. This lack of initiative, or laziness, supposedly served to keep Mexicans in a "culture of poverty."

Anthropologists have tended to view Mexicans (and Latino culture in general) as "traditional." According to this negative stereotype, certain cultural attributes— MACHISMO, *envidia* (envy), the extended family, respect for one's elders, and a fatalistic attitude (linked to Catholicism)—create dysfunctions in a modern, postindustrial society.

Popular Images. Magazines and newspapers have not treated Mexicans any more fairly. From the mid-nineteenth to the mid-twentieth century, the U.S. press routinely portrayed Mexicans as "inferior," "half-civilized," and lazy. It was not unusual for the Roman Catholic church to be criticized for its role in keeping Mexicans "backward." The image of the "GREASER" appearing in *The Atlantic Monthly* in 1899 is a good example. This portrayal accented the dark skins and "Indian" features thought to be typical of an inferior race.

During the 1920's, when immigration from Central and South America was being debated in the U.S. Congress, numerous articles on the topic appeared in such leading magazines as *The North American Review*, *The Saturday Evening Post*, and *Time*. These articles continued through the 1930's and created a variety of stereotypes. Latinos were portrayed as "irresponsible," "distrustful," "childish," and "unwashed." "WETBACKS" were seen as "ants" illegally streaming into the United States and as a potentially divisive element. Latinas were viewed as "submissive" and lacking independence and importance. Latino marriages were viewed as "loose"; it was usual, according to these magazines, for Latino marriage partners to have three or four other relations.

By the 1960's, popular images of Latinos revolved around socioeconomic characteristics. Members of specific ethnic groups were viewed as homogeneous; for example, Puerto Rican migrants to the United States were seen as coming entirely from the impoverished, lower strata of Puerto Rican society. Puerto Ricans were thus portrayed as blue-collar, semiskilled or unskilled workers who lacked the business, financial, and middle-class elements needed to exert greater control over their environment.

Conversely, Cuban migration was seen as coming from the upper social and economic strata of Cuban society. Cubans fleeing the regime of Fidel CASTRO in the 1960's brought capital, skills (financial, managerial, business, and educational), and entrepreneurial values that enabled them to prosper and achieve socioeconomic success in the United States. The MARIELITOS, about 120,000 immigrants who arrived in the United States during the 1980 MARIEL BOAT LIFT, were mostly of lower socioeconomic status. Some had criminal histories. A new stereotype of Cubans emerged in response to this wave of immigration.

In the 1990's, the influx of immigrants from El Salvador, Honduras, Guatemala, and Mexico was viewed by many U.S. citizens as coming from the lower classes and the peasantry of Central America. There was little attempt on the part of most U.S. observers to differentiate among these heterogeneous ethnic groups.

U.S. stereotypes of Latinos have tended to focus on people of Mexican descent. (James Shaffer)

Television and Film. By the 1960's, some Latino stereotypes were beginning to fade from public view, but prejudicial attitudes were still expressed in popular entertainment media. The most widespread perception, according to Joe Feagin in *Racial and Ethnic Relations* (1984), was the Latino criminal stereotype. This image was perpetuated into the 1990's in such television shows as *Miami Vice*, *L.A. Law*, and *NYPD Blue*. The ruthless Colombian drug lord, a frequent villain in television and film, was only the most popular of such images.

Media advertising also often showed Latinos in a negative light. The "Frito Bandito" advertisements, for example, implied that Mexicans were criminals; one deodorant company used a picture of a grubby looking Mexican bandit accompanied by the words, "If it works for him, it will work for you." Tequila advertisements in college newspapers included a game featuring characters representing negative stereotypes of Mexicans: the lazy peon in a large sombrero sleeping on a burro, the border-town prostitute, the sleepy border guard, and the thieving bandito.

In the film industry, the 1920 silent version of *Zorro* provides an early illustration of negative stereotyping of Latinos. Latinos, especially Mexicans, were depicted as cruel, lazy, prone to drunkenness, arrogant, of low morals, disrespectful of women, and otherwise reprehensible. A 1940 remake of *Zorro* simply added to the stereotypes of the earlier version.

Bordertown (1935), *Juarez* (1939), *Vera Cruz* (1954), *Bandido* (1956), *Villa Rides* (1968), and *The Wild Bunch* (1969) are examples of films that contributed to the stereotype of the "brutal" Mexican revolutionary. Perhaps the most common Latino stereotype in film, however, is that of the bandit. Even when such a character is depicted as a hero—as in the popular 1930's and 1940's films about the Cisco Kid—the bandit image was central. Added to the bandit image is a language stereotype. Latino characters in such films typically displayed an inability to speak English without an accent.

Latinas. Latinas are typically stereotyped as docile, passive, hard-working, forgiving wives and mothers. They are often presented as victims of violent, unfaithful males. In reality, the indigenous elements of Latino culture support matriarchy and strong cultural roles for women.

Conclusion. Latinos have suffered from more than their share of negative stereotypes. Historically, the Latino mentality has been characterized as lazy, primitive, and fatalistic. Latino families have been characterized as hypermasculine, Latinas have been portrayed as passive and of loose morals, and the general Latino population has been depicted as criminal in nature. Such pervasively negative stereotyping has been widely criticized by scholars and activists.

—*David Camacho*

SUGGESTED READINGS: • Carlson, Lewis H., and George A. Colburn. *In Their Place: White America Defines Her Minorities, 1850-1950*. New York: John Wiley and Sons, 1972. • Fitzgerald, Roosevelt. "Stereotypes of Mexicans Projected in Selected Films." *National Social Science Journal* 1, no. 5, pp. 36-53. • Herrera-Sobek, Maria, ed. *Beyond Stereotypes: The Critical Analysis of Chicana Literature*. Binghamton, N.Y.: Bilingual Press, 1985. • Martinez, Tomás. "Advertising and Racism: The Case of the Mexican American." *El Grito* 2 (Summer, 1969): 3-13. • Sanchez, Joseph P. *The Spanish Black Legend: Origins of Anti-Hispanic Stereotypes*. Albuquerque, N.Mex.: National Park Service, Spanish Colonial Research Center, 1990.

Sterilization of women: The most common method of sterilization for women is cutting, tying, or burning the Fallopian tubes. Sterilization may be voluntary or involuntary, depending on the conditions under which it takes place. Informed consent to sterilization has been a key issue for women of Mexican and Puerto Rican descent in the United States.

Background. Sterilization entails the disruption of the reproductive process by obstructing the possible unification of an ovum with a sperm. Although ways of reversing the surgery have been explored, it generally has been an irreversible method of birth control and family planning.

Throughout the history of birth control procedures and eugenics laws (laws regulating reproduction), sterilization has been mandated for those considered to be unfit to bear children. In the United States, it was clear by the early 1960's that the term "unfit" encompassed a disproportionately high number of working-class and poor women, especially African Americans, Native Americans, Puerto Ricans, and Mexican Americans.

Madrigal v. Quilligan. In 1975, twelve women of Mexican descent filed a suit against the University of Southern California-Los Angeles County Medical Center, charging the center with coercing them to be sterilized. Such coercion, the women stated in separate testimonies, included asking them to sign forms (written in English) that they were unable to read, inadequately outlining the implications of the procedure, obtaining consent from their husbands, sterilizing them while performing a cesarean section, or threatening to withhold medication unless they consented to be sterilized.

During the trial, it was revealed that encouraging women to consent to a sterilization procedure was an unwritten policy of the center, which had a clientele consisting primarily of poor Latinas. Funding for the center, in the case of poor women, was provided by the federal government. The judge ruled in favor of the doctors, arguing that the sterilizations were largely a result of misunderstandings between the Spanish-speaking patients and the medical staff, whose knowledge of Spanish was limited.

La Operación. From the 1950's to the late 1970's, sterilization was promoted as a desirable form of birth control for women living in Puerto Rico. By 1968, it was estimated that more than one-third of the women on the island between twenty and forty-nine years of age had been sterilized. The pervasiveness of sterilization as the main form of birth control in Puerto Rico was such that Puerto Rican women living on the island could refer to the procedure simply as "la operación," which in English means "the operation."

One study of island-born and mainland-born Puerto Rican women showed that among Puerto Rican women living in New York City, those born on the island were sterilized at a rate that was approximately the same as the rate on the island and higher than the sterilization rate of Puerto Rican women born on the mainland. Nevertheless, the use of sterilization for birth control among Puerto Rican women living in the United States appears, overall, to be higher than the rate of its use by all U.S. women.

There are a number of possible reasons for the persistently high rates of sterilization as a birth control method among Puerto Rican women. Knowledge of alternative, reversible methods of birth control may be restricted, such that Puerto Rican women do not have access to such information; the women may be involuntarily sterilized; or alternative birth control methods may be consciously rejected.

Informed Consent. As a result of cases of abuse, the Department of Health, Education, and Welfare instituted a set of guidelines in 1974 that made the docu-

Latinas have often been pressured to consent to sterilization procedures. (James Shaffer)

mentation of informed consent much more rigorous. These guidelines included the stipulation that women were to obtain extensive information about the procedure in the language they speak and understand most, and that they were to wait for seventy-two hours between the time they gave consent and the time of the sterilization.

In 1975, the Committee to End Sterilization Abuse (CESA) was formed to monitor the process by which poor women, particularly women of African American, Mexican, and Puerto Rican descent, were encouraged or coerced into being sterilized, or were sterilized involuntarily. Through coalitions with other concerned groups, CESA lobbied for legislation that would ensure that informed consent was obtained before sterilization surgery was performed.

—*Dionne Espinoza*

SUGGESTED READINGS: • Del Castillo, Adelaida. "Sterilization: An Overview." *Mexican Women in the United States: Struggles Past and Present*, edited by Magdalena Mora and Adelaida R. Del Castillo. Los Angeles: Chicano Studies Research Center Publications, University of California, 1980. • Gonzalez, Maria, et al. "'The Operation': An Analysis of Sterilization in a Puerto Rican Community in Connecticut." In *Work, Family, and Health: Latina Women in Transition*, edited by Ruth E. Zambrana. Bronx, N.Y.: Hispanic Research Center, Fordham University Press, 1982. • Hernandez, Antonia. "Chicanas and the Issues of Involuntary Sterilization: Reforms Needed to Protect Informed Consent." *Chicano Law Review* 3, no. 3 (1976): 3-37. • Lopez, Iris O. "Sterilization Among Puerto Rican Women in New York City: Public Policy and Social Constraints." In *Cities of the United States: Studies in Urban Anthropology*, edited by Leith Mullings. New York: Columbia University Press, 1987. • Rodriguez-Trias, Helen. "Sterilization Abuse." *Women and Health* 1 (May/June, 1978): 30-31. • Salvo, Joseph J., Mary G. Powers, and Rosemary Santana Cooney. "Contraceptive Use and Sterilization Among Puerto Rican Women." *Family Planning Perspectives* 24 (September/October, 1992): 219-223. • Shapiro, Thomas M. *Population Control Politics: Women, Sterilization, and Reproductive Choice*. Philadelphia, Pa.: Temple University Press, 1985. • Vélez-I., Carlos G. "The Nonconsenting Sterilization of Mexican Women in Los Angeles: Issues of Psychocultural Rupture and Legal Redress in Paternalistic Behavioral Environments." In *Twice a Minority: Mexican American Women*, edited by Margarita B. Melville. St. Louis, Mo.: C. V. Mosby, 1980.

Storni, Alfonsina (May 29, 1892, Sala Capriasca, Switzerland—Oct. 25, 1938, Mar del Plata, Argentina): Poet. In 1896, Storni's family emigrated to Argentina and settled in the city of San Juan. In 1907, Storni joined a theatrical company. She toured with the group for a year. By the age of eighteen, she had obtained a certificate as a primary school teacher from the normal school of Coronda, and the next year she began teaching in Rosario.

An independent single mother, Storni made a life for herself in Argentina and wrote the major part of her vast poetical work there. She eventually developed breast cancer and committed suicide at the age of forty-six.

Storni's work can be divided into two periods. The first produced four volumes: *La inquietude del rosal* (1916), *El dulce daño* (1918), *Irremediablemente* (1919), and *Languidez* (1920), the beginning of Storni's mature work, which was more metaphysical in nature. The second period followed with *Mundo de siete pozos* (1934) and *Mascarilla y trébol* (1938). Storni was one of Argentina's outstanding poets for more than twenty years. She has been labeled as Argentina's first feminist poet.

Street vendors: Street vending has been a means of economic survival for many people throughout history. As businesses, retail stores, and supermarkets developed, they replaced street vendors in delivering various goods.

In the 1980's, the United States experienced an economic decline. Factories began closing down and moving abroad, particularly from the industrial Midwest and the East Coast. With the economic recession came declines in wages and the number of full-time jobs. Increasingly, jobs required secondary and postsecondary education. The Latino population as a whole suffers from low levels of education, making the job search even more difficult. Undocumented workers faced an even more difficult task. The IMMIGRATION REFORM AND CONTROL ACT OF 1986 imposed sanctions on employers who hired them, and they often did not speak English fluently, closing off many opportunities.

In the 1990's, increasing numbers of documented and undocumented Latinos found themselves selling foods and material goods on the streets as a means of economic survival. In major metropolitan areas, Latinos sold fruit and flowers on busy streetcorners and on freeway ramps. On commercial strips, street vendors sold fruits, their native foods, car accessories, home

A young Mexican American street vendor in turn-of-the-century Arizona. (Ruben G. Mendoza)

decorations, audio tapes, and homemade arts and crafts, thus bringing the mall out to the sidewalks. This type of vending is common in many countries in Latin America, where markets are more personal and less commercialized. Some cities, notably New York, allow vending by persons with permits, and pushcarts are relatively common. Competition from street vendors who do not have to pay rent on store space, however, has angered some merchants, who push to put street vendors out of business.

The continuous influx of immigrants into Los Angeles, as one primary destination, made it difficult for Latinos there to find jobs during the 1980's and 1990's. Many Latinos had jobs that paid the minimum wage or less; street vending helped them supplement their income. Although some major U.S. cities had legalized street vending by the early 1990's, city council members in Los Angeles viewed street vending as infringing on the rights of merchants. Los Angeles had passed a law in 1930 prohibiting sales on public property and making street vending a criminal misdemeanor.

To begin legalizing street vending in Los Angeles, Councilman Michael Woo announced the formation of the Los Angeles Street Vending Task Force on July 7, 1989. The task force designated three areas for legalized street vending. Street vendors were required to have a permit, along with a health certificate if they sold food. Street vending is not permitted anywhere else in Los Angeles. Violation of these regulations or selling in a nondesignated area subjected the vendor to criminal prosecution.

Different cities and areas took different approaches to street vending. In areas where it was illegal, Latinos, along with others, nevertheless engaged in it because they saw no other means of survival or no more attractive job opportunity, even with the risks involved. It provided one of the least expensive ways for a person to begin a business.

Student movement: Latino students, primarily of Mexican and Puerto Rican descent, participated in various international youth movements and in civil rights movements in the United States beginning in the 1960's. They protested the racial discrimination that they believed structured their lives, seeing differential treatment of their communities throughout society and in the educational system in particular.

Background. During the 1960's, a youth movement with national and international dimensions came together to promote social change. Students formed a major part of this youth movement. Recognizing the implications of the socializing process of education, students questioned not only the educational system as an autonomous unit but also the overall system composed, in their view, of a number of social institutions, including the government, the legal system, education, and some churches. Students also allied themselves with poor and working-class people protesting widespread unemployment and unfair working conditions.

Mobilization of Latino Student Movements. National liberation movements in Africa and Cuba, U.S. movements for the civil rights of African Americans, the escalation of U.S. intervention in Vietnam, and student movements in Puerto Rico and Mexico encouraged students of Puerto Rican and Mexican descent in the United States to mobilize. Demonstrations, walkouts, and conferences were the main channels through which students contested the discriminatory practices they perceived in the educational system.

In the southern states, discriminatory practices included the segregation of African Americans from white students. Differential treatment also manifested itself in the educational curricula, in which histories of African Americans were absent from textbooks or were presented in a biased manner. In the Northeast and in the Southwest, Latino students recognized the injustice of their differential treatment, which included unnecessary enrollment of Latino students in remedial courses, prohibitions against speaking the Spanish language on school premises, and promotion of curricula that neglected or gave biased views of Latino histories and cultures.

Various community-based youth, high school, and college student groups emerged around these issues of discrimination in education. These groups included the MEXICAN AMERICAN YOUTH ORGANIZATION, UNITED MEXICAN AMERICAN STUDENTS, Mexican American Student Confederation, ASPIRA, Puerto Ricans Involved in Student Activities, and the Puerto Rican Student Movement. As the 1960's wore on, more extreme forms of resistance propelled a number of these organizations to consolidate into radical student groups.

Drawing upon examples of national liberation movements in other countries and on the example of black nationalism, the Latino student movement formulated its own philosophies of nationalism, giving rise to student groups that called themselves, in the Southwest and part of the Midwest, El MOVIMIENTO ESTUDIANTIL CHICANO DE AZTLÁN and, in the Northeast, the Puerto Rican Student Union/Union Estudiantil Boricua. Student movements engaged in ongoing

Latino students at the City University of New York protest budget cuts. (Hazel Hankin)

debates among themselves about the appropriate platform to represent the interests of Latino students. For example, some objected to a platform of nationalism if it did not allow for the expression of international solidarity with poor and working-class peoples.

Others in the Latino student movement were less concerned with debates regarding the incompatibility of nationalist and working-class movements but were not necessarily hostile to ideas of nationalism. Their primary goal was to make access to health care and housing available to poor and working-class members of their communities. Latino student groups developed organizing strategies and goals that paralleled those of the African American Civil Rights movement.

In some cases, students followed the example of the Student Nonviolent Coordinating Committee (SNCC). The SNCC worked against segregation in the South through sit-ins, freedom rides to desegregate buses, and voter registration drives. Students for a Democratic Society also provided a model for student mobilization with its militant demand for the fulfillment of democracy and the securing of human rights. Although their goals and strategies often paralleled those of African American students, Latino students made clear their assertion of Latino culture and history as key elements of their struggles.

Gains of the Movement. One lasting impact of the student movements in the United States was the implementation of programs, support systems, and departments that centered on the needs of poor and minority students. These programs included educational opportunity programs for low-income students and affirmative action programs that seek to bring more students from racial minority groups into universities. CHICANO STUDIES PROGRAMS, PUERTO RICAN STUDIES PROGRAMS, and various courses oriented to the Latino experience have been added at a number of colleges and universities.

The addition of support systems, programs, and departments that center on the intellectual and emotional needs of Latino students occurred unevenly. Many of the gains related to education were in constant danger of eradication or were neglected, such that the number of faculty and staff was not increased to meet the needs of growing Latino populations.

In 1993, resurgence of Latino student movements occurred across the country. At Cornell University, students of African and Latino descent—including those of Puerto Rican, Dominican, Colombian, and Mexican heritage—protested not only cuts in financial aid but the lack of tenured Latino faculty at the university. Latino students in the State University of New York system staged sit-ins to protest state budget cuts that would affect them. Students at the University of California, Los Angeles, went on a hunger strike, demanding that a Chicano studies department be approved and funded. These demonstrations, in addition to a number of student-initiated movements for Latino studies at smaller private colleges, underlined the ongoing student struggle for an empowering education.

—*Dianne Espinoza*

SUGGESTED READINGS: • Gómez-Quiñones, Juan. *Mexican Students Por La Raza: The Chicano Student Movement in Southern California, 1967-1977.* Santa Barbara, Calif.: Editorial La Causa, 1978. • Muñoz, Carlos, Jr. *Youth, Identity, Power: The Chicano Movement.* London: Verso, 1989. • Sale, Kirkpatrick. *SDS.* New York: Random House, 1973. • Zinn, Howard. *SNCC: The New Abolitionists.* Boston: Beacon Press, 1964.

Suárez, Mario (b. Jan. 12, 1925, Tucson, Ariz.): Short-story writer. Suárez's father, Francisco Suárez, was originally from the Mexican state of Chihuahua. He had visited the United States on several occasions before moving to Tucson permanently in the 1920's. Suárez's mother, Carmen Minjárez, was from Hermosillo, Mexico.

Upon receiving his high school diploma, Suárez enlisted in the United States Navy. In 1946, he enrolled

at the University of Arizona, where his interest in literature developed, and in 1952 he received his degree in liberal arts from that institution. He also attended California State University, Fullerton, where he eventually earned his teaching credentials. In 1970, he was appointed to the faculty of California State Polytechnic University, Pomona.

Suárez's first published stories appeared in the *Arizona Quarterly* in 1947. These stories focused on Chicanos living in barrios of the 1940's. In 1948 and 1950, *Arizona Quarterly* published three additional sketches. Suárez's unique contribution to Chicano literature is his examination of reality with the intent of reproducing it accurately, in the minutest detail, and also of making it comprehensible on a more than superficial level.

Suárez, Virgil (b. 1962, Havana, Cuba): Writer. Suárez spent time in Madrid, Spain, as a young child. At the age of eight, he emigrated with his family from Cuba to the United States. He grew up in Los Angeles and in 1980 was graduated from high school there. He received a B.A. in English from California State University, Long Beach. In 1987, he was graduated with an M.F.A. in creative writing from Louisiana State University, where he later taught.

Suárez's first novel, *Latin Jazz* (1989), chronicles the experiences of a family that leaves Cuba to settle in Los Angeles after Fidel CASTRO comes to power. The novel depicts one family member's incarceration in a Cuban prison and his eventual release to the United States, as well as problems faced by the immigrants' children in the United States. Suárez is also the author of the novel *The Cutter* (1991) and a collection of short stories, *Welcome to the Oasis and Other Stories* (1992). He has also edited an anthology of fiction titled *Iguana Dreams: New Latino Fiction* (1992). His work has contributed much to the development of a Latino cultural identity in fiction.

Suárez, Xavier L. (b. May 21, 1949, Las Villas, Cuba): Public official. After attending Villanova University to study engineering and graduating first in his class, Suárez went on to Harvard Law School and the John F. Kennedy School of Government, also at Harvard. He earned his law degree and a master's degree in public policy in 1975. In addition, Suárez holds an honorary law degree from Villanova University School of Law.

After graduation, Suárez moved to MIAMI, FLORIDA, to begin practicing law and to lay the foundation

Miami mayor Xavier Suárez campaigns for reelection. (AP/Wide World Photos)

for a run at citywide office. In 1985, he became the first Cuban American to be elected as mayor of Miami. He was reelected to second and third terms in 1987 and 1989. During his service, Suárez spoke to the new-found significance of Latino voters on both local and national levels. He also spoke out against the impediments of large electoral districts for county commissioner and school board elections. President George Bush appointed him to the board of directors of the Legal Services Corporation.

Suárez y Romero, Anselmo (Apr. 21, 1818, Havana, Cuba—Jan. 7, 1878, Havana, Cuba): Writer and critic. Suárez y Romero attended primary school at a Dominican boarding school but later attended a Presbyterian school, then the Seminary of San Carlos. He received his law degree from the University of Havana. He taught at various universities in Havana in the areas of literature and political economy.

Suárez's *Francisco*, written in 1839 but not published until 1880, is an intentionally grim picture of slavery in Cuba. It is one of the earliest fictional works from the Americas, along with Felix Tanco Bosmeniel's *Petrona y Rosalia* (written in 1838, published in 1925) and Cirilio Villaverde's early sketch of Cecilia Valdés, later elaborated into a long novel of that name. British abolitionist Richard R. Madden, who visited Cuba from 1837 to 1839 to survey slave conditions on the island, was given a copy of Suárez's work and subsequently produced some copies of the novel in 1840.

Suárez also published critical essays on the works of other writers. His nature essays were weaker than his other prose, using excessive, lyrical romantic style and lush vocabulary. Most of Suárez's works, historically significant in their portrayal of slavery in Cuba, remain in manuscript in the Cuban Biblioteca Nacional.

Substance abuse: Latinos, like other Americans, experienced increasing problems of substance abuse during the late twentieth century. Although problems of substance abuse in general are not particular to the

Latino community, aspects of substance abuse among Latinos differ from those of other populations.

Defining the Problem. Determining the exact prevalence of drug abuse in Latino communities is fraught with methodological problems. Most research articles dealing with alcohol and substance abuse in Latino communities pertain to survey results, outpatient and inpatient drug treatment data, archival data, and arrest records. Most drug use records pertain to illicit drugs and ignore legal drug use. True estimates of drug abuse or use are therefore impossible to determine.

Another problem is use of the broad terms "Hispanic" and "Latino," which some researchers have suggested have nothing to do with ethnic identity. Researchers thus cannot pin problems of substance abuse to a "Latino" identity. In addition, some statistics on substance abuse are not collected or categorized in ways that allow separation of data pertaining to Latinos.

Contradictory Evidence. It is not surprising then that studies of licit and illicit drug use in the Latino community contain contradictory findings. One study of substance abuse among Latino adolescents, published in the mid-1980's, indicated alarming increases compared to white and black adolescents. A survey published by the National Institute on Drug Abuse in 1992, however, showed that a smaller proportion of Latinos (29.2 percent) than of non-Hispanic whites (37.7 percent) responded that they had ever used any illicit drug. Only 10.8 percent of Latinos reported using illicit drugs during the past year, compared to 11.3 percent of white respondents. Researchers have pointed to the similar rates, among Latinos and non-Latinos, of use of illicit drugs. They have suggested that acculturation to American society may help explain that similarity.

The National Institute on Drug Abuse reported in 1990 that between 1985 and 1988, the number of Latinos aged twelve and older who had ever used illicit drugs rose 29 percent. The percentage of Latinos who had ever used cocaine rose from 7.3 percent to 11 percent.

Links to Health Problems. Substance abuse has been linked to various health problems. For example, as of December, 1989, half of more than eighteen thousand Latinos who had developed ACQUIRED IMMUNE DEFICIENCY SYNDROME (AIDS) had used illicit intravenous drugs. In 1989, 70 percent of cases of children under the age of thirteen with AIDS were linked to mothers who had abused intravenous drugs or had sex with an intravenous drug abuser. About one-fourth of intrave-

nous heroin or cocaine users never used bleach or alcohol to clean their needles before injection. This placed them at high risk for HIV infection.

Research also has established that illicit drug use is a major cause of death among Latino males and contributes significantly to high infant mortality rates and low birth weight in Puerto Rican children. According to a National Institute of Drug Abuse study published in 1988, nearly 18 percent of emergency room incidents for Latinos involved heroin or morphine, a higher percentage than for any other ethnic group. In 1988, Latinos accounted for 13 percent of deaths resulting from drug abuse in twenty-seven metropolitan areas. In 1987, 16 percent of all Americans in drug treatment were Latinos, but an estimated 40 percent of Latinos who used drugs intravenously had never been in treatment.

Characteristics of Latino Substance Abuse. Latinos have higher rates than other groups of abuse of certain drugs, including heroin, morphine, inhalants, and PCP. Betty Crowther's 1972 study of patterns of drug use among Mexican Americans showed less experimentation with drugs than among other groups. Mexican Americans in that study had a much higher propensity

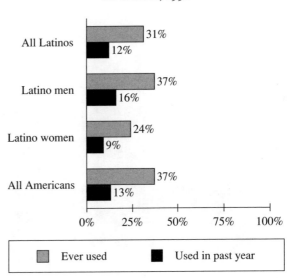

ESTIMATED ILLEGAL USE OF DRUGS BY LATINOS TWELVE YEARS OF AGE OR OLDER, 1991

Source: Data are from Marlita A. Reddy, ed., *Statistical Record of Hispanic Americans* (Detroit: Gale Research, 1993), Table 426.

Note: Illegal use of drugs includes use of marijuana, inhalants, cocaine, hallucinogens, and heroin as well as nonmedical uses of psychotherapeutics.

to use marijuana and heroin than did non-Hispanic whites in the same study.

Inhalant abuse also has been associated disproportionately with Latino youth. This abuse began in the 1950's with the sniffing of model airplane glue and continued with inhaling fumes from aerosol cans.

Comparisons Among Latino Groups. One review of findings on the use of illicit drugs by Latinos pointed to a crisis among adolescent and young adult Mexican Americans and Puerto Ricans. It confirmed earlier studies showing that Mexican Americans and Puerto Ricans are more likely to use marijuana and cocaine than are Cuban Americans, and that Mexican American youths are more likely to use inhalants than are Puerto Rican youths.

The use of licit drugs for nonmedical purposes generally has been found to be higher among Mexican Americans than among non-Hispanic white adolescents. The HISPANIC HEALTH AND NUTRITION EXAMINATION SURVEY, conducted in the 1980's, found that cocaine and marijuana use was higher among young, single, male Puerto Ricans and Mexican Americans whose primary language was English rather than Spanish. Poorer youth tended to abuse illegal drugs less than did wealthier youth. This finding strongly suggests that drug abuse is linked to acculturative stress associated with loss of identification with the parents' culture of origin. Further consequences of illicit drug use include a link to high rates of criminal activity and to dropping out of school.

One study from the early 1990's showed that drug availability was not always the main reason why youths abused drugs. Instead, close friends more often influenced an individual to abuse drugs. Substance abuse in general and among Latinos in particular, however, has various causes and no simple explanation. Prevention and treatment programs therefore must address multiple causes of substance abuse, with attention paid to cultural factors. —*Juan Garcia-Castañón*

SUGGESTED READINGS: • Crowther, Betty. "Patterns of Drug Use Among Mexican Americans." *International Journal of the Addictions* 7, no. 4 (1972): 637-647. • De La Rosa, M. R., J. H. Khalsa, and B. A. Rouse. "Hispanics and Illicit Drug Use: A Review of Recent Findings." *International Journal of the Addictions* 25 (June, 1990): 665-691. • Guinn, Robert. "The Phenomenology of Marijuana Use Among Mexican American Youth." *Journal of Psychedelic Drugs* 9

Latino street mural depicting aerosol substance abuse and its consequences. (Ruben G. Mendoza)

(October/December, 1977): 341-343. • Leal, Anita. "Hispanics and Substance Abuse: Implications for Rehabilitation Counselors." *Journal of Applied Rehabilitation Counseling* 21 (Fall, 1990): 52-54. • Mayers, Raymond Sanchez, Barbara Lynn Kail, and Thomas D. Watts, eds. *Hispanic Substance Abuse.* Springfield, Ill.: Charles C Thomas, 1993. • National Institute on Drug Abuse. Division of Epidemiology and Prevention Research. *National Household Survey on Drug Abuse: Population Estimates 1991.* Rockville, MD: Author, 1992. • National Institute on Drug Abuse. Division of Epidemiology and Statistical Analysis. *National Household Survey on Drug Abuse: Main Findings, 1985.* Rockville, MD: Author, 1988. • Padilla, E. R., A. M. Padilla, A. Morales, E. L. Olmedo, and R. Ramirez. "Inhalant, Marijuana, and Alcohol Abuse Among Barrio Children and Adolescents." *International Journal of the Addictions* 14 (October, 1979): 945-964. • Santisteban, Daniel A. "Toward a Conceptual Model of Drug Abuse Among Hispanics." In *Mental Health, Drug and Alcohol Abuse: An Hispanic Assessment of Present and Future Challenges*, edited by J. Szapocznik. Washington, D.C.: COSSMHO, 1979. • Schinke, S., M. Orlandi, D. Vaccaro, R. Espinoza, A. McAlister, and G. Botvin. "Substance Use Among Hispanic and Non-Hispanic Adolescents." *Addictive Behaviors* 17, no. 2 (1992): 117-124.

Sunny and the Sunliners: Tejano music group. Led by Sunny Ozuna, Sunny and the Sunliners is a premier Tejano group from southern Texas. They began playing together in the 1960's.

Sure-Tan, Inc. v. National Labor Relations Board (467 U.S. 883, 1984): Labor litigation. In this case, argued on December 6, 1983, and decided on June 25, 1984, the Supreme Court ruled on labor practices related to reporting employees to the IMMIGRATION AND NATURALIZATION SERVICE.

The National Labor Relations Board had found that Sure-Tan engaged in unfair labor practices by reporting certain employees that the employer knew to be undocumented aliens. The reporting was done in retaliation for the employees' union activities.

The Court of Appeals for the Seventh Circuit agreed that Sure-Tan had violated labor law but modified the remedial order issued by the National Labor Relations Board. The ruling of the appeals court was appealed to the Supreme Court.

The Court ruled that Sure-Tan had committed an unfair labor practice. It also ruled that the court of appeals had exceeded its limited authority under the NATIONAL LABOR RELATIONS ACT. The appeals court had directed the National Labor Relations Board both to impose an award of back pay (without regard to the employees' actual economic losses or legal availability for work) and to draft reinstatement offers in Spanish. The Court found both of these directions to be beyond the scope of authority of the appeals court. Part of the Supreme Court decision said that private persons do not have a legally recognized interest in securing enforcement of immigration laws.

Syphilis: Sexually transmitted disease. Syphilis, along with several other sexually transmitted diseases (STDs), can be treated with antibiotics. If left untreated, it has severe adverse effects on the person who has been infected.

Syphilis, ACQUIRED IMMUNE DEFICIENCY SYNDROME (AIDS), gonorrhea, and chlamydia trachomatis are among the most common STDs. According to a 1993 surveillance report issued by the Centers for Disease Control, chlamydia trachomatis is the most common sexually transmitted bacterial pathogen in the United States. The incidence of gonorrhea among Latino adolescents has been declining gradually. The only exceptions are for females between the ages of ten and fifteen. Among Latinos, rates of infection have been highest among adolescents between the ages of fifteen and nineteen in the northeastern part of the United States.

According to a 1993 surveillance report issued by the Centers for Disease Control, there was a syphilis epidemic between 1986 and 1990, when there were more than fifty thousand cases documented. Shortly thereafter, a decline was noted. Declines were noted in both the number and the rate of reported cases in every racial group and in both sexes. The rates for Latinos in 1991 were 15.5 (per 100,000 population) for males and 9.1 for females, compared to 138.2 for black males and 106.5 for black females. The rate for non-Hispanic whites was 2.4 for males and 1.6 for females.

Geographically, there has been a decline in all regions except the South. Probable reasons cited for the continued higher levels of disease transmission in the South were higher levels of poverty and poor access to health care services. Reasons for the decline in incidence elsewhere are unclear; there has been little documentation concerning activities that may reduce the incidence of infection.

A few studies give some indication that education may be making a difference. It was initially thought that Latino males would oppose condom use. This has not been supported by research. Since the spread of AIDS in the heterosexual population, there has been a steady increase in cases among Latinos, especially among Latinas and children. Because STDs can be transmitted in some of the same ways as AIDS, Latinos were therefore also likely to be at risk for syphilis. If teen pregnancy is any indicator of sexual activity among Latino adolescents, then the risk for any STD is fairly high. One study published in 1993 examined gender differences in sexual attitudes and behaviors among Latinos and white unmarried adults. The study found that Latinas reported fewer sexual partners but that the non-English-speaking Latinas also reported lower use of condoms than did the white women. Latinos were less likely than others to believe they could prevent AIDS with condom use.

The literature on Latinos and syphilis is sparse, indicating a need for further research. As of early 1994, the literature had not yet addressed differences among the Latino groups in terms of incidence.

T

Tabaqueros: Workers who produce tobacco products, particularly cigars. A large number of Latinos have served in the tobacco industry, which in the United States is located predominantly in the Southeast (*see* CIGAR MANUFACTURING). In 1944, cigar rollers and tobacco strippers formed the second largest bloc of union members in the United States when they joined with the UNITED CANNERY, AGRICULTURAL, PACKING AND ALLIED WORKERS OF AMERICA to become the Food, Tobacco, Agricultural, and Allied Workers of America. Latinas, who have been the majority of the tobacco work force, have contributed significantly to leadership of that union.

Tacla, Jorge (b. Santiago, Chile): Artist. Tacla moved to New York City in 1981. He held six solo shows there in the following ten years. He painted figurative works, as shown in his 1988 exhibition "To His Image and Likeness," until 1991, when he began to combine global awareness and quantum physics. A representative oil-on-canvas work with this influence is *Curvature of Space.*

Tacla also paints landscapes with expressionist and Chinese influences. These generally are large and multipaneled, on unprimed linen or canvas for color. He sometimes includes photographic negatives, notations, and physical addenda in collage-like work. Tacla is

A cigar factory in Miami, Florida. (Impact Visuals, Jack Kurtz)

known for the dots and dashes that crisscross many of his works, representing the fragmentation of the modern world.

Taco: Mexican ANTOJITO consisting of a folded tortilla with savory filling. The essence of the taco is a filling wrapped with a corn tortilla. Most tacos consumed in Mexico are of this simple variety. Diners in the United States, however, are more familiar with a slightly more complex version also known in Mexico. In this version, the folded and filled tortilla is fried. Fillings include shredded meat, beans, vegetables, brains, shark meat, and numberless other items.

Taft-Hartley Act. *See* **Labor-Management Relations Act**

Tagging and taggers: Tagging is the use of GRAFFITI to publicize a group or personal identity. Some studies and observers indicate that Latino youths engage in tagging to a greater extent than do non-Hispanic white youths and perhaps more than other youthful members of minority groups.

Origins. The origins of tagging as a specific practice are unclear. Graffiti of one type or another has existed for centuries. Tagging as a means of laying claim to territory or simply putting one's identity before the public eye began to be practiced on a significant scale in the 1960's.

Sometime in the late 1960's, a teenager bearing a felt-tipped pen began to write his nickname and house number on walls and subway cars in New York City. The idea soon evolved into a fad and came to be called tagging. By the early 1970's, the activity exploded into an art form, with New York City subways the primary target for energetic Puerto Rican graffiti masters such as Chino; Master Jaster, who got his name from his favorite brand of permanent ink, Flo-Master; and IZ THE WIZ. They were joined by African Americans and other youthful miscreants who, armed with marker pens and aerosol paint cans, scribbled and sprayed themselves into national attention.

Spray paint, which quickly replaced the felt-tipped pen as the favorite medium, provided a quick means of marking a large surface. Colorful signatures spread over the walls, the doors, and sometimes the windows of the city's subway cars. Taggers' nicknames, enigmatic to the police and the general public but known to many of the artists and their friends, provided the common basis of design, which was elaborated on by each artist according to individual style.

Tagging soon became a group endeavor. Many of the most prolific crews (organized teams of taggers) made headlines. Among them were OTB (Only the Best), TVS (The Vamp Squad), and WBLS (We Bomb Like Stars). Subway cars decorated in flamboyant multicolored graffiti known as "wildstyle" moved through tunnels and across bridges—which were also awash in spray-painted decoration—like enormous painted caterpillars.

The Spread of Tagging. Much to the chagrin of most law enforcement officials, the stylized swirls and blends of color born in the South Bronx spread across the United States, covering buildings, bridges, and highways in every urban center. Tagging took hold in Los Angeles, especially, with an intense passion. The long history of gang-related graffiti in EAST LOS ANGELES and elsewhere on the east side of the city dated to the PACHUCO era in the 1940's (*see* GANGS AND GANG ACTIVITY). The city's horizontal sprawl, abandoned industrial spaces, and temperate climate made it ideal for itinerant teams of taggers, many of whom preferred to call themselves writers, bombers, or mobbers. Freeway overpasses, dividers, and signs were particularly attractive places to spray fanciful signatures and designs. As the practice of tagging spread, many taggers began to consider themselves more as artists, signing their names artistically or even creating artworks to which they signed their names.

For a long time, taggers from the East Coast claimed superiority over West Coast writers because New York City's official semitoleration of the activity allowed graffiti artists to develop inventive, complex inscriptions. Intense rivalries of styles were forged in the subway tunnels. New York City began large-scale eradication efforts in the 1980's. By the 1990's, it had largely removed GRAFFITI from its five-thousand-car subway fleet. A combination of police tactics developed to deter vandals, the emergence of new car-cleaning products, the authorities' use of night-vision goggles, and the employment of hidden video cameras brought about a relatively clean subway system.

Profile of Taggers. Although some get caught up in violent acts, most taggers are non-gang-aligned thrill seekers associated with the rap-driven hip-hop subculture. Latino gang graffiti incorporated stylized medieval writing (such as Old English, German Gothic, and other angular forms of calligraphy) and developed a coded script that included distortions and substitutions of the Roman alphabet designed to mark territory.

Taggers commonly spray paint or write their monikers in an effort to self-advertise to friends, other tag-

Tagging is often perceived as an eyesore. (Impact Visuals, David Schulz)

gers, and the public. Their main objective is to write on as much property as possible. Many taggers scribble their insignias on anything and everything. Desires for self-promotion and to increase a crew's name recognition frequently overshadow an emblem's aesthetic validity.

CHAKA, probably the most famous tagger, tagged more than ten thousand locations, causing more than $500,000 in property damage from Southern California's Orange County to Oakland and San Francisco before his arrest at the age of eighteen. Born in Nicaragua, he was influenced by Los Angeles' first recog-

nized graffiti crew, the Bomb Squad. Its members were almost all youths of Central American birth or background, living in the Pico-Union area west of downtown or on the city's east side. After being referred to a state mental institution, incarcerated, sent to the sheriff department's "boot camp," getting shot, and running into other trouble, CHAKA turned to religion and entered a drug rehabilitation center in 1994.

At the other extreme, Charles "Chaz" Bojórquez began "bombing" (going on painting sprees) with his moniker and an unsigned skull figure, crossing its fingers and wearing a wide-brimmed fedora. He later became a renowned gallery artist after catching the attention of the film and advertising industries. He worked on several films and created advertising logos and commercial backgrounds. He considered tagging of the 1990's to be immature and childlike.

Types of Tagging. Most graffiti artists perceive simple tagging as at the bottom of a three-tier system of street writing and painting. Graffiti murals, at the top, are often referred to as "pieces" (short for masterpieces) and typically embody message, technique, and care that warrant a measure of aesthetic admiration. Gang territorial markings, just below "piecing," are often referred to as *placas* or *plaqueasos* (plaques or signs) by gang members. Often illegible to the casual observer because of their cryptic nature, their beauty is measured by their neatness, their originality within the context of established forms, and the alignment and design of their letters. *Placas* delineate turf boundaries and define the culture within a specified neighborhood. Most of the markings now called tagging are considered eyesores, marring the urban landscape with narcissistic scrawls crudely put together.

Conclusion. Tagging does not occur in a vacuum but is linked to crime, poverty, substandard education, faltering families, unemployment, systemic racism, and the crisis of identity experienced particularly by members of minority groups. Without another outlet to channel their creative energy and express their identities, taggers will continue their vandalism. Although some of the creations of taggers might be considered art, most are considered graffiti, to be removed at sometimes considerable cost. By the early 1990's, tagging and other forms of graffiti had spread into Mexico and Central America.   —*Ignacio Orlando Trujillo*

SUGGESTED READINGS: • Alland, Alexander. *The Artistic Animal: An Inquiry into the Biological Roots of Art.* Garden City, N.Y.: Anchor Books, 1977. • Chalfant, Henry, and James Prigoff. *Spraycan Art.* New York: Thames and Hudson, 1987. • Cockcroft, Eva, John Weber, and James D. Cockcroft. *Toward a People's Art: The Contemporary Mural Movement.* New York: E. P. Dutton, 1977. • Reisner, Robert. *Graffiti: Two Thousand Years of Wall Writing.* New York: Cowles Books, 1971. • Romotsky, Jerry, and Sally R. Romotsky. *Los Angeles Barrio Calligraphy.* Los Angeles: Dawson's Book Shop, 1976. • Shusterman, Richard. *Pragmatist Aesthetics: Living Beauty, Rethinking Art.* Oxford, England: Blackwell, 1992. • Vigil, James Diego. *Barrio Gangs: Street Life and Identity in Southern California.* Austin: University of Texas Press, 1988.

Tamales: ANTOJITO consisting of a steamed ball of filled corn dough. Tamales are quintessential fiesta food, since they take a long time to make and are best made in large quantities. The basic *tamal* begins with MASA spread inside a pliable corn husk. A filling is placed onto it, and the husk is folded and steamed. Most tamales are savory, usually with spiced meat fillings; some have sweetened dough and fillings of fruit or fresh corn. They vary from tiny tamales of the north, scarcely two inches long, to enormous yard-long tamales of the Huastec region. In some areas, tamales are available for sale only on certain days, Sunday in many parts of Mexico and Saturday in the American Southwest and Southern California. People in eastern Mexico and parts of Central America make tamales in banana leaves and call them *vaporcitos*; Venezuelans call theirs *hallacas*. Puerto Rican, Cuban, and other Caribbean cuisines include some tamales, usually called *pasteles*. The Anglo-American term "tamale" is a backformation from the Spanish plural "tamales" and is not used in Mexico; the correct singular is *tamal*.

Tamayo, Rufino (b. 1899, Oaxaca, Mexico): Artist. Tamayo moved to Mexico City in 1911. From 1919 to 1921, he attended the Academy of Fine Arts there.

Tamayo was appointed the head of ethnography at the National Museum of Archaeology in 1921. He taught painting at the National School of Fine Arts in Mexico City in 1928 and 1929, and in 1932 he became head of the Department of Plastic Arts at the Secretariat of Education in that city. For twenty years beginning in 1936, Tamayo lived in New York City off and on. He taught painting at the Dalton School in 1936 and at the Brooklyn Museum in 1946.

In 1933, Tamayo did his first mural for the Mexican National Music Conservatory. He painted several murals in Mexico and the United States in 1936, with murals following at Smith College (1943), in Dallas (1953), and in Houston (1955-1956). Later he painted murals on the UNESCO building in Paris (1958), on walls in Israel (1963), and for the Mexican Pavilion at Expo 67 in Montreal, Canada (1967). He also produced lithographs for the Ford Foundation in 1964. Among Mexican muralists, Tamayo is known not for his political content but for his solid art technique and production.

Tamayo's first solo exhibition was in Mexico in 1926. He had retrospectives at the Palace of Fine Arts in Mexico City in 1948 and 1968. He exhibited at the Venice Biennale in 1950. He won the grand prize at

Rufino Tamayo in 1990 with one of his later works, The Mockers. (AP/Wide World Photos)

the São Paulo, Brazil, Biennale in 1953, received the Guggenheim Foundation prize and the international prize at the Biennale of Mexico in 1960, and won the national prize presented by the president of Mexico in 1964. His work has been exhibited around the world and is held in the collections of numerous large museums.

Tampa, Florida: It is said that Tampa Bay was discovered by a pirate. In fact, the first European reference to the area comes from the log of a shipwrecked Spaniard of the sixteenth century who lived for a time among the local Indians; his profession as a pirate, however, has never been confirmed.

Tampa's official history begins with the arrival of Juan PONCE DE LEÓN, the Spanish explorer who searched in vain for the fabled Fountain of Youth. Ponce de León entered FLORIDA by way of Tampa Bay in 1513. Following him were missionaries, opportunists, and adventurers.

Florida was granted U.S. statehood in 1845. Tampa's first boom in population occurred in the last years of the nineteenth century, when a group of Cuban cigar manufacturers arrived. YBOR CITY, which lies north of the downtown area, was founded by the cigar makers in 1886 as a center for manufacturing. Thousands of mostly Spanish-speaking immigrants came to work in the cigar factories (*see* CIGAR MANUFACTURING). By 1900, they had transformed Tampa into the world's largest manufacturer of Cuban cigars and Ybor City into a highly civilized, multiethnic community. During the SPANISH-AMERICAN WAR (1898), the city of Tampa was employed briefly as a staging point for Theodore Roosevelt and his "Rough Riders" as they voyaged to Cuba.

Although the city remained primarily Hispanic in character, the private clubs, ballrooms, theaters, and restaurants reflected its ethnic diversity. Ybor City became relatively affluent, but its prosperity was based on the health of the cigar trade. In 1900, Tampa's cigar production peaked at 111 million units. In the decades that followed, many of the factories closed. Several factors exacerbated this process of decline. First were improvements in technology. By the 1920's, thousands of cigars could be rolled by machine in the time it took to create fifty by hand. This, coupled with the increasing popularity of cigarettes and the effects of the Great Depression, sent the area into a long, downward spiral that continued for many years.

In a state notorious for economic booms and busts, Tampa managed to weather most difficulties relatively well. Beginning in the 1980's, the city grew steadily in population and status as a population shift to the Sunbelt gained momentum. In the wake of Tampa's sudden success, YBOR CITY achieved a kind of economic afterlife. This new prosperity was based mostly on tourism, one of Tampa's core industries.

Tampa's evolution from sleepy southern backwater to urban giant occurred virtually overnight. Businesses relocated by the hundreds to the Gulf Coast, where land and labor costs were significantly lower than those in other parts of the United States. Workers arrived from other U.S. cities as well as from Europe and the island nations of the Caribbean. By 1990, the Tampa metropolitan area had a Latino population of nearly 140,000, about evenly split in fourths among Cuban Americans, Puerto Ricans, Mexican Americans, and other Latinos.

Tango: Argentine song and dance genre. Influenced by the *milonga* (African dance of syncopated rhythm) and the habanera, the tango, played in a minor key, bears emotional texts sung by a vocalist accompanied typically by violin, flute, guitar, or accordion. The original tango in two-four time later spread throughout Europe, with more complex rhythms evolving. Three types became popular: *tango milonga* (purely instrumental), *tango romanza* (romantic texts, sung or instrumental), and *tango canción* (dramatic, pessimistic texts with accompaniment). The tango is danced in tight embrace, with smooth, gliding steps, sharp movements, and haughty poses that assert the masculinity of the man and the subdued role of the woman.

Tanguma, Leo (b. c. 1945): Muralist. Tanguma paints monumental murals, inspired by the work of David Alfaro SIQUEIROS, whom he met in 1972. The Chicano muralist's works treat contemporary subjects with radical political content. Tanguma's work is politically controversial, and he has had commissions canceled because of political opposition. His panels have been refused, his murals have been repainted, and his studio and home were burned. He has been harassed by law enforcement officials and rejected by the art community.

Tanguma's works include *The People's Judgement Against Institutionalized Brutality and Racism: Rebirth of Our Nationality* (1973), a 240-foot by 18-foot work done with 150 assistants; *Towards a Humanitarian Technology for la Raza* (1972, destroyed); *Americanization of a Chicano* (1974, destroyed); and *Humanity in Harmony with Nature* (1981). Tanguma is known for his radical politics and the harsh discrimination from which he and his art have suffered as a result.

Taos, New Mexico: Taos is one of the oldest settlements in New Mexico and in the United States. It is the

LATINO POPULATION OF TAMPA, FLORIDA, 1990

Total number of Latinos = 139,248; 6.7% of population

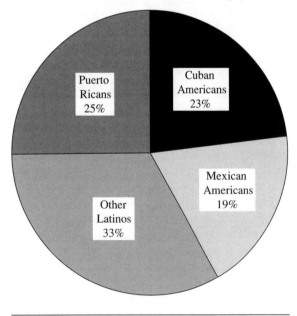

Puerto Ricans 25%
Cuban Americans 23%
Mexican Americans 19%
Other Latinos 33%

Source: Data are from Marlita A. Reddy, ed., *Statistical Record of Hispanic Americans* (Detroit: Gale Research, 1993), Table 111.
Note: Figures represent the population of the Tampa-St. Petersburg-Clearwater, Florida, Metropolitan Statistical Area as delineated by the U.S. Bureau of the Census.

Dancers of the tango use a tight embrace. (Impact Visuals, Donna DeCesare)

Taos is the site of the mission of St. Francisco de Asis. (James Shaffer)

county seat of Taos County. It combines three communities: a majority-culture economic center, a Pueblo village, and an old Spanish farming center. The city is about fifty-five miles northeast of Santa Fe.

Taos refers to several different features in New Mexico. It is the name of a mountain range, a mountain, a canyon, a valley, a stream, a county, and three towns. The area was first visited by the Spanish in 1540, when Francisco Vázquez de CORONADO traveled through the territory. In 1598 it became one of the seven mission districts designated by Juan de OÑATE.

Spanish settlers came to Taos as early as 1615, as indicated by a sign in the plaza. There has been a continuous Spanish/Mexican presence in the area since that time, except for the decade after the Pueblo Revolt in 1680. The area was reconquered for the Spanish by Diego de VARGAS in 1692.

Revolt and rebellion are a distinct part of Taos history. Geographic features contributed much to these events. The land itself is poor and rocky. The climate features cold winters and limited rainfall, so there is a short growing season. Farming and herding of both sheep and cattle were main means of subsistence. Agricultural products included cereal grains and beans. As the land was overworked by both planting and grazing, the soil became sterile, making subsistence difficult.

The area is surrounded by natural geological barriers, mountains in particular. As a result, it was isolated from the mainstream Spanish political influence from Mexico City. This isolation caused the area to develop a particularly independent quality. After the Pueblo Revolt, or POPÉ'S REVOLT, of 1680, a second revolt by the Pueblo Indians was attempted in 1696. The early 1700's saw a Comanche attack. A second Comanche attack occurred in 1760.

The revolts and rebellions resulted in a unique feature of Taos history, a dearth of historical documents. During the Pueblo Revolt of 1680, Indians destroyed most of the historical documents and other papers of the area. Other valuable papers were burned during a revolution during the 1840's. Once the revolts were subdued, the town prospered as a trading center. The fur trade was active in the area in the 1820's.

In 1898, two artists, Bert Phillips and Ernest Blumenschein, were traveling south in New Mexico when their wagon wheel broke about twenty miles outside Taos. During their forced stay in the area, they decided to end their journey at Taos. This was the beginning of the well-known "art colony" of Taos that survives into the present. Artists enjoy the climate and the unique beauty of the area. In addition, the town serves the region as a trade and economic center for nearby farms and ranches.

Taos Rebellion (Jan. 19, 1847): The Taos Rebellion broke through the façade of acceptance that at first characterized the occupation of New Mexico by U.S. troops during the MEXICAN AMERICAN WAR. The uprising showed the extent of the resentment the *nuevomexicanos* felt toward their captors.

The stage was set for the Taos Rebellion in August, 1846, with General Stephen W. Kearny's capture of Santa Fe. The town was taken over without a shot fired, and Kearny immediately set about to establish good relations between the *nuevomexicanos* and his troops. He appointed Charles Bent, a longtime resident of New Mexico, as governor and pledged that U.S. citizenship would be extended to the people of New Mexico. To all appearances, the Mexicans and heads of the local Native American pueblos accepted the new government.

Kearny, convinced he was no longer needed in New Mexico, set out in September with the bulk of his army to aid the war effort in California. Troops in Santa Fe were further depleted when Colonel Alexander W. Doniphan led a body of men south toward Chihuahua.

Beneath the seeming peace, resentments seethed. In late December, an extensive, well-organized plan to free Santa Fe from U.S. rule was uncovered barely in time to prevent a bloody uprising. The plot involved not only former Mexican soldiers but also local priests and many of the region's highly respected, influential residents. With the suppression of this rebellion, U.S. authorities once again assumed that matters were well in hand.

On January 19, 1847, Governor Bent was murdered and scalped on his way to Taos to visit his family. More than a dozen other Americans were slain that same day in nearby towns and ranches. The assassinations immediately precipitated an uprising of the *nuevomexicanos*, both Native Americans and Mexicans. They were led by Pablo Montoya of Taos (who years earlier had played a major role in a revolt against Governor Albino Pérez, another outsider appointed to assume military and civil command of the region) and Tomasito, the Taos Indian leader, who may have been supported by local priests. The rebels eventually numbered approximately fifteen hundred.

Colonel Sterling Price quickly gathered 479 troops from Santa Fe and Albuquerque and rode toward Taos to suppress the rebellion. After winning a battle at La

Cañada on January 24 and another at the Embudo pass on January 29, Price followed the rebels to Pueblo de Taos. On February 3 and 4, Price's troops bombarded the pueblo, but its adobe walls were too thick for the cannon to penetrate. The soldiers eventually hacked holes in the walls so their artillery could shell the pueblo interior. Screened by the smoke from the shelling, the soldiers stormed the rebels. The U.S. troops suffered light casualties in the encounter; the rebels lost 150 men before surrendering. This effectively ended the revolt, although several skirmishes followed in the next few days.

The insurrection leaders were tried, and fifteen were sentenced to death. The fairness of the trial is still disputed, as is the matter of whether the Taos Rebellion was an extension of the thwarted Santa Fe plot. Evidence suggests that the Taos Rebellion was spontaneous, rather than carefully plotted. Both incidents, however, demonstrate the hostility the *nuevomexicanos* harbored for the U.S. troops occupying their land.

Tapia, Luis (b. 1950, Santa Fe, N.Mex.): Artist. Little art instruction was offered in the public schools that Tapia attended. Even during his one year at New Mexico State University, he had no formal art instruction. Tapia began making santos around 1970, when he became aware of Latino issues surrounding the Civil Rights movement. He modeled his work after SANTOS at the Folk Art Museum in Santa Fe, but unlike earlier *santeros*, he used bright colors for his figures. His use of bright colors shocked some viewers, but he believed that his works were more authentic than unpainted santos or those that had been artificially aged.

Tapia has also worked on the making and restoration of furniture and was involved in major restoration projects. One of his most important projects was the church at Ranchos de Taos.

Tarango, Yolanda (b. Sept. 26, 1948, El Paso, Tex.): Association executive. Tarango has been an active civic and church leader and administrator within the Hispanic community. She worked as a counselor for the emotionally disturbed at the St. Joseph Center from 1970 to 1973. After she received her B.A. in education in 1973 from the Incarnate Word College in San Antonio, she was a teacher at St. Mary's School.

Tarango served in the youth and young adult ministry in the diocese of El Paso from 1973 to 1979 and attended the Catholic Theological Union in Chicago in 1983. In the 1980's, Tarango was the director of pastoral education of the MEXICAN AMERICAN CULTURAL CENTER, founder and director of the Visitation House Homeless Shelter, director of the School of Ministry of the West Side Parish Coalition, and director of volunteers for the Sisters of Charity of the Incarnate Word. She attended the John F. Kennedy School of Government at Harvard University in 1988.

Tarango's community service has included being a board member and chairperson of the National Assembly of Religious Women, national coordinator of Las Hermanas, a board member of the Mary's Pence Women's Foundation, and a member of Mujeres Para el Dialogo and Hispanas Unidas. She is the author of *Hispanic Women: Prophetic Voice in the Church* (1988).

Teachers and teaching styles: Teachers and teaching styles affect the learning of students of all races and cultural backgrounds. By virtue of their own cultural backgrounds, teachers may favor certain cognitive styles over others, making it easier or more difficult for certain students to learn.

In many school settings, the teachers are primarily Anglo and the students primarily Latino. Educators must consider the world for which education is preparing the student and whether the world of the student is appreciated properly by the educational system.

Cultural values contribute much to cognitive styles, and these cognitive styles influence how students learn. When teachers come from one cultural background and students from another, the results may include failure to learn, high dropout rates, poor performance on standardized tests, and high levels of retention at grade level. None of these outcomes, in this case, can be attributed completely to the students. Instead, schools have failed to teach in the ways in which students best learn.

Among the documented differences in cognitive style between Anglos and Latinos are those of incentives and motivation. For example, research based on Mexican Americans has shown that Latinos are more cooperative in school tasks, while Anglo students are more competitive. Latinos also have more need for affiliation (interaction with others and membership in a social group) than Anglos. Latino students also exhibit more of a desire to emulate role models.

Cultural differences also tend to show up in intellectual areas. Anglos outperformed Latinos on tests dealing with Piaget's conservation tasks (mass, weight, volume), but Latinos did better than Anglos on tasks involved with imaginative stories.

Latino teachers can bring to the classroom styles of teaching and learning different from those of many Anglos. (James Shaffer)

Research tends to show Latinos as more "field dependent" (better at relational thinking) than Anglos, while Anglos tended to be "field independent" (better at analytical tasks). Most school environments favor the "field independent" style, thus disadvantaging Latino students, whose culture contributes to the development of a "field dependent" style. Most standardized tests reward the analytic cognitive style, leading to identification of Latino students as low in achievement and ability.

Situations in which students and teachers are of the same types tend to result in more favorable learning outcomes; each group also assigns better evaluations to individuals of the same type. Teachers and students with the same cognitive style (and perhaps the same cultural background) therefore might enjoy working together, with students learning more as a result.

Research on teaching styles thus indicates that teachers with backgrounds in different cultures, especially Latino, need to be recruited so that teachers' styles can match students' learning styles. Teacher education must create more sensitivity to the variety of learning and teaching styles and give a place to relational thinking along with the traditionally valued analytical thinking. Some experts recommend bicognitive development, by which teachers encourage all students to draw from both analytical and relational styles and use the one most appropriate to the task at hand. Bicognitive development would provide more equity for students of all cultural backgrounds because each student's cultural contribution would be valued.

Teatro Campesino: Theater group. El Teatro Campesino began performing in 1965 in the agricultural fields

Teatro Campesino performances featured minimal props and strong messages. (Lou DeMatteis)

of Delano, California, during César CHÁVEZ's first attempt to organize farmworkers into a labor movement. Although a long theater tradition existed in the Latino world, the creation of a labor theater that focused on the political and cultural concerns of farmworkers was unique.

The creator of El Teatro Campesino was Luis Miguel VALDEZ, who had performed with the San Francisco Mime Troupe. He joined Chávez in organizing strikes in the lettuce fields and in the grape boycott. Valdez's dramatizations of workers' lives popularized their cause. Students, activists, and artists formed small theater groups that spread the ideas of the farmworker movement throughout the United States. Many of Valdez's performances in the fields showed the conflict between workers and growers, often through satirical portrayals.

By 1968, Valdez had left the agricultural fields and begun to create theater for all Chicanos, not only for farmworkers. He believed that he could strengthen the newly emerging identity of Chicanos by dramatizing the social and political problems that affected all Mexican Americans (*see* CHICANO MOVEMENT). He com-

bined the philosophy of El Teatro Campesino with the style of touring Mexican theater groups that had been popular in the Southwest since the late nineteenth century. He wrote many works to celebrate the bilingual-bicultural identity of Chicanos.

Many theater groups sprang up to follow the footsteps of Valdez. They presented *actos*, dramas of one act, written by Valdez or by other emerging dramatists. *Actos*, a collection of Valdez's short plays, was published in 1971. Chicano theater festivals held in 1976 contrasted sharply with the images presented by the official celebrations of the U.S. bicentennial. In that same year, some Chicano theater groups broke away from the model of El Teatro Campesino. They incorporated new methods and themes into their repertoires, and each group developed its own style. El Teatro Campesino turned toward religious mysticism as the focus for its productions. Criticism of this focus caused El Teatro Campesino to withdraw from the Chicano theater movement before the end of the 1970's.

El Teatro Campesino was a unique creation that filled the needs of a people striving to forge a new identity within mainstream U.S. culture. It helped Chicanos to see themselves as a unified group with a common language, a common past, and common goals. It was created as theater for the people, and it brought theater to them in the fields where they spent their lives. It helped Mexican Americans to rediscover the folklore, music, history, and artistry of their past, and it prepared mainstream audiences for Chicano themes in theater, music, and cinema.

Teatro de la Esperanza (San Francisco, Calif.): Professional theater group. This Chicano theater group began in 1969 at the University of California at Santa Barbara. It was a student theater group affiliated with Movimiento Estudiantil Chicano de Aztlán until 1971. Gradually moving away from the student base, it became a community-based group and full-time professional theater by about 1976, with international touring beginning in 1978. In 1986, the theater relocated to the Mission District of San Francisco, California. Teatro de la Esperanza brings bilingual/bicultural Chicano experience to the community and has been instrumental in leadership of the theater coalition TENAZ (Teatro Nacional de Aztlán).

Teatro Nacional de Aztlán (TENAZ): Association of Latino theaters. TENAZ was founded in 1971 in the midst of the farmworkers' struggle and the Chicano movement. It was led originally by Teatro Campesino, which split from TENAZ in 1975. Leadership has since been shared among member groups. The group's main activities include producing the TENAZ festival, which occurs every two years or so in the United States or Mexico and features various Latino theater groups' works. TENAZ serves as a coalition to promote Latino theater and communication among Latino theater groups. TENAZ has also produced special events such as the Youth Teatro Festival in Puerto Rico.

Tecatos: Chicano drug addicts. *Tecatos* are Chicanos addicted to heroin or other drugs. The term was created by pachucos around the 1940's. At that time, drug use and addiction proliferated in urban settings such as East Los Angeles, California, and Chicago, Illinois.

Tehuana costume: Traditional Mexican costume from Tehuantepec. The *tehuana* costume is a traditional dress worn by women from the town of Tehuantepec, in the state of Oaxaca. This distinct costume consists of a tunic called a *huipil*, a dark sateen or velvet skirt with flounces, and a headdress called a *huipil grande*. The *huipil*, which dates from pre-Columbian times,

and the skirt are richly embroidered with floral or geometric designs. Flounces commonly are made of organdy or tulle, but the finest feature handmade lace. The *huipil grande* is made of lace, has tiny sleevelike attachments, and is heavily starched so that it frames the face.

Tejano Conjunto Festival (San Antonio, Tex.): Styled as the largest festival of its kind in the world, the Tejano Conjunto Festival draws more than forty thousand people annually. The unique *conjunto* style of music originated in northern Mexico and South Texas at the end of the nineteenth century, when Mexicans and Mexican Americans living in the area adopted the button accordion of the German settlers, combining it in ensembles with the Spanish twelve-string bass guitar, or *bajo sexto*. Using a variety of European rhythms with native musical forms, *conjunto* music became popular in the 1920's.

Over the years, *conjunto* music has become highly diversified and both individualized and regionalized. Tejano *conjunto* music, played in Texas, is now distinct from *norteño conjunto*, played in northern Mexico. Tejano *conjunto* music itself can be divided into three styles: San Antonio, Coastal Bend (or Corpus Christi), and Valley. It also has traditional, popular, and progressive forms.

San Antonio remains the center for *conjunto* music and is to it what New Orleans is to jazz. The Tejano Conjunto Festival was organized there in 1982 by the Guadalupe Cultural Arts Center with the express purpose of introducing *conjunto* music to new audiences. The festival, held in Rosedale Park, Mission County Park, and Market Square, features ethnic food, folk art and craft booths, children's games, and dancing in addition to *conjunto* music. It is at this festival that accomplished musicians are inducted into the Conjunto Music Hall of Fame.

Tejano Music Awards (San Antonio, Tex.): In creating the Tejano Conjunto Festival, the Guadalupe Cultural Arts Center of San Antonio stipulated that one purpose was to afford "proper recognition to those artists who pioneered" the unique, Chicano musical genre of Tejano *conjunto* music. The organization established the Conjunto Music Hall of Fame, which annually inducts artists in the field and honors their contributions with festival performances. Inductions have now become part of the festival's opening night ceremonies. By 1994, the Conjunto Music Hall of Fame had inducted twenty-nine members.

Raymond Telles, Jr., became U.S. ambassador to Costa Rica in 1961. (AP/Wide World Photos)

Telles, Raymond L., Jr. (b. Sept. 15, 1915, El Paso, Tex.): Government official. After being educated at the International Business College and the University of Texas at El Paso, Telles, a Mexican American, started seven years of public service as a cost accountant and Justice Department administrator.

During World War II, Telles served in the Air Force, principally as chief of the lend-lease program to Latin American countries. In the Korean War, he achieved the rank of lieutenant colonel.

In 1948, Telles was elected as El Paso County Clerk, serving until taking the office of mayor in 1957. He served two terms as mayor. In 1961, President John F. Kennedy appointed Telles as ambassador to Costa Rica. Telles was influential in bringing Costa Rica into the Central American Common Market. In 1967, President Lyndon B. Johnson appointed Telles to chair the U.S. Section of the Joint U.S.-Mexico Commission for Border Development and Friendship. President Richard M. Nixon appointed Telles to the Equal Employment Opportunity Commission in 1971. Telles served for five years.

Tenayuca (Brooks), Emma (b. 1916, San Antonio, Tex.): Labor organizer. During the 1930's, Tenayuca was a strong advocate for a fair wage for pecan shellers in San Antonio, Texas, and was a leader of the PECAN SHELLERS' STRIKE (1938) before being replaced by Luisa MORENO. A devout Communist, she was well educated and charismatic. She was admired but not taken seriously by government leaders. In the early 1930's she married a Houston Communist, Homer Brooks, but she retained her birth name and saw him only on occasional weekends. As a founder of the militant Workers Alliance, she led demonstrations at City Hall and at the state capitol, and she was arrested several times. Because of her courage and dynamic speaking, her followers called her *La Pasionaria*, for the Communist Passion Flower of the Spanish Civil War. After a violent clash between her Communist supporters and local patriotic societies, Tenayuca left Texas for California, but she was not well received by activists there. She disappeared from the public eye in 1939. She earned a college degree and returned to San Antonio to teach elementary school.

Tenochtitlán: Capital city of the Aztec empire. Located in Central Mexico, Tenochtitlán was the political and religious center of the Aztecs. The Aztecs, originally from the area that is now the southwestern United States, migrated to central Mexico in the beginning of the thirteenth century. They founded Tenochtitlán in 1325. From that center, they conquered other city-states and created an empire.

Tenochtitlán's structure impressed the Spaniards who saw it in 1519. The city was situated on a small island on a lake, and waterways provided the main form of transportation. Canals and bridges linked different parts of the city.

When Hernán CORTÉS conquered the Aztec empire, he established the colonial capital at the site of Tenochtitlán. Mexico City, the capital of modern Mexico, is on the same site.

Teotihuacán: Archaeological site northeast of Mexico City. A major civilization flourished in Teotihuacán between the beginning of the Christian era and the year 650, when Toltecs invaded. The origin and language of the Teotihuacanos are unknown. It is also unclear whether this city, more than ten square miles in size, had political control of a larger area. Teotihuacán influenced most of Mesoamerica, most noticeably in the worship of the god QUETZALCÓATL, whom the Aztecs venerated. Teotihuacán's most impressive structures are the pyramids of the Sun and the Moon, which rise 200 and 140 feet respectively.

Tertulia: Daytime social gathering for conversation. The *tertulia* in Mexico derives from the event of the same name in Spain. In Spain, people assemble near the middle of the day at a café, particularly to discuss politics or to converse. The Mexican *tertulia* differs from its Spanish counterpart in that it is restricted to the larger towns and cities and does not necessarily take place in a café. In rural Mexico, a *tertulia* is an evening party for teenagers with music, food, and dancing.

Texas: As the second largest U.S. state (exceeded in geographic area only by Alaska), Texas is home to the nation's second largest Latino community. Its 4.34 million Latino residents (1990 U.S. census) composed 26 percent of the state's population.

Spanish Exploration. Latino history dominates the history of Texas. In the sixteenth century, Spaniards began an era of exploration of Texas coastlines and inner territories. Increasing numbers of conquistadores came from southern Spain, the Canary Islands, and Cuba. The conquistadores vanquished the Indians in Texas, establishing Roman Catholic missions, military forts, and a cattle ranching heritage. The subsequent historical development of what is now the state of Texas has been largely the result of Spanish influence, the loss of the territory to Mexico, merger with the United States, and ever-increasing numbers of immigrants, primarily from Mexico.

Spanish history accounts for about two-thirds of the recorded history of Texas. A 1519 expedition headed by Alonzo ÁLVAREZ DE PINEDA first charted the coastline of Texas. A more influential early expedition was headed by Pánfilo de NARVÁEZ, who was sent in 1527 by the governor of Cuba to explore the coastline along the Gulf of Mexico. Most of these Spaniards died or returned to Cuba, with the exception of a group of survivors headed by Álvar Núñez CABEZA DE VACA. Cabeza de Vaca's *La Relación*, published in Spain in 1542, was the first book ever written about Texas and its native people.

These writings of adventures in Texas territory set the stage for intense interest in Texas treasuries of gold and diamonds. A 1541 military expedition, with a cavalry headed by Francisco Vázquez de CORONADO, was sent to find the seven cities of CÍBOLA, the cities of gold reported by Cabeza de Vaca. This expedition into the Great Plains and western Texas lasted more than a

year. Coronado's negative report on Texas discouraged settlement in territories north of the Rio Grande for nearly a century and a half. During this period, most expeditions to Texas were directed by friars and had a goal of gaining religious converts among the indigenous peoples.

The first appearance in any known document of the name of Tejas or Texas (both pronounced "tay hass" in old Spanish) was in the reports of the religious expedition of 1650 headed by Hernán Martín and Diego del Castillo. Traveling along the Colorado River of Texas, the expedition was met by Indians, who greeted the Spaniards by saying *techias*, meaning "friends." The Spaniards reported reaching the outer boundaries of an extensive Indian nation called Tejas. Many of the descendants of these Indians and Spaniards proudly call themselves Tejanos, and their unique cultural heritage is referred to as Tejano culture.

Fray Francisco Hidalgo perhaps had the largest influence in the permanent occupation of Texas by Spain when he founded the Presidio del Rio Grande in 1701. This was the main gateway to Texas for the next 150 years. French expeditions, prompted by requests from Fray Hidalgo, renewed Spain's interest in Texas and led to establishment of four missions in eastern Texas in 1716.

Settlements. The first group of civilian colonists to settle in Texas came from the Canary Islands and Cuba in 1731. These immigrants founded the town that was later called San Antonio. Their settlement had the first organized civil government in Texas.

After three centuries of Spanish rule of Texas and following Mexico's independence in 1821, the Mexican-born Spaniards called Creoles became Texas' ruling class. The Creole rulers approved a plan proposed by Moses Austin to bring Anglo settlers into Texas. They gave his son, Stephen F. Austin, a land grant that initiated a rapid immigration from the United States.

During subsequent years of unrest in the Mexican government, thousands of Anglos moved to Texas. They outnumbered Mexicans by a factor of four within a period of fifteen years. This Anglo majority revolted and declared independence from Mexico on March 2, 1836. Four days later, Mexico's new dictator, General Antonio López de Santa Anna, arrived in San Antonio, leading an army composed primarily of several thousand conscripted Indians and mestizos from Mexico. More than a thousand of these men died in the famous Battle of the Alamo, in which the nearly two hundred defenders of the Alamo mission were defeated. The only recorded Texas-born people who died defending

An 1868 photo shows the Alamo as a working mission. (Institute of Texan Cultures)

the Alamo were eight Mexican liberals who opposed Santa Anna's suspension of the Mexican Constitution of 1824. The remaining defenders were Anglos, most of whom had been in Texas for only a few weeks or months.

Tejanos became a disfranchised ethnic minority. Their Texan descendants, who never crossed the Mexican border, are among the poorest people in Texas and are regarded as foreigners in their native land.

Spanish place names have been fixed to most geographic areas and political maps of Texas over centuries of Hispanic heritage. Spanish and Mexican influence shows in the language, food, music, and folklore of Texas. These influences are so familiar that they are seldom recognized as Latino; instead, they are considered to be uniquely Texan.

Mexican Americans. Ten years after the declaration of Texas' independence, the United States declared war with Mexico. Its forces occupied Mexican territory and killed thousands of civilians, destroying town after town. Mexico was defeated and signed the TREATY OF GUADALUPE HIDALGO in 1848. Under the terms of this treaty, more than half of Mexico's territory was sold to the United States for $15 million. The Mexican territory sold included Texas, California, Nevada, Utah, and parts of Arizona, Colorado, Kansas, New Mexico, Oklahoma, and Wyoming. This treaty created a new category of people, Mexican Americans, who lived north of the new border. They were forced to accept American citizenship or move from their land.

It was not until 1906 that large numbers of Mexicans started to cross the northern border demarcated by the Treaty of Guadalupe Hidalgo. The depressed Mexican economy prompted the beginning of this migration, and the 1910 MEXICAN REVOLUTION, which killed several million people, increased the flow of people. More than a quarter of a million Mexicans moved into Texas during the next ten years.

By 1929, more than one million Mexicans had crossed the border into the United States. About 10 percent of the Mexicans who moved to Texas could be classified as wealthy. Many of them started influential colonies in San Antonio and El Paso. The majority of the migrants were poor, with few skills and little education.

Postwar Experience. Around the time of World War II, a new generation of Mexican Americans moved to major Texas cities. After the war, veterans in Texas founded the AMERICAN G.I. FORUM, which grew to encompass hundreds of chapters. The group hoped to erase any differences in treatment between Mexican American veterans and others. The G.I. Bill contributed to the success of thousands of Mexican Ameri-

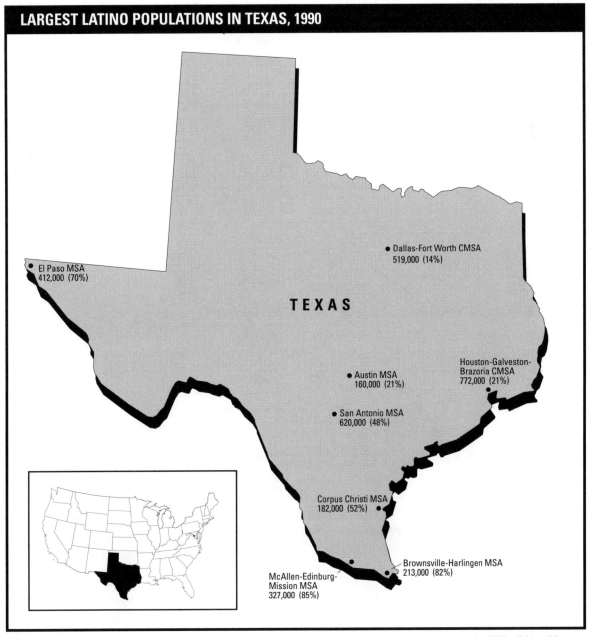

LARGEST LATINO POPULATIONS IN TEXAS, 1990

El Paso MSA
412,000 (70%)

Dallas-Fort Worth CMSA
519,000 (14%)

TEXAS

Houston-Galveston-
Brazoria CMSA
772,000 (21%)

Austin MSA
160,000 (21%)

San Antonio MSA
620,000 (48%)

Corpus Christi MSA
182,000 (52%)

Brownsville-Harlingen MSA
213,000 (82%)

McAllen-Edinburg-
Mission MSA
327,000 (85%)

Source: Data are from Marlita A. Reddy, ed., *Statistical Record of Hispanic Americans* (Detroit: Gale Research, 1993), Table 109.
Note: MSA = Metropolitan Statistical Area; CMSA = Consolidated Metropolitan Statistical Area. Numbers below location names are the Latino population of the area and the percentage of the area's population that is Latino.

cans who attended college. Education brought economic success and encouraged political participation. Raymond TELLES, a war veteran from El Paso, was elected mayor of that city in 1957, making him the first Mexican American mayor of a major city in the Southwest in the twentieth century.

In the late 1960's, a new generation of Latino youth began to refer to themselves as Chicanos. They joined the growing CIVIL RIGHTS MOVEMENT, advocating equality for Latinos and pride in Mexican heritage. In Texas, several political and student groups were created, such as La RAZA UNIDA PARTY, El MOVIMIENTO ESTUDIANTIL CHICANO DE AZTLÁN, and the MEXICAN AMERICAN LEGAL DEFENSE AND EDUCATION FUND.

A significant event for Latino politics was the foundation of the SOUTHWEST VOTER REGISTRATION EDUCATION PROJECT by William VELÁSQUEZ of San Antonio. This group hoped to empower Latinos through voting. Under Velásquez's leadership, the project contributed to an increase of 125 percent in the number of Latino voters between 1975, the year of its founding, and 1988.

Legal challenges and other efforts by these new groups, including disputes over the boundaries of election districts, resulted in an increase in the number of elected Latinos from 565 in 1973 to 1,611 in 1988. By

1993, there were 2,030 Latino elected officials in Texas, including five members of the U.S. Congress: Henry Bonilla, Eligio "Kika" DE LA GARZA, Henry B. GONZÁLEZ, Solomon P. Ortiz, and Frank Tejeda. Among the Latinos with the longest tenure as elected officials were Henry B. GONZÁLEZ of San Antonio, Tati SANTIESTEBAN of El Paso, and Ben Reyes, the mayor of Houston. Mexican Americans from Texas appointed to the highest federal government offices included Lauro F. CAVAZOS, who was made secretary of education in 1988. President Bill Clinton appointed former San Antonio mayor Henry CISNEROS as secretary of housing and urban development and Federico F. PEÑA as secretary of transportation in 1993.

Latino Demographics. The historical influence of Spaniards and Mexicans permeates all aspects of Texas life, but it is dominant in the southern portion of the state, where Latinos constitute a higher proportion of the population. Areas in Texas with populations that are more than 80 percent Latino include the consolidated metropolitan statistical areas of Laredo, McAllen-Edinburg-Mission, and Brownsville-Harlingen. More than 70 percent of Latinos in Texas live in nonborder counties.

Historically, most of the first Mexican immigrants were *VAQUEROS*, *pastores*, and braceros who lived in rural areas. By 1990, however, approximately 80 percent of Latinos in Texas lived in metropolitan areas. More than half of the growth of the Latino population in Texas from 1980 to 1990 was from new immigrants, primarily Mexicans.

The Latino population is younger than the population as a whole, with one-third of Latino Texans under the age of fifteen. The higher birthrates and relative youth of the Latino population, along with immigration, were expected to increase the proportion of Latinos in the Texas population to 29.5 percent in the year 2000 and 41 percent in the year 2030. Mexican-origin Latinos accounted for about 90 percent of the Latinos in Texas in 1990.

About one-fourth of the Latinos in Texas lived below the poverty line in 1990. Among older Latinos, 31 percent lived in poverty. Mexican American families had more members, on average, than did those in other groups. The percentage of Latinos in Texas without health insurance in 1994 was about three times the national figure. Latinos also showed lower health service utilization than other groups. This lack of utilization was attributed to factors including illiteracy and lack of acculturation. Most incoming Mexican immigrants are poor and move slowly into the middle class.

LATINO POPULATION OF TEXAS, 1990

Total number of Latinos = 4,339,905; 26% of population

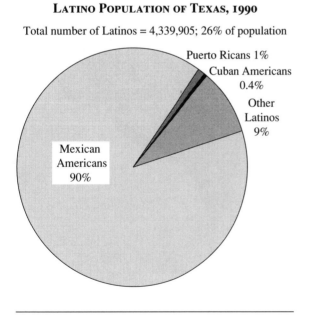

Puerto Ricans 1%
Cuban Americans 0.4%
Other Latinos 9%
Mexican Americans 90%

Source: Data are from Marlita A. Reddy, ed., *Statistical Record of Hispanic Americans* (Detroit: Gale Research, 1993), Table 106.

Note: Percentages are rounded to the nearest whole number except for Cuban Americans, for whom rounding is to the nearest 0.1%.

Many Mexicans cross the border into Texas daily, both with and without legal authorization. (Impact Visuals, Christopher Takagi)

The average level of education for Latinos is the lowest of all ethnic groups in Texas, with a median of about eight school years. In 1993, Latinos accounted for 35 percent of the student enrollment in Texas school districts. Graduation rates of Latinos from Texas high schools are typically half those of Anglos; the attrition rate in Texas public schools was 48 percent for Latinos in 1993.

The U.S. institution of higher education with the largest Mexican American population enrolled is the University of Texas at Austin, where Latinos made up 12.8 percent of the approximately fifty thousand students enrolled in 1994. More than 20 percent of first-year Latino students at the University of Texas were dismissed or dropped by the end of the year, and 46.2 percent of Latino students failed to graduate in 1992 after six years of enrollment.   —*F. Gonzalez-Lima*

SUGGESTED READINGS:

• Jamail, Milton H., and Margo Gutierrez. *The Border Guide: Institutions and Organizations of the United States-Mexico Borderlands*. Austin, Tex.: Center for Mexican American Studies, 1992. Includes a selected bibliography and information on borderlands topics, including border communities, government, media, chambers of commerce, and educational resources.

• Kanellos, Nicolás, ed. *The Hispanic-American Almanac*. Detroit: Gale Research, 1993. A one-stop source of information on Latinos, covering a broad range of Hispanic culture. Based on research by a national team of eminent scholars.

- Kingston, Mike, ed. *1994-1995 Texas Almanac.* Dallas: Dallas Morning News, 1994. Facts and figures on Texas history, politics, government, population, education, health care, science, religion, and other topics. Provides an industrial guide.
- Reddy, Marlita A., ed. *Statistical Record of Hispanic Americans.* Detroit: Gale Research, 1993. The most comprehensive database of statistics on the Latino population.
- Shorris, Earl. *Latinos: A Biography of the People.* New York: W. W. Norton, 1992. Describes the historical backgrounds and experiences of the diverse groups of Latinos residing in the United States.
- Simons, Helen, and Cathryn A. Hoyt, eds. *Hispanic Texas: A Historical Guide.* Austin: University of Texas Press, 1992. Scholarly essays on the history and cultural heritage of Hispanic Texas and a geographic guide to historical sites and events.

Texas Folklife Festival (San Antonio, Tex.): Cultural event. Held in early August on the grounds of the Institute of Texan Cultures, on Hemisphere Plaza in HemisFair Park, the Texas Folklife Festival, begun in 1970, celebrates the diverse cultural heritages of the state's citizens and draws more than 100,000 visitors each year to sample the culture and folkways of more than thirty ethnic groups in Texas. A major focus is on Mexican and Mexican American music (MARIACHI and *CONJUNTO*), and most of the artists featured are Mexican or Mexican American. The festival also features dance, folk arts and crafts, living history demonstrations, and, notably, ethnic Tejano foods, such as *pan de campo, tripitas, mole de guajolote*, ENCHILADAS, *QUE-SADILLAS*, and FAJITAS.

Texas Good Neighbor Commission: Volunteer agency. The Texas Good Neighbor Commission is a voluntary state organization dealing with local matters affecting relations between the United States and Mexico. The federal presence along the border is designed to maintain a legally defined boundary, but harmony there exists in large part as a result of voluntary associations and informal agreements.

Although the commission has official sanction and funding from the government, most of its work is accomplished by volunteers. Its goals are defined vaguely in terms of promoting goodwill, understanding, and mutual development. It is difficult to assess the commission's effectiveness. Although frequent educational and cultural exchanges have been arranged, the major importance of the commission is

in maintaining open channels of communication at a binational, unofficial level.

Texas Proviso (1952): Amendment to the IMMIGRATION AND NATIONALITY ACT OF 1952. Under the terms of the proviso, employment of alien laborers was defined as not being "deemed to constitute harboring." Employers could not be punished solely for providing jobs to illegal aliens. Because the proviso affected the hiring of migrant workers in the American Southwest, it had a direct effect on Latinos: Employers who could not be punished for harboring illegal aliens also could not be forced to comply with fair employment practices. Some legislators were unhappy that the proviso watered down the intent of the Immigration and Nationality Act of 1952, which was designed to reduce the influx of illegal immigrants.

Texas Rangers: Militia that grew out of Texan independence. Stephen Austin organized the Texas Rangers in 1823 to protect settlers on the Texas frontier. They evolved into a paramilitary force during the TEXAS REVOLT and were charged with both protecting settlers from Indian raids and enforcing independence from Mexico.

The Rangers concerned themselves with cattlemen's funds and rustlers. They acted, in effect, as a police force for the landowners. Mexican Americans in Texas were often the victims of Ranger law enforcement. The Texas state government reorganized the Rangers in 1874. Forces were expanded to nearly one thousand during World War I but fell to fewer than one hundred by the 1930's.

In the twentieth century, the Rangers were plagued by scandal resulting from their political involvement. During a strike by melon workers in 1967, the Rangers employed harassment to quell unionization efforts. The Supreme Court ruled against their actions in *MEDRANO V. ALLEE* (1967).

Texas Revolt (1835-1836): Texas' battle for independence. In the Texas Revolt, the largely Anglo-American residents of the region called Texas rebelled against Mexican authority and won independence for their new Republic of Texas.

At the same time that Mexico was winning its independence from Spain (in 1821), settlers from the United States began to immigrate into the Mexican region called Texas. Led by Stephen F. Austin and others, hundreds of Anglo-American families began to settle along the lower Brazos and other streams. Sev-

The Battle of the Alamo was a key event in the Texas Revolt. (Robert Fried)

eral Mexican colonizers were also active, including Martín de León, who founded Victoria, Texas.

By the mid-1830's, the Anglo-American settlers made up a clear majority of the area's population, numbering about thirty thousand. They also controlled about five thousand African American slaves. At the same time, Indians in the region numbered about fourteen thousand, while fewer than five thousand Mexicans lived in Texas. The Mexican government expressed concern that the Anglo-American population was growing dominant in the region and that these settlers showed little interest in adopting the Spanish language or embracing the Roman Catholic faith. In 1830, the Mexican administration attempted to cut off American immigration while encouraging Mexican and European colonization in Texas. The Anglo-Americans, however, remained in the majority.

The Texas Revolt grew out of cultural clashes between Anglos and Mexicans, the U.S. colonists' desire to protect the institution of slavery, and the Anglo-Americans' anger at the rise in 1835 of President Antonio López de Santa Anna, widely regarded as a dictator. Most of the Mexicans living in Texas sided with

Santa Anna's government, although some chose to support the U.S.-born rebels.

In the spring of 1835, the Texas rebels won a number of small engagements, forcing the Mexican army to abandon Goliad and San Antonio. In early March of 1836, a conference at Washington-on-the-Brazos declared Texas independent and wrote a constitution for the new republic.

On March 6, the Texas Republic met a severe setback in the Battle of the ALAMO, as Mexican troops stormed the Alamo and all the defenders were killed. Excellent military leadership by General Sam Houston led to the eventual defeat of Santa Anna at the Battle of SAN JACINTO, where the Texans employed the rallying cry "Remember the Alamo!"

Texas remained an independent republic for nearly ten years and won the diplomatic recognition of the United States and a number of European nations. In 1846, the United States Congress overcame its reluctance to add a new slave state. The Texans' petition to join the United States led to annexation and statehood for Texas.

The Texas Revolt changed the region's history. For almost ten years, the Republic of Texas endured as a weak and indebted nation. Not long after joining the United States, Texas joined the other Southern states in the disastrous U.S. Civil War. For Latinos, the Texas Revolt eventually brought U.S. citizenship, although a majority of Latinos living in Texas at the time would have preferred to remain Mexican citizens.

Texas Tornados: Tex-Mex/country-rock band. The Texas Tornados are Freddy FENDER, Leonardo "Flaco" JIMÉNEZ, Augie Meyers, and Doug Sahm. These four successful solo artists joined in 1989 to form the Texas Tornados, who play a Tex-Mex mix of rock, country, CONJUNTO, rhythm and blues, and ballad styles. Fender plays guitar; Jiménez button accordion; Meyers the Vox organ, keyboards, accordion, and bajo sexto; and Sahm guitar. All four are vocalists. Their several albums have crossed musical boundaries to appear on the rock, Latin, and country *Billboard* charts. The group has toured throughout the United States.

Tex-Mex: Many Mexican Americans consider themselves to be both U.S. citizens and members of *La Raza*, or "the race." In Mexico, *La Raza* refers to a glorious destiny linked to national strength. Economic and social conditions, however, have altered Texas Mexicans' concept of their destiny. Tex-Mex culture, language, and food reflect a blending of traditional Mexican influences with the culture of Anglo Texans. The culture has been adopted by Latino and non-Latino Texans, and elements have spread outside the state.

The Spanish of the Southwest reflects the influence of English. Many English words are used in the daily language of those speaking a Tex-Mex dialect, and many anglicisms or modified English words are found in that dialect. The Tex-Mex words *troca*, *brecas*, and *parquear*, for example, are derived from their English counterparts "truck," "brakes," and "to park." Another phenomenon is the use of a literal translation from English to Spanish when an expression does not have an adequate equivalent in Spanish. For example, "high school" becomes *escuela alta*, "yard" becomes *yarda*, and "chance" becomes *chanza*. Through borrowed expressions, the Tex-Mex dialect reflects the influence of Anglo culture.

Tex-Mex food resembles that common in northern Mexico. The main vegetables include squashes, tomatoes, onions, and corn. Reflecting the influence of In-

Restaurants have commercialized Tex-Mex food. (Bob Daemmrich)

dian culture, corn is often washed through lime after cooking. This process, called slaking, is used in the creation of a beverage called *pulque* and is responsible for the distinctive flavor of some chips, tortillas, and bread.

Like Mexican food, Tex-Mex food includes mashed pinto beans and cheese. Mexicans often use cheese made from goats' milk; the Tex-Mex adaptation is to use cheese processed from cows' milk. The main spices found in Tex-Mex food are coriander, cumin, garlic, and jalapeño peppers.

Tex-Mex food shows Spanish as well as Indian influences. Beef, poultry, rice, cinnamon, wine, and olive oil are all Spanish influences. The generous portions of meat contained in Tex-Mex dishes, however, derive from Anglo culture and tastes.

Tex-Son Garment Strike (Feb. 24, 1959-April, 1962): Strike by Mexican American garment workers. The strike began on February 24, 1959, after Tex-Son, a major manufacturer of boys' clothing, fired several hundred workers in San Antonio and moved most of its operations to Mississippi, where wages were lower and unions nonexistent. The company received the enthusiastic support of the Southern Garment Manufacturing Association. The INTERNATIONAL LADIES' GARMENT WORKERS' UNION (ILGWU) had eight hundred members in the San Antonio plant; they led the walkout.

Strikers received $20 a week in benefits from the union. The strike became violent when picketers threw eggs at Tex-Son owner Harold Franzel, and the police were called to restore order. Over the next few days, the police beat hundreds of strikers and arrested two union leaders, Sophie Gonzáles and Georgia Montalbe. Garment workers picketed stores and held parades throughout the remainder of the year, but the company hired dozens of strikebreakers. Union benefits were not enough to keep strikers clothed and fed. Most found other jobs. The last picketers disappeared from the street in front of Tex-Son by April, 1962.

Theater and drama, Cuban American: Cuban American drama has its roots in nineteenth century New York, New York, and Tampa, Florida. With the arrival of large numbers of Cubans in the United States after the CUBAN REVOLUTION (1959), it developed in diverse yet distinct ways.

Before the Cuban Revolution. Since the nineteenth century, the United States has been a haven for exiled Cuban artists and intellectuals. Before 1959, Tampa

and New York City were the main centers for writers such as the poet and independence leader José MARTÍ and the priest Félix Varela. Some Cuban American playwrights, actors, and theatrical entrepreneurs adhered to a serious repertoire of Spanish plays and European and American works in translation; others used the theater as a vehicle for sociopolitical protest. Many preferred lighter theatrical forms including the ZARZUELA (a type of folkloric operetta), vaudeville, and farce (*obras bufas*).

As early as the 1820's, a Hispanic culture was being nurtured by Cuban residents of Manhattan. Romantic dramas and comedies of manners were written and produced. Some examples are José María HEREDIA's *Abufar o la familia árabe*, Gertrudis Gómez de Avellaneda's *Baltasar*, and José Martí's *No lo quiero saber*. During the first four decades of the twentieth century, New York Cubans also witnessed the birth of theatrical groups such as the Club Lírico Dramático Cubano and the Compañia de Bufos Cubanos, as well as the appearance of theaters such as Teatro Hispano and Teatro Campoamor. Some of the Cuban actors who achieved fame were Juan C. Rivera, who specialized in *gallego* roles, depicting a stereotypically cranky, stingy Spaniard, and Alberto O'FARRILL in *negrito* comic roles, portraying stereotypical Afro-Cubans.

In Tampa, the theater developed differently. Cubans who migrated there in the nineteenth century and founded YBOR CITY were primarily cigar manufacturers and their workers. The practice of employing *lectores* (readers) in cigar factories to read good literature to the workers produced a rather literate working class. These tobacco workers formed mutual-aid societies—the Centro Obrero, the Círculo Cubano, and the Afro-Cuban Unión Martí-Maceo—that included entertainment committees, amateur acting groups, and impressive theaters. Some members became professional actors.

During the Great Depression, the only Spanish-language company funded by the Federal Theater Project was established in Tampa. The theater review *La Revista* was established, and touring acting companies began including Tampa on their itineraries. The repertoire consisted primarily of zarzuelas, operettas, Spanish plays and operas, variety acts, comedies, melodramas, and dramas of social protest, often dealing with labor issues.

Developments Since 1959. Following Fidel CASTRO's takeover of Cuba in 1959, many Cubans fled to the United States. The Cuban American theatrical scene began to change, and several important groups were founded. In New York, INTAR (International Arts Relations) was founded to promote a new drama and playwrights who wrote in English. INTAR sponsored the Playwrights in Residence Laboratory, funded by the Ford Foundation and directed by the dramatist María Irene Fornés. Fornés, who was born in Cuba and trained in Paris, wrote many plays, including *Tango Palace*, the Obie Award-winning *The Conduct of Life*, *Mud*, and *Abingdon Square*. In Los Angeles, the BILINGUAL FOUNDATION FOR THE ARTS was founded. It produced Leopoldo Hernández's *Martínez*, an eclectic play about marginal characters struggling to retain their self-respect.

MIAMI, FLORIDA, the capital of the Cuban exile community since the early 1960's, was another matter. Comic satire and farce thrived, probably as a relief from the traumatic experience of exile. In the late 1960's, two small theaters, Las Máscaras, began staging farces with political commentary reflecting anti-Castro sentiments or the colorful aspects of the Miami exile experience. Zarzuelas also were well received by the Miami Cuban community, as shown by the success of the company Pro-Arte Grateli, founded by Pili de la Rosa. Every year it presented several zarzuelas and operettas well loved by older Cubans, for example, *María la O* and *Cecilia Valdés*.

Serious drama eventually developed in Miami. In 1972, Teresa María Rojas founded Teatro Prometeo at Miami-Dade Community College. It staged classical works from various dramatic traditions, often in Spanish translation. Mario Ernesto Sánchez's Avante Theater and other theaters with a more serious repertoire, such as Teatro de Bellas Artes and Sala Teatro Casanova, also thrived. In the early 1980's, noted actor José FERRER became artistic director of the Coconut Grove Playhouse and introduced a Hispanic program to this important Miami theater. In 1984, a coalition of Miami-based Cuban theaters, Acting Together, was formed under the auspices of the Metro-Dade Cultural Affairs Council.

Recent Voices. A new generation of Cuban American playwrights sprang up after the 1970's. They wrote principally in English, and their themes, techniques, and genres were varied. Some plays dealt with the contemporary Cuban experience in Cuba and the United States, such as Uva Clavijo's *With All and for the Good of All* (about the problems of Cuban exiles in post-Castro Cuba) and Gonzalo Rodríguez's *Algunos prefieren fresas, otros chocolate* (concerning sexual and artistic repression in revolutionary Cuba). In *Birthday Present*, Al Septién analyzes the cultural dif-

ferences separating younger Cubans from their elders, as does Renaldo Ferradas in *Birds Without Wings*. In *Broken Eggs*, Eduardo Machado writes about the tensions of Cuban exiles dealing with the mores of a new culture. Other playwrights explored nonethnic, more general themes, as did Ramón Delgado in *The Flight of the Dodo*, a symbolic play that explores the dehumanizing effect of monotonous work on the human psyche. José Peláez wrote in *Cadillac Ranch* about alienated New Jersey youths, one Italian and one Cuban, in search of their identity. Michael Alasá—librettist, lyricist, and director of DUO, a Spanish-English ensemble theater in New York—wrote many diverse plays, including *Sloth*, a one-act musical farce, and the trilogy *The Shining Path*, which traces artistic and political revolutions from the court of Czar Nicholas to the guerrilla movement in the Peruvian Andes.

Cuban American playwrights represent both modern dramatic conventions—realism, naturalism, expressionism, and existentialism—and contemporary forms—theatrical ensembles, absurdist plays, theater of social commentary and protest, and ethnic drama. Given the fecundity and diversity of Cuban American drama, optimism about its future is justified.

—*Robert Carballo*

SUGGESTED READINGS: • Cortina, Rodolfo J., ed. *Cuban-American Theater*. Houston: Arte Público Press, 1991. • Kanellos, Nicolás. *Hispanic Theatre in the United States*. Houston: Arte Público Press, 1984. • Kanellos, Nicolás. *A History of Hispanic Theatre in the United States: Origins to 1940*. Austin: University of Texas Press, 1990. • Osborn, M. Elizabeth, ed. *On New Ground: Contemporary Hispanic-American Plays*. New York: Theatre Communications Group, 1987. • Pottlitzer, Joanne. *Hispanic Theater in the United States and Puerto Rico: A Report to the Ford Foundation*. New York: Ford Foundation, 1988. • Zalacaín, Daniel, ed. *New Beats: Seven One-Act Hispanic American Plays*. New Brunswick, N.J.: Slusa, 1990.

Theater and drama, Latin American: Latin American theater dates back to the tradition of Spanish (peninsular) theater as well as to ritual performance in pre-Columbian America. Among Aztecs and Maya in Mesoamerica, ritual dances were staged on religious holidays, for example, to commemorate mythical battles among cultural heroes. In the Andean region, the Inca elite periodically organized festivals with performances honoring past rulers. The anonymous *Rabinal Achí*, a Mayan-Quiché dance drama sung and per-

Ritual dances, such as this one re-created by Mexican dancers, form part of early theater history. (James Shaffer)

formed with masks, may be the only pre-Hispanic play that survived the impact of conquest and colonization untouched by European influence. The play, which presents the ritual battle between enemy warriors, was first recorded in the mid-nineteenth century but probably dates back to the fifteenth century.

Missionary Theater. When the first Catholic missionaries arrived in Latin America in the early sixteenth century, mendicant orders relied on theatrical performance as a tool for the conversion of the indigenous population. Franciscans and Jesuits staged ritual representations of scenes of saints' lives, such as the beheading of St. John the Baptist. Missionaries often took extreme measures to convert Indians. In 1559, for example, Jesuits in Lima exhumed indigenous skeletons and cadavers to depict graphically the resurrection of the dead for their performance of *Historia alegórica del Anticristo y el Juicio Final.*

Criollo Theater of the Early Colony. During the sixteenth and early seventeenth centuries, Spanish immigrants and their descendants (*CRIOLLOS*) developed a theater patterned after Spanish models. The best-known playwright of that period is Fernán González de Eslava. His *entremeses* (short plays, light in tone, usually performed between acts of a longer play) are memorable because of their abundant references to historic events and social customs.

During the seventeenth century, the Baroque period in literature and the arts, theater companies from Spain traveled to the colonies to present the latest dramas. Although competing with dramatists such as Lope de Vega and Calderón de la Barca was difficult, Latin America produced important playwrights. Although the work of Mexican dramatists Juan Ruiz Alarcón and Sor Juana Inés de la CRUZ closely followed peninsular models, the beginnings of a Mexican consciousness can be found in their plays. Sor Juana's drama, which encompasses work both sacred and secular in focus, is a good example. Although her comedy of intrigue *Los empeños de una casa* (1684?), about the complexities of love and jealousy, contains few references to the American colonies, her shorter plays often include indigenous characters and references to Mexican customs. Her *Loa al divino Narciso* (1690) begins with a *tocotín*, an indigenous dance. Her *Sainete segundo*, which deals with the problematic relationship among playwright, actors, and audience, makes humorous references to the lisp in Castilian Spanish.

Developments in the Eighteenth Century. During the eighteenth century, Spanish Golden Age theater continued to be popular in Latin America. The increasing influence of French culture during the reign of the House of Bourbon (since 1700) could also be seen in the frequent stagings of French drama. Although few new Latin American playwrights emerged, this period saw the construction of lavish theater houses in major urban centers such as Mexico City, Lima, and Santiago de Chile.

Theater, initially linked to the Roman Catholic church, came into increasing conflict with the church hierarchy over issues of morality. Parallel to the stirrings of independentist sentiment toward the end of the century, the stage was becoming an arena for political discourse. The popular classics of the Baroque period continued to be staged, and seventeenth century dramatic conventions had a strong influence on eighteenth century theater. On the other hand, particularly in the second half of the century, the reform of theater according to neoclassical guidelines produced plays that respected the classic unities of time, space, and action, and were often moralizing in nature. Among the few playwrights of that period whose work is still read today is Peruvian Pedro de Peralta y Barnuevo, whose work is written in part in the neoclassic vein but still shows Baroque influence.

Of particular interest was the resurgence in Peru of a theater rooted in the indigenous experience. Most of this theater was written at least partly in Quechua, the language of the Inca. The anonymous play *Ollántay* was staged in 1780 close to Cuzco, the ancient capital of the Inca empire, in the wake of the largest indigenous revolt in the Spanish colony. Its performance was prohibited after the suppression of the rebellion. The play was European in form but took its inspiration from Inca tradition. In the play, Ollántay is a valiant military leader in the service of Inca Pachacutic. When the Inca ruler denies Ollántay the right to marry his daughter Estrella (Ksi Cóyllur) because of his lower social standing, Ollántay turns against him and thus threatens the unity of the Inca empire.

Another anonymous play of this period was *Usca Páucar*. This play defended the moral values of Christianity, in an effort similar to that found in earlier missionary theater. The protagonist has to choose between pagan indigenous culture, personified by the devil to whom he sells his soul, and a humble life as a poor Christian. The play ends with a praise to the Virgin.

In Argentina, the beginnings of a national theater with a strong regionalist interest were evident in plays such as *El amor de la estanciera*, attributed to Juan Bautista Maciel. This *sainete* (humorous one-act play, popular in character) highlighted the qualities of the Argentine rural CRIOLLO in contrast to the materialism of the foreigner.

Independence and the Development of a National Theater. The struggle for independence from Spain during the first three decades of the nineteenth century brought theatrical activity to a virtual halt. Although political ties between Spain and Latin America were broken, cultural ties remained strong. French and Spanish plays of the Romantic period succeeded neoclassical drama on Latin American stages.

Few Latin American playwrights of the early nineteenth century are known today. Among the few is Cuban Gertrudis Gómez de Avellaneda (1814-1873), whose plays stand out for the depth of characterization (for example, *Baltasar*, 1858). Significant for the development of a national theater were plays written in the vein of *costumbrismo*, a literary current within Romanticism that focused—usually in a humorous or satirical manner—on the depiction of social customs and popular fashions. In his play *Contigo pan y cebolla* (1833), Mexican Manuel Eduardo de Gorostiza ridiculed the infatuation of young, well-to-do women with the heroines of melodramatic romanticism. Doña Matilde marries the wealthy Don Eduardo only when the latter pretends that his uncle disinherited him because of his refusal to marry the woman his relative had selected for him. Manuel Ascensio Segura, who is considered to be the father of Peruvian theater, criticized the military establishment in comedies such as *La Pepa* (1834) and *El Sargento Canuto* (1839). One of his best-known plays is *Na Catita* (1856), a play critical of the impressionability of women led by materialistic interests and easily fooled by appearances. Chilean Daniel Barros Grez (1834-1904) cast a satirical look on the blind imitation of urban customs by a provincial family in *Como en Santiago* (1875). The dichotomy between rural and urban environment remained an important theme in Latin American theater throughout the nineteenth and twentieth centuries.

In Argentina, trends that started in the late eighteenth century with plays such as *El amor de la estan-*

ciera developed into early *gauchesco* theater. This theater focused on the gaucho, the roaming cattle herder of the Argentine pampa, as a sometimes ridiculed, sometimes revered symbol of national identity. José Podestá's *Juan Moreira*, a play based on Eduardo Gutiérrez's novel of the same name, was a popular pantomime about the adventures and misfortunes of the gaucho protagonist. In 1886, it was staged with dialogue. It was a successful early example of a theater constantly adapting to the suggestions and demands of the audience.

The Early Twentieth Century. At the turn of the century, the River Plate region of Argentina was one of the few areas in Latin America noted for the production of an original theater, reflective of the young nation's cultural and social conflicts and development. Roberto Payró, Gregorio de Laferrére, and Florencio Sánchez are three of the authors of the "golden decade" of River Plate drama.

The best-known work of the prolific Uruguayan author Florencio Sánchez is *Barranca abajo* (1906), a tragedy that has been called the requiem to the traditional gaucho lifestyle. Don Zoilo, the protagonist, represented an era when the relationship between rural man and his land was still untouched by the city dweller's encroachment on land and the moral and cultural values associated with it. He loses his land and his family to a new social order, in which there is no room for his lifestyle. In the process, he is stripped of even his identity. Don Zoilo in the end is nothing more than "*el viejo Zoilo*," the old Zoilo, with empty hands and a noose for the final obliteration.

Few plays written during this period in other parts of Latin America are still read today. Some noted playwrights who wrote in the realist vein of nineteenth century theater were the Chileans Antonio Acevedo Hernández and Armando Moock, the Cubans José Antonio Ramos and Marcelo Salinas, and the Mexican Gamboa brothers (Federico and José Joaquín). In Chile, Moock wrote comedies that today are considered overly melodramatic. His popular play *La serpiente* (1920)—adapted to the Hollywood screen as *Cobra* (1925), with Rudolph Valentino and Nita Naldi in stellar roles—depicted women as the destroyers of men's creative genius. Antonio Ramos' play *Tembladera* (1906), with its symbol-laden depiction of a Cuba involved in a ferocious battle for economic and cultural survival, continued to hold the interest of readers in the late twentieth century. Protagonist Joaquín Artigas, son of the administrator of the hacienda *Tembladera*, opposed selling the land to North Americans. In his

fight for the land, he symbolized the future of an autonomous Cuba, unfettered by the ghosts of the Spanish past and North American interests.

During the first decades of the twentieth century, cheap imitations of Spanish melodrama were the order of the day, with few exceptions. The Castilian accent was preferred on stage. It was not until after World War I that conscious efforts were made to address Latin American reality with a new and original theatrical language.

The Search for a New Dramatic Expression: 1920 to 1950. At the end of the 1920's, there was a strong reaction against the decadence of the professional theater. The European avant-garde played a crucial role in this process. European dramatists such as Luigi Pirandello, George Bernard Shaw, and Federico García Lorca all left their indelible imprint on Latin American theater, as did Freudian psychoanalysis, Marxism, and French existentialism. Experimental and independent theaters such as the Teatro Ulises in Mexico (1928), the Teatro del Pueblo in Buenos Aires (1930), La Cueva in Cuba (1937), and El Grupo Areyto in Puerto Rico (1938) provided the space for the staging of foreign avant-garde plays and the work of new Latin American playwrights.

In the River Plate area, a dramatic movement strongly influenced by Italian models appeared: the *grotesco criollo*. It reflected the alienation experienced in sprawling Buenos Aires by thousands of European—mainly Italian—immigrants at the beginning of the century. The bitter comment on the total failure of the characters' aspirations in a society that distorted them emotionally echoed a similar experience portrayed in the theater of the Puerto Rican migration to New York in the 1940's and 1950's. Two of the best known dramatists of the *grotesco criollo* are Defillippis Novoa and Armando Discépolo. In Discépolo's *Mateo* (1923), the protagonist Miguel doggedly holds on to a traditional lifestyle doomed to disappear in an urban, increasingly mechanized environment. Mateo, Miguel's carthorse, eventually—and tragically—loses out against the machine, in the same way as honesty and friendship vanish where only the dishonest survive. Roberto Arlt (1900-1942) was another Argentinean influenced by Italian dramatist Pirandello. He addressed the anguishing routine of everyday life in the city, from which the imagination offers a liberating, but also dangerous, escape. In *Los trescientos millones* (1932), a domestic servant flees into a dreamworld of love and riches. In the end, suicide seems to provide the only true escape. *La isla desierta* (1937) addressed the fear of losing control and of assuming responsibility for one's actions and life. A group of office workers, unable to stand up for a more humane living environment, are in the end punished for their lack of courage.

In Argentina, an important sector of experimental theater viewed the art as a vehicle for social and political consciousness raising. The members of the Mexican Teatro Ulises, in contrast, regarded theater first and foremost as artistic expression and refused to use theater as a tool for social change. Teatro Ulises and Teatro Orientación, although seldom commercially successful, today are considered to have established the foundation for the development of Mexican theater of the twentieth century.

Teatro Ulises was founded by playwrights Xavier Villaurrutia, Celestino Gorostiza, and Salvador Novo, among others. Their purpose was to create a universalist theater. It was short-lived but provided the basis for the Grupo de los Contemporáneos, a loose association of dramatists among whom Novo, Villaurrutia, and Rodolfo Usigli stand out. They were widely criticized for their stand against the fanatic nationalism after the Mexican Revolution (1911-1920). Octavio PAZ wrote that Villaurrutia's theater was the psychological portrayal of a traditional middle class, in which no ideological or generational conflict existed. In plays such as *Sea usted breve*, *¿En qué piensas?*, and *Parece mentira* (1943), Villaurrutia represented the banality of everyday life, love, and family relationships with surrealist overtones.

Usigli was one of the best-known Latin American playwrights. His plays attempted to demythologize Mexican history. In *El gesticulador*, first staged in 1947 after difficulties with censorship, Usigli analyzed the tragic consequences of hero worship and the resulting distortion of Mexican reality. Pressed by economic hardship and his own political idealism, the unemployed professor César Rubio decides not to clear up an American scholar's error that identifies him with a long-lost hero of the Mexican Revolution. In his trilogy *Corona de sombra* (1947), *Corona de luz* (1960), and *Corona de fuego* (1961), Usigli presented an antihistoric analysis of three great moments in Mexican history: the French occupation and the episode of Maximilian and Carlotta, the miracle of the appearance of the Virgin of GUADALUPE, and the trauma caused by the SPANISH CONQUEST.

Although Mexico and Argentina were traditionally the two Latin American regions with the most active theater life, other areas caught on during the 1950's

and 1960's. Chilean theater began in the early 1940's, with the founding of experimental theaters at the Universidad de Chile (Instituto de Teatro de la Universidad de Chile, ITUCH) and the Universidad Católica (Teatro Experimental de la Universidad Católica, TEUC) in 1941 and 1943, respectively. In Puerto Rico, the work of Emilio S. Belaval, founder of the group Areyto (1938), was seminal for the development of a highly nationalistic theater.

Major Trends and Themes After 1950. In the latter half of the twentieth century, Latin American theater gained increasing recognition both at home and abroad. During and after the 1960's, this interest was associated with the popularity of the novel of the "boom," an explosion of literary creativity. By the 1990's, Latin American theater was widely studied at American universities, and numerous festivals were held to celebrate the genre. One well-known example was the yearly Theater Festival sponsored by the Casa de las Américas in Havana, Cuba.

A genre sensitive to its sociopolitical and cultural context, Latin American theater in this period reflected increasingly polarized societies. The power of the colonial heritage, represented by institutions such as the military and the church, was waning. Revolutionary movements in Guatemala, Bolivia, Cuba, and Nicaragua had shaken the neocolonial world order. Alarming urban growth, coupled with the abandonment of a rural lifestyle, had brought extraordinary socioeconomic difficulties and cultural conflict. Despite the obvious hardships facing playwrights whose work was scarcely rewarded, and who in most countries had to cope with covert and overt censorship, Latin American theater generally strove to mirror critically the contradictions of its environment. Although often regionalist in focus, the genre became increasingly universal in appeal. Diverse in form and content, this theater more often than not reflected a spirit that was both aesthetically and politically revolutionary.

Many of the prominent themes dealt with in this theater were apparent in earlier periods. The following list is a small sample of the wealth of themes and plays. The city as an environment that alienates and dehumanizes the individual, and the harrowing routine of everyday life, were the focus of many Argentine plays, such as Osvaldo Dragún's *Historias para ser contadas* (1957) and *El amasijo* (1968), and Roberto Cossa's *Los días de Julián Bisbal* (1966). This theme often overlapped with another one: the horror of the passage of time, as in Cuban Virgilio Piñera's play *Dos viejos pánicos* (1968), René Marqués' *Los soles trun-*

cos (Puerto Rico, 1958), and Julio Ardiles Gray's *Ceremonia inútil* (Argentina, 1975).

The frustration engendered by the fruitless attempts of the weak individual to struggle against an overpowering, repressive system was reflected in Agustín Cuzzani's *Una libra de carne* (Argentina, 1957), Dragún's *Historias para ser contadas*, and José Triana's *La noche de los asesinos* (Cuba, 1966). The individual's fear of assuming responsibility for his or her own dignity results in tragedy for the protagonists of Francisco Arriví's *Medusas en la bahía* and *Sirena* (Puerto Rico, 1957, 1959) as well as those of Griselda Gambaro's *Decir Sí* (Argentina, 1974).

In Chile, several authors showed a profound interest in class conflict and cast a critical, often satirical, look upon a self-righteous middle class. Examples are Sergio Vodanovic's trilogy of one-act plays, *Viña* (1964), and Egon Wolff's *Los invasores* (1963) and *Flores de papel* (1970). For obvious political reasons, in Argentina and Colombia physical and psychological torture, as the extreme representation of political repression, were addressed as in Eduardo Pavlovsky's *El señor Galíndez* (Argentina, 1973), in several of Gambaro's plays, such as *Información para extranjeros* (1973), and in Enrique Buenaventura's *Los papeles del infierno* (Colombia, 1977). Gender relations were the focus of Piñera's *Dos viejos pánicos*, Chilean Jorge Díaz's *El cepillo de dientes* (1961) and *La orgástula* (1969), and Dragún's *El amasijo* (1968).

Although Latin American theater in the latter half of the twentieth century drew on a solid indigenous tradition, the influence of European and North American experimental theater should not be ignored. The absurdist theater of Eugène Ionesco and Samuel Beckett left its mark on the work of many dramatists, among them Chilean Jorge Díaz. In *El cepillo de dientes*, language was distorted to the extreme of noncommunication. The two protagonists are caught in the cyclic ritual of married life, in which their own private battles and the language of television and radio commercials erode meaningful communication. Antonin Artaud and his ideas on theatrical performance as ritual inspired plays such as Triana's *La noche de los asesinos*. In this circular play, three siblings rehearse the murder of their parents in an attempt to subvert an order no longer expressive of their needs.

German playwright Bertolt Brecht's ideas on epic theater were seminal for many Latin American playwrights. In *Historias para ser contadas*, Dragún followed Brecht's precepts when he portrayed the effects of an alienating urban environment on characters desperate from hunger, illness, and loneliness. Actors assumed different roles and commented on the action, thus inviting the audience to participate and to analyze the reasons behind this human misery. In Mexico, Vicente Leñero developed the documentary drama, following the tradition of Brecht and Peter Weiss. In plays such as *Pueblo rechazado* (1968), theater became an open forum that presented alternative and often contrasting viewpoints on a concrete historical event rather than offering solutions.

The North American avant-garde of the late 1960's, with the Living Theater and the experimental work of consciousness-raising theater, also left their imprint on Latin American drama. In Mexico, the Centro Libre de Experimentación Teatral y Artística (CLETA) was founded in 1973. In Nicaragua, Alan Bolt and his group Nixtayolero sparked the appearance of hundreds of communitarian theater groups that attempted to analyze community problems and recapture the indigenous past. In Cuba, the Teatro Escambray (founded in 1968) helped implement government policy after the revolution. In Columbia, in the 1990's, the company La Candelaria addressed the urgent issues of the time, such as drug-related violence (*El paso*, 1988).

All these groups concentrated their interest on collective creation. They made the effort to take the theater to the audience, rather than the audience to the theater. Often, this audience had never attended a play before. Street corners, schools, churches, and community centers, both in the cities and in the countryside, became performance spaces. The liveliness and fervor of these groups in turn became influential for Latino theater in the United States, particularly the Chicano theater movement of the 1960's and 1970's.

Trends of the 1980's and 1990's. In some areas, collective creation continued to be one of the most popular and widespread types of theater in the 1990's. The playwright, who earlier had seemed to retreat into the background, reclaimed some ground during the 1980's and in the 1990's, adapting to the needs of the ensemble. Groups such as the Peruvian Telba and Teatro de Ciudad based their performances on texts provided by one or two authors. In Mexico, playwrights such as Sabina Bergman, Oscar Liera, Juan Tovar, and Oscar Villegas wrote drama that gave the director, the set designer, and the actor the role of coauthors. Along with this trend came the appearance of a new generation of highly successful directors who staged universal classics, contemporary plays, and works of collective creation. Many of these directors gained international recognition. Mexican Jesusa Rodríguez stirred the theater world at home and abroad with her controversial adaptation of the old myth in *Donna Giovanni* (1986).

Each new generation of playwrights seemed to be committed to critically analyzing Latin American society, almost always at odds with the political and artistic establishment. The study of the consequences of exile in the work of Chileans Jaime Miranda and Ramón Griffero, the revolutionary theater of Albio Paz in Cuba, the continued uncovering of the weaknesses of Argentine democracy from an increasingly feminist viewpoint in Greiselda Gambaro's plays, and the critique of political corruption in the work of Felipe Santander in Mexico all were proof of one of the connecting threads of Latin American drama: its unrelenting commitment to social change. Undeterred by the many faces of censorship, the liveliness of late twentieth century Latin American theater countered the common contention that theater was a dying art. —*Anna Witte*

SUGGESTED READINGS:

- Bravo-Elizondo, Pedro. *El teatro hispanoamericano de crítica social*. Madrid: Playor, 1975. Gives a useful introduction to socially committed theater in Latin America. The first part explains European avant-garde influence on Latin American drama. The second part studies plays by selected dramatists.
- Colecchia, Francesca, and Julio Matas, eds. and trans. *Selected Latin American One-Act Plays*. Pittsburgh: University of Pittsburgh Press, 1973. Good, although brief, introduction to selected twentieth century plays.
- Dauster, Frank, Leon Lyday, and George Woodyard, eds. *9 dramaturgos hispanoamericanos: Antología del teatro hispanoamericano del siglo XX*. 3 vols. Ottawa, Canada: GIROL Books, 1983. Excellent selection of plays, with introductory essays by the editors.
- Luzuriaga, Gerardo, and Richard Reeve, eds. *Los clásicos del teatro hispanoamericano*. Mexico: Fondo de Cultura Económica, 1975. One of the best anthologies to date. Spanish drama from pre-Hispanic times to the 1950's. Useful introductory essays.
- Lyday, Leon F., and George Woodyard, eds. *Dramatists in Revolt: The New Latin American Theater*. Austin: University of Texas Press, 1976. Contains excellent interpretive essays on Latin American dramatists of the twentieth century. Includes Brazilian drama.
- Pérez Coterillo, Moisés. *Escenarios de dos mundos: Inventario teatral de Iberoamérica*. 4 vols. Madrid, Spain: Centro de Documentación Teatral, 1988. Exhaustive survey of theater of the Spanish-speaking world, in the form of interpretive essays and reviews.

Emphasis on late nineteenth and twentieth centuries.

- Versényi, Adam. *Theatre in Latin America: Religion, Politics, and Culture from Cortés to the 1980's*. Cambridge, England: Cambridge University Press, 1993. Excellent critical theater history. Emphasizes the relationship between theater and the church, from missionary theater to the use of theater in liberation theology.

Theater and drama, Mexican American: Mexican Americans have produced theatrical works as expressions of religious and cultural identity, sociopolitical reality, and social protest. This theater is specific to the portrayal of the Mexican American experience and, therefore, differs from the theater of other Latino subgroups.

Origins. The origins of Hispanic theater in what is now the United States can be traced to 1598 and the dramatic representations of the colonizers who arrived in New Mexico. The early settlers performed both secular folk dramas and religious plays known as *pastorelas*, or shepherd's plays. *Pastorelas* represent the shepherds' voyage to pay tribute to the newborn Christ child. The tradition of the *pastorela* survived, and such plays were performed annually at Christmas into the late twentieth century.

In addition to folk dramas, theater flourished through professional theatrical troupes that toured California and the southwestern United States, performing works in Spanish during the second half of the nineteenth century and into the twentieth century. A large number of Hispanic theaters emerged prior to 1940 in cities with large Hispanic populations, such as Los Angeles, California; San Antonio, Texas; New York, New York; and Tampa, Florida. What distinguishes this early theater from what would follow is that it was intended to be entertainment and professed no social or ideological elements, although it did at times poke fun at the "GRINGO" population.

Chicano Theater. Chicano theater is distinct from traditional Mexican or Mexican American roots. Although *pastorelas* conserved the religious, and to some extent cultural, traditions of Mexican Americans, it was not until the inception of Chicano drama that the theater began to be used for political means. The term "Chicano" itself implied a certain cultural, social, historical, economic, racial, and ideological identity. Included in this identity was the notion that one must fight for the social advancement of the Chicano people as a whole. One method of joining in such a social struggle was theatrical performance.

Lo'il Maxil, a troupe from Chiapas, Mexico, performs a folk play. (Impact Visuals, Tom McKitterick)

The Chicano theater movement was founded during the height of the general social upheaval of the 1960's. Luis Miguel VALDEZ, the son of migrant farmworkers, is acknowledged as the father of Chicano theater. In 1965, he went to Delano, California, in order to start a farmworkers' theater group and at the same time assist César CHÁVEZ's farm labor union.

Valdez and His Actos. Then a recent graduate of San Jose State College, Valdez began organizing simple improvisational skits, called *actos*, with the workers in the fields. This term not only refers to the literal theatrical act but also implies a call to action, in this case joining the farmworkers' union. Valdez's purposes were to incite the workers into protesting against the miserable living and working conditions to which they were subjected and to allow them to vent their frustrations by acting out satirical situations related to their collective social reality. Each brief *acto* was a political statement, a declaration of dissent.

The *acto* by nature was not only didactic but also a highly political, and therefore ideological, form of theater. It is readily compared to Bertolt Brecht's didactic theatrical pieces as well as to revolutionary Russia's agitprop theater, which had considerable influence on the proletarian theater of the 1930's in the United States.

Valdez's newly formed group, El TEATRO CAMPESINO (the farmworker's theater), never followed set scripts. Actors improvised basic situations or conflicts related to daily life in the fields. The typical *acto* pitted the underdog *huelguistas* (strikers) against a powerful team of antagonists composed of the *patrón* (boss), the *esquiroles* (scabs), and at times the COYOTE (labor contractor). Typical of these early *actos* were *Las dos caras del patroncito* (1965; the two faces of the boss) and *La quinta temporada* (1966; the fifth season).

El Teatro Campesino soon developed into a much larger phenomenon that took it beyond the farcical sketches in the fields. It separated from Chávez's labor union in 1967. The group began to incorporate urban themes. In 1971, Valdez outlined the five principal goals of the *acto* as a theatrical genre. These were to inspire the audience to social action, illuminate specific points about social problems, satirize the opposition, show or hint at a solution, and express what people are feeling. Some urban themes portrayed in the later *actos* of El Teatro Campesino include submission to and assimilation into the dominant Anglo cul-

Along with his many actos, *Luis Valdez wrote several full-length dramas including* La Bamba!, *about singer Ritchie Valens.* (AP/Wide World Photos)

ture, as in *Los vendidos* (1967; the sellouts); the failure of the American educational system to meet the needs of the Chicano student, as in *No saco nada de la escuela* (1969; I don't get anything out of school); and the Vietnam War, as in *Vietnam Campesino* (1970) and *Soldado razo* (1971; buck private).

Other Forms of Theater. Although the *acto* was the first form of theater to be created and employed by El Teatro Campesino, it was not the only one. The *acto* was followed by a dramatized reworking of the Mexi-

can *CORRIDO*, or ballad. Each play was based on a popular *corrido*, which the actors would depict as a narrator sang the ballad. At times the actors employed dialogue taken directly from *corrido* lyrics. *El fin del mundo* (1974; the end of the world) followed this format. It was the *corrido* of Raymundo Mata, whose life and death served as a metaphor for the end of the world.

The third theatrical form used by Valdez and his Teatro Campesino is the *mito*, or myth. The theatrical *mito* is based on larger-than-life allegorical figures juxtaposed to real-life characters. The *mito* features characters such as Superstition, Winter, or El Sol (The Sun). The *mito* is a dramatic parable that unfolds before the spectator; it can be more ritualistic than dramatic in form. The *mito* also incorporates indigenous beliefs and deities, thereby rooting Chicano identity in the indigenous history of Mexico.

Bernabé (1970) was Valdez's first *mito*. It tells the story of Bernabé, who is mentally retarded and yet is to be admired for his innocence and honesty. Bernabé is visited by different Aztec deities and undergoes a transformation. *Dark Root of a Scream* (1971) is perhaps Valdez's best-developed *mito*. It continues the Vietnam theme of the earlier *actos* as it uncovers Chicano history through a young Chicano who died in Vietnam.

Valdez also wrote full-length dramatic pieces that had effects not only within the Mexican American community but also nationally. These pieces created Valdez's reputation as one of the foremost dramatists in the United States. His most famous work is *Zoot Suit* (1978), which met with wide critical and public acclaim and was his first work to afford him economic success. It was the first Chicano play to be performed on Broadway and in 1981 was made into a motion picture directed by Valdez himself. It deals with the PACHUCO culture of the 1940's. Also among Valdez's well-known plays are *Bandido* (1982), a musical revision of the history of the famous nineteenth century bandit Tiburcio VÁSQUEZ, and *I Don't Have to Show You No Stinking Badges* (1984).

Significant Theater Groups. Even though Valdez and El Teatro Campesino are cornerstones of Chicano theater, they do not stand alone. A number of Chicano theater groups sprang up following Valdez's lead, performing plays that reflected the Chicano experience in the United States. In 1971, these groups formed a coalition known as EL TEATRO NACIONAL DE AZTLÁN, or TENAZ. *Tenaz* is a Spanish word meaning "tenacious" or "persistent"; the group's name thus represents the determination and perseverance of the Chicano theater movement.

Of the many Chicano theater companies of the late twentieth century, at least two merit mention for their contribution to the advancement and development of Chicano theater. The first, El TEATRO DE LA ESPERANZA (the theater of hope), was formed in 1971. Its first performances consisted of El Teatro Campesino's *actos*. The group later collectively began to write original docudramas based on actual events. *Guadalupe* (1974), named for a town in California, is based on a series of events concerning discrimination against Hispanic schoolchildren. Another play by this group is *La víctima* (1976; the victim), a docudrama based on the mass deportation of Mexicans from the United States in the 1920's. This historical reference had a strong contemporary resonance, as the same thing was happening to undocumented workers in the 1970's.

El Teatro de la Gente (the theater of the people) was formed in 1970 by students and was based in San Jose, California. Its first major production, in 1973, was *El corrido de Juan endrogado* (the ballad of doped-up Juan), written by the group's director, Adrian Vargas. It spoke to the problem and danger of drugs in the Mexican American barrios and also debunked the ideal of the American success story.

Chicano Playwrights. An often-forgotten Chicano playwright of the 1970's is Nephtalí de León. Although his plays employ some of the same techniques established by Valdez, de León went a step further. His plays tend to be less didactic and more intellectually searching, at times leaning toward existential analyses of the purpose of life. They raise many questions yet offer few solutions. His work signaled a movement away from Valdez's early agitational plays toward a focus on the strictly dramatic elements of theatrical production.

Carlos MORTON is another major playwright who emerged in the early 1970's. Many of his plays are political in nature, but like those of de León, they show considerable dramatic skill. His most famous work is *Las many muertes de Richard Morales* (1977), which was later reworked and titled *The Many Deaths of Danny Rosales* (1983). Under that title, it won the Hispanic Playwrights Festival Award in 1986. Morton often looked to earlier dramatic models for his works. A prime example is his 1983 play *Johnny Tenorio*, the story of a modern Don Juan. It is based loosely on Tirso de Molina's *El burlador de Sevilla* (1630; the joker of Seville) and José Zorilla's *Don Juan Tenorio* (1844).

One of the most important innovations in Mexican American/Chicano theater was plays written and produced by women. Estela PORTILLO TRAMBLEY's *The Day of the Swallows* (1971) is considered to be the first Chicano play written by a woman, for women. Portillo paved the way for later dramatists such as Denise CHÁVEZ, Cherríe MORAGA, and Diana Saenz, all of whom have enjoyed considerable critical acclaim and success in dealing with issues of specific concern to women and in portraying Chicana reality as they have experienced it.

Chicano actors reenact the birth of Christ in a teatro performance. (Ruben G. Mendoza)

Impact. Prior to the late 1970's, theater produced by Mexican Americans was of little importance on a national level. That began to change with the advent of CHICANO STUDIES PROGRAMS on university campuses and the inclusion of Chicano literature as a valid area of study within literature departments. Through the efforts of pioneers such as Luis VALDEZ, Chicano theater and Mexican American theater in general gained a wide following among both critics and the theater-going public.　　　　　　　—*Darrell B. Lockhart*

SUGGESTED READINGS:

• Feyder, Linda, ed. *Shattering the Myth: Plays by Hispanic Women.* Selected by Denise Chávez. Houston: Arte Público Press, 1992. An important anthology of works by contemporary female playwrights, representative of the growing corpus of theater that portrays the Latina experience.

• Garza, Roberto J., ed. *Contemporary Chicano Theatre.* Notre Dame, Ind.: University of Notre Dame Press, 1976. An anthology of early plays by Chicano playwrights.

• Huerta, Jorge A. *Chicano Theater: Themes and Forms.* Tempe, Ariz.: Bilingual Press/Editorial Bilingüe, 1990. A well-researched and comprehensive study of Chicano theater. Focuses largely on the theater of Luis Valdez. Contains photo illustrations and an extensive bibliography.

• Huerta, Jorge A., ed. *Necessary Theater: Six Plays About the Chicano Experience.* Houston: Arte Público Press, 1989. An anthology of plays considered to be foundational texts of Chicano theater.

• Kanellos, Nicolás. *A History of Hispanic Theatre in the United States: Origins to 1940.* Austin: University of Texas Press, 1990. A monumental work tracing the history of Hispanic theater in the United States. A meticulously researched and comprehensive study accompanied by photo illustrations.

• Kanellos, Nicolás. *Mexican American Theater: Legacy and Reality.* Pittsburgh, Pa.: Latin American Literary Review Press, 1987. An interesting study of various themes pertaining to Mexican American theater, including Chicano theater, folklore, popular culture, and the Mexican American circus.

• Morton, Carlos. *Johnny Tenorio and Other Plays.* Houston: Arte Público Press, 1992. Morton's second anthology of plays. Introduction by Lee A. Daniel.

• Morton, Carlos. *The Many Deaths of Danny Rosales.* Houston: Arte Público Press, 1988. Morton's first anthology of plays.

• Valdez, Luis. *Luis Valdez—Early Works: Actos, Bernabé, and Pensamiento Serpentino.* Houston: Arte Público Press, 1990. A valuable anthology of *actos* performed by Valdez's Teatro Campesino. Also contains one of his first full-length plays and his poetic meditation on the purpose of Chicano theater.

• Valdez, Luis. *Zoot Suit and Other Plays.* Houston: Arte Público Press, 1992. An anthology of Valdez's most important and successful full-length works. All are deeply rooted in the search for Hispanic identity. Introduction by Jorge Huerta.

Theater and drama, Puerto Rican: Puerto Rican theater and drama in the United States (U.S.-Rican theater) is deeply rooted in Puerto Rico's rich theatrical tradition. Since the 1930's, this theater has been a direct reflection of the political and cultural conflicts that were and are a consequence of the presence of the United States on the island and the difficult situation of Puerto Rican immigrants in the New York City area.

Theater and National Identity. Puerto Rican theater since the early decades of the twentieth century has been closely linked to the cultural, political, and economic vicissitudes of that nation. In this context, three dates are particularly significant. On October 18, 1898, Puerto Rico became a satellite of the United States as a result of the SPANISH-AMERICAN WAR; in 1917, the JONES ACT conferred United States citizenship on all Puerto Ricans without prior referendum on the island; and in 1952, Puerto Rico's colonial status was confirmed with its establishment as protectorate of the United States.

Identity problems brought about by the imposition of a foreign culture on the island have been recognized by playwrights since the 1910's, for example in Eugenio Astol Bussati's *Tres banderas* (1912), which introduced a motif that would reappear in Puerto Rican theater until the 1980's: that of a masked identity. Spanish colonial heritage, the presence of the United States, and the problematic immigrant experience in NEW YORK CITY are predominant themes in Puerto Rican theater. Beginning in the 1980's, these themes were replaced in the U.S.-Rican community by a focus on a new identity that assimilates the Afro-Caribbean and Hispanic heritage and Anglo-American culture.

Puerto Rican Drama Before 1954. One cannot truly speak of Puerto Rican drama until the 1930's, when renewed interest in Puerto Rican culture sparked interest in theater as a vehicle for the search for a national identity. In 1939, Emilio S. Belaval founded the seminal company Areyto. The year before, the Ateneo Puertorriqueño organized a contest of native dramatists that produced three noteworthy plays. Among these, Manuel Méndez Ballester's *El clamor de los surcos* and Fernando Sierra Berdecía's *Esta noche juega el jóker* addressed issues still important in the 1970's and 1980's. *El clamor de los surcos* initiated a long series of plays identifying Puerto Rico's source of national culture with the land.

It is in the relationship of the individual to the land that, in the author's perception, Hispanic and North American value concepts clash. The dichotomy between Hispanic idealism and North American materialism resurfaces in plays by René MARQUÉS, Pedro Juan SOTO, Luis Rafael SÁNCHEZ, and others. *Esta noche juega el jóker* is one of the first plays to address the cultural conflicts to arise with the Puerto Rican migration to New York, though Sierra Berdecía's view of this experience is more positive than that reflected in Marqués' *La carreta* (1953) or Soto's *El huésped* (1956). Paramount in the development of Puerto Rican theater since the 1950's was the founding of the Instituto de Cultura Puertorriqueña at the end of that decade. The institute began sponsoring annual theater festivals in 1958.

During the 1950's and 1960's, three tendencies predominated in island drama: the social realism of Marqués' *La carreta*, the psychological realism of Francisco Arriví's trilogy *Máscara puertorriqueña* (1955-1960), and the "grotesque" (*teatro del grotesco*) of Arriví's *Cóctel de don Nadie* (1964). Although the two best-known Puerto Rican dramatists, Marqués and Arriví, address similar issues, they differ in style and focus. Marqués concentrates his attack on the inhumane materialism of North American society and hails the *JÍBARO*, the peasant of Hispanic descent, as a symbol for Puerto Rican identity. Arriví seeks reasons for his nation's lack of identity in the inherent racism of a society that denies its African roots. Marqués' social realism seemed to have the most immediate impact on the Puerto Rican community in New York, but Arriví's plays about the psychological scars left by racism and the resulting self-hatred had a lasting effect on U.S.-Rican theater.

Development of Puerto Rican Theater in the United States. The phases Marc Zimmerman establishes for Latino literature apply largely to Puerto Rican drama in the United States. The first phase, which Zimmerman calls the attempt to replicate homebase literary culture, can be observed in the popularity of *orquestas rumberas* (rumba orchestras) and *teatro bufo* (a type of farce of Cuban origin) in New York during the 1920's and 1930's. Theaters of this epoch were the Teatro Hispano, Teatro Campoamor, and Teatro Puerto Rico.

Increased Puerto Rican migration to New York in the 1940's and 1950's was reflected, during the second phase, in theater that explored racism and culture clash experienced by the immigrants and that focused on the affirmation of roots in island culture. The characteristics Zimmerman points out as typical of literature of migration and immigration—social orientation, didacticism, and bitterness—are present in representative plays of this period: Marqués' *La carreta*, Soto's *El huésped* (1956), and Méndez Ballester's *Encrucijada* (1958).

In these plays, the predominant image is of New York as a monstrous machine that mercilessly sacrifices its victims in the name of progress and the American way of life. *Encrucijada*, like *Esta noche juega el jóker* before it, foreshadows the inevitable absorption of the Puerto Rican into Anglo-American culture. *La carreta* depicts the harrowing journey of a peasant family first from the countryside to San Juan, and from there to New York, which they leave again after facing humiliation and death. The staging in 1954 of *La carreta*, first in Spanish and in 1966 in English, with Miriam COLÓN and Raúl JULIA in leading roles, was so successful that actress Colón and director Roberto Rodríguez founded the company Nuevo Círculo Dramático, devoted to the staging of Spanish and Latin American plays. Although short-lived, this company laid the foundations for the seminal work of the PUERTO RICAN TRAVELING THEATER. Founded by Colón in 1967, it became one of the centers of theatrical activity in New York.

It is difficult to speak of U.S.-Rican theater before the 1970's and a new generation of playwrights born in the United States. Yet one author, island-born Jaime CARRERO, was successful in bridging the gap between island and mainland drama. Beginning in the 1960's, he wrote plays both in Spanish for the Puerto Rican and in English for the New York stage. Plays such as *Flag Inside* (1966), *Pipo Subway no sabe reír* (1973), and *FM Safe* (1979) address issues including the draft of Puerto Ricans during the Vietnam War and the stresses and tensions experienced by members of the Puerto Rican community in New York.

In *FM Safe*, the return to the island remains a possibility, but that possibility is relinquished in favor of the struggle to "make it" in New York. Carrero in this sense is a pioneer of the NUYORICAN or neo-Rican identity, a term he coined in 1964. He is a forerunner of the third phase of Puerto Rican drama in the United States, equivalent to Zimmerman's "literature of set-

Miriam Colón appears in the play Fanlights *in 1980.* (AP/Wide World Photos)

tlement." During this phase, playwrights still look back to their roots in island culture, and issues concerning the immigration experience still are addressed, but now from a new angle, with a newly found awareness of other Latino communities and an existing Latino tradition behind them.

As important as the staging of *La carreta* was for the previous phase of Puerto Rican theater in New York, so were two events in the 1970's for the third phase of its development: the New York Drama Critics Circle Award for best American play of the 1973-1974 season for Miguel PIÑERO's *Short Eyes*, and the staging of Edward Gallardo's *Simpson Street* in 1979. Piñero (1946-1988) began writing *Short Eyes* while he was serving time in Ossining Correctional Facility. The play was first staged by The Family, a group of convicts and ex-convicts, under the direction of Marvin Félix Camillo. It depicts prison life as a reflection of the social and racial tension, and the violence, extant in American society as a whole. Among Piñero's other plays, *The Sun Always Shines for the Cool* (published 1984) stands out as the vivid portrayal of an urban community of hustlers, pimps, and prostitutes in which love, wisdom, and repentance still have a place as part of the struggle for survival and betterment.

Piñero and poet/playwright Miguel ALGARÍN were the founding members of the NUYORICAN POETS' CAFÉ on Manhattan's Lower East Side (Losaida). In the 1970's, the café was one of the focal points of U.S.-Rican theatrical activity. As an informal gathering point for poets and playwrights, it facilitated first readings and stagings for works that in many cases never were published or staged by professional theater groups. The café also helped introduce innovative dramatic technique, organizing performances of collective creation and improvisational workshops. Since the 1970's, other groups including The Family, Teatro Otra Cosa, and the Puerto Rican Bilingual Workshop (founded 1973) have been instrumental in furthering the development of U.S.-Rican theater. Another extremely important promoter of this theater has been Joseph Papp, director of the New York Shakespeare Festival, who facilitated the production of large numbers of plays by Latino authors.

Gallardo's *Simpson Street*, staged at the end of this fruitful decade by Colón's company, was a milestone in the movement to return Hispanic theater to the people. The reception in New York was so enthusiastic that the play toured Spain and several Latin American countries. *Simpson Street* pits mothers against children in the struggle for survival in the Nuyorican commu-

nity. Unable to bridge the emotional and cultural gap between them, Michael Rodríguez at the end of the play leaves his mother in order to begin a new life in California. The play condemns the defeatism expressed by some of the female characters, who convince themselves of the hopelessness of their situation and drown their sorrows in alcohol. In Gallardo's *Women Without Men* (1985), the protagonist (Soledad) wins her struggle against a domineering mother, herself a victim of internalized racism, when she takes off her white makeup at the end of the play, recognizing and accepting herself. Gallardo's plays contain strong reminiscences of earlier Puerto Rican plays such as Méndez Ballester's *Encrucijada* and Arriví's *Vejigantes*, thus underlining the debt of U.S.-Rican theater to its roots in island drama.

Trends of the 1980's and Beyond. Simpson Street has often been cited as the play that marks the end of the PUERTO RICAN DIASPORA. Nevertheless, memories of the island persisted in U.S.-Rican theater of the 1980's. Although affirmation of Puerto Rican identity is usually not the central focus of the play anymore, characters still appear who identify with island culture, rejecting the North American experience. José Rivera's *The House of Ramón Iglesia* (1983) describes the plight of a family torn by broken dreams, nostalgia for the island, and the appeal of the American lifestyle. The lack of communication between Javier, who embraces U.S. culture, and his mother, who refuses to learn English and eventually returns to the island, is a painful reminder that some old wounds may never heal. Federico Faguada's *Bodega* (1986) depicts a similar conflict between Máximo Toro, whose dream is to own the "Superbodega," a liquor store in the South Bronx, and his wife, Elena, who wants to return to the island. When Max is killed, Elena decides to stay and fight.

U.S.-Rican theater of the 1980's and 1990's seems to go beyond nationalisms in its depiction of a culture more self-critical and removed from earlier island and male-centered discourse. A good example is Migdalia Cruz's play *Miriam's Flowers* (published 1992), which addresses the problematic role of Latina women immersed in and mutilated by a highly religious (Catholic) culture that emphasizes suffering and self-sacrifice. National identifications are irrelevant in this play, which reaches out to all Latina women and is in this sense an excellent example for current trends in U.S.-Rican and Latino theater in general. The last decade of the twentieth century saw the increasing popularization and mainstreaming of this theater, evident in the filming of *Short Eyes* and *The House of Ramón Iglesia* as well as in the numerous publications of drama anthologies.   —*Anna Witte*

SUGGESTED READINGS:

• Kanellos, Nicolás, ed. *Hispanic Theatre in the United States.* Houston: Arte Público Press, 1984. Contains seven articles on Hispanic theater, two of which also address U.S.-Rican drama. To date the best introduction to Latino theater.

• Kanellos, Nicolás, and Jorge A. Huerta, eds. *Nuevos Pasos: Chicano and Puerto Rican Drama.* Houston: Arte Público Press, 1989. One of the best anthologies of its kind. Contains plays by playwrights of the 1970's (among them Carrero and Piñero). Brief but thorough introductory essay.

• Montes-Huidobro, Matías. *Persona: Vida y máscara en el teatro puertorriqueño.* San Juan, Puerto Rico: Editora Corripio, 1984. Contains an exhaustive history of the major authors of Puerto Rican (island) drama. Emphasis on detailed textual analysis of plays from 1914 to 1983.

• Morton, Carlos. "The Nuyorican Theatre." *The Drama Review* 20, no. 1 (1976): 43-49. Discusses key figures of Nuyorican theater in the 1970's. Describes technical innovation in this theater and efforts of the Nuyorican Poets' Café in this context.

• Zimmerman, Marc. *U.S. Latino Literature: An Essay and Annotated Bibliography.* Chicago: MARCH/Abrazo Press, 1992. Contains an excellent essay on the development of Latino literature, with specific information on U.S.-Rican literature. Excellent and complete bibliography.

Thomas, Piri (b. Sept. 30, 1928, New York, N.Y.): Writer. Thomas' mother, Dolores Montañez, was from Bayamón, Puerto Rico. His father, Juan Thomas, was born in Oriente Province, Cuba, but after immigrating to Puerto Rico considered himself Puerto Rican. Thomas grew up during the Depression, in the streets of New York's Spanish Harlem. Thomas' parents encouraged their children to maintain their Puerto Rican identity, but Piri, the oldest, often was perceived as African American because of his dark skin color.

From his youth, Thomas was involved in petty theft, gangs, and later drug sales. He served seven years in prison for attempted armed robbery and felonious assault. He earned his high school equivalency diploma in prison, where he also studied bricklaying and began reading and writing.

Two months after meeting an editor at Alfred A. Knopf, Thomas received a grant to finish writing his autobiography, *Down These Mean Streets.* It was published in 1967. He also wrote two other autobiographical narratives, *Saviour, Saviour Hold My Hand* (1972) and *Seven Long Times* (1974), as well as several plays, a collection of short stories, and a volume of poetry. In addition to being the first U.S.-born writer of Puerto Rican descent to break into mainstream publishing, Thomas also became a prominent spokesperson for the Puerto Rican community.

Tiant, Luis, Jr. (Luis Clemente Tiant y Vega; b. Nov. 23, 1940, Marianao, Cuba): Baseball player. The son of one of Cuba's greatest pitchers, Tiant began his professional career as a right-handed pitcher in the Mexican Leagues in 1959. His first year was miserable, but he returned in 1960 with an impressive 17-7 record. In 1962, the Cleveland Indians organization bought Tiant's contract, and he made the move to U.S. baseball.

Debuting in the majors with the Indians in the middle of the 1964 season, Tiant compiled a 10-4 record with a 2.83 earned run average (ERA) as a rookie. In 1966, he led the American League with five shutouts.

Although he was a successful major league pitcher, Tiant began changing his throwing style, turning away from the plate during his delivery to create a hesitation-style pitch. His assortment of moves and arm angles earned for him the nickname "The Man of Many Motions," and his varied style proved even more confusing to hitters. In one July, 1968, game, he struck out 19 batters in 10 innings to set an American League record. That year, he led the league with a 1.60 ERA and nine shutouts on his way to an excellent 21-9 record. After the Indians asked him to forgo winter league play in Mexico, however, Tiant seemed to fall apart, leading the American League with 20 losses.

Plagued by injuries, Tiant was traded to the Minnesota Twins and, after only one season in Minnesota, to the Boston Red Sox. Tiant then began a successful comeback that saw him again become one of the American League's top pitchers for most of the 1970's. In 1972, he compiled a 15-6 record and a league-leading 1.91 ERA, earning for him Comeback Player of the Year honors. He won 20 games or more three times for the Red Sox and again led the league in shutouts in 1974. A year later, the Red Sox won the American League pennant, and Tiant finally got the chance to pitch in front of his father, whom Cuban dictator Fidel Castro allowed to leave the country for the World Series. Tiant won two games in the Series, but the Red Sox lost to Cincinnati.

Luis Tiant, Jr., made a brief return to the major leagues in 1982 following a stint playing in Mexico. (AP/Wide World Photos)

A three-time All-Star, Tiant became a free agent in 1979. He pitched for the New York Yankees, Pittsburgh Pirates, and California Angels before retiring following the 1982 season with a career record of 229-172, 2,416 strikeouts, and a 3.30 ERA.

Tienda, Marta (b. Aug. 10, 1950, Donna, Tex.): Educator. Tienda has written widely on immigrant workers, particularly those from Mexico. She edited *Hispanics in the U.S. Economy* (1985) and coedited, with Frank Bean, *The Hispanic Population of the United States* (1987). She has also served as editor of the *American Journal of Sociology*.

Tienda earned her B.A. in Spanish from Michigan State University in 1972. Her M.A. (1975) and Ph.D. (1975) in sociology are from the University of Texas at Austin. She was a migrant services worker for the Michigan Department of Social Services in 1971 and an assistant to the director of the Michigan Cooperative Extension Service in 1972. In 1976, she joined the faculty of the University of Wisconsin at Madison, rising to the rank of associate professor in 1980 and full professor in 1983. She served as a visiting professor at Stanford University in 1987 and became a professor at the University of Chicago in 1989.

Tierra Amarilla: Town in New Mexico. Tierra Amarilla, a town with fewer than five thousand inhabitants in 1990, is located north of Santa Fe. Its origin dates to the Spanish settlement of New Mexico in the eighteenth century. It came to national attention in 1967, when Reies López TIJERINA and the Alianza movement led a protest movement, arguing that the United States was not living up to the spirit of the TREATY OF GUADALUPE HIDALGO. This treaty guaranteed the land grants of the people residing in the region prior to its takeover by the United States.

Tigres del Norte, Los: Music group. The members of Los Tigres del Norte immigrated to the United States from Sinaloa, Mexico, in the late 1960's. In 1970 they produced their first hit, and they remained on *Billboard* magazine's regional Mexican Top 10 list for more than twenty years. They are arguably the leading group of their style, *MÚSICA NORTEÑA*. The group is made up of three brothers, Hernan, Jorge, and Raul Hernandez; their cousin; and a friend. Themes in their songs include immigration and contraband. They have recorded various albums, toured throughout the United States and several Latin American countries, and appeared in films in which their music is featured.

Tijerina, Reies López (b. Sept. 21, 1926, near Falls City, Tex.): Activist and community organizer. Born into a migrant family with eight children, Tijerina grew up in migrant camps and had little formal education. At the age of nineteen, he attended a Texas Bible school, then became a circuit preacher in the Assembly of God church. According to Tijerina, preaching throughout the Southwest showed him the miserable situation of his people.

Tijerina came to believe that the cure for this misery was ownership of land. In the early 1950's, he spent time in Mexico researching Spanish and Mexican land grants. He moved to New Mexico and, on February 2, 1962, organized the Alianza Federal de Mercedes (Federal Alliance of Land Grants) and the land-grant movement.

Tijerina is best known for his work surrounding the land-grant struggle. The Alianza was part of a history of efforts to reclaim land and water rights based on the TREATY OF GUADALUPE HIDALGO (1848), which ended the Mexican American War. At its peak in 1965, the Alianza claimed twenty thousand members. Its initial efforts were legal in nature, but after little success working through court proceedings, the Alianza resorted to militant confrontations. One such incident was the KIT CARSON NATIONAL FOREST TAKEOVER on October 15-22, 1966. His supporters occupied the Echo Amphitheater area in the forest to proclaim the rights of land grant claimants.

The most noteworthy of these militant incidents occurred on June 5, 1967. The Tierra Amarilla courthouse was raided by Alianza members. The incident ended with a shootout between law enforcement agents and Alianza members. As a result of this incident, Tijerina was charged with kidnapping and assault to commit murder, destruction of federal property, and assault on two officials. Conducting his own defense, Tijerina was acquitted of the lesser charges in December of 1968.

Tijerina was successfully prosecuted for his actions at the Echo Amphitheater. He was sentenced to a two-year prison sentence in February, 1969. In January, 1970, he was convicted on assault charges stemming from the courthouse raid, receiving sentences of one to five years and two to ten years.

After serving two years at the federal prison in Springfield, Missouri, Tijerina was released on parole in July, 1971. As part of his parole, Tijerina agreed to cease activity within the Alianza. Without Tijerina's leadership and organizational skills, the Alianza's efforts were crippled. The Alianza lost its influence, and Tijerina disappeared into obscurity.

Reies López Tijerina at Alianza headquarters in 1968.
(AP/Wide World Photos)

During his most effective years, from 1962 to 1967, Tijerina made important contributions to the efforts of the Chicano movement and its attempts to empower the Mexican American community. His charisma added to the political rhetoric of the time. He eloquently preached ethnic self-identity, justice and fairness for Chicanos, and working for the good of the community. Tijerina offered hope during a time when the dismal socioeconomic conditions of Chicanos were being challenged and the ideological protestations known as CHICANISMO were being raised. Much of the cultural nationalism of Chicanos can be attributed to Tijerina.

Tijuana, Mexico: Located twenty miles south of San Diego, just across the border between California and Mexico, Tijuana is Mexico's northernmost and fourth largest city. It is situated in BAJA CALIFORNIA, a semi-arid peninsula about eight hundred miles long. Tijuana's history and affairs are intimately linked to those of the United States.

Early History. In the early nineteenth century, José Maria de Echeandia, a Spaniard, obtained rights and property to develop a rancho in the area. The rancho became Rancho de Tijuana. The name Tijuana likely comes from two Spanish words, "Tia" and "Juana" (literally, "Aunt Jane"). A picturesque woman by this name is supposed to have come from Sonora to the ranch as a cook, and people referred to the area using her name. By 1840, the Rancho de Tijuana was the largest of six cattle ranches in the area.

From its earliest history, Tijuana has been closely tied to the United States. The first formal contact was in 1871, when U.S. officers began to patrol the border area. Shortly thereafter, customs officers were permanently stationed at facilities on the border. In 1889, about two thousand American gold miners passed through Tijuana on their way to reported goldfields to the south. In 1906, John D. Spreckels built a railroad from San Diego to Yuma, Arizona. The railroad crossed the Mexican border and had a station in Tijuana. This connected the city more closely to the United States than to the Mexican capital nearly two thousand miles away.

Increasing Ties to the United States. During the MEXICAN REVOLUTION (1910-1921), the Liberal Party shifted its headquarters from Mexico City to Los Angeles, California. It allied itself with the INDUSTRIAL WORKERS OF THE WORLD (a labor union), and about half of its membership was American. In May, 1911, the party captured Tijuana with the aid of American mercenaries but was soon driven out by the Mexican army.

By 1915, Tijuana had a population of about one thousand and was a relatively modern city. Extensive contact with the United States began when tourists attending the San Diego Exposition of 1915-1916 visited Tijuana. In response, a gambling casino was built and entertainment attractions were developed in Tijuana. These included musical shows, bullfighting, and cockfighting, as well as boxing and horse racing, both of which were illegal in California. The racetrack was built and operated by an American. Prostitution and other vices also flourished. Much of this enterprise was controlled by the American ABW Corporation, which was a major financial power in Tijuana through the 1920's, along with the American promoters Baron Long and James Cofforth.

Prohibition, which banned alcoholic beverages in the United States in 1920, was the single greatest boon to Tijuana's economy. Drinking remained legal in Mexico. Entertainers and celebrities flocked regularly to the city, along with large numbers of tourists. On July 4, 1920, an estimated sixty-five thousand Americans visited Tijuana. In 1931, more than four million Americans crossed the border into Tijuana.

Although a combination of the Great Depression and restrictions imposed by the Mexican government caused a significant decrease in border crossings in the 1930's, World War II produced another boom. In addition, the BRACERO PROGRAM (1942-1964) stimulated Mexican migration to Tijuana. Under this program, Mexican contract workers were permitted to enter the United States to perform agricultural work to alleviate labor shortages. During this period, U.S. capital played only a moderate role in Tijuana's development. Mexican businesspeople were in primary control of the local economy.

The Modern Era. By the early 1950's, Tijuana was a wide-open city offering every form of vice and activities that were illegal in the United States, such as prostitution, drugs, gambling, pornography, and abortion. It catered primarily to a clientele of Southern Californians, servicemen stationed in San Diego, and tourists.

Over the years, various forces transformed Tijuana from a seamy border town to a somewhat modern urban city. Pressure from the Mexican and U.S. governments helped curb Tijuana's excesses. Introduction in 1965 of the BORDER INDUSTRIALIZATION PROGRAM (also known as the *maquiladora* program) resulted in the construction of labor-intensive, export-oriented assembly plants along the border. About three-quarters of these plants were foreign-owned in the 1990's, and of those about 90 percent were American-owned. Most produced textiles, clothing, automotive goods, and electronic products. Although the *MAQUILADORAS* have provided jobs and revenue, they pay very low wages, and many resemble sweatshops. They have contributed to extensive environmental pollution through discharge and illegal dumping of industrial wastes.

Tourism remained Tijuana's main source of revenue in the late twentieth century. Local government has worked hard to promote the growth of family tourism.

Illegal border crossings from Tijuana became more common toward the end of the twentieth century. (AP/Wide World Photos)

The downtown area has been extensively rehabilitated, landscaped, and modernized to the point that it resembles a giant shopping mall. Many Tijuanans regularly cross the border to work or shop in the United States, and many Mexican Americans in California pass through the city en route to visit relatives. The city has also become an important center of contemporary border culture involving Latino artists, poets, musicians, and others (*see* BORDER REGION AND CULTURE).

Tijuana had a population of 495,000 in 1993. Along with rapid growth came a host of social problems. Tijuana is a key point of departure for illegal border crossers into the United States, raising political issues with the U.S. government. The city has considerable poverty, squalor, and crime associated with the work of COYOTES and others who assist illegal immigrants. Corruption in municipal government is rampant. Tijuana's fortunes will continue to rise or fall depending in large part on relations of the city, and Mexico as a whole, with the United States.   —*Laurence Miller*

SUGGESTED READINGS: • Barry, Tom, ed. *Mexico: A Country Guide*. Albuquerque, N.Mex.: Inter-Hemispheric Education Resource Center, 1992. • Box, Ben, ed. *Mexico and Central American Handbook*. New York: Weidenfield and Nicolson, 1989. • Price, John A. *Tijuana: Urbanization in a Border Culture*. Notre Dame, Ind.: University of Notre Dame Press, 1973. • Rudolph, James D., ed. *Mexico: A Country Study*. 3d ed. Washington, D.C.: Government Printing Office, 1985. • Young, Margaret Walsh, ed. *Cities of the World*. 4 vols. Detroit: Gale Research, 1982.

Timbales: Pair of single-headed drums of Cuban origin. *Timbales*, or kettledrums as they are often called, have metal shells of shallow diameter (between twelve and twenty inches) and screw-tensioned plastic heads. The two drums, tuned to different pitches, are clamped to a stand reaching the musician's waist. From a standing position, the player beats the drums with two sticks, producing sharp, definite notes. It is customary to hang two *cencerros* (metal cowbells) nearby; when played with the drumsticks, they add percussive variety to the instrument. *Timbales* are an important part of Latin American urban popular music ensembles.

Tío Taco: Stereotype. Tío Taco is both a derogatory term for a Chicano and a type of law. As a derogatory term, it is interchangeable with Tío Tomás, or "Uncle Tom," and describes someone who serves Anglo culture at the cost of losing his or her own culture. This meaning of Tío Taco revolves around a stereotype of

Mexican people as complacent, submissive, lazy individuals ready to accept a second-class position in life. Tío Taco also refers to informal laws enacted against Mexicans and Mexican Americans through which Anglos control the educational and economic systems, thereby holding the power to deny certain privileges to Chicano workers.

Tiple: Small guitar. The four courses of triple metal strings of the *tiple* are meant to be strummed rather than plucked. The instrument is common in Colombia and also is found in Guatemala, Puerto Rico, and Venezuela with a few variations. The Colombian *tiple* has four courses of strings, and the Guatemalan one may have up to five strings. In Puerto Rico, the *tiple* has four or five single strings, and in Venezuela it has five double or triple courses. The string tuning also varies; as many as sixteen accepted tuning patterns exist. The *tiple* is paramount in song accompaniment.

Tirado, Romualdo (b. Spain): Actor, producer, and writer. Tirado spent fifteen years acting in Mexico before moving to Los Angeles in the late 1910's to establish his career in the United States. One of the central figures in early Los Angeles theater, Tirado was devoted to expanding opportunities for Hispanic artists and audiences. During the 1920's, he established contests to find and present the work of emerging dramatists. As a performer, he had a stock *peladito* comic persona, a sympathetic underdog that he played in such popular original *revistas* as *De México a Los Angeles* and *Tirado bolshevique*.

In 1930, Tirado adapted Mariano Azuela's epic novel of the Mexican Revolution, *Los de abajo* (1916), for the stage. During the Depression, Tirado continued producing plays at churches and also began his own film production company. He continued producing and performing into the 1940's, appearing in New York and San Francisco as well as Los Angeles.

Tizol, Juan (Vicente Martínez; Jan. 22, 1900, San Juan, Puerto Rico—Apr. 23, 1984, Inglewood, Calif.): Jazz trombonist and composer. Tizol received musical instruction at an early age and quickly learned how to play most of the instruments of the orchestra. He preferred to play the valve trombone, a popular instrument on the island at the turn of the century, and joined the Municipal Band of San Juan.

At the age of twenty, Tizol moved to the United States, where he worked with the pit band at the Howard Theater in Washington, D.C. He also contracted with the Theatre Owners Booking Association, which booked acts around the United States.

Duke Ellington heard Tizol in the late 1920's and invited him onto a radio broadcast performance. Ellington was impressed with Tizol's warmth and melodic playing. Tizol joined Ellington's orchestra in 1929, thus beginning a productive musical collaboration. Together they composed such songs as "Caravan" and "Pyramid," with an oriental tinge, and the Latin-flavored "Conga Brava" and "Perdido." Tizol also played with the Harry James band and made recordings with Nat "King" Cole, Nelson Riddle, and Louis Bellson.

Tjader, Cal (Callen Radcliff, Jr.; July 16, 1925, St. Louis, Mo.—May 5, 1982, Manila, Philippines): Percussionist. Tjader, a Swedish American, began his professional career with pianist Dave Brubeck. In 1949, he joined British pianist George Shearing's quintet, which also included Willie Bobo (*TIMBALES*), Mongo Santamaría (congas), and Armando Peraza (BONGOS). The quintet had a large popular success with its definitive bop and Latin jazz sound. These musicians were very influential in the 1960's and 1970's fusion music. Each of them also had successful individual careers.

Cal Tjader became a major figure in Latin music. (AP/ Wide World Photos)

Tjader's productive career as pianist, percussionist, composer, and bandleader brought him together with artists Alvino Rey, Lalo Schifrin, Donald Byrd, Kenny Burrell, Stan Getz, Hank Jones, Eddie Palmieri, Tito PUENTE, Scott Hamilton, and Ray BARRETTO, to name a few. Tjader participated in the First Latin Music Festival at Madison Square Garden in New York City in 1972.

Tjader has a large discography in print. His albums include *Mambo with Tjader*, *Ritmo Caliente*, and *Mas Ritmo Caliente* from the 1950's in addition to *Cal Tjader Plays Mucho*, *The Cal Tjader Sextet*, *La Onda Va Bien* (Grammy winner in 1980), and his last album *Good Vibes* (1982).

Tolan Committee hearings: On April 22, 1940, the U.S. House of Representatives passed a resolution calling for the formation of a congressional committee to investigate problems associated with the interstate migration of indigent persons, to be known as the Select Committee on the Interstate Migration of Destitute Citizens. It was later referred to as the Tolan Committee, for its chairman, Congressman John Tolan (D-California).

The committee was formed in response to increasing social and economic problems stemming from the dramatic increase in the number of agricultural migrant families resulting from the Great Depression, increased agricultural mechanization, and soil erosion. In the Midwest and West, newly displaced native-born white migrants were competing with one another and with an already established migrant labor force, mostly Mexican, for a dwindling number of jobs. The problem was especially acute in California, which was overwhelmed by a surplus of labor and was experiencing a social and economic crisis as increasing numbers of people fell below the poverty line. The committee's purposes were to examine the problem, allocate federal funds to the areas most affected, and make recommendations for legislation to alleviate the situation. More than three million words of oral and written testimony were received during the course of the year-long investigation.

The committee held hearings in seven regions of the country. Testimony by specialists in agricultural economics and rural welfare told a story of marginalized workers and unorthodox business practices made worse by lack of government regulation. The majority of expert witnesses recommended broadening existing legislation to include farm labor, which traditionally had been exempt from government regulation. Wit-

The Tolan Committee heard evidence concerning "stoop" labor and other conditions of farm work. (Filipino American National Historical Society)

nesses also cited the need to expand medical programs for migrants and institute school attendance laws as a means of reducing child labor. They also identified certain states' settlement laws (requiring various periods of residency before an individual qualified for public assistance) as the most serious problem facing migrant workers.

Much of the investigation examined the interstate migration of Mexican workers. Mexican immigrants had flooded into the United States in the decades before the Depression, recruited by labor representatives of large sugar firms to plant and harvest sugar beets. With the onset of the Depression, labor surpluses in industry and agriculture suddenly displaced this vulnerable migrant labor force. During the 1930's, the flow of labor actually reversed as Mexicans and Mexican Americans moved south of the border. In spite of the labor surpluses, a demand for Mexican labor persisted. Long-distance recruiting by northern employers of Mexican agricultural workers in Texas kept a steady stream of Mexicans moving north to places such as California, Michigan, and Minnesota to plant and harvest sugar beets. Employers there preferred recruiting Mexican labor from Texas because local non-Hispanic workers demanded improvements in the deplorable wages and working conditions offered.

The Tolan Committee found that after Mexican laborers were in the fields, they were given substandard accommodations and a grueling work schedule of manual "stoop" labor. Mexican workers often were required to remain between planting and the harvest season, unable to collect money or accept other work. The investigation also revealed exploitative practices of labor contractors, who recruited large groups of Mexican families and individuals and sometimes forced them to stand for long periods in overcrowded trucks with inadequate sanitation. To make matters worse, Mexican laborers were typically charged a fee for their transportation, which was deducted from their pay.

On April 3, 1941, the Tolan Committee submitted a report to Congress containing a number of recommendations to improve the social and economic welfare of migrant agricultural workers. Recommendations included new legislation to regulate interstate labor contractors and private employment agencies engaged in interstate commerce, the continued improvement of standards of housing and sanitation for agricultural workers through establishment of new Farm Security Act camps in areas with the greatest increases in the use of migrant labor, and the establishment of a new category of public assistance under the Social Security Act to provide relief to workers on farms.

Tomatillo: Green tomatolike fruit used mostly in Mexican sauces. The tomatillo is a green fruit native to Mexico and the adjacent American Southwest. It is used in the cooking of both areas. Tomatillos are vaguely similar to unripe tomatoes in taste and culinary characteristics, though they are somewhat more tart and have a distinctive flavor. Like tomatoes, tomatillos are used primarily in sauces. Most Mexican red sauces are based on tomatoes and use ripe (red) chiles, and green sauces usually are based on pureed tomatillos and use unripe (green) chiles. Tomatillos are not closely related to tomatoes.

Tomato: Red fruit (often treated as a vegetable) used widely in Latin America, especially for sauces. Tomatoes were domesticated in tropical America and were eaten widely by many Indian tribes and peoples, including the Aztecs, who called them *tomati*. Tomatoes are eaten in all Latin American countries today, in salads, as garnishes, and particularly as the basis for red sauces. The prominence of the tomato (and, in some places, its partner, the TOMATILLO) led native Latin American sauces to focus on vegetable purees as bases. This focus has been continued in modern folk cooking in Mexico and elsewhere.

Torres, Art (b. Sept. 24, 1946, Los Angeles, Calif.): Legislator. Born and reared in East Los Angeles, Torres, a Mexican American, completed his undergraduate studies at the University of California, Santa Cruz,

Art Torres. (AP/Wide World Photos)

and earned a law degree at the University of California, Davis. He later laid the groundwork for what would be a career in public service by serving as a John F. Kennedy teaching fellow at Harvard University. Torres was first elected to the California State Assembly in 1974 and served there until his election to the state senate in 1983.

During his service in the state senate, Torres dedicated his time and energy to the improvement of education at all levels, particularly through legislation to address the problem of high school dropouts. Torres was also elected to the Council on Foreign Relations of New York and participated in the National Commission on International Migration and Economic Development, which recommends federal policy regarding Latin America.

Torres, Esteban Edward (b. Jan. 27, 1930, Miami Ariz.): Legislator. The son of a Mexican-born miner, Torres found his life shaped by childhood events. When he was six years old, his father was deported for union-organizing activities. His family moved to East Los Angeles. Despite a flirtation with gang life, Torres was graduated from high school before joining the army and serving in Korea. After his discharge, he landed an assembly line job and attended California State University.

During his factory work in the 1950's, Torres became active in the United Autoworkers Union. He founded The East Los Angeles Community Union (TELACU), which became one of the nation's largest antipoverty organizations. After losing a 1974 House primary, Torres was named ambassador to the United Nations Educational, Scientific, and Cultural Organization (UNESCO) by President Jimmy Carter. He was elected to Congress in 1982 and established himself as an advocate for consumers, fair and open lending practices, and safe disposal of hazardous waste. He served on the House Appropriations Committee.

Torres, José Luis (b. May 3, 1936, Playa de Ponce, Puerto Rico): Boxer. Torres began his boxing career while serving in the U.S. Army. Fighting in the 1956 Melbourne Olympics, Torres lost to the dominant light

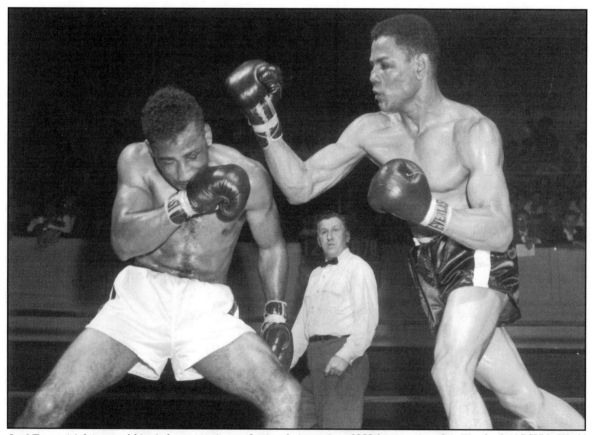

José Torres (right) scored his sixth consecutive professional victory in a 1958 bout against Otis Woodard. (AP/Wide World Photos)

middleweight of the time, Laszlo Papp, and took home the silver medal.

Torres continued to fight in armed forces competition for two more years. In 1958, he won the Amateur Athletic Union championship in his weight class. He turned professional and won the light-heavyweight title in 1965 with a knockout of Willie Pastrono. He successfully defended his title four times, becoming a hero in Puerto Rico.

A loss in a fifteen-round decision against Dick Tiger in December of 1966 marked the end of Torres' career. Turning to writing after his retirement, Torres penned a biography of Muhammad Ali. He later served as the boxing commissioner for the state of New York.

Torres-Gil, Fernando (b. June 24, 1948, Salinas, Calif.): Government official. Born to parents who were migrant farmworkers, Fernando Torres-Gil was reared in California. He earned his Bachelor of Arts degree from San Jose State University and his Ph.D. in social policy from Brandeis University.

Torres-Gil is a nationally recognized expert on public policy issues concerning health and long-term care, gerontology, ethnicity, human services, rehabilitation, and disabilities. He served as staff director of the House Select Committee on Aging in 1978. From 1990 to 1992, Torres-Gil served as a member of the Social Security Administration's Supplemental Security Income Modernization Task Force. He served as a policy adviser to Bill Clinton's presidential campaign in California and served on the Clinton transition team. He was nominated by President Clinton on February 23, 1993, as the first assistant secretary for aging in the Department of Health and Human Services. He also served on the White House Working Group on Welfare Reform.

Tortilla: Thin, griddle-baked corn sheet. Tortillas are eaten like bread or as a wrapper for other food. They are an ancient Mexican dish known to the Aztecs as *tlaxcalli*. They are made from MASA and traditionally are patted to regular thinness between the palms. The

A tortilla stall in Merida, Mexico. (Hazel Hankin)

thin circles are cooked on a *COMAL* or similar griddle with no fat until they are dry and start to scorch at a few points. For centuries, tortillas have been eaten like bread as a standard accompaniment to country meals. They also are used as flexible food wrappers, as for TACOS and *FLAUTAS*. In northern Mexico, *tortillas de harina* are made with wheat flour, lard, baking powder, and water, and many northern Mexicans prefer them to the corn version. Outside Mexico and Central America, a tortilla usually is an egg omelette.

Tortilla Curtain Incident (1978-1979): U.S.-Mexico border dispute. The incident centered on a proposed fence, to be built on the border between Mexico and the United States. Conflict began in October, 1978, with newspaper reports that described plans to build the fence. The fence's designer, a Texas contractor, described it as being twelve feet high, with a five-foot section made of sharp metal that would reportedly cut off the toes of anyone attempting to climb it. The upper seven-foot section would be chain link and barbed wire. The sixteen-mile fence would replace a six-mile existing one, covering spots were crossings occurred frequently.

The series of newspaper articles enraged the Mexican government and some Mexican American groups. In Mexico, the press incorrectly reported that fourteen thousand troops were to accompany the new fence to keep out border crossers. In addition, the incident occurred in the midst of a U.S. government review of policies toward Mexico, including migration and trade barriers. In this political climate, the proposed fence appeared to the Mexican government as a U.S. ploy to stop migration and pressure Mexico to sell its petroleum products at lower prices.

Mexican Americans organized demonstrations and formed a "Coalition Against the Fence" in El Paso, Texas. Intensified enforcement against illegal commuters added to Mexican Americans' anger. From January to March, 1979, the status of the fence was undecided. Changes in plans for the fence were made known by Associate Attorney General Michael Egan in El Paso. The Southwest Border Region Commission recommended against the fence.

In April, 1979, the Immigration and Naturalization Service revealed a new and revised plan for the fence. It was to be lower, with the sharp metal part redesigned, the barbed wire left out, and the proposed length shortened to eight miles. The Mexican government, when consulted, did not state any objections to the new fence, and the incident was resolved.

Tostada: Mexican *antojito*. Tostadas are made all over Mexico, with many regional variations. All begin with a corn tortilla, fried in oil until slightly crisp. It is topped with the region's specialty: meat, cheese, SALSA, GUACAMOLE, lettuce, TOMATO, onion, *FRIJOLES REFRITOS*, or any combination. Outside Mexico, "tostada" usually refers to a slice of toasted bread.

Tostones: Fried plantain slices. Plantains are starchy, so they take well to frying. *Tostones* are one-inch rounds of plantain fried once, then flattened and fried again. This double-frying produces crisper results than the single-frying of plantains that occurs in English-speaking parts of the Caribbean. *Tostones* are eaten extensively in Puerto Rico and Cuba. Though less common, they also are made along the Central American Caribbean coast from Belize to Venezuela. They usually are eaten as snacks.

Toys. *See* **Games and toys**

Track and field sports: Many successful Latin American track and field athletes have competed on the teams of U.S. universities; there have been, however, only a relative handful of Latino track and field stars.

Brief History. When the Spanish arrived in Central and Latin America, they found that various physical activities, among which was running, were popular and actively engaged in by the indigenous population. By the mid-1800's, formal track and field events from Europe and the United States had become popular. Indigenous running games provided a firm foundation for track and field sports in Latin American nations.

Also imported from the United States, around the beginning of the twentieth century, were organized athletic clubs, the restructuring of school curricula to include physical education, the founding of national sport associations, and the establishment of training facilities. Unlike a number of other imported sports (for example, boxing, soccer, baseball, and horse racing), track and field remained almost exclusively an amateur sport in Latin American countries, as well as in the United States, until late in the twentieth century. This resulted in part because track and field sports never attained the mass spectator appeal of some other sports.

Several Latin American countries also affiliated early on with emerging international sports federations and events, the most important of which were the Olympics and the Pan American Games. Chile was one of thirteen countries represented at the first modern Olympics in 1896. Cuba and Mexico have competed since 1900, and Mexico hosted the Olympics in 1968. Eventually all Latin American countries participated in the Summer Olympics.

Perceived Benefits. Involvement in track and field and other sports was believed to be beneficial in improving physical health, aiding spiritual and moral development, teaching discipline, encouraging national identity, earning international respect and status, and serving certain political purposes. For example, a one hundred-kilometer race by two Tarahumara Indians in Mexico in 1926 was run both to encourage inclusion (although unsuccessfully) of such long-distance events in the 1928 Olympics and to counter what Mexico perceived as lack of attention to its national merits. The San Blas half marathon in the rural Villa de San Blas de Illescas in Puerto Rico is a community-backed and community-building event ranking in popularity with major baseball and cycling events.

Adding to track and field's luster among Latin Americans is its favorable treatment in literature. Alejandro Gandara wrote a fictional account, *La media distancia* (1984), of a runner nearing the end of his career. The runner speculated on his past triumphs and agonies and the true meaning of success in athletics. In Gabriel Ruiz de Las Llanos' *La marathon* (1977), a fictional Argentine runner gives an account of his experiences of pain, solitude, pride, ambition, discipline, and fulfillment as he runs a marathon. The author suggests that the marathon is a metaphor for life.

Prominent Athletes. Latin American countries, in particular Cuba, Brazil, and Mexico, have emerged as powers in track and field, in part as a result of interest in and concentration on the sport. Many athletes from these countries have attended American colleges and universities with strong track and field teams. For example, Joaquim Cruz, Agberto Guymares, and Jose-Luis Barbosa attended the University of Oregon. Cruz won the eight hundred- and fifteen hundred-meter races at the 1984 National Collegiate Athletic Association meet and the gold medal in the eight hundred meters for Brazil at the 1984 Olympics in Los Angeles, California. Other noted athletes who attended American universities are Ruben Reina, a middle-distance runner for the University of Arkansas; Juan de la Garza, who threw the javelin for Texas A&M; pole vaulter Jose Guerra from the University of Texas; Arturo Barrios, a long-distance runner who competed for Texas A&M and remained in the United States; and Puerto Rican pole vaulter Edgar Diaz, who competed for Louisiana State University.

Athletes who do not attend U.S. schools can still receive exposure through participation in American-sponsored meets. For example, Cuban high jumper and world record holder Javier Sotomayor and sprinter Andres Simon participated in the 1991 Snickers Millrose Games in New York City and the Mobil 1 meet in Fairfax, Virginia. Saboador Garcia of Mexico won the New York Marathon. Olga Appell won the Los Angeles Marathon. The United States thus offers Latin American runners opportunities for higher levels of competition and exposure, and in the case of college athletes, for education and training.

Latino Track and Field Athletes. Despite the large population of Latinos in America, relatively few have achieved prominence in track and field sports. The most prominent are middle- to long-distance runners. Alberto SALAZAR (who was born in Havana, Cuba, but came to the United States as a youngster after the Cuban Revolution) competed for the University of Oregon. He won the New York Marathon and held the

Alberto Salazar set a record for the Boston Marathon in his 1982 victory. (AP/Wide World Photos)

world record in the marathon. Doug Padilla competed for Brigham Young University and held American records at three thousand and five thousand meters and at two miles. Joe Falcon attended the University of Arkansas. He was the 1987 cross-country champion and later won the Bislett Mile in Norway.

Contributions of these and a few other prominent Latino athletes aside, American track and field is dominated by African Americans and non-Hispanic whites. It appears that the higher profile, more lucrative sports with more mass appeal (boxing, horse racing, and baseball) have provided the preferred venues into sport for the best Latino athletes.

—*Laurence Miller*

SUGGESTED READINGS: • Arbena, Joseph L., ed. *Sport and Society in Latin America: Diffusion, Dependency, and the Rise of Mass Culture.* New York: Greenwood Press, 1988. • Gandara, Alejandro. "The Middle Distance." *Arete: The Journal of Sport Literature* 4, no. 1 (1986): 1-8. • Jordan, Tom. "Padilla: A Man of Quiet Faith." *Track and Field News* 34 (March, 1981): 25. • Meserole, Mike, ed. *The 1994 Information Please Sports Almanac.* Boston: Houghton Mifflin, 1994. • Thatcher, Paul. "T&FN Interview: Alberto Salazar." *Track and Field News* 36 (January, 1984): 78-80.

Travel literature: Written accounts by European travelers expanding the frontier in North America had a major influence on subsequent settlement patterns in a given territory. During the long period of Spanish exploration, conquest, and settlement in northern New Spain, for example, many explorers gained inspiration and ideas from the accidental adventures of Álvar Núñez CABEZA DE VACA. In 1528, Cabeza de Vaca began an expedition to Florida that developed into an eight-year inland journey. Found in 1536 by fellow Spaniards as he roamed through what became northern Mexico, Cabeza de Vaca shared his imprecise, yet fascinating, discoveries. The story of his unintentional journey was printed in Spain in 1542, and word of his travels circulating throughout the Spanish world gave impetus to the expeditions of both Francisco Vázquez de CORONADO in New Mexico and Hernando DE SOTO in Florida. Eventually, fables about the seven mythical cities of Cíbola to the north inspired the Spanish and Mexican people to conquer and settle what later became the state of New Mexico.

During the nineteenth century, travel literature played a significant role in developing the early colonists' fascination with the land and people in the western part of what is now the United States. Expansionist U.S. officials developed an interest in owning these lands and sent covert expeditions into Spanish-held territories. Men such as Zebulon Pike, Thomas Freeman, and Peter Custis began exploring these regions as early as 1806. More thorough investigations of Mexican territories and culture followed the 1821 opening of the SANTA FE TRAIL. Visits by non-Hispanics to the northern region of Mexican territory between 1821 and 1846 resulted in a dramatic increase in the writing and distribution of travel literature throughout the United States. James Ohio Pattie (*The Personal Narrative of James O. Pattie of Kentucky*, 1831), Mary Austin Holley (*Texas: Observations, Historical, Geographical, and Descriptive*, 1833), Josiah Gregg (*Commerce of the Prairies*, 1844), and George Wilkins Kendall (*Narrative of the Texan Santa Fe Expedition*, 1844) were among the most significant authors writing on Texas and New Mexico. In California, Richard Henry Dana (*Two Years Before the Mast: A Personal Narrative of Life at Sea*, 1840), Alfred Robinson (*Life in California*, 1846), and Walter Colton (*Three Years in California*, 1850) wrote popular accounts of Californio culture.

Many scholars researching the genre of travel guides have detected the racist and ethnocentric sentiments prevalent in the United States during this period. Travel authors frequently disparaged the Mexican people, depicting them as swarthy, indolent, and immoral. Non-Hispanic writers often held Mexican women to constrictive Victorian standards and criticized them for their "unbridled passion" and "immorality" based on their appearance and dress. Upper-class Mexican women, on the other hand, often were held up as "true women," far removed from public life and positions of power.

Travel literature generally reflected the most prevalent sentiments of mainstream culture. Influenced by anti-Catholic, anti-Spanish sentiments that persisted through the colonial and revolutionary periods, and repulsed by the mixed-blood status of mestizos, Anglos believed it was their "MANIFEST DESTINY" to displace Mexican and Indian people residing in North America. U.S. travel literature that reinforced these prejudices played a significant role in justifying the MEXICAN AMERICAN WAR of 1846-1848.

Treaty of El Chamizal (November, 1970): Established the boundary between the United States and Mexico. The Rio Grande marks an official boundary between the United States and Mexico. In 1836, after

U.S. ambassador Thomas Mann (left) and Foreign Affairs Minister Manuel Tellos exchange copies of the Treaty of El Chamizal. (AP/Wide World Photos)

Texas won its war for independence from Mexico, the Rio Grande was established as the dividing line between the new Lone Star Republic and Mexican territory. When Texas became a state in 1845, the old border was retained. Because of flooding and erosion, the river changed course many times. Mexico and the United States engaged in sometimes bitter disputes over small amounts of land that ended up on different sides of, or in the middle of, the river.

In 1963, at the direction of President John F. Kennedy, negotiators signed a convention that seemed to resolve the problem. The document was not formally recognized by the United States until seven years later, when the Senate ratified the Treaty of El Chamizal. The treaty granted the Chamizal region, then north of the Rio Grande but formerly south of it, back to Mexico.

Treaty of Guadalupe Hidalgo: Signed on February 2, 1848, at the village of Guadalupe Hidalgo near Mexico City, the Treaty of Guadalupe Hidalgo ended the MEXICAN AMERICAN WAR and granted the United States nearly half of Mexico's territory, encompassing California, New Mexico, Arizona, and Texas.

End to the War. The war between Mexico and the United States had been declared in May, 1846, after U.S. president James K. Polk ordered General Zachary Taylor to cross the Nueces River in Texas and occupy territory claimed by Mexico. The U.S. military had success on the battlefield in northern Mexico, and California was seized, but the Mexicans were unwilling to sue for peace because the U.S. terms demanded surrender of much of Mexican territory.

After futile attempts at negotiation, the United States decided to attack central Mexico and capture Mexico

General Antonio López de Santa Anna led Mexico and its forces during the Mexican American War. (Library of Congress)

City. General Winfield Scott invaded the port city of Veracruz in March, 1847, and began a march toward the capital. After defeating the Mexicans at Cerro Gordo, Scott reached Puebla, only eighty miles from Mexico City. President Polk had appointed Nicholas TRIST, the chief clerk of the State Department, to accompany the army as a commissioner empowered to negotiate with the Mexicans. The Americans attempted to open negotiations with the Mexicans, but no one would accept the correspondence because the Mexican congress had passed a law declaring anyone who negotiated with the United States to be a traitor.

General Antonio López de Santa Anna, the president of Mexico and leader of its armies, was an unscrupulous politician who had both defended his country heroically and betrayed it in war. In exile when the war began, he had bargained with the Americans for safe passage to Mexico, where he would seek to end hostilities quickly. Instead, he took over the government and led troops against the United States. Now, faced with Scott's army so close to the capital, Santa Anna secretly sent word to Trist that he would begin negotiations to end the war if he were paid ten thousand

STATES & TERRITORIES FORMED FROM THE MEXICAN CESSION & GADSDEN PURCHASE

dollars. Scott and Trist finally agreed to pay the amount and stopped operations while awaiting negotiations. Santa Anna, however, was unable to overcome strong public opinion against negotiations, and hostilities resumed.

In August, 1847, Scott reached the outskirts of Mexico City. He and Trist attempted one more time to negotiate, but the terms—that Mexico give up all claims to territory north of the Rio Grande and cede both New Mexico and California for a set payment— were unacceptable to the Mexicans. The Mexican government was willing to surrender Upper California and relinquish claims to Texas but demanded an independent buffer state between the Rio Grande and the Nueces River and refused to cede New Mexico. In addition, Mexico insisted that the United States prohibit slavery in any territory taken from Mexico. With no hope for a negotiated peace, Scott attacked Mexico City and occupied it on September 14, 1847.

Signing of the Treaty. Santa Anna retreated with the remnants of his army, and the government was left in disarray. Trist found no one with whom he could negotiate. In the meantime, political pressure in Washington led Polk to recall Trist and demand that Mexico initiate future negotiations. Although officially recalled on October 6, 1847, Trist did not receive the letter until after an interim president had been elected in Mexico and commissioners had been appointed to negotiate a peace treaty. Trist ignored his instructions when they arrived in mid-November and, believing that a delay would only weaken the provisional government and lead to guerrilla warfare, he met with the Mexicans.

By late January, 1848, fearing his removal, Trist threatened to end negotiations and demanded an immediate agreement. On February 2, 1848, the Treaty of Guadalupe Hidalgo was signed. Its twenty-three articles spelled out the terms of settlement: removal of U.S. troops, surrender of Mexican territory, setting of navigation rights, and ratification procedures. The most important part of the document granted the United States territory in Texas, New Mexico, and California in return for a payment of fifteen million dollars. The U.S. government also agreed to assume American claims against Mexico of more than three million dollars.

The United States, as the victor in the war, had gained its objectives; moreover, in spite of his lack of authority at the time, Trist had achieved his goal. Polk, although furious with Trist, accepted the treaty as politically expedient. On March 10, 1848, the U.S. Senate ratified the Treaty of Guadalupe Hidalgo by a vote of thirty-eight to fourteen.

It took Mexico longer to ratify the treaty. Many Mexicans were horrified at the potential loss of so much territory. After rancorous debates, the Mexican congress ratified the treaty on March 25. By June, American troops had evacuated Mexico City.

Impact. The signing of the Treaty of Guadalupe Hidalgo was the most significant event in the relationship between Mexico and the United States in the nineteenth century. The treaty gave the United States control of nearly half of Mexico's territory, led to an anger that colored Mexico's relations with the United States well into the twentieth century, and fulfilled the goals of Americans who wanted a nation that spanned the continent. The United States justified its actions by claiming that Mexico had not developed the territory and by implying American superiority. Mexicans felt betrayed and were surprised that their neighbor would seek to destroy the Mexican nation for gain. The discovery of gold in California shortly after the MEXICAN AMERICAN WAR confirmed the Mexicans' belief in American greed and duplicity and helped them to forget that they had long neglected their northern frontier.

—*James A. Baer*

SUGGESTED READINGS: • Bauer, K. Jack. *The Mexican War, 1846-1848.* New York: Macmillan, 1974. • Eisenhower, John S. D. *So Far from God: The U.S. War with Mexico, 1846-1848.* New York: Random House, 1989. • Henry, Robert Selph. *The Story of the Mexican War.* New York: Frederick Ungar, 1961. • Schroeder, John H. *Mr. Polk's War: American Opposition and Dissent, 1846-1848.* Madison: University of Wisconsin Press, 1973. • Singletary, Otis A. *The Mexican War.* Chicago: University of Chicago Press, 1960.

Treaty of Paris (1898): Concluded hostilities between the United States and Spain in the SPANISH-AMERICAN WAR. Spain gave up all claims in the Caribbean to Cuba and to Puerto Rico. In the Pacific, Spain relinquished its claims to the Philippines and to Guam. As a result of this treaty, the United States gained new claims to far-flung territories and became responsible for the welfare and government of the Spanish-speaking populations in these territories. Many residents of the territories began migrating to the United States in search of employment, thus increasing the Spanish-speaking population of the United States.

Treaty of Velasco (1836): Peace treaty. This document was signed by Mexico and the independent government of Texas, which had defeated Mexican forces and captured General Antonio López de Santa Anna at the Battle of San Jacinto on April 21, 1836. The treaty recognized the independence of Texas from Mexico and provided for the withdrawal of Mexican troops to the territories south of the Rio Grande. Although a secret agreement between the two sides indicated that Mexico might give in to the demand that this southern boundary be made permanent, the Mexican government refused to acknowledge this provision officially. Some people of Mexican descent decided to abandon their lands in Texas after it established its independence, but many others stayed and eventually became residents of the United States when Texas was admitted to the union in 1845.

Tres Reyes Magos (Three Kings Day): Tres Reyes Magos, January 6, coincides with the Feast of the Epiphany, the last of the twelve days of Christmas. It celebrates the arrival of the three wise men in Bethlehem and the revelation to them, by Mary, of Jesus as the Christ child. It concludes the religious observance of Christmas in most predominantly Catholic countries and in Hispanic American communities in the United States.

The celebrations may involve a performance of *Los Tres Reyes*, a traditional nativity play. A feast often is involved, featuring, as a dessert, *Rosca de los Reyes*, or Three Kings Bread (called King Cake in Louisiana), made with nuts, raisins, candied fruit, grated lemon, and orange peels in addition to the usual ingredients. The bread is shaped into a ring to represent a crown, and baked inside is a small plastic baby figure representing the Christ child. The finder of the effigy is supposed to have good luck in the coming year, and in recompense for that good fortune is expected to host a party on the Feast of Candelaria, which falls on February 2.

Although in many Hispanic communities the Anglo traditions of Christmas trees, Santa Claus, and gift

The 1988 Tres Reyes Magos celebration sponsored by New York City's El Museo del Barrio. (Impact Visuals, H. L. Delgado)

giving have been adopted, in Mexico and elsewhere in Latin America the older Spanish tradition of giving gifts to children on January 6 is still in vogue, particularly outside the larger cities. In many border communities in Mexico and the United States, both traditions are observed.

Treviño, Jesús Salvador (b. Mar. 26, 1946, El Paso, Tex.): Filmmaker. Treviño established himself as a leading filmmaker by treating subjects and issues of importance to Latinos. His documentaries include *Salazar Inquest* (1970), *Chicano Moratorium* (1970), *America Tropical* (1971), *Have Another Drink, Ese* (1977), and *One Out of Ten* (1979).

In 1972, Treviño documented the national convention of La Raza Unida Party in *La Raza Unida*, and his *Yo Soy Chicano* became the first nationally televised Hispanic documentary. *Raíces de Sangre* (1977) explored life on the border. *Seguín* (1982) gave a Hispanic perspective on the history of the Alamo.

Treviño's 1985 *Yo Soy Chicano* examined the social and political progress achieved by Chicanos during the 1970's and 1980's. In 1989, he received the Directors Guild of America Award for Best Dramatic Daytime Show for the documentary *Gangs*. In addition to his own projects, Treviño has directed episodes of the television series *Gabriel's Fire*, *Lifestories*, and *Mathnet*.

Trevino, Lee Buck (b. Dec. 1, 1939, Dallas, Tex.): Golfer. The son of an impoverished Mexican American couple, Trevino grew up near the back fairways of

Lee Trevino, after sinking a putt on his way to victory in the 1984 PGA Championship. (AP/Wide World Photos)

the Glen Lakes Country Club and began learning the game at the age of six. He left school after the seventh grade to work at the club; at the age of fifteen, he shot a 77 in his first full round of golf.

While serving in the U.S. Marine Corps from 1957 to 1961, Trevino played in service tournaments. After his discharge, he worked as a golf instructor and club professional, and he won the Texas State Open in 1965. He broke into the Professional Golfers Association (PGA) ranks at the 1966 U.S. Open, finishing in fifty-fourth place. In 1967, he improved to fifth in the Open and was named the tour's Rookie of the Year.

Trevino emerged as a star with a smashing win at the 1968 U.S. Open, becoming the first golfer to shoot four subpar rounds in the tournament's history. In 1971, he captured victories at the U.S., British, and Canadian Opens to earn PGA Player of the Year, Associated Press Athlete of the Year, and *Sports Illustrated*

Sportsman of the Year honors. His many other victories include the 1972 British Open, 1977 and 1979 Canadian Open, and 1974 and 1984 PGA Championship titles. In 1970, 1971, 1972, 1974, and 1980, Trevino won the Vardon Trophy as the PGA player with the lowest yearly scoring average.

Trevino was struck by lightning at the 1975 Western Open and was left with severe back problems. Highly popular among his fellow golfers and fans, he remained one of golf's top players and drawing cards. After his fiftieth birthday, Trevino began playing on the PGA Senior Tour, and he soon came to dominate it. He also continued to play in Skins Games and to provide golf analysis for television. In 1981, he was inducted into the PGA/World Golf Hall of Fame.

Trillo, Manny (Jesus Manuel Marcano y Trillo; b. Dec. 25, 1950, Caridito, Venezuela): Baseball

Manny Trillo throws from second base to complete a double play. (AP/Wide World Photos)

player. A right-handed-hitting second baseman with tremendous defensive range, Trillo made his major league debut with the Oakland A's in 1973. After a trade took him to the Chicago Cubs in 1975, he became a regular, playing four seasons before another trade sent him to the Philadelphia Phillies in 1979.

Trillo's defensive excellence with Philadelphia earned for him three Gold Glove Awards in four seasons. In 1980, he batted a solid .292 for the world champion Phillies and was named the Most Valuable Player of the National League playoffs. Two years later, he set several fielding records (since broken) at second base, including consecutive error-free games in a season (89), consecutive errorless chances accepted (479), and single-season fielding percentage (.9937).

A three-time All-Star with the Phillies, Trillo was traded to the Cleveland Indians in 1983 and became the first player chosen to starting All-Star teams in consecutive years for different leagues. He retired in 1987 after seasons with the Montreal Expos, San Francisco Giants, and Cincinnati Reds.

Trio Borinquen: Music trio. Rafael Hernández founded Trio Borinquen in New York City in 1926. A skilled musician and prolific composer, Hernández was a creator of the trio and small-ensemble style of Puerto Rican music popularized in New York City in the 1920's and 1930's. Hernández's songs were based on traditional Puerto Rican styles as well as more modern styles of BOLERO, GUARACHA, RUMBA, and SON. The trio also played Dominican and Cuban songs. Trio Borinquen was popular in New York City as well as in Latin America, where it gained popularity through recordings.

Trio los Panchos: Music trio. One of the most famous trios of Latin music, Trio los Panchos formed in 1944 when duo Alfredo Gil and Chucho Navarro added a third member to their act. Various musicians filled that third position. The trio brought increased recognition to Mexican popular music and played throughout the United States, Mexico, and Latin America. They played BOLEROS, creating a model for trios that was imitated by many groups throughout Latin America. Their instruments included guitars, *requinto*, and some percussion, and their music featured three-part vocal harmonies. Trio Los Panchos recorded about forty albums.

Trist, Nicholas (June 2, 1800, Charlottesville, Va.— Feb. 11, 1874, Alexandria, Va.): Diplomat. In April, 1847, President James K. Polk chose Trist, who had risen to the post of chief clerk and de facto undersecretary of the State Department, as peace commissioner to Mexico. Trist seemed well suited for the task of concluding a treaty that would end the MEXICAN AMERICAN WAR. He knew Spanish, was familiar with Latin American culture, and had acquired some diplomatic experience as resident consul in Havana during the 1830's.

Trist's mission ran into several obstacles. His quarrel with General Winfield Scott upon arrival in Mexico in May, 1847, delayed for a time the opening of negotiations. After American troops captured Mexico City in September, 1847, President Polk, eager to obtain more land, ordered Trist to break off discussions and return home. Trist, however, believed that refusal to negotiate at that time would prove disastrous to the Mexican political administration, which desired peace. Any further delays might allow the pro-war faction a chance to take over the government and renew hostilities. Trist ignored Polk's order and negotiated the TREATY OF GUADALUPE HIDALGO, which was signed in February, 1848.

Trova: Song contest indigenous to Mexico and New Mexico. *Trova*, from the Spanish *trovador* (troubadour), appeared in northern Mexico and New Mexico as an improvisational musical genre derived from song contests that originated in the Spanish and Portuguese courts. Much as the troubadours met in the presence of kings to compete, troubadours traveling from Chihuahua to New Mexico would engage in competitions, singing their long repertoires of *décimas de amor* (ten-line love songs), religious *DÉCIMAS*, and *TROVAS* (improvised verses), singing alternately to one another. *Trovas* are still heard in many Latin American countries, particularly in Peru and Chile.

Trujillo Herrera, Rafael (b. 1897, Durango, Mexico): Playwright. Trujillo Herrera immigrated to Los Angeles in 1926. During a career that spanned half a century, he wrote nearly one hundred plays, including full-length and one-act pieces, and supported himself solely through the theater. His radio plays of the early 1930's include such works as *Pancho Villa*, *La serenata de Los Angeles*, and *Doña Clarines en Jaligú*. In 1933, he began directing his own radio show.

Trujillo Herrera's three- and four-act plays include *Revolución*, *Estos son mis hijos*, *La hermana de su mujer*, *Cuando la vida florece*, *A la moda vieja*, *Juan Tenorio*, and *Una luz en las tinieblas*. In 1940, in association with the Works Progress Administration, he produced *El bandido*, which was later published under the title *Revolución*.

During the 1960's, Trujillo Herrera had his own Los Angeles publishing company, Editorial Autores Unidos. He also served as director of the Instituto Norteamericano de Intercambio Cultural. As an outgrowth of his work there, in 1974 he founded the Teatro Intimo.

Tucson, Arizona: Second largest city in Arizona. Tucson was home to about 117,000 Latinos in 1990, according to the U.S. census. They constituted about 29 percent of the city's population. The larger Metropolitan Statistical Area including Tucson had a lower proportion of Latinos.

In 1775, Hugo O'Conor, a commandant inspector for the Spanish Crown, founded a PRESIDIO (fort) at what was called San Agustín de Tucson. Presidios were established to fight off Apache warriors during the Spanish colonization of Mexico. In 1776, Tucson was colonized by people who came from the presidio at Tubac, about forty miles to the south. Some of these were Spaniards, and others were MESTIZOS (people of mixed Native American and European blood).

Prior to establishment of the presidio, the site had contained a mission. Father Eusebio Francisco KINO arrived there in 1694, and in 1699 he first used the name Tucson on a map. The mission collapsed and was rejuvenated several times prior to O'Conor's selection of the site for a presidio.

Tucson was acquired by the United States in the GADSDEN PURCHASE of 1854. Few Anglos settled in Tucson immediately following the purchase. They saw few resources and perceived Hispanic people as dirty and lazy. The few Anglos who did settle often married Hispanic women and took advantage of the agricultural and mining techniques developed long ago. The Hispanic population remained a majority until the twentieth century. Despite their numbers, Hispanic people continued to lose political power.

Esteban OCHOA was elected as Tucson's mayor in 1875, but during the 1890's and early 1900's only one Mexican American, Mariano Samaniego, was elected to the state legislature. Two Mexican Americans were elected to the city council during these years.

During the Mexican Revolution (1910-1921), Mexican nationals began immigrating to Tucson. Tucson's population of foreign-born Hispanics increased almost 75 percent. New Hispanic associations emerged during World War I and the 1920's. The 1930's were difficult for the Hispanic population of Tucson. Many Hispanics worked as laborers, a job category hit particularly hard by the Depression. The 1940's saw little economic improvement for Tucson's Hispanic population. The percentage of Hispanics in unskilled jobs was slightly higher than during the 1920's. As late as the early 1970's, Tucson neighborhoods and schools were racially segregated.

According to the 1990 census, Hispanics were the largest minority group in Tucson. Mexican Americans were the largest subgroup of Latinos in the city, accounting for 92 percent of the Hispanic population.

Hispanic influences are present throughout the city in organizations such as Chicanos por la Causa, the Latin American Social Club, and the Tucson Metropolitan Hispanic Chamber of Commerce. The University of Arizona hosts the Mexican American Studies and Research Center, the Latin American Area Center, and the Hispanic/Chicano Resource Center. Manuel Pacheco, a Mexican American, served as president of the university in the early 1990's. Tucson's largest school district operated several bilingual magnet schools and programs. Cultural organizations included the Instituto de Folklore Mexicano, which teaches folkloric dance. Other Hispanic cultural influences could be found in shrines (*nichos*) in Hispanic neighborhoods. Although

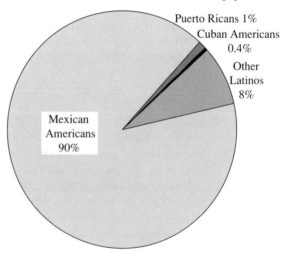

LATINO POPULATION OF TUCSON, ARIZONA, 1990

Total number of Latinos = 163,262; 24% of population

Puerto Ricans 1%
Cuban Americans 0.4%
Other Latinos 8%
Mexican Americans 90%

Source: Data are from Marlita A. Reddy, ed., *Statistical Record of Hispanic Americans* (Detroit: Gale Research, 1993), Table 111.

Note: Figures represent the population of the Metropolitan Statistical Area as delineated by the U.S. Bureau of the Census. Percentages are rounded to the nearest whole number except for Cuban Americans, for whom rounding is to the nearest 0.1%.

A drawing by Cal Peters of the early walled city of Tucson. (Arizona Historical Society)

Hispanic influences could be seen throughout the city, including its businesses, Hispanics were still largely underrepresented in local government.

Tucson International Mariachi Conference (Tucson, Ariz.): The Tucson International Mariachi Conference is basically a music festival and professional conference inaugurated in 1982 by the Tucson Festival Society and other community groups. It quickly came under the sponsorship of La Frontera Center. Its proceeds have been used to help fund mental health services at the center.

In Mexico, MARIACHIS were originally small itinerant or "strolling" folk orchestras limited to the various kinds of string instruments, ranging from large guitars to the tiny *vibuela*. They later evolved into ensembles using both brass and string instruments and now often include coronets, trumpets, and a *guitarrón*, a cross between a bass fiddle and a guitar.

The conference in Tucson focuses on mariachi music and *baile folklórico*, or folk dancing, and it offers educational workshops in which professional mariachi musicians and *folklórico* instructors teach these traditional folk arts. Workshops are sometimes closed to the general public, but many events are open to all visitors, including major concerts at the Tucson Convention Center, featuring mariachi groups; the Garibaldi Fi-

Folk dancing demonstrations are part of the conference's entertainment. (James Shaffer)

esta, which re-creates the Garibaldi Plaza of Mexico City in downtown Tucson, with folk music and dancing as well as food and game booths; a major art exhibit and demonstration of crafts by artisans from Mexico, Texas, and Arizona; and a major parade.

Turquoise Trail: Name given to the trade route linking central Mexico with the American Southwest. The route emerged during pre-Columbian times, in part to facilitate the distribution of turquoise throughout Mesoamerica.

Turquoise was one of the most precious stones of ancient Mesoamerica, rivaling jade and its sacred beauty in Mayan Central America. Mesoamericans cherished turquoise, believing its blueness to contain both sky and water. The principal sources of turquoise lay far north of the Mexican centers of civilization. To obtain the treasured stone, the Indian peoples of Central Mexico traded with the inhabitants of what is now the southwestern United States, where turquoise was mined in New Mexico, Arizona, and Nevada, and south of New Mexico, near the border of Sonora and Chihuahua at Casas Grandes. Trade routes evolved to link the turquoise-producing regions with southern consumers.

Although turquoise has been found among burial goods in Guerrero, Mexico, dating to 600 B.C.E., widespread demand for the gemstone developed during the Classic period (200 to 800 C.E.). A main center of turquoise-working was Alta Vista in Zacatecas. It lay in the Chalchihuites area, the site of many ancient mines that yielded azurite, cinnabar, malachite, and hematite, along with native copper. Mesoamericans also imported turquoise, perhaps small quantities at first, from nearby sources and then large amounts from the Cerrillos mines on Turquoise Mountain in north-central New Mexico. By 700 C.E., Alta Vista carried on a substantial trade along an early inland version of the Turquoise Trail, which ran through the dry, lightly populated lands northward from Zacatecas toward

New Mexico and onward to Cerrillos. Traders distributed processed turquoise from Alta Vista south to Teotihuacán, Cholula, and Oaxaca.

The more famous version of the Turquoise Trail went along the populous west coast of Mexico. It emerged at the end of the Classic period and coincided with the rise of new distribution and processing centers. In the mid-tenth century, the Anasazis in the Chaco Canyon gained control of the export into Mexico of unworked turquoise from Cerrillos and other southwestern mines. They began to process turquoise, adopting beveling and mosaic techniques invented in Chalchihuites. Mexican merchants brought quetzal feathers and copper bells, among other trade goods, along with Mesoamerican ideas and technologies to exchange for turquoise. The collapse of Anasazi culture in the twelfth century coincided with the Chaco Canyon's loss of control over turquoise distribution.

In the centuries leading up to the Spaniards' arrival, trade along both trails increased, with turquoise flowing as far away as the Yucatán. Throughout Mesoamerica, turquoise remained a sacred stone. Aztecs presented Hernán CORTÉS with a mosaic turquoise mask of the god QUETZALCÓATL. The trails, meanwhile, linked northern Mexico with the central heartland. In 1540, for example, Francisco Vázquez de CORONADO took his expedition along the coastal Turquoise Trail in search of the land of CÍBOLA. He discovered instead that the trail led to the land of the sacred blue stone.

U

UCLA student demonstration for a Chicano Studies department (Apr. 24, 1990—June 7, 1993): Students associated with El Movimiento Estudiantil Chicano de Aztlán (MECHA) at the University of California, Los Angeles (UCLA) held demonstrations supporting establishment of a Chicano Studies department at UCLA.

The Chicanos Studies Program was formed in 1969 to combat anti-Mexican sentiment at UCLA. After twenty-one years of minimal funding for the program, UCLA Chicano and Latino professors, MECHA representatives, and community, labor, and business leaders formed the United Community and Labor Alliance Coalition. In December, 1990, this group wrote a proposal for the establishment of a Chicano Studies department. Chancellor Charles Young ignored the proposal, and the Committee on Undergraduate Courses and Curricula of the Academic Senate rejected it. For two years, the coalition worked to develop a new pro-

posal, which was submitted in January, 1992. It was reviewed and approved in the spring of 1992 by the Academic Senate Committee and the Spanish, economics, and history departments. On April 28, 1993, Chancellor Young announced his rejection of the proposal to establish a Chicano Studies department, setting off a protest movement on campus.

On May 11, 1993, a rally was organized in front of the faculty center to protest the dissolution of the Chicano Studies Research Library. Conscious Students of Color and MECHA took over the center and organized a sit-in to protest closing the Chicano Studies Research Library, budget cuts, and failure to establish a Chicano Studies department. Ninety-nine students were arrested by Los Angeles and university police officers, and eighty-three students spent more than a day in jail.

In response to the arrests, on May 12, more than one thousand people attended a rally supporting establish-

The demonstrations concerning the Chicano studies curriculum at UCLA drew a variety of students. (Impact Visuals, Ted Soqui)

ment of the department and release of the arrested students. In the days to follow, politicians protested the arrests and fines of the incarcerated students. On May 14, state senators Tom Hayden and ART TORRES joined assemblywomen Marguerite Archei and Hilda SOLIS in a meeting with Chancellor Young and other administrators. The politicians demanded that all charges against the students be dropped and that the Chicano Studies department be created.

Another rally on campus was organized on May 21. Actor Edward James OLMOS; representatives of MOTHERS OF EAST L.A.; state legislators Hilda Solis, Art Torres, and Tom Hayden; and Congresswoman Lucille Roybal-Allard (*see* ROYBAL FAMILY) spoke to a crowd of more than one thousand people.

A hunger strike was organized on May 25 in response to Chancellor Young's continued refusal to approve a Chicano Studies department. A professor and six students vowed not to eat solid food until the department was established.

On June 5, students, professors, politicians, community members, union members, and others gathered at Olvera Street to march in solidarity with the hunger strikers. Thousands gathered for a twenty-one-mile march to UCLA. A rally was held at the end of the march, at which hunger strikers and community and political activists spoke to the crowd.

On June 7, after many meetings with the hunger strikers, community members, and politicians, Chancellor Young approved the proposal to establish the department. The thirteen-day hunger strike ended with a dinner for the hunger strikers, dancing, singing, and victory speeches. Most of the protesters' terms were met, and the César Chávez Center for Interdisciplinary Instruction in Chicana/o Studies was formed.

Ugarte y Loyola, Jacobo (c. 1721, the Basque Provinces, Spain—Aug. 20, 1798, Guadalajara, Mexico): Soldier and administrator. Little is known of Ugarte's early life other than his noble birth and 1732 entry, as a cadet, into the Royal Guard. In 1740, Ugarte began service in the regular army, campaigning bravely in Italy and Austria. He became an ensign in 1746 and then a lieutenant in 1762. In 1767, Ugarte's accomplishments, for example in the Seven Years War, led to his promotion, in one step, from lieutenant to colonel. In that year, he also became the governor of Coahuila, beginning a thirty-one-year career in Spanish America.

In 1778, Ugarte, by then a brigadier general, left Coahuila to become governor of Sonora (1779-1784). In 1784 and 1785, Ugarte governed Puebla, which he

left to become commandant general of the internal provinces (1786-1790). In 1791, field marshal Ugarte became commandant general of Nueva Galica. He retained this post until his death.

Ugarte fought bravely and sensibly to pacify the Indians throughout his career. He was an honest, hardworking official who sought the best for his subordinates and subjects, frequently helping out with his own funds. Ugarte was an excellent administrator, exemplified in Nueva Galica by his institution of public improvements, inauguration of the second university in NEW SPAIN (the University of Guadalajara), and introduction of hospital reform, new crops, and city planning.

Ulibarrí, Sabine (b. Sept. 21, 1919, Tierra Amarilla, N.Mex.): Writer. Ulibarrí was reared in Tierra Amarilla, where he attended public elementary and secondary schools. He was reared in a completely Spanish-speaking environment, and literary Spanish was an important part of his childhood. His father would often read Spanish literature to the family.

Ulibarrí received his bachelor's (1947) and master's (1949) degrees in Spanish from the University of New Mexico. During the next nine years, he studied and taught at the University of California, Los Angeles, from which he was awarded a doctorate in 1959.

In addition to publishing scholarly works, textbooks, and essays, Ulibarrí published two books of poetry in 1966: *Al cielo se sube a pie* and *Amor y Ecuador*. He has also produced two collections of short stories: *Tierra Amarilla* (1964; English translation, 1971) and *Mi Abuela Fumaba Puros: My Grandmother Smoked Cigars* (bilingual edition, 1977). All of his creative work was originally written in Spanish. Ulibarrí's thoughts on crucial social issues such as bilingual-bicultural education are respected by the local and national Chicano communities.

Unauthorized workers: "Unauthorized," "undocumented," and "illegal" are all terms used in the United States to describe foreign nationals holding or actively seeking U.S. jobs without the legal authorization to do so. Before the IMMIGRATION REFORM AND CONTROL ACT OF 1986 (IRCA), unauthorized workers were often referred to as undocumented workers. After the IRCA required all persons hired to present documentary proof of their legal right to work in the United States, there was a proliferation of false documents, most often forged driver's licenses and permanent resident alien (I-551) visas. By the 1990's, most U.S.

workers not legally entitled to hold jobs had work authorization documents. The U.S. government and most researchers therefore refer to them as unauthorized workers.

Most unauthorized workers enter the United States across the Mexico-U.S. border, without inspection. Others enter the United States legally, often as tourists, and then violate the terms of their entry by working. The number of unauthorized resident aliens is not known with certainty but was estimated by the IMMIGRATION AND NATURALIZATION SERVICE (INS) to be four million in October, 1994, and increasing by 300,000 annually. An estimated 60 to 80 percent of those unauthorized residents were unauthorized workers.

Macroeconomic Effects. Unauthorized workers earn wages and consume public services, and they usually pay taxes. The overall balance of their effects on the economy may be positive or negative, in both the short term—within ten years or so of their arrival—and over longer time periods. Many of the factors to be weighed are hard to measure, making it difficult to isolate the effects of some three million unauthorized workers on economic indicators such as the rate of increase in wages and profits, the development and spread of labor-saving and productivity-increasing technologies, and the entrepreneurial vigor of the economy in a U.S. labor force of 130 million.

There is general agreement that the most important effects of unauthorized workers are distributional, meaning that their effects on particular U.S. workers and industries are more important than their overall contributions to the size of the U.S. economy and labor force. The President's Council of Economic Advisers summarized the economic effects of immigrant workers in a 1986 report. Although immigrant workers were found to increase output, their addition to the supply of labor caused wage rates in the immediately affected market to be bid down. Native-born workers who competed with immigrants for jobs therefore could experience reduced earnings or reduced employment.

The Council of Economic Advisers emphasized that even if unskilled immigrants displace similar Americans from jobs and depress wages, they can still provide a small benefit to the U.S. economy as a whole. The availability of immigrant workers may increase opportunities and raise wages for complementary U.S. workers, as occurs when the availability of immigrant laborers makes feasible a construction project that employs American carpenters and electricians. Immigrant workers spend at least some of their wages in the United States, creating jobs for American citizens. The

Council of Economic Advisers' report concluded that, as a general rule, increases in output brought about by immigration outweigh reductions that may occur in the wages of workers who compete with immigrants. The comments from that report, it should be noted, refer to immigrant workers but not specifically to unauthorized workers.

Microeconomic Effects. Three major kinds of studies examine the effects of unauthorized immigrants on the wages and job opportunities of other workers. Case studies rely on interviews with employers and workers to investigate particular situations. Econometric studies correlate the estimated number of unauthorized immigrants in a city with the wages and unemployment rates of U.S.-born workers to determine whether cities with more such immigrants offer other workers lower wages and fewer jobs. Economic mobility studies chart the earnings progress of immigrants, including unauthorized immigrants, after their arrival in the United States to determine the relative importance of education, skill in use of the English language, age, and other factors in explaining an immigrant's economic mobility in the United States.

Case studies often conclude that unauthorized immigrant workers displace Americans and depress wages and working conditions. Many such studies emphasize how the labor markets in industries such as agriculture and janitorial services can become dependent on unauthorized workers and isolated from other U.S. labor markets.

Case studies often find that in so-called "ethnic enclave" industries, the unauthorized immigrant workers might have been hired by accident or by design. The immigrants persist in high-turnover farmworker, maid, or laborer jobs, while American workers quit. The immigrants then offer to bring their friends and relatives to fill vacancies, and in this manner the immigrant network becomes the supplier of new workers.

After unauthorized immigrants come to dominate a work force, the language and culture of the workplace may change. Authorized American workers who might have accepted low-wage and unpleasant jobs, at least temporarily, no longer learn about them.

Econometric Studies. Econometric studies begin from the assumption that the more immigrants in a city, the higher should be the unemployment rate and the lower should be wage levels for other workers who are similar to the immigrants. The surprise is that they find few such "negative" labor market effects. Analyst George Borjas has asserted that modern econometrics cannot detect evidence that immigrants have a sizable

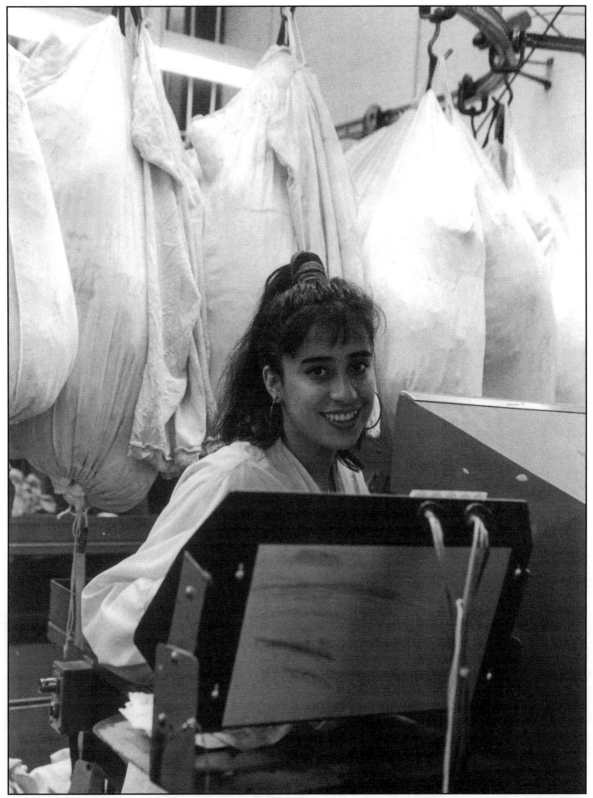

Unauthorized workers become dominant in some workplaces through use of informal networking and because other workers leave. (David Bacon)

Many farm jobs are filled through informal channels, with openings never advertised. (AP/Wide World Photos)

adverse impact on the earnings and employment opportunities of natives in the United States.

For example, most studies have found that a 10 percent increase in the immigrant work force reduces wage rates by less than 5 percent. The MARIEL BOAT LIFT, for example, increased Miami's labor force by 7 percent in 1980, but econometric studies could find no differences between wage and job opportunities for American workers in Miami in the early 1980's.

More recently, econometric studies have been challenged by geographers who have noted that persons similar to unauthorized workers in education and skills tend to move away from, or not move into, areas with large numbers of such workers. The workers who remain may not be affected by unauthorized workers, they argue, because they are in jobs whose wages are not affected by immigration, such as government or manufacturing jobs with pay scales established on a nationwide basis. Furthermore, the case studies sometimes find that immigrant workers are given lower wages in a manner not reflected in the employer-reported wage data typically used in econometric studies. A foreman, for example, may require immigrant workers to pay for daily rides to work.

Agriculture. The overall labor market effects of unauthorized immigrants are probably small, although they may be significant in particular industries and areas. Agriculture is probably the U.S. industry most dependent on unauthorized workers. An estimated 20 to 40 percent of the country's two million farmworkers are unauthorized workers, despite the legalization through AMNESTY of one million farmworkers in 1987-1988. Agriculture used to represent an easy-entry job for American students and housewives. As of the early 1990's, 60 percent of all farmworkers and 90 percent of the new entrants to the farm work force were immigrants.

In most areas, authorized Americans do not learn about farm jobs. There is little employer advertising for grape or peach pickers because crew bosses recruit immigrant workers through networks that bypass most U.S. citizens. In the fields, most instructions are given in Spanish, so an English-only worker would be out of place.

Instead of asking whether immigrants help or hurt American workers in the labor markets where both work, the most important question may be whether their earnings catch up to those of other workers. In a series of pioneering economic mobility studies, Barry Chiswick found that legal immigrants who arrived in the 1950's and 1960's initially earned less than Americans with the same education, but after fifteen to twenty years, these immigrants typically earned more than their American counterparts.

More recent analyses paint a less cheerful picture. George Borjas has argued that today's immigrants include so many unskilled workers that they lower average U.S. incomes. His analysis of Census of Population data indicates that unauthorized immigrant men arriving in the United States from Mexico will earn about 15 percent less during their lifetimes than comparable non-Hispanic white native men. Further, because the typically large immigrant families exhibit a higher propensity to go on welfare, they threaten to increase the cost of public assistance.

Inequality. Unauthorized workers may also affect America's "competitiveness." Secretary of Labor Robert Reich defined competitiveness as rising living standards for most Americans, linking economic growth with economic equality. In 1978, a white male college graduate earned 49 percent more than a white man with only a high school diploma, yet both were considered middle class. Today, this gap has widened, so that the college graduate earned 82 percent more in 1992.

Most unauthorized workers have little education. Large numbers of them therefore accentuate this growing earnings inequality. Unlike most Americans, immigrants, both legal and illegal, tend to be bunched at the extremes of the educational distribution: They tend to be either college graduates or high school dropouts.

The traditional view is that general economic growth helps both rich and poor. This did not happen in the 1980's. The highest-earning 25 percent of American families got about half of the national income, while the lowest-earning 25 percent, with incomes of less than $22,000, got about 6 percent.

Immigration is only one of several factors responsible for increased earnings inequality. Most studies attribute at least some of the decline in inflation-adjusted (real) wages—they fell 2.6 percent from 1989 to 1993—to the expansion of low-wage service jobs and the increasing globalization of the U.S. economy, reflected in both rising trade and increased immigration. Other studies point to technologies that require more skills, the decline of unions, and tax cuts for the wealthy.

Optimal Unauthorized Immigration? Unauthorized immigrants cannot replace investments in human and physical capital as the basic engines of economic growth, nor can the presence of three or four million unauthorized immigrants lead the United States to ruin. Economic arguments about unauthorized immigration

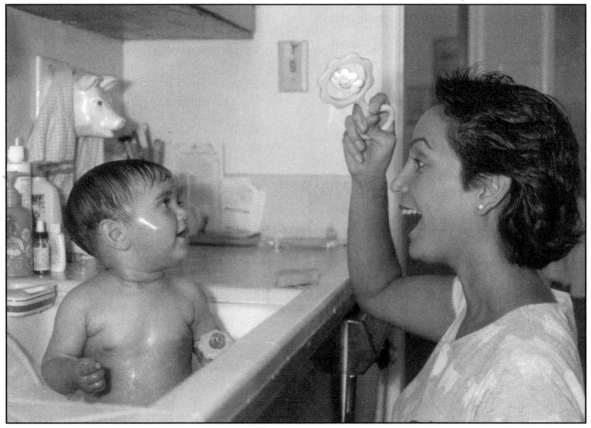

Unauthorized workers fill many of America's low-wage jobs, such as in child care and cleaning. (Robert Fried)

inevitably become debates over what kind of economy Americans want. Tolerating unauthorized workers eager for jobs expands U.S. employment, because there is rarely a one-for-one displacement of Americans by immigrants. Millions of immigrants are eager for employment in the United States, including jobs such as cleaning American houses and tending America's children and elderly. The argument for increased immigration states that workers should be allowed in if they are willing to do these jobs cheaply, thus lowering the cost of services.

Admitting immigrants involves trade-offs. More immigrants lead to more jobs and economic activity. Those jobs, however, may be at the bottom of the economic spectrum. Opponents of increased immigration argue that the United States should not allow itself to become a low-wage economy.

Policy Perspectives. U.S. policymakers repeatedly have illustrated that they do not want to adopt every policy that maximizes the number of jobs and the total amount of production. The United States has decided to sacrifice some jobs in order to have higher labor standards and a cleaner environment.

Immigration policy has similar trade-off effects. More unskilled immigrants would mean more jobs but also more inequality. Increased immigration would also pose the challenge for the future of ensuring that the children of farmworkers, maids, and other immigrants receive an equal chance to achieve the American Dream.

The major argument in favor of more immigration is that the immigrants and most Americans can benefit without significant costs. The major arguments against immigration, especially unskilled immigration, are that it hurts the most vulnerable American workers and can distort the development of the economy. These effects of immigrants, however, are likely to be small in the context of the $6 trillion U.S. economy.

The history of immigration to the United States and successful integration into U.S. society leads to optimistic predictions concerning unauthorized workers arriving today. There is no reason that history must repeat itself, however, and those raising questions have legitimate worries.

The United States may very well have valid reasons for controlling the growth of its immigrant work force.

The existence of unauthorized workers means that the controls, to some extent, are not effective.

—*Philip Martin*

SUGGESTED READINGS: • Borjas, George J. *Friends or Strangers: The Impact of Immigrants on the U.S. Economy*. New York: Basic Books, 1990. • Briggs, Vernon, Jr. *Mass Immigration and the National Interest*. Armonk, N.Y.: M. E. Sharpe, 1992. • Martin, Philip L. *Trade and Migration: NAFTA and Agriculture*. Washington, D.C.: Institute for International Economics, 1993. • Martin, Philip L., and Elizabeth Midgley. *Immigration to the United States: Journey to an Uncertain Destination*. Washington, D.C.: Population Reference Bureau, 1994. • Massey, Douglas S., Joaquin Arango, Graeme Hugo, Ali Kouaouci, Adela Pelligrino, and J. Edward Taylor. "Theories in International Migration: A Review and Appraisal." *Population and Development Review* 19 (September, 1993): 431. • U.S. Congress. Senate. Committee on the Judiciary. Subcommittee on Immigration and Refugee Policy. *Final Report of the Select Commission on Immigration and Refugee Policy*. Washington, D.C.: Government Printing Office, 1981. • U.S. Council of Economic Advisers. *Economic Report of the President*. Washington, D.C.: Government Printing Office, 1986.

Underclass debate: This social science and public policy debate addresses the underclass theory of urban poverty in the United States. Although the debate focuses on African Americans, applicability of the theory to Latino POVERTY has been widely analyzed.

A Theory of Urban Poverty. The underclass debate concerns the causes and consequences of urban poverty in the United States. The underclass theory seeks to explain deteriorating social conditions in large industrial centers such as Chicago, New York City, and Detroit. The most influential theory of the underclass was developed by sociologist William Julius Wilson in his book *The Truly Disadvantaged: The Inner City, the Underclass, and Public Policy* (1987).

The central argument of the underclass theory is that persistent poverty is the result of a number of interrelated factors, including certain behaviors, the social environment, and economic conditions. According to this theory, persistent poverty is associated with increasing rates of social dislocation, which takes the forms of inner city joblessness, teenage pregnancy, out-of-wedlock births, female-headed families, welfare dependency, and serious crime. Such behaviors reflect changes in the social environment of inner-city neighborhoods, or ghettos. Specifically, these areas have experienced an outmigration of middle- and working-class people, which has contributed to the concentration of poverty.

At a broad level, economic restructuring is considered to be the main force behind underclass poverty. The shift from a manufacturing to a service economy in major U.S. urban centers in the 1970's is blamed for a substantial decrease in the availability of jobs for low-skilled inner-city residents. The effect of living in an overwhelmingly impoverished environment characterized by high levels of joblessness is that individuals are deprived of role models and resources, such as access to informal job networks.

Liberal Versus Conservative Interpretations. The underclass theory has generated debate in the social sciences and other disciplines, including sociology, economics, political science, social welfare, and public policy studies. The main area of contention concerns the causes of persistent, concentrated poverty in America. Generally, the debate is split between liberal and conservative views.

The liberal perspective is that poverty is the product of structural forces; that is, lack of opportunity is the main cause. This perspective supports Wilson's hypothesis that changes in the structure of the economy have decreased the availability of jobs for certain groups and in certain areas, particularly African Americans living in central cities. The liberal view also emphasizes the role of discrimination at all levels, including education, employment, and housing. Along the same lines, liberals believe that a major cause of poverty in the United States is an inadequate welfare system that is not effective at getting families out of poverty.

Conservatives argue that poverty is not so much a result of social barriers as a product of dysfunctional attitudes and behaviors that keep people from working. They maintain that jobs are available, but as a result of a defeatist attitude, the poor choose not to work or to progress. According to this view, social welfare programs have exacerbated the problem by creating dependency among the poor.

Latino Poverty and the Underclass. Although the underclass model focuses on African Americans, Latinos have been an important part of the underclass debate. Some aspects of contemporary Latino life parallel those of African American life. Both groups are highly urbanized, both have seen a loss of jobs as a result of economic restructuring, and both have experienced extremely high rates of poverty and social dislocation.

Neighborhoods can become ghettos because people from the middle classes choose to move away, leaving the poor behind. (David Bacon)

Latinos often do not benefit from workplace protections, particularly if they are undocumented. (Impact Visuals, Les Stone)

Theorists argue that because the underclass theory of poverty focuses on the case of inner-city African Americans, it needs to be reframed to take into account issues specific to Latinos. Some of the fundamental factors involve the diversity within the Latino population, the continual influx of immigrants, and the economic context for Latinos.

First, unlike African Americans, who for the most part share a common ancestry and historical background in the United States, the Latino population is composed of diverse groups with distinct histories. Mexican Americans, Puerto Ricans, Cuban Americans, Central Americans, and other Latino subgroups were incorporated into the United States during different historical periods and under different circumstances. In addition, U.S. government policy toward different groups ranged from supportive, with economic assistance provided for resettlement in the United States, to utilitarian, with immigrants viewed as a source of cheap labor. As a consequence, poverty among different populations of Latinos stems from different historical roots.

Second, in contrast to the case of African Americans, poverty among Latinos is strongly related to new

flows of immigrants. Therefore, poverty for Latinos is associated with different dynamics. One consequence of immigration is that new, poor immigrants occupy poor neighborhoods, while older immigrants move on as they improve their social status. Latino immigrants often work for wages lower than those of other U.S. residents, driving down prevailing wage rates. At the same time, some new and returning immigrants revitalize Latino communities by bringing in new capital and setting up small businesses.

Third, the economic conditions that shape Latino poverty vary from those that shape African American poverty. The economic status of people of Mexican origin along the U.S.-Mexico border, for example, is influenced by fluctuations in the economy of Mexico. In MIAMI, FLORIDA, a growing segment of Cuban-owned business is an important source of jobs for Cuban Americans. Economic restructuring is only partly responsible for the employment status of Latinos; foreign economic factors and motivation within the community also play roles.

Theorists argue that the causes and consequences of African American and Latino poverty are distinct. They contend that in order for the underclass theory to be useful in understanding Latino poverty, these different dynamics need to be taken into account.

Impact. The underclass debate brought the problem of poverty in the United States to the forefront of social science research and stimulated large amounts of public policy analysis, but it did not result in any immediate policy action. During the presidency of George Bush (1989-1993), no major social welfare legislation was enacted.   —*Yolanda C. Padilla*

SUGGESTED READINGS: • Jencks, Christopher. *Rethinking Social Policy: Race, Poverty, and the Underclass.* Cambridge, Mass.: Harvard University Press, 1992. • Massey, Douglas S. "Latinos, Poverty, and the Underclass: A New Agenda for Research." *Hispanic Journal of Behavioral Sciences* 15 (November, 1993): 449-475. • Mead, Lawrence M. *The New Politics of Poverty: The Nonworking Poor in America.* New York: Basic Books, 1992. • Moore, Joan, and Raquel Pinderhughes, eds. *In the Barrios: Latinos and the Underclass Debate.* New York: Russell Sage Foundation, 1993. • Wilson, William Julius. *The Truly Disadvantaged: The Inner City, the Underclass, and Public Policy.* Chicago: University of Chicago Press, 1987.

Undocumented people: UNEMPLOYMENT, POVERTY, and civil wars have motivated Latin Americans to migrate north in search of improved living conditions.

Those seeking to escape often exceed the number legally permitted to enter the United States and Canada. Desperation pushes many immigrants to cross borders illegally.

Many people from Mexico and Latin America view the United States and Canada as utopias. As the conditions in their home environments deteriorate, escape appears to be the only hope for survival. A certain number of visas are granted, but the number is smaller than the number of people seeking a better life. When survival is at stake, people turn to illegal methods to enter these lands of opportunity.

History. On December 27, 1847, the first U.S. immigration law was established by Colonel R. B. Mason. This law proclaimed that Mexicans from Sonora could no longer enter California. This law became obsolete in 1848, at the end of the MEXICAN AMERICAN WAR. At that time, the United States bought the remaining Mexican territories for $15 million. This annexation of the Southwest was granted by the TREATY OF GUADALUPE HIDALGO. The Mexicans living in these territories were forced to become inhabitants of the United States or to leave the territory.

Several lures brought Mexicans north. They came to mine gold, to build railroads, and to work in agriculture. The flight to U.S. farms grew particularly large during the decade beginning in 1910. A violent revolu-

Availability of jobs building railroads encouraged Mexicans to immigrate. (Museum of New Mexico, Emil Bibo)

Undocumented Immigrants Apprehended by the Border Patrol
(selected years, 1944-1990)

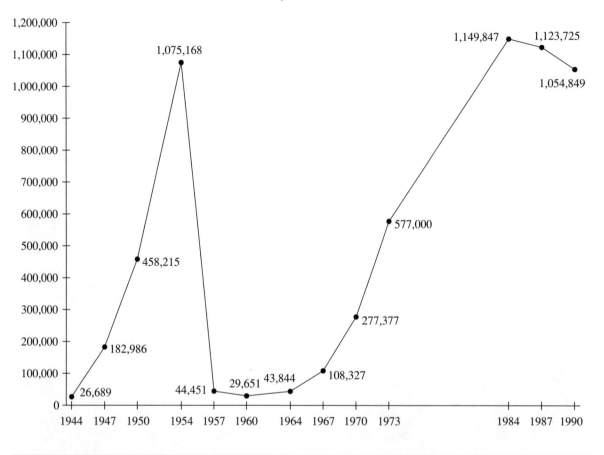

Source: Data are from Mario Barrera, *Race and Class in the Southwest: A Theory of Racial Inequality* (Notre Dame, Ind.: University of Notre Dame Press, 1979), p. 123; and Marlita A. Reddy, ed., *Statistical Record of Hispanic Americans* (Detroit: Gale Research, 1993), Tables 25 and 26.

tion in Mexico and a world war encouraged about 220,000 Mexicans to enter the United States during these years.

In 1924, Congress created the Border Patrol to enforce new laws concerning immigration that included small quotas. At that time, Mexicans paid a head tax to enter the United States. They crossed the border in large numbers to work for U.S. farmers and industrialists. In 1942, an agreement with the Mexican government allowed 4.8 million braceros to enter the country seasonally to work on farms and ranches. The Bracero Program, instituted in response to war-related labor shortages, encouraged many Mexicans to come to the United States. The number desiring entry surpassed those permitted, so illegal crossings of the border occurred.

In 1964, the Bracero Program ended. Mexicans still saw job opportunities across the border, and illegal immigration flourished throughout the 1970's and 1980's. To gain some control over this situation, Congress passed the U.S. Immigration Reform and Control Act of 1986. This law gave legal resident status to nearly three million undocumented or illegal residents through an amnesty program for longtime residents. In conjunction with this amnesty program, a stiff penalty was stipulated for employers who hired undocumented people. This law proved ineffective, however, and the number of illegal immigrants to the United States from Mexico increased to an estimated 900,000 in 1980.

Other Hispanic populations contributed to the estimated two million undocumented persons in the United

Salvadorans have fled oppressive conditions in their homeland. (Impact Visuals, Ted Soqui)

States in 1993. (Estimates vary widely.) Mexico contributed 45 percent of that total, according to some estimates. Other Latin American countries and the Caribbean area accounted for 23 percent. Many Cubans entered the United States in the 1940's and 1950's to escape the oppression of the regime of Fulgencio Batista. Another wave of CUBAN IMMIGRATION occurred in the 1960's as a result of the CUBAN REVOLUTION. A third wave surrounded the 1980 MARIEL BOAT LIFT. Undocumented immigration was part of each wave. Puerto Ricans represent another group of immigrants, but documentation is not an issue because Puerto Ricans have been United States citizens since 1917, when the JONES ACT was passed.

Salvadorans and Guatemalans represent a large group of undocumented persons. A stream of refugees passes from El Salvador through Guatemala and from Guatemala into Mexico, then into the United States. In December, 1983, a U.S. government official estimated that 300,000 to 500,000 Salvadorans and 60,000 Guatemalans lived in the United States without legal resident status. The 1980 census estimated that 1,380,000 undocumented persons from Mexico and other Latin American countries were living in the United States.

The Passage. People coming from Central and South America often travel by land until they reach the border between Mexico and the United States. Many of these migrants work on Pacific Coast plantations in Guatemala and gradually drift northward across the Usumacinta River into Mexico, where they find work on the coffee plantations of Chiapas. These migratory workers risk being deported as they travel the hundreds of miles to the United States border.

At the U.S. border, these migrant workers often hire "COYOTES," professionals at smuggling people across the border. The process of being smuggled across often brings devastating consequences. In July, 1980, fifteen persons being smuggled across the Arizona desert were abandoned by their coyote. The immigrants had no supplies to survive a trek across the desert. With inadequate water and shoes unfit for hiking, thirteen of the group died. Another set of border crossing fatalities occurred in Texas in 1982. Immigrants being smuggled in a freezer truck were unable to open the door from the inside, and several persons died of asphyxiation. Another incident occurred in Houston in 1983. Several Salvadorans were found murdered because they had not paid the coyote. These incidents illustrate that securing the services of a coyote is no guarantee that a U.S. destination will be reached safely.

Not everyone pays a coyote for assistance in crossing the border. Instead, many undocumented people group together and rush the fence that divides Mexico from the United States. In groups of one hundred or more, they climb over the fence and then go in various directions to evade the border guards. Some are caught, but they try again. Others cross the border alone or in small groups, hoping to avoid notice.

Many U.S. residents along the border are acting to curb illegal entries. One such group is called Light Up the Border, founded by Muriel Watson, the widow of a Border Patrol officer. This group lines up hundreds of cars and turns on their lights at a specified hour to spotlight those trying to sneak across the border.

Persons coming from many Central and South American countries apply for VISAS to enter the United States for a designated period of time. These visas may be granted for purposes of education, work, and family visitation. When visas expire, many persons choose not to return to their homelands. They stay in the United States as undocumented persons.

Once in the United States, immigrants often head for cities where large groups of others from their country reside. Cities such as Los Angeles and San Francisco, California; Miami, Florida; Washington, D.C.; and Houston, Texas, are popular destinations. When immigrants enter the United States, they may have family or friends who can shelter them; however, some have no personal connections and must rely on safe homes, places where they can hide out for a period of time. These residences offer a place to sleep and bathe; at times, meals are prepared for clients, who pay from ten to twenty dollars a day. Immigrants find out about these safe homes through word of mouth or through coyotes or *pasadores*, guides who sell their services once a crossing has been made.

Dream Versus Reality. Reality rarely lives up to expectations for new arrivals without documentation. They dream of freedom and economic opportunity, but without documentation to prove legal status, illegal immigrants are restricted in their choices of jobs. Very often, undocumented people find themselves in the least desirable positions, as low-paid housekeepers, hotel maids, construction laborers, and farmworkers. After seeing the reality in contrast to the dream, many opt to return to their home countries.

Some are lucky. The reality in the United States or Canada may seem like heaven in contrast to the devastation of their home environments. They return home on visits with encouraging reports for their friends and relatives, stimulating more border crossings with tales

Housing for undocumented people is sometimes far below the standards applied for others. (Impact Visuals, Philip Decker)

of jobs that pay more for a day's work than many homeland workers can earn in a week. For some who leave devastated countries for a better life, new environments may not be all that was envisioned, but the immigrants refuse to adjust their dreams of El Norte. They cling to their fantasies and maintain hope for the future.

Living Conditions. Many undocumented people choose to share shelter out of economic necessity or to save money to send home. Although conditions may be crowded, these individuals also find security in a group. Language, shared customs, and common experiences lend psychological and emotional support in an unknown environment. In addition, financial responsibilities can be shared within the group when necessary.

Social Services. Many undocumented people avoid drawing attention to themselves so that their status is not found out. A myth exists claiming that illegal immigrants drain the resources of welfare and social service agencies funded by U.S. taxpayers. Many refugees rely heavily on welfare and Medicaid, but undocumented people are barred from most forms of government assistance. Illegal immigrants avoid con-

tact with public officials, relying on one another and on people from their home countries for assistance.

Schools, however, suffer the consequences of overcrowded conditions, ethnic strife, and language barriers. Many taxpayers blame these conditions on undocumented people. If undocumented students were barred from schools, however, the negative conditions would not disappear. The number of legal immigrants in the United States requires schools to deal with language issues and ethnic strife regardless of attendance by undocumented children.

Another service undocumented people use is medical care. Because medical treatment is so expensive in the United States and because undocumented people cannot qualify for Medicaid, emergency rooms in hospitals are often filled with undocumented people in need of medical services. Documented residents complain about overcrowded conditions when they need emergency medical treatment, claiming that undocumented people use the emergency centers for illnesses that are not "emergencies." Humanitarians respond that a country cannot turn its back on people seeking medical assistance. Humanitarianism aside, provision of medical treatment for undocumented people lessens the spread of disease throughout the whole population, providing a benefit to documented residents.

The Struggle for Success. After working long hours each day, many undocumented people attend night classes in order to learn English. They realize that the first obstacle to job advancement is lack of skill in use of the English language. The process of language acquisition can be difficult, because many immigrants live with people who speak only their native languages. They are not forced to use English on a daily basis and, therefore, may take years to become proficient in English. Their employment opportunities are limited as long as they lack proficiency in use of English.

Along with survival and language difficulties, undocumented persons must cope with various prejudices. Undocumented people have become scapegoats in the search for causes of societal ills. Public concern has been expressed openly, and many politicians have presented legislation to gain control over the two million people who enter the United States illegally each year. Undocumented people, many people suggest, take jobs away from those with legal status (*see* UN-AUTHORIZED WORKERS). Undocumented residents respond that they accept jobs that others will not perform, as housekeepers, laborers, and field workers. Some people claim that undocumented workers accept

California's Proposition 187, passed in 1994, extended prohibitions on use of social services by undocumented people. (David Bacon)

wages that are "too low," thus pushing down wages for documented persons. Undocumented people also are blamed for contributing to gang violence, graffiti, and crime. As social conditions worsen in urban environments, undocumented immigrants increasingly are blamed.

Many undocumented people must deal with the psychological and emotional traumas of leaving family and friends behind. Some plan occasional trips to visit those left behind, but years may separate these visits. Visits home present risks in reentering the United States. Time spent apart from family members, along with an altered living environment, often causes familial roots to become severed. To lessen the pain of missing the family back home, some persons start families in the United States, thus having two families, one on each side of the border. This adds to the financial strains on undocumented workers as they contribute funds toward running two households. The financial strain may necessitate reliance on social services to the extent that they are available, perhaps to a household member with documentation or citizenship.

Cultural Transfer. Public schools offer some bilingual programs to keep students progressing academically, but English is generally used for official business and educational purposes. Because of the dominance of English and the lack of recognition of cultural differences, immigrants are subtly pressured to abandon their own cultures and languages in exchange for those of the mainstream. The process of ACCULTURATION often causes psychological and emotional tension. All immigrants, but particularly undocumented immigrants who must avoid official attention and therefore tend to function within ethnic enclaves, can come to feel split between two cultures.

Some immigrants choose to establish or join strong ethnic communities so that they feel more at home. These ethnic communities may have their own food stores, newspapers, and banks, but these neighborhoods often become slums as they alienate themselves from the mainstream economic system.

An alternative is cultural assimilation. Immigrants may choose to drop their native culture in order to adapt to the new social environment. This disregard for cultural heritage is a loss to the individual and to the social environment, which could benefit from fresh ideas and different cultural perspectives.

Adult newcomers cannot fully release their background and experiences, nor can they fully understand the intricacies of the new culture. They adapt on superficial levels in regard to behavior but not in regard to beliefs and values. Immigrants are caught between outward social decorum and personal values revealed in the privacy of their homes.

The children of immigrants are also caught in this conflict because society expects these children to conform to the new environment. The children may be in conflict with parents concerning which value system to adopt and may encounter cultural confusion as they are torn between peers and traditions. In the case of Latinos, children may speak Spanish at home and English at school, thus coming to see the home as a separate environment. These children often turn away from their home environments but often do not feel a close bond with native residents. As a result, some turn to gangs to find a sense of belonging (*see* GANGS AND GANG ACTIVITY).

Legal Implications. The laissez-faire attitude toward immigration that opened doors to newcomers was replaced by a quota system in 1921. Restrictions were justified by economic arguments that immigrants could not be absorbed into the labor pool. In reality, cultural selection also played a role. The dominating groups in the United States feared that American culture would be diminished by cultural diversity, so quotas favored immigrants from countries that had already established a strong presence in the United States. In Canada, immigrants had to be literate, possess a considerable sum of money, and maintain an employment contact.

Some undocumented immigrants to the United States attempt to marry citizens so that they can legally remain in the United States. U.S. law also states that any child born in the United States is a U.S. citizen. This birthright qualifies the child for social services not given to undocumented persons. (*See* CITIZENSHIP, PATHS TOWARD.)

Some undocumented people were granted AMNESTY by the IMMIGRATION REFORM AND CONTROL ACT OF 1986. They could apply for citizenship after five years if they met certain requirements. These requirements included legal admittance into the country for permanent residence, age of eighteen years or more, residency in the United States for five years or more, good moral character, proficiency in English, knowledge about American history and government, and lack of membership in any organization that advocates the overthrow of the government by violence or the doctrines of communism.

When an undocumented person is discovered by the IMMIGRATION AND NATURALIZATION SERVICE, he or she is held in a detention camp. If the person signs a

Border Patrol agents take into custody a truckload of suspected undocumented people. (AP/Wide World Photos)

voluntary departure form, he or she is transported to the border of his or her home country and released. In some cases, a hearing is required to determine the status of the individual. Various advocacy groups are involved in the protection of undocumented persons who are apprehended. One such group is the National Center for Immigration Rights in Los Angeles, California.

Impact on Canada and the United States. Immigrants, whether legal or illegal, have an effect on their countries of destination. Children may swell enrollments in public schools, and BILINGUAL EDUCATION programs may face greater burdens. Academic progress within classrooms may slow as a result of accommodation of language differences. Teachers can progress only as rapidly as students can absorb material. Immigration may also present problems of cultural conflict that can lead to violence. On the positive side, students in multicultural schools are exposed to new ideas and value systems that aid in the acceptance of various people and traditions.

Large immigrant populations, when concentrated in particular areas, can cause changes in the physical appearance of urban environments. Store signs and architecture can reflect new cultural influences, and neighborhoods can take on some of the appearance of the country of origin.

Perhaps the greatest effect of immigrants on a society comes in the realm of economics. CALIFORNIA, with its large undocumented population, is a good example. In the early 1990's, Governor Pete Wilson of California presented an immigration-aid request to President Bill Clinton asking for $1.7 billion for education programs, $300 million for Medi-Cal reimbursements, and $300 million for the incarceration of illegal immigrants, who accounted for 13 percent of the population in state prisons. Clinton rejected Wilson's request, questioning estimates of the size of the undocumented population. Many taxpayers in California are outraged that more federal funding is not given to California to reimburse the state for the money spent on federally mandated services for undocumented immigrants.

When unemployment increases, blame is placed on undocumented workers. California's Senator Dianne Feinstein claimed in the early 1990's that 1.3 million Californians were out of work; at the same time, an estimated 1.3 million undocumented people had settled in California. No correlation logically can be drawn between the two figures, but implied or sug-

Undocumented people have been cited as contributing to the problems of graffiti and gang activity. (Impact Visuals, David Schulz)

gested linkages made by government officials illustrate how undocumented immigrants are made scapegoats during economic hard times.

Many people claim that ethnic strife is tearing Canada and the United States apart. They blame undocumented people for contributing to problems of gangs, drug use, graffiti, and overcrowding in schools and urban areas. Because they believe that illegal immigrants are harming the quality of life, many citizens want to limit official compassion toward and public expenditures on behalf of undocumented people. They have grown tired of providing a safe haven for the desperate people of the world.

Political Actions. Various measures have been taken to gain control over illegal immigration. For example, Senator Feinstein suggested that a one dollar toll be levied on all border crossings in order to finance an expansion of the United States Border Patrol. Kathleen Brown, California's state treasurer, called on President Clinton to send undocumented persons in United States prisons back to their home countries. Governor Wilson of California proposed cutting health care to undocumented pregnant women, denying citizenship to children born to illegal immigrants, and expelling undocumented children from public schools. On July 27, 1993, President Clinton proposed an increase in the number of Border Patrol agents and a speedier resolution of political asylum cases (*see* ASYLUM POLICIES). Six hundred agents were added.

In December, 1993, the LATINO NATIONAL POLITICAL SURVEY found that 65 percent of Hispanics believed that too many immigrants were entering the United States. As the government tightens controls against illegal immigration, barriers are also implemented against legal immigrants. Senator Alan Simpson of Wyoming proposed that the ceiling for legal immigrants be dropped from the 1992 figure of 830,000 to 300,000.

Those defending illegal immigrants claim that government officials who are up for reelection use undocumented people as an issue to gain votes. In economically difficult times and in crowded urban environments, citizens look for answers. Federal and state officials claim that curbing the problem of undocumented immigrants will solve the problems of urban areas.

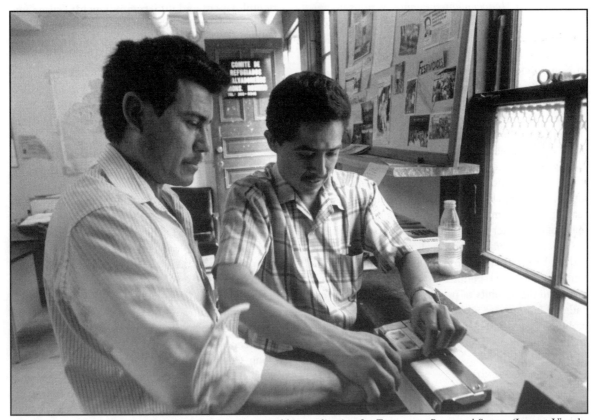

A Salvadoran immigrant has fingerprints taken as part of his application for Temporary Protected Status. (Impact Visuals, Donna DeCesare)

Myths About Illegal Immigration. Many myths exist in regard to illegal immigration. One study conducted in the early 1990's reported that Mexicans composed only 55 percent of the undocumented people in the United States, contradicting popular beliefs that illegal immigration is primarily a "Mexican" problem. Most undocumented people not from Mexico enter with visas but stay beyond those documents' expiration dates. The same study estimated that only 200,000 or 300,000 illegal entrants each year become permanent residents.

The report stated that undocumented people composed 6 percent of the U.S. labor force and agreed that this addition tended to push wages and consumer prices downward. Research also indicated, however, that these same people consumed goods and services, boosting the economy. In 1990, the President's Council of Economic Advisers concluded that "the long-run benefits of immigration greatly exceeded any short-run costs."

Contrary to some perceptions, U.S. policy on immigration did not, in the early 1990's, always change in the direction of restriction. The IMMIGRATION ACT OF 1990, for example, expanded quotas by 40 percent.

Support for Undocumented People. Various organizations offer support for undocumented people as well as legal immigrants. One such group, Mujeres Unidas y Activas, was founded by a refugee from El Salvador in San Francisco, California. The group supported community projects, education, and job training as well as offering support to immigrants who feel isolated and fearful in their new environment.

Emily Goldfarb, director of the Coalition for Immigrant and Refugee Rights and Services in the early 1990's, was concerned that in order to win votes, political leaders encouraged resentment toward immigrants, both legal and illegal. She claimed that by making immigrants scapegoats, politicians let people place blame rather than finding effective solutions.

Global Migration. A new reality now faces Canada and the United States. These countries no longer represent specific ethno-cultural groups. Technology has increased the mobility of people around the world, and national borders are no longer effective as barriers to mobility. Issues associated with undocumented people are therefore likely to increase in importance.

—*Linda J. Meyers*

SUGGESTED READINGS:
- Congressional Quarterly, Inc. "Common Myths About Illegal Immigration." *CQ Researcher*, April, 1992, 374. Presents seven myths about illegal immigration and responds with factual information.
- Conniff, Ruth. "The War on Aliens." *Progressive* 57 (October, 1993): 22. Gives views from those opposing legal and illegal immigration, followed by responses supporting immigration.
- Davis, Marilyn P. *Mexican Voices/American Dreams.* New York: Henry Holt, 1990. This collection includes oral histories from immigrants, both legal and illegal, from coyotes and *pasadores*, and from family members on both sides of the border. Davis includes excellent background information on the history of immigration and on the living conditions spurring immigration.
- Graham, Otis L. *Illegal Immigration and the New Reform Movement.* Washington, D.C.: Federation for American Immigration Reform, 1980. Presents the case for reform of U.S. immigration laws.
- Leone, Bruno, ed. *Illegal Immigration.* San Diego, Calif.: Greenhaven Press, 1994. Articles debate issues of illegal immigration, giving perspectives from immigrants and from the citizens and governments of destination countries.

Undocumented workers. *See* **Unauthorized workers**

Unemployment and underemployment: During January, 1994, about 1.2 million Latinos were unemployed, about 11 percent of the Latino labor force at the time. By comparison, the unemployment rate among the non-Hispanic white population during January, 1994, was 5.8 percent. The higher Latino unemployment rate represents a long-term tendency in the American economy. To understand it, one must examine both historical patterns and causes.

Patterns of Latino Unemployment. From 1950 to 1990, unemployment rates among Latinos exceeded the unemployment rates of non-Hispanic whites, for both men and women. In 1950, for example, the unemployment rate of Latino men was 12 percent, while that of non-Hispanic white men was 5.1 percent. For women, the unemployment rates in 1950 were 8.9 percent among Latinas and 3.6 percent among non-Hispanic whites.

There are significant differences in the historical unemployment rates of the various Latino subgroups. The average Latino unemployment rate in 1990 was 9.6 percent for men and 11.5 percent for women. Among Cuban Americans, however, unemployment was much lower, 6.5 percent for men and 7.1 percent for women. By contrast, the unemployment rates among people of Dominican and Puerto Rican descent in the United States were the highest for the Latino subgroups considered. In 1990, about 16 percent of

LATINO UNEMPLOYMENT, 1950-1990
(persons 16 years of age or older)

| | Unemployment Rate (percentage of labor force) | | | |
| | Latinos | | Non-Hispanic Whites | |
Year	Male	Female	Male	Female
1950	12.0	8.9	5.1	3.6
1960	7.2	7.5	4.4	5.0
1970	6.1	8.7	4.0	4.1
1980	7.9	10.8	5.2	6.1
1990	9.6	11.5	5.0	4.8

Source: Data for 1980 and 1990 are from U.S. Department of Commerce, *1980 and 1990 United States Census of Population and Housing Public Use Microdata Samples.* Data for 1950, 1960, and 1970 are from Gregory DeFreitas, *Inequality at Work: Hispanics in the U.S. Labor Force* (New York: Oxford University Press, 1991), p. 80.

both Dominican American men and women were unemployed.

Unemployment rates vary significantly by age, with the youngest members of the labor force prone to higher levels of unemployment. Latinos are no exception. In February, 1994, the unemployment rate for the overall Latino population was 10 percent, but among Latinos sixteen to nineteen years old, the rate was 25.2 percent, and among Latinos twenty to twenty-four years old, it was 11.9 percent.

The unemployment rate varies over time according to cycles of economic activity. Some evidence suggests that the unemployment rate of Latinos is more volatile than that of the non-Hispanic white labor force. This means that in recessionary times, unemployment among Latinos rises proportionally more than unemployment among non-Hispanic whites. In addition, many people who would prefer to work full-time have only part-time positions, and many people are working in jobs that are below their skill levels. Both groups are referred to as "underemployed."

Factors Influencing Unemployment Rates. Many variables influence whether a person is unemployed at any given moment in time and whether any employment is full-time or part-time. In general, people with more skills or skills of higher levels will receive more job offers, at higher rates of pay, than will less-skilled people. Higher-skilled people are also generally less prone to unemployment unless there is a downturn in their occupation and they are unwilling to search for jobs outside that occupation. An individual's skills may include academic, school-related skills as well as out-of-school skills acquired through on-the-job training or vocational programs.

The importance of skills in determining an individual's chances for employment has risen over time in the United States. Major changes in production and technology beginning in the 1960's require a more skilled work force. Some urban affairs experts argue that in central cities, where educational attainment lags compared to the suburbs, a growing skills mismatch has emerged between the skills of the local work force and the requirements of the employers in the area. For example, according to the final report of the 1988 Cuomo Commission on Trade and Competitiveness, a group of New York City banks had pledged, in 1986, to fill 250 entry-level positions with graduates from South Brooklyn high schools. By June, 1987, only about one hundred graduates had been hired. Most of those interviewed had failed the entry-level test, the equivalent of an eighth-grade math exam.

The significance of skills in determining employment is magnified when the supply of unskilled jobs declines sharply. The flight of manufacturing to the suburbs, to cities in the South and West, and to other countries has been associated with a sharp elimination of high-paying, blue-collar employment in cities of the Northeast. For many urban Latino and African American communities that relied on such jobs, the exodus of manufacturing to other regions generated a spatial mismatch, in which attractive employment opportunities for unskilled workers disappeared in local, central city labor markets.

The empirical evidence supporting the skills mismatch and spatial mismatch hypotheses is somewhat mixed. In general, there is some support for both hy-

UNEMPLOYMENT AMONG LATINO SUBGROUPS, 1990
(persons 16 years of age or older)

| | Unemployment Rate (percentage) | |
Ethnic Group	Male	Female
United States, overall	6.2	6.2
Latino population, overall	9.6	11.5
Central Americans	8.2	11.2
Cuban Americans	6.5	7.1
Dominican Americans	16.2	16.8
Mexican Americans	9.8	12.0
Puerto Ricans (mainland)	11.9	13.8
South Americans	6.7	8.8

Source: Data are from U.S. Department of Commerce, *1990 United States Census of Population and Housing Public Use Microdata Samples.*

potheses, although results depend on gender, the racial and ethnic group considered, the particular location, and the time period examined. The high unemployment rate of Puerto Ricans in the 1970's and 1980's, for example, has been traced to the shift of manufacturing away from the Northeast, where most of the mainland Puerto Rican population is located.

Immigration and Unemployment. A large share of the Latino population residing in the United States consists of first-generation immigrants. Among persons of Mexican ethnicity, for example, as many as one in three were born in Mexico. Americans have long debated the extent to which immigrants "take jobs away" from previous residents. Most technical studies on the issue have been unable to identify significant negative effects of immigrants on the employment of local residents.

One such study, by Princeton economist David Card, examined the Miami labor market in the aftermath of the MARIEL BOAT LIFT in 1980, when more than 125,000 Cuban immigrants arrived in Miami. About half of the Mariel immigrants settled permanently in Miami, increasing the Miami labor force by about 7 percent. This represented a major change in the Miami economy. The study found that the Mariel immigrant flow did not cause a perceptible increase in the unemployment of less-skilled African Americans or other workers. In fact, there was a remarkably rapid absorption of the immigrants into the Miami labor market. Labor-intensive industries absorbed the newcomers without raising unemployment rates among previous workers.

Although the impact of immigrants on the employment of other workers has not been found to be nega-

tive, anti-immigrant sentiment historically rises during periods of recession and high unemployment. Research shows that recent immigrants tend to have higher unemployment rates than the average. This is a consequence of temporary adjustment difficulties facing newcomers in the American labor market. The longer an immigrant has been in the United States, the less likely it is that the person will be unemployed. For example, male immigrants who arrived in the United States before 1970 had an unemployment rate of 5.4 percent in 1990, compared to a rate of 9.3 percent for male immigrants who had arrived in the United States between 1985 and 1990 and a rate of 7.4 percent for those who had arrived between 1980 and 1984. A similar pattern held for immigrant women.

Employment Discrimination. Immigration factors and lower job skills cannot completely explain the higher unemployment rates of Latinos relative to the non-Hispanic white population. Studies suggest that labor market DISCRIMINATION against Latinos may explain an important part of their higher unemployment rates.

A 1989 study by the Urban Institute for the U.S. government analyzed the extent of employment discrimination against Hispanic U.S. citizens in Chicago and San Diego. It carefully matched pairs of individuals, one Latino and one Anglo, in all personal characteristics other than ethnicity that could influence the hiring decision. These persons were then sent to apply for low-skilled, entry-level jobs. Their experiences through the hiring process were measured and compared. The study found evidence of widespread discrimination against Latino applicants, who received unfavorable discriminatory treatment from three out of every ten employers, with Anglos receiving 33 percent more interviews than Latinos and 52 percent more job offers.

The Underground Economy. Most employment figures cited are based on census-type surveys carried out by government agencies. To the extent that these surveys may undercount employment in underground or informal economies, their estimates of unemployment rates for Latinos may not be accurate. Persons involved in the underground economy, especially UNAUTHORIZED WORKERS (also referred to as undocumented workers and illegal aliens), tend to hide their economic participation for fear of criminal prosecution. Many of these workers are underemployed, working intermittently at day labor or a few hours a week in a job not kept on the employer's tax records.

Explicit information on the informal sector is scarce

UNEMPLOYMENT RATES OF IMMIGRANTS IN THE UNITED STATES, 1990		
	Unemployment Rate *(percentage of labor force)*	
Year of Arrival in the United States	Male	Female
1985-1990	9.3	13.5
1980-1984	7.4	9.5
1975-1979	7.3	9.0
1970-1974	7.3	8.4
Before 1970	5.4	5.6
Native born	6.1	5.9

Source: Data are from U.S. Department of Commerce, *1990 United States Census of Population and Housing Public Use Microdata Samples.*

The underground economy of work done or sales made for cash payments distorts unemployment figures. (David Bacon)

and based on limited surveys. Evidence suggests that participation in the underground economy has long-term adverse effects on the official labor market employment of young males. Unfortunately, the short-term income received by unskilled, young Latinos in urban areas through illegal or unrecorded activity sometimes exceeds the income that they can earn in the official labor market. Economist Richard Freeman has calculated that men with limited skills involved in illegal activity can earn twice as much as those whose jobs are legal. This income gap spurs the short-run growth of underground employment, which also leads to longer-term withdrawal from the official labor market.   —*Francisco L. Rivera-Batiz*

SUGGESTED READINGS:

• Card, David. "The Impact of the Mariel Boatlift on the Miami Labor Market." *Industrial and Labor Relations Review* 43 (January, 1990): 245. Studies the effects of the Mariel immigration flow on the earnings and unemployment of workers in the Miami labor market.

• DeFreitas, Gregory. "Ethnic Differentials in Unemployment Among Hispanic Americans." In *Hispanics in the U.S. Economy*, edited by George Borjas and Marta Tienda. Orlando, Fla.: Academic Press, 1985. Discusses the determinants of differences in unemployment rates among various groups of Latinos in the United States.

• Ehrenberg, Ronald. *Modern Labor Economics: Theory and Public Policy*. 5th ed. New York: Harper-Collins College Publishers, 1994. A thorough survey of the theory and evidence on the functioning of labor markets.

• Falcon, Luis M., and Charles Hirschman. "Trends in Labor Market Position for Puerto Ricans on the Mainland: 1970-1987." *Hispanic Journal of Behav-*

ioral Sciences 14 (February, 1992): 16. Examines unemployment and other labor force trends for Puerto Ricans in the United States.

- Freeman, Richard B. "Crime and the Employment of Disadvantaged Youths." In *Urban Labor Markets and Job Opportunity*, edited by George E. Peterson and Wayne Vroman. Washington, D.C.: The Urban Institute Press, 1992. Determines interactions between employment in illegal activity and employment in the official labor market.
- Freeman, Richard B., and David A. Wise, eds. *The Youth Labor Market Problem: Its Nature, Causes, and Consequences*. Chicago: University of Chicago Press, 1982. Articles describe and examine issues surrounding youth unemployment in the United States.
- Ortiz, Vilma. "Latinos and Industrial Change in New York and Los Angeles." In *Hispanics in the Labor Force: Issues and Policies*, edited by Edwin Melendez, Clara Rodriguez, and Janis Barry Figueroa. New York: Plenum Press, 1991. Examines whether the skills mismatch and spatial mismatch hypotheses apply to the cases of Latinos in New York and Los Angeles.
- Peterson, George E., and Wayne Vroman, eds. *Urban Labor Markets and Job Opportunity*. Washington, D.C.: The Urban Institute Press, 1992. Articles analyze the various causes and consequences of unemployment in urban areas of the United States.
- Rivera-Batiz, Francisco L. "Quantitative Literacy and the Likelihood of Employment Among Young Adults in the United States." *Journal of Human Resources* 27 (Spring, 1992): 313. Examines the impact of literacy skills in influencing the likelihood of unemployment spells among young adults in the United States.
- Tienda, Marta. "Puerto Ricans and the Underclass Debate." *The Annals of the American Academy of Political and Social Science* 501 (January, 1989): 105. Discusses the reasons for the comparatively high unemployment rates of Puerto Ricans in the United States. Also discusses the impact of economic restructuring on unemployment.

Unión Patriótica Benéfica Mexicana Independiente: Mutual aid society. This organization was established in 1913, with members mostly working-class immigrants from Mexico. Chapters were located in Southern California. The union's main function was to provide basic services for the community. It offered illness and death benefits, assisted poor families, held social activities such as dances and holiday celebra-

tions, and occasionally sponsored fund-raisers. La Union Femenil Mexicana, established in 1926, was an auxiliary organization formed by some of the society's female members. The auxiliary group, working in coordination with the main group, sponsored social and cultural events.

United Cannery, Agricultural, Packing and Allied Workers of America (UCAPAWA): Labor union. UCAPAWA organized Mexican American and Mexican farm and food processing workers, especially women in Southern California canneries. The union represented a model of democratic trade unionism and offered unprecedented opportunities for local leadership among people of color, particularly Mexicans. In its heyday, UCAPAWA was the seventh largest union affiliated with the Congress of Industrial Organizations (CIO), and from its beginnings at a 1937 Denver, Colorado, convention, the union promulgated policies of local control, mutual aid, and tolerance. The Denver delegates reflected the racial and regional diversity characterizing UCAPAWA. Mexican, Japanese, and Filipino farmworkers from California; African American sharecroppers from Missouri; and New York mushroom canners, among others, helped create this union. In the UCAPAWA pledge, members swore "never to discriminate against a fellow worker because of creed, color, nationality, religious or political belief."

With regard to organizing Mexican workers, the UCAPAWA, under the leadership of union representative Luisa MORENO and local activist Emma TENAYUCA, negotiated the successful settlement of the San Antonio PECAN SHELLERS' STRIKE of 1938. Moreno also worked among agricultural laborers in Texas and Colorado. During the late 1930's, UCAPAWA made valiant efforts to unionize Mexican, Filipino, white, and African American workers in California fields.

In 1939, led by veteran organizer and Communist Party leader Dorothy Ray Healey, more than four hundred cannery operatives, the majority of whom were Mexican and Russian Jewish women, staged a successful strike at the California Sanitary Canning Company. Exemplifying rank-and-file activism, Carmen Bernal Escobar headed the secondary boycott; after the strike, she became a head shop steward. Two years later, Moreno, as vice president of UCAPAWA, consolidated the organizing within Southern California canneries. The Los Angeles rank and file formed Local 3, the second largest UCAPAWA affiliate. In 1943, twelve of the fifteen elected positions in Local 3 were held by women, eight by Mexicanas. This local also negotiated innovative benefits, such as a hospitalization plan and free legal advice.

In many respects, UCAPAWA was a "woman's union." By 1946, 66 percent of its contracts nationwide had clauses specifying equal pay for equal work and 75 percent provided for leaves of absence without loss of seniority, an important issue in cases of maternity leave. At one Southern California plant, women walked off their jobs, in part over the lack of child care facilities. Management-financed day care became part of their contract.

UCAPAWA changed its name in 1944 to the Food, Tobacco, Agricultural, and Allied Workers of America (FTA) to reflect the recruitment of African American tobacco workers in the South. After World War II, the union became embroiled in jurisdictional battles with both the American Federation of Labor (AFL) and the Teamsters. Accusations of Communist influence, or red-baiting, by rival unions, management, and politicians as well as an apathetic National Labor Relations Board accounted for the union's demise. In 1950, UCAPAWA/FTA was one of ten unions expelled from the CIO for alleged Communist domination. Several organizers openly identified with the Communist Party, and others seemed more circumspect about their party membership. According to Moreno, "UCAPAWA was a *left* union, not a Communist union." Moreno herself was red-baited and left the United States in 1950 under the status "voluntary departure under warrant of deportation." UCAPAWA's legacy rests in its unwavering commitment to democratic trade unionism and its successes among Mexican workers in the Southwest, particularly among cannery women.

United Farm Workers of America: After decades of disappointments, the union movement headed by Chicano leader César CHÁVEZ succeeded in organizing farmworkers within the framework of the American Federation of Labor-Congress of Industrial Organizations (AFL-CIO). The forerunner of the United Farm Workers' movement was the NATIONAL FARM LABOR UNION (NFLU), formed in 1947. When NFLU Local 218 tried to strike against orchard owners in California in 1947, it discovered its vulnerability. With the support of Congressman Alfred Elliot, growers led by the Di Giorgio Corporation sought legislative condemnation of what they said was the unrepresentative nature of the NFLU.

By the mid-1950's, the NFLU had begun using a different approach. This change centered on lingering negative effects of the BRACERO PROGRAM, which had been instituted to bring temporary Mexican laborers to the United States during World War II. The continuing flow of braceros into the labor market hampered union efforts to maintain what were perceived to be reasonable rates of pay for the majority of farmworkers.

Early Stages of La Causa. The name of César CHÁVEZ became inseparable from the nucleus of the United Farm Workers of America. Chávez, son of an Arizona Mexican American migrant worker and former member of the NFLU, became associated in the 1950's with the San Jose, California, branch of a Chicano social assistance and civil rights program called the COMMUNITY SERVICE ORGANIZATION. As its executive director, Chávez tried unsuccessfully to convince the group and its board of directors, who were concerned primarily with urban issues, to consider the plight of Mexican American agricultural workers. His failure led to a decision to start a new movement. Chávez chose the grape-growing "capital" of Delano, California, to organize self-help for marginalized Mexican American farmworkers. He knew he faced not only two giant agricultural companies, the Di Giorgio and Schenley corporations, but also dozens of small private grape growers. Both groups kept profits at a maximum by exploiting farmworkers' dependency on whatever wages they could garner.

The Delano Grape Strike. Chávez's association became a full-fledged movement when the famous DELANO GRAPE STRIKE was launched in September, 1965. Chávez's organization, the NATIONAL FARM WORKERS ASSOCIATION, joined forces with the Agricultural Workers Organizing Committee. By August, 1966, after a nonviolent resistance effort involving consumer boycotts and political lobbying, the two unions merged as the United Farm Workers Organizing Committee (UFWOC) and affiliated with the AFL-CIO.

As the standoff between grape pickers and the California growers began to gain national attention in 1966, a variety of organizations declared their support for the strike. Volunteer organizers came to Delano from varied groups including the Stewart Mott Spectamur Agendo Foundation (backed by a variety of liberal New York philanthropists) and numerous student activist groups more often associated with the Civil Rights movement, such as the Student Nonviolent Coordinating Committee.

At the same time that supports welled in liberal circles, signs of coming difficulties emerged. Within the broad AFL-CIO labor organization itself, a difference of opinion began to form concerning which fac-

Larry Itliong led the Agricultural Workers Organizing Committee, which went on strike before the National Farm Workers Association. (Filipinos: Forgotten Asian Americans *by* Fred Cordova)

tion of farmworkers to support, Chávez's group or former members of the Independent Workers Association, which had affiliated with the National Farm Workers Association in June, 1966. When decisions were made to provide AFL-CIO contributions to keep the Delano strike going, material support was split, implying unwillingness to recognize the two farmworkers' movements as actually being united. Such concerns underlined the fact that *La Causa* could be seen from different perspectives.

Organizers faced another type of potential division in the fields. Workers who performed different types of processing or transport jobs might align their interests with other more conservative unions (specifically the Teamsters Union). In addition, rivalries existed between ethnic groups in the work force. Filipino workers were numerous in the grape-growing area and, if they did not agree with the Chicano-oriented UFWOC, could weaken what Chávez hoped would be a single front to obtain social justice.

A different source of support for Chávez's cause came in the form of a public boycott against non-

UFWOC grapes at market counters. *La Causa* could count most on liberal sympathizers to boycott growers who used nonunion labor in an attempt to beat the strike. Supporters staged numerous demonstrations across the country. Some even blocked normal supermarket business by obstructing cashier lines with deliberately fabricated problems that took hours of managers' time to iron out. This often happened in clear view of bewildered consumers who otherwise might never have known of the grape strike.

The grape strike nearly lost ground on several occasions, when the Di Giorgio Corporation encouraged the Teamsters Union to develop so-called "sweetheart" (or alternative) contracts for workers who might be wooed away from the grape strike (*see* DI GIORGIO FRUIT CORPORATION STRIKE). Di Giorgio tried several times to have a farmworkers' vote to decide between Chávez's movement and the "sweetheart" contracts supported by the Teamsters. Efforts by the UFWOC brought fresh Chicano workers into the region to bolster voting power. By then, Chávez apparently showed willingness to "deradicalize" *La Causa*, at least to a

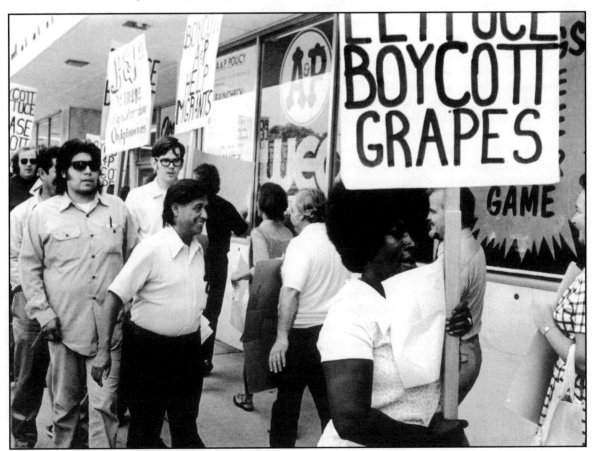

César Chávez joins picketers protesting the sale of produce not picked by UFW members. (AP/Wide World Photos)

degree that could earn the farmworkers a higher level of support from the national union organization.

From Delano to a Wider Field. Bolstered by what some called its broader base of political legitimacy, the UFWOC extended its strike campaign to other areas of California and Arizona in 1969. It began to see signs of eventual victory. Although early talks with hesitant growers in the Coachella Valley broke down in the summer of 1969, the tide clearly shifted early in 1970, when forty Coachella growers signed history-making contracts. Six more months were needed for twenty-six Delano growers, representing half of California's table grape crops, to concede that the CHÁVEZ movement was winning.

The campaign of the UFWOC did not end when the grape strike succeeded. As the 1970's began, Chávez bid for higher wages in the lettuce industry. Thousands of strikers left the fields. Boycott teams were dispatched to dozens of cities as 1971 began.

The UFWOC was recognized as a full-fledged AFL-CIO Union, under the name of United Farm Workers of America (UFW), in February, 1972. The UFW was stronger than its predecessor organization had been in the 1960's. Millions of dollars were available to provide relief for strikers. Special investigating teams uncovered signs of foul play not only by growers but also by Teamster Union rivals. In contrast to the 1960's, the Teamsters could now be confronted officially through high-level AFL-CIO channels. The UFW lost many contracts to the Teamsters before finding organizational strength and resources to prevent raiding.

Although UFW labor disputes still had a long way to go, major gains would come in the mid-1970's. Aid from Governor Jerry Brown of California yielded the 1975 AGRICULTURAL LABOR RELATIONS ACT, the nation's second (after Hawaii's) state legislation package guaranteeing clear rights for farm labor contract negotiation and extension of unemployment insurance for those displaced by the turmoil of strikes.

Despite an uneven record through the rest of the 1970's and into the 1980's, the UFW's struggle to defend Mexican Americans and other underprivileged farmworkers became a major chapter in U.S. history. The union's contribution to American labor history was dramatically interrupted, but certainly not removed, by the death of Chávez in the summer of 1993.

—*Byron D. Cannon*

SUGGESTED READINGS: • Acuña, Rodolfo. *Occupied America: A History of the Chicanos.* 2d ed. New York: Harper and Row, 1981. • Gómez-Quiñones, Juan. *Chicano Politics.* Albuquerque: University of New Mexico Press, 1990. • Jenkin, Craig. *The Politics of Insurgency.* New York: Columbia University Press, 1985. • Kushner, Sam. *Long Road to Delano.* New York: International Publishers, 1975. • Pitrone, Jean M. *Chávez, Man of the Migrants.* Staten Island, N.Y.: Alba House, 1971.

United Mexican American Students (UMAS): Student activist organization. UMAS was established in 1967 at Loyola Marymount University in Los Angeles. In its first year, various chapters formed in Southern California. By 1969, it had spread to other parts of the Southwest and one chapter in the Midwest. UMAS stressed education, concentrating on recruitment and retention of college students. It played an important role in the East Los Angeles school strike (the BLOW-OUT) in 1968 and was heavily involved with the Mexican American community, assisting high-school students in defending themselves from racism in school and offering tutoring services. Two of the thirteen Mexican American activists arrested for "conspiracy to disturb the peace" in connection with the Blowout were UMAS members. UMAS also supported César CHÁVEZ and the farmworkers' struggle. At the Santa Barbara Conference on Higher Education in 1969, the majority of UMAS chapters changed their name to MOVIMIENTO ESTUDIANTIL CHICANO DE AZTLÁN (MECHA).

United Neighborhoods Organization (UNO): Community activist group. UNO was founded in 1975 in East Los Angeles, California. Its leaders were Bishop Juan Arzube and Father Pedro Villaroya, who organized the group along with pastors of twenty-two Catholic parishes and ten Protestant churches. UNO aimed to bring Mexican American residents together to discuss solutions to community problems such as housing, inadequate infrastructure, education, health, and unfair insurance practices. UNO was modeled after its sister organization in San Antonio, COMMUNITIES ORGANIZED FOR PUBLIC SERVICE (COPS). UNO received much less support from the Catholic archdiocese and thus was not as strong or as well-organized as COPS. UNO continued to work for justice in the Mexican American community.

Urista-Heredia, Alberto Baltazar. *See* **Alurista**

Urrea, Teresa (Oct. 15, 1873, Rancho Santana, Sinaloa, Mexico—Jan. 11, 1906, Clifton, Ariz.): Curandera. Urrea was the illegitimate child of Tomás Urrea, the son of a prominent Sinaloan family. Defeat in local politics drove the Urrea family to Sonora, and Tomás settled with his family in a ranch called Cabora.

At the age of fifteen, Teresa Urrea suffered a seizure that left her comatose for two weeks. Upon regaining consciousness, she informed family and friends that she had been charged by the Virgin Mary to cure, comfort, and console her fellow humans.

Urrea's preachings molded a cult of followers in the small mountain village of Tomochic, Chihuahua. In 1891, villagers rebelled against Porfirio Díaz's government in protest against a newly installed mayor who grazed his sheep on their pastures and forced them to work at reduced wages in nearby haciendas. After crushing the villagers, who claimed that Urrea had inspired their uprising, Díaz drove her into exile in the United States in 1892.

Urrea's teachings encouraged resistance to the Porfirian state and to the Catholic church in Mexico. Subsequent Mexican rebels against Díaz's government continued to invoke her name, even after her death from tuberculosis in 1906. Urrea may thus have played a role in the inception of the 1910 MEXICAN REVOLUTION.

Urueta, Cordelia (b. Sept. 16, 1908, Coyoacán, Mexico): Painter and diplomat. Urueta's first trip abroad was in 1920 and 1921. She traveled to Argentina because her father, the ambassador from Mexico, was ill. Her next trip, to New York in 1929, was to take care of her own health problems. That trip also resulted in her first exhibition, arranged by her uncle, a poet who saw her drawings. She met José Clemente OROZCO and Rufino Tamayo in New York during that trip. In 1938, she married Gustavo Montoya, also a painter.

Urueta represented her country as a diplomat in Paris in 1938 and in New York in 1939. Her next exhibition, in 1964, was the first one at the Museum of Modern Art in Mexico City. She has also exhibited at the Biennale of São Paulo, Brazil (1969), at the museums of modern art in Kyoto, Japan, and Mexico City (1975), and at the Petit Palais in Paris.

During 1932, Urueta taught painting at the Primary School of the ministry of education in Mexico and drawing in Mexico City in 1943, when she began to paint more. In 1955, she was appointed art producer at the Mexican National Institute of Fine Arts. Urueta's work is largely portraits and landscapes, done in oils on canvas.

V

Vacunao: Cuban dance form with African influence. An old dance that claimed the name of RUMBA was the *vacunao*, a courtship dance characterized by a flirtatious woman at the mercy of a persistent man, resolving in a successful conquest. African traits can be observed in the convulsive steps of the *vacunao*, which exhibits a rapid twisting of the hips and legs performed by the man and rapid turns and hand-crossing movements (symbolizing a covering of her nudity) executed by the woman. The *vacunao* ranks together with the rumba Colombia as one of the many "old rumbas" that permeated Cuba before the popular rumba.

Valadez, John (b. 1951, Los Angeles, Calif.): Painter. Valadez's parents are of Mexican descent. He was the older of their two children and grew up with his mother and brother in Boyle Heights, California. An introverted child, Valadez has said that he spent many hours during his childhood imagining, drawing, and play-acting. He always sympathized with the underdog. He was graduated from Huntington Park High School in 1969 and attended East Los Angeles Junior College, where he became involved in the CHICANO MOVEMENT.

Valadez participated in the theater group MACCA (Mexican American Center for Creative Arts), whose leader was Emilio Delgado, who later was a leading actor on the *Sesame Street* television show. The group performed works such as a dramatization of Rodolfo "Corky" GONZÁLES' poem *I Am Joaquín* (1967) in prisons and community centers. Valadez studied art, history, and painting with Roberto Chavez and Luis LaNetta and was graduated from California State University at Long Beach with a B.F.A. in 1976.

Valadez does figurative work dealing with self-identity and Chicanos. He does not emulate the Mexican muralists; instead, he addresses the city around him. From the mid-1970's into the 1980's, Valadez did murals for the Long Beach Parks and Recreation Department with neighborhood children, two city murals, murals for the graphics department of a record company, and a banner for the United Farm Workers Third Constitutional Convention in Fresno in 1977. His *Broadway Mural*, along a busy Los Angeles street, followed in 1982.

Valadez's group work, with Carlos Almaraz, Barbara Carrasco, Leo Limón, and others, includes the mural *Zoot Suit*, done when the Mark Taper Forum presented Luis Valdez's play of that name in 1978. Valadez, Almaraz, Frank Romero, and Richard Duardo founded the Public Arts Center in Highland Park, California, in order to have studio space and access to cooperative mural projects. Thereafter, Valadez began to paint smaller studio works such as narrative paintings and portraits in pastel and oil. His *Preacher* (1983) is a pastel on paper.

Valdés, Jorge E. (b. Apr. 18, 1940, Matanzas, Cuba): Government official. Valdés was graduated from the Instituto de Matanzas in Cuba with a bachelor's degree. He moved to Florida and was elected as the mayor of Sweetwater in 1978, becoming the first Cuban American mayor in Florida's history.

As mayor, Valdés' interests were varied, including economic development, municipal planning, health and environmental issues, criminal justice, and issues of importance to the area's young people. In 1981, he was elected as county commissioner for Metro-Dade County, breaking new ground once again. Valdés was the first Cuban American to hold the position of county commissioner in Florida. He served as the chairman of the community affairs committee and on the Metropolitan Planning Organization, the health and human services committee, the Dade-Miami Criminal Justice Council, and the board of directors of the South Dade branch of the Young Men's Christian Association (YMCA).

Valdez, Luis Miguel (b. June 26, 1940, Delano, Calif.): Playwright and director. Valdez won a playwriting contest in 1961 with his play *The Theft*. He produced his first play, *The Shrunken Head of Pancho Villa*, in 1964 while attending San Jose State University. He also worked with the San Francisco Mime Troupe, leaving the group in 1965 to work with César CHÁVEZ.

Bringing his theatrical skills to the labor movement, Valdez founded El TEATRO CAMPESINO, which revived Hispanic stage traditions such as the *revista*, the CARPA, and the comic *peladito* character. His plays, including *Zoot Suit* (1978) and *I Don't Have to Show You No Stinking Badges* (1986), deal with such issues as Chicano gangs, stereotypes, and prejudice. In addition, he has adapted works of other Hispanic writers, such as Rodolfo "Corky" GONZÁLES' *I Am Joaquín* and Rudolfo

Luis Valdez. (Arte Público Press)

Anaya's *Bless Me, Ultima.* Valdez's film directing credits include *I Am Joaquín* (1969); *Zoot Suit* (1982), for which he also wrote the screenplay adaptation; and *La Bamba* (1987), in which he also performed. In 1987, he wrote *Corridos!*, a dramatization of traditional Mexican narrative ballads, for public television.

A founding member of the California Arts Council, Valdez has earned numerous awards, including an Obie and an Emmy. He has taught in the University of California system and has edited several anthologies of Chicano writing.

Valens, Ritchie (Richard Valenzuela; May 13, 1941, Pacoima, Calif.—Feb. 3, 1959, near Mason City, Iowa): Singer. Valens was the first major Hispanic American rock star and a legend whose career was one of the shortest in American popular music history.

Ritchie Valens in a photograph taken ten days before his death. (AP/Wide World Photos)

Valens' mother rented a dance hall so that he could perform. At the age of seventeen, he wrote the song "Donna" for his high school sweetheart Donna Ludwig. Valens would show up at high school pep rallies with his green electric guitar and his band, the Silhouettes.

Valens' recording career was launched in September, 1958, with "Come On, Let's Go." That song was followed by "Donna," "That's My Little Susie" and his rock and roll version of "La Bamba." He skyrocketed to stardom and was soon being compared with Elvis Presley. The plane crash that killed Valens, along with singer Buddy Holly and disc jockey J. P. "Big Bopper" Richardson, is considered to be one of the greatest single tragedies in popular music.

In 1990, Valens was honored by a star on the Hollywood Walk of Fame. The Ritchie Valens Music Scholarship was established to help support young Latinos enrolled in college programs in music.

Valenzuela, Fernando (Fernando Valenzuela y Anguamea; b. Nov. 1, 1960, Etchohuaquila, Mexico): Baseball player. A star pitcher in Mexico by the age of eighteen, Valenzuela took U.S. baseball by storm. After winning the Mexican League Rookie of the Year Award in 1979, the portly left-handed pitcher signed with the Los Angeles Dodgers. He raced through the Dodgers' minor league system, making his big-league debut with eighteen scoreless innings of relief pitching at the end of the 1980 season.

An injury to Los Angeles star Jerry Reuss led the Dodgers to use Valenzuela as the team's opening day starter in 1981, and the twenty-year-old rookie responded by shutting out the Houston Astros, beginning a remarkable string of eight victories without a loss. He drew capacity crowds wherever he pitched and proved especially popular with the Dodgers' large contingent of Latino fans; the media dubbed the phenomenon "Fernandomania." He finished the strike-shortened 1981 season with a 13-7 record, a fine 2.48 earned run average, and league-leading totals of 180 strikeouts and 8 shutouts. The Dodgers went on to win the World Series, and Valenzuela became the first player to win both the Rookie of the Year and Cy Young awards in the same year.

Valenzuela's trademark pitch was a screwball, a reverse curveball that made him equally effective against right-handed and left-handed hitters. He earned National League All-Star honors each year through the 1986 season; that year, he led the league with 21 wins and earned a Gold Glove Award. In succeeding years,

Fernando Valenzuela won the first eight games he pitched in the major leagues. (AP/Wide World Photos)

he suffered from shoulder injuries that diminished his effectiveness, but he rebounded in the 1990 season to pitch a no-hitter against the St. Louis Cardinals. He was nevertheless released by the Dodgers before the 1991 season; he pitched for the California Angels and Baltimore Orioles and in the Mexican League before returning to the National League in 1994 with the Philadelphia Phillies.

Valenzuela, Luisa (b. Nov. 26, 1938, Buenos Aires, Argentina): Writer. As the daughter of Luisa Mercedes Levinson, a writer, Valenzuela was initiated at an early age into the world of the written word, working for magazines and practicing journalism. In 1958, when she was twenty, she left her native Buenos Aires to become the Paris correspondent for the Argentine daily *El Mundo*. There she also wrote programs for

Radio Television Française and participated in the intellectual life of the then-famous Tel Quel group and the structuralists.

In 1961, Valenzuela returned to Buenos Aires and joined the staff of Argentina's foremost newspaper, *La Nación*. In 1969, she attended the University of Iowa's Writers Workshop on a Fulbright grant, and in 1972 she obtained a scholarship to study pop culture and literature in New York City.

Valenzuela's novels include *El gato eficaz* (1972), *Aqui pasa cosas raras* (1975; *Strange Things Happen Here*, 1979), *Como en la guerra* (1977; *He Who Searches*, 1979), *El señor de Tacuru* (1983; *The Lizard's Tail*, 1983), and *Novela negra con argentinos* (1990; *Black Novel with Argentines*, 1992). Valenzuela is considered a formidable addition to the ranks of female Magical Realists, along with Clarice Lispector and Cristina Perri Rossi.

Vallejo, César (Mar. 16, 1892, Santiago de Chuco, Peru—Apr. 15, 1938, Paris, France): Writer. Vallejo was the youngest of eleven children. His parents were Francisco de Paula Vallejo and María de los Santos Mendoza. His primary studies were in the small schools of his town, from 1900 to 1905. He showed a passion for books as a child.

When he had completed half of his studies at the Colegio de San Nicolás, in Huamachuco, he matriculated at the school of letters of the University of La Libertad in Trujillo. He was not able to support himself and before the end of the year returned home, where he assisted his father in his law activities. In 1913, Vallejo entered the School of Philosophy and Letters at the University of La Libertad and obtained a position as a teacher. During this time he wrote poetry, which he published in the local press.

In 1918, Vallejo published his first book of poetry, *Los heraldos negros* (*The Black Heralds*, 1990). He also contributed to various literary journals. His major collections of poetry are *Poemas en prosa* (1930) and *Poemas humanos* (1939; *Human Poems*, 1968). He also wrote several plays, a collection of essays, and a novel, *El tungesteno* (1931; *Tungsten*, 1988). Vallejo's poetry, consumed with passion and suffering, reveals the complex intellectual, emotional, and spiritual qualities that characterize his later work.

Vallejo family: California historical figures. The Vallejos excelled as social, civil, military, and political leaders of nineteenth century California. Ignacio Vicente Vallejo (1748-1832), a resident of Jalisco, Mexico, par-

ticipated in the Rivera y Moncada California expedition in 1774. For his services, Ignacio was awarded a large land grant near modern Watsonville, California. This established the Vallejo properties in the area.

Ignacio and his wife, Maria, became parents to Mariano Guadalupe Vallejo on July 7, 1808, in Monterey, California. Mariano was thus a second-generation Californio. Early in life, like his brothers José and Salvador, he was selected for training as a soldier and political leader. At the age of fifteen, he commanded a small unit with the Monterey garrison. By the age of twenty-one, he was a political and military leader of some note and commanded several hundred troops in field operations against Indians near San Jose mission. In 1830, he supported the Californios in opposition to the Mexican governor.

In 1832, Mariano married Francisca Benicia Carrillo (1815-1891), whose sister, María de la Luz, wed Vallejo's brother José, thereby allying two important families of Californios. He was made a general and put in command of northern California as a precaution against Russian imperialism, as well as being administrator of the Solano mission during the period of secularization. In these capacities and in this remote region, Mariano Vallejo created a fiefdom within the new pueblo of Sonoma that he founded. He established vineyards and made the first wine from the region.

Salvador Vallejo was born on January 1, 1813, in Monterey. He established himself early as a successful rancher. Through Mariano's influence, he was appointed a militia captain, and in 1836 he commanded a post in Sonoma. He served as colonial administrator of the Solano mission. In 1836, Salvador led California volunteers against Indians in Arizona. He was known as a rough, hard-drinking, and recklessly brave soldier. He died in 1876 in Sonoma, California.

José de Jesus Vallejo, born in San Jose on January 20, 1798, was grantee and later successful claimant of the Arroyo de la Alameda. He was military commander of San Jose as well as of an artillery battery at Monterey, in 1818. He also served as government administrator and postmaster of San Jose. He died in 1882 in San Jose, California.

Rosalia, the sister of Mariano Vallejo, was born as Maria Paula Rosalia on January 25, 1811, in Monterey. She married Jacob Primer Leese, an early trader and shipowner. The birth of Rosalia Leese (April 15, 1836), their daughter, is recorded as the first birth to American parents in Yerba Buena.

Rosalia harbored a dislike for American nationalism, especially after the Bear Flag incident involving her brothers in Sonoma. Jacob Leese's exploitation of Rosalia's dowry led to marital difficulties and eventually to separation. He was not reconciled to Rosalia's children until near his death at the age of eighty-three. Rosalia died on July 30, 1889, in Monterey.

Vallejo land grants evolved into urban centers of modern Vallejo, Benicia, and Petaluma. In 1852, the state legislature accepted the Vallejos' offer to create a state capital at the location where the Napa River empties into San Pablo Bay. After one week, legislators found the available facilities inadequate and relocated to Sacramento. Vallejo land later prospered as the site of the Mare Island Naval Shipyard and a merchant marine academy. It offers beautiful vistas and unique environmental attractions.

When the BEAR FLAG REVOLT (1846) broke out, Mariano and Salvador were seized and jailed at Sutter's Fort for two months. Later, under American administration, Mariano was appointed by the military governor to the territorial council and as Indian agent for northern California.

In 1849, Mariano was one of eight Californios elected to the constitutional convention. He was elected to the new state's first senate. In the early 1850's, he was one of the first Californios to file for validation of his land grants. His joy at confirmation in 1855 was short-lived because squatters and speculators appealed this favorable decision all the way to the U.S. Supreme Court. This appeal invalidated his title to the large Soscol land grant. The expenses involved in defense of his property caused family fortunes to decline. His son Platon was the first Spanish-speaking Californian to earn an M.D. degree and later served in the Union Army.

In the 1870's, Mariano Vallejo devoted himself to writing a history of California as he continued his advocacy of the rights of Hispanics. He died on January 18, 1890, in Sonoma, California, owning only 280 acres of his once large landholdings. His *Recuerdos históricos tocantes a la Alta California* (historical memoirs concerning Alta California) is a definitive work on California culture between 1769 and 1849.

The Vallejos were dominant figures among early colonizing Californios. They showed friendliness toward Anglo-Americans and were committed to the peaceful transition of Mexican-controlled California to the United States. Under American occupation, established and respected settlers such as the Vallejos were brought into positions of authority. As a family, they favored government by native-born leaders and did much to achieve California's later political stability and economic prosperity.

Valse: Genre of waltz. The *valse*, a product of Latin American colonial aristocracy, was popular as a social dance form in the nineteenth century. It bears some relationship to the waltz that swept Europe during the same century. The *valse* is performed in three-four time by ensembles featuring harp, violin, and various instruments from the guitar family such as the TIPLE (twelve strings), CUATRO (four strings) and *bandola* (flat-backed lute). The *valse* is danced with two steps per measure, with light gliding steps and turns. In Colombia, the *valse* gave rise to the *torbellino* and *pasillo*, and in Peru to the *vals criollo*, a purely vocal genre.

Vando, Gloria (b. New York, N.Y.): Poet. Vando is one of the few female poets within the group referring to themselves as NUYORICANS. Vando grew up in a bilingual and bicultural environment, then moved west and settled in a suburb of Kansas City, Missouri, with her husband Bill Hickok, who is also a writer.

Vando's first book, *Promesas: Geography of the Impossible*, was published by ARTE PÚBLICO Press in 1993. The book explores the disparity between promises and reality as perceived by Puerto Ricans. Although the poems in the book have themes of powerlessness, loss, and forgetting, the book ends with the idea that happiness can be found within oneself.

Vando has won many awards for her poetry and served on the literature panels of the National Endowment for the Arts and the Kansas Arts Commission. In addition to crafting her poetry, Vando began working as editor-in-chief and publisher with Helicon Nine in 1977. The company produced a journal of women's arts and letters.

Vando Rodriguez, Erasmo (June 2, 1896, Ponce, Puerto Rico—?): Political activist, theatrical producer, actor, and writer. At the age of six, Vando moved with his aunt and uncle from Ponce to San Juan. His mother was hospitalized at the time. At the age of sixteen, he was expelled from school for refusing to pledge allegiance to the flag of the United States. He worked in his own businesses (a general store and a café) before traveling to the United States in 1918 as part of a group of several hundred Puerto Ricans who were contracted to work at Camp Jackson in Columbia, South Carolina, as part of the United States' effort in World War I. There, he organized a protest against the proposed segregation of the white and black Puerto Ricans.

In 1919, in New York, he organized a strike at the hotel where he worked, losing his job for his efforts. He went on to work in a laboratory where colors and essences for candies were made, a post he held for twenty-three years. He also took part in the founding of the Nationalist Youth of Puerto Rico (Juventud Nacionalista Puertorriqueña), the members of which later became part of the Puerto Rican Nationalist Party (PARTIDO NACIONALISTA DE PUERTO RICO), of which he was president at various times. He was a founding member and leader of many other political, cultural, and charitable organizations, including the Pro Puerto Rican Independence Association (Asociación Pro Independencia de Puerto Rico), Centro Obrero Español (Spanish Workers' Center), and Club Pomarrosas, which distributed toys to children in New York and Puerto Rico at Christmas.

Vando worked as the society editor for the weekly newspaper *Semanario Gráfico*. He worked as a columnist and as a reporter for New York's Spanish-language newspapers, including *El Mundo* and *El Día*. He also was instrumental in founding the Puerto Rican association of writers and reporters (Asociación de Escritores y Periodistas Puertorriqueños) in 1939.

In theater, he was a director, producer, actor, and playwright. He presented musicals and plays, many of which dealt with Hispanic themes, in New York (including Carnegie Hall), in regional theaters around the New York State area, and in Puerto Rico. His *Love in El Batey* was presented in Puerto Rico and in New York City.

He returned to Puerto Rico in 1945, continuing his work in theater, journalism, and politics. He was a founding member and a member of the board of directors of the Puerto Rican Independence Party (PIP, or the PARTIDO INDEPENDISTA PUERTORRIQUEÑO). He continued to write poetry.

Vaquero: Mexican herdsman. In Mexico, indigenous *vaqueros*, or herdsmen, were key laborers among the Maya, Huichols, and Tarahumara. Once horses were brought to the Americas by Spaniards, *vaqueros* were needed to run the large cattle-raising estates. They soon learned to master and train horses. The *vaquero charro*, a consummate rider skilled in breaking horses, was a direct descendant of these first indigenous *vaqueros*. North American cowboys and RODEOS have been traced to the Mexican *vaqueros* who settled in the area that is now the state of Texas.

Modern rodeo and charreada *competitions celebrate the skills of* vaqueros. (Ruben G. Mendoza)

Vargas, Diego de: (Diego de Vargas Zapata Luján y Ponce de Leon; Nov. 8, 1643, Madrid, Spain—Apr. 4, 1704, Bernalillo, N.Mex.): Soldier and adventurer. Vargas, originally a wealthy Spanish noble of Madrid, served Spain all his life. At first a courtier in Madrid, he next served as an officer in several Italian military campaigns. In 1664, Vargas married Beatriz Pimentel of Torrelaguna. Then, immigrating to New Spain, he became mayor of Teutila, in Oaxaca, and administrator of the royal quicksilver (mercury) supply. Vargas' main endeavor was a stormy career as the governor of New Mexico. There, he regained for Spain control of New Mexico, lost after Indian revolts ending in the early 1680's.

Vargas served two terms as New Mexico's governor. During the first (1692-1696), he conquered many antagonistic Indian tribes. This led to relative peace until 1696, when another Indian revolt occurred. Blamed on Vargas, the revolt led to loss of his position and his imprisonment. By 1701, Vargas had been freed and exonerated. In 1703, he began another term as governor. Trouble with the Indians again occupied much of Vargas' time, and he again began to pacify them. He was not, however, fated to complete the effort, falling ill on campaign and dying several days later. Vargas' endeavors in New Mexico included rebuilding Santa Fe, constructing many churches and convents, and establishing numerous permanent settlements.

Vargas Llosa, Mario (b. Mar. 28, 1936, Arequipa, Peru): Novelist. Vargas Llosa was born into a middle-class family. When his parents separated, he lived for a time in Cochabamba, Bolivia, where his grandfather was consul. After his parents reconciled, the family moved to Lima, where he attended a parochial secondary school. This experience provided the background for his short novel *Los cachorros* (1967; *The Cubs*, 1979, in *The Cubs and Other Stories*).

From 1950 to 1952, Vargas Llosa attended a military school in Lima but revolted against its harshness and male chauvinism. He transformed this experience into a novel, *La cuidad y los perros* (1963; *The Time of the Hero*, 1966). In 1952, he completed high school. He worked for a local newspaper and wrote his second novel, *La casa verde* (1966; *The Green House*, 1968). His third major novel, *Conversación en la catedral* (1969; *Conversation in the Cathedral*, 1975), focuses on Peru's social environment. Other major novels include *La tía Julia y el escribidor* (1977; *Aunt Julia and the Scriptwriter*, 1982), *La guerra del fin del mundo* (1981; *The War at the End of the World*, 1984), *The*

Real Life of Alejandro Mayta (1986), and *¿Quien mato a Palomino Molero?* (1986; *Who Killed Palomino Molero?*, 1987). He has also written plays, critical studies, and short stories. Vargas Llosa's major contribution to Latin American literature has been his passionate, articulate literary rebellion against society's ills, particularly those of the Peruvian middle class.

Varo, Remedios (1913, Spain—1963): Painter. Varo left Spain for France during the Spanish Civil War in the late 1930's, then traveled to Mexico during the Nazi occupation of France in the 1940's. The daughter of a hydraulic engineer, she studied drawing and mathematics at the Academy of San Fernando in Madrid, Spain. Varo's first, short marriage began in 1932 and ended in divorce. In 1936, she married a French surrealist poet. That marriage also ended in divorce, and she was married again in 1953.

During the 1930's and 1940's, Varo worked as a commercial artist, interior decorator, costume designer, potter, and nature illustrator in France and Venezuela. She began to paint oils on masonite and canvas in 1953 and completed about one hundred paintings before her death from a heart attack.

Varo won first prize in the Salon of Women Painters and exhibited in the International Exposition in Tokyo in 1962. Her work has been the subject of a posthumous retrospective and a book.

Varo, whose works are mostly in private collections, combined feminism and nature in a surrealist mode. Feminist critics in the United States have posthumously canonized her images as embodying the female "quest" for meaning and finding it in the regeneration of the earth.

Vasconcelos, José (Feb. 28, 1882, Oaxaca, Mexico—June 30, 1959, Mexico City, Mexico): Philosopher and writer. The five-volume autobiography by Vasconcelos has been referred to as one of the best sociocultural studies of twentieth century Mexico. The first four volumes appeared during the 1930's, with the last published in 1959. Vasconcelos wrote in the fields of history, biography, and sociology as well as producing some fiction.

Vasconcelos studied law and was a 1905 graduate of Mexico's Escuela Nacional de Jurisprudencia. He supported the MEXICAN REVOLUTION and was a cofounder of the Ateneu de la Juventud in 1909. That group, devoted to the revival of culture, survived only until 1914 but had a long-lasting influence.

Vasconcelos wanted to end Porfirio Díaz's dictatorship through the free exercise of the vote and repre-

José Vasconcelos ran for the presidency of Mexico in 1929. (AP/Wide World Photos)

sented Francisco Madero in Washington, D.C. Back in Mexico, he was arrested by order of Victoriano Huerta. Upon his release, he served Venustiano Carranza, but the two later became bitter enemies.

Later, as rector of the Universidad Nacional, Vasconcelos promoted reestablishment of the Ministry of Education, which he headed from 1920 to 1924. He resigned from the ministry to run for the governorship of Oaxaca; he alleged fraud after losing the election. Following his defeat, he traveled throughout Europe and lectured at several U.S. universities.

In 1929, Vasconcelos ran for the presidency of Mexico against Pascual Ortíz Rubio. He lost that election and again alleged fraud. He left the country to live in the United States, waiting for his supporters to rebel, but they never did. He traveled throughout Central America, with returns to the United States, but was forbidden to enter Mexico. In 1938, when his U.S. residency permit expired, Mexico allowed him entry. After returning to his homeland, Vasconcelos directed the National Library and the Library of Mexico. He was a founding member of El Colegio de México, wrote regularly for newspapers and magazines, and lectured throughout Latin America and the United States. He developed and expressed the opinion that Latin America would develop a new and superior race of people. Although he later repudiated that idea, he continued to call for a synthesis of Latin American cultures.

Vasquez, Luis (Oct. 3, 1795, St. Louis, Mo.—1868, Westport, Mo.): Businessman. Vasquez, the son of a Spaniard, was born a subject of King Charles IV. After the death of his father, Vasquez began to work in the skin and fur business. After years of experience working for others and dealing with Indian tribes, Vasquez went into business with a partner, Jim Bridger.

Vasquez and Bridger established a fort in 1838. The fort became a center of trading in Colorado. In 1838, he organized an expedition following the Santa Fe Trail and Arkansas River before heading north. He sold the fort in 1842 and established Fort Bridger with his partner in Wyoming. They engaged in trading operations there from 1842 to 1855. Vasquez returned briefly to St. Louis, where he was married in 1846. In 1855, Vasquez sold his interests to the Mormons. Fort Bridger was subsequently a strategic point for the Pony Express; the Pony Express building there was later reconstructed, with a museum built adjoining it.

Vásquez, Richard (b. June 11, 1928, Southgate, Calif.): Writer. Vásquez was reared in a family of ten children

in the San Gabriel Valley, on the outskirts of Los Angeles. Having lived in various parts of the Los Angeles area, he sought, early in life, to widen his life experiences. At the age of seventeen, he enlisted in the Navy. He later worked in construction. In 1959, his interests led him to journalism, although he had no formal training in the field. He eventually became a full-time reporter for several different newspapers. In addition to his journalistic duties, he wrote more than five hundred articles on Chicano history and folklore.

From 1965 to 1970, Vásquez held several jobs, including historian for a book publisher and account executive for a public relations firm. He was the first Mexican American to hold the latter position at his firm. During this period, he wrote two novels: *Chicano* (1970) and *The Giant Killer* (1978). His third novel, *Another Land*, was published in 1982. Although the epic novel *Chicano* received a mixed critical reception, it is one of the best-selling Chicano novels ever written. It has been used by many Chicano literature and sociology classes taught in high schools, community colleges, and universities.

Vásquez, Tiburcio (Aug. 11, 1835, Monterey, Calif.—Mar. 19, 1875, San Jose, Calif.): Bandit. Born to a respected Californio family, Vásquez received at least an elementary education and became fluent in both English and Spanish. In 1852, Vásquez escaped from a lynch mob after shooting a sheriff. His reputation as an outlaw grew immensely after 1870. Vásquez then began a four-year spree of cattle rustling and robbery that made him notorious throughout California.

The robbery and killing of three men at Snyder's Store in Tres Pinos in 1873 raised a statewide alarm. Authorities in central California began to weave a net around Vásquez, who had little choice but to shift his activities to the Los Angeles region. Many Californios were alarmed after several of Vásquez's holdups, which they feared would ignite racial violence against them. As a result, Vásquez was betrayed and captured near La Brea in April, 1874. While in jail, Vásquez justified his activities on the grounds that he had set out only to avenge Anglo injustice. This explanation did not persuade the jury, which sentenced him to death by hanging. Vásquez's execution nearly brought to an end the activities of Spanish-speaking bandits in California but also deepened racial tensions in the state.

Vatican II (1962-1965): Council that established the most wide-ranging reforms in Catholic church history. The Vatican's Second Ecumenical Council (Vatican II),

Opening ceremonies of the Second Ecumenical Council, in St. Peter's Basilica. (AP/Wide World Photos)

in which twenty-five hundred bishops participated, is generally recognized for opening up the church to the modern world and to improved relations with other religions. The changes it instituted affected Catholics around the world, including Latinos, who make up a significant portion of American Catholics.

When Pope John XXIII convened Vatican II, he realized that reforms were long overdue. Church officials had noted the influence of the Civil Rights movement in the United States, in which religious leaders took an active role, as well as the influence of the views of John F. Kennedy, the first Catholic president of the United States, who believed in more freedoms and opportunities for the disenfranchised. In Latin America, support was growing among priests and scholars for a liberation theology that advocated for the needs of oppressed peoples. The Catholic church was under attack for being out of touch with the world's problems because it was too preoccupied with spiritual matters and was overly hierarchical and authoritarian in its approach.

In the past, the church had placed its spiritual commitment and role as a sacramental body above other obligations to society. With Vatican II, the church declared that it is of this world, rather than some higher spiritual world, and made up of a community of equals. Symbolic changes included changing the position of the altar, so that the priest faced the congregation, and allowing priests and nuns to wear ordinary clothing.

A greater focus on the plight of poor people emerged from Vatican II. Poverty and illiteracy were recognized as keeping a large number of people, including Latinos, marginalized from mainstream society. Vatican II called for the elimination of inequalities based on income and possessions. Its rulings opened the door for Catholic priests and lay persons to seek ways to address the problems of poverty, low socioeconomic status, and inadequate political representation among Latinos and other disadvantaged groups.

The council also recognized the needs of an increasingly diverse population of Catholics. It made provisions for Spanish and bilingual Spanish-English worship. As a result of Vatican II, dioceses expanded their pastoral activity that was adapted to Latino cultures, and the church began naming a few Latinos as bishops and priests.

Vázquez de Ayllón, Lucas (c. 1475, Toledo, Spain—Oct. 18, 1526, Winyah Bay, S.C.): Explorer and settler.

Ayllón arrived on Santo Domingo in 1502 and became a wealthy judge in the colonial administration. He was interested in exploration and settlement of new territories. In 1520, he sent a vessel under the leadership of Francisco Gordillo to Florida. Gordillo's mission was to explore the area and establish friendly relations with the natives. Gordillo, however, decided to capture slaves and returned to Santo Domingo without exploring the coast.

Ayllón's disappointment led to his own expedition in 1526, with a mission of establishing a settlement. More than five hundred men and women, including black slaves and three Dominican missionaries, joined the expedition.

Ayllón's ship landed on the coast of South Carolina, where he founded the settlement of San Miguel de Guadalupe. Conditions there were unfavorable, and many of the Spaniards succumbed to disease. The first winter brought many hardships. Ayllón himself died in October of 1526. The survivors, numbering about 150, were forced to abandon the settlement. It has been claimed that Ayllón's settlement was at the same site as the later Jamestown, but this claim has been refuted.

Vega, Ana Lydia (b. Dec. 6, 1946, Santurce, Puerto Rico): Short-story writer. Vega spent her childhood and adolescence in Santurce, Puerto Rico. Her father, a businessman and a poet, was self-taught. The family's move to urban Río Piedras during her teenage years inspired in Vega nostalgia for the countryside of Santurce. She attended a Catholic high school, and it was there that she began to write.

She studied at the University of Puerto Rico, where she majored in French. She completed her master's and doctorate in comparative literature at the University of Provence in France. Upon her return to Puerto Rico, Vega, with several collaborators, developed a method for teaching French to Spanish-speaking students.

Vega's first book of short stories, a collaborative effort with Carmen Lugo Filippi titled *Virgenes y mártires* (1981), contained irreverent tales that penetrated universal feminine secrets in the context of colonialism. Her second collection of stories, *Encancaranublado y otros cuentos de naufragio* (1981), a work of Caribbean inspiration, won the Casa de las Américas prize in Havana in 1982. Her third book, *Pasión de historia y otras historias de pasión* (1987), is a collection of humorous stories. Vega's narrative skill lies in her blending of history and fiction to tell the hidden story of Puerto Rico's rural and urban reality.

Vega, Bernardo (1885, Puerto Rico—1965): Writer. Vega chronicled the experience of emigration from Puerto Rico to the United States in his *Memorias de Bernardo Vega* (1977), written in 1940. He made the crossing in 1916, on the *Coamo*. Vega, a cigarmaker, wrote about the custom of *la lectura*, whereby employees of cigar factories would hire someone to read to them while they worked. The practice flourished in the cigar factories of New York, New York, as well as in Florida. Vega's work is important because he wrote about the city as someone who intended to stay there, rather than to return to Puerto Rico.

Vega's 1977 memoirs are in the picaresque genre, using a first-person narrator for a story of adventure and travel. The book also contains sections discussing history. Vega specifically included people otherwise excluded from written history because of their radical stances or because of their gender. In the latter case, he mentions the importance of women in liberation movements. He also discusses the ideological split between those who desired independence for Cuba and Puerto Rico and those who wished them to be annexed by the United States. The book discusses the life of Puerto Ricans in New York City from many perspectives.

Vega worked at organizing the cigarworkers of New York City and in the Puerto Rican Socialist Party there. He also wrote for the newspapers *El Gráfico*, *El Nuevo Mundo*, and *Liberación*.

Vega, Ed (Edgardo Vega Yunqué; b. May 20, 1936, Ponce, Puerto Rico): Writer. Vega lived in Ponce until his family moved to the Bronx, New York, in 1949. He was reared in a devout Baptist home, his father having been a Baptist minister. After graduation from high school, he renewed his early literary interest while in the Air Force by attempting to write a pornographic book for his G.I. friends. He failed and became frustrated by his awkwardness as a writer. After being discharged from the service, he studied for two years under the G.I. Bill at Santa Monica College in California. In 1969, Vega completed his studies in political science at New York University. Subsequently, he worked in a number of social service programs but finally returned to academic life, holding teaching positions at various universities.

In 1977, Vega began publishing short stories in magazines and journals. He later published a book of short stories, *Mendoza's Dreams* (1987); a novel, *The Comeback* (1985); and a second book of short stories, *Casualty Report* (1991). His works draw on English-

and Spanish-language traditions as well as common events in the lives of Puerto Ricans in the barrios.

Vega, Salvador: Painter. Vega is a Chicano working from a studio in Casa Aztlán, a community center in the Pilsen neighborhood (Little Mexico) of Chicago, Illinois. He has provided free art workshops to Pilsen residents.

Vega participated in the Benito Juárez High School mural with Jaime Longoria, Malú ORTEGA Y ALBERRO, Marcos RAYA, and José Oscar Moya. His show "Birth of the Earth," at Chicago's Museum of Contemporary Art in 1981, broke the tradition of the Chicago muralists stylistically. For example, his *Man Enjoying the Sun* is an abstract work.

Velasquez, Baldemar (b. Feb. 15, 1947, Pharr, Tex.): Labor leader. Velasquez, of Puerto Rican background, focused on the needs of migrant farmworkers, who were still struggling for basic rights at the close of the twentieth century. In 1967, he became the founder and president of the FARM LABOR ORGANIZING COMMITTEE (FLOC). Through the FLOC, he negotiated better living conditions for migrant workers employed by large food companies. In the 1980's, negotiations with the companies stalled over issues involving pay and mechanization. Directed by the FLOC, migrant leaders in Ohio began a boycott of Campbell Soup products, culminating in a one-hundred-mile march to the state capital to dramatize their demands. Velasquez also turned to the churches for support. The resulting contracts were credited to his efforts. He continued to work for workers' rights and in 1990 was granted a John D. and Catherine T. MacArthur Foundation Fellowship, the most prestigious of his many honors and awards.

Velasquez, Jorge Luis, Jr. (b. Dec. 28, 1946, Panama City, Panama): Jockey. One of the top jockeys of the 1970's and early 1980's, Velasquez began his riding

Jorge Velasquez wins his sixth race of the day at Belmont Park in 1981. (AP/Wide World Photos)

career in 1963. He was soon a dominant rider in Panama and was often compared to the famous Panamanian jockey Braulio Baeza. In 1965, Velasquez followed in Baeza's footsteps and began racing in the United States. In 1969, he was the leading money-winner among U.S. jockeys.

In 1978, Velasquez, aboard Alydar, finished second to Affirmed in all three Triple Crown races. In 1981, Velasquez won both the Kentucky Derby and the Preakness aboard Pleasant Colony. Still active in the 1990's, Velasquez had moved to high positions on all-time lists of career victories and money won.

Velásquez, William (May 8, 1944, Orlando, Fla.—June 15, 1988, San Antonio, Tex.): Civil rights activist. Velásquez, a Mexican American, was assistant director for the NATIONAL COUNCIL OF LA RAZA in the early 1970's. He founded the nonprofit SOUTHWEST VOTER REGISTRATION EDUCATION PROJECT (SVREP) and served as its executive director for fourteen years.

Velásquez was exposed to politics early, assisting as a teenager in his uncle's campaign for election to a school board. He received his bachelor's degree in economics from St. Mary's University while simultaneously organizing Hispanic youth. Velásquez forfeited a nearly completed master's degree in econom-

William Velásquez. (AP/Wide World Photos)

ics from St. Mary's to organize striking farmworkers in the Rio Grande Valley in Texas.

In 1970, Velásquez was named field director of the Southwest Council of La Raza in Phoenix, the predecessor to the National Council of La Raza. In 1971, in Washington, D.C., he became the group's assistant director in charge of fund-raising and organizing. From 1972 to 1974, Velásquez organized the Southwest Voter Registration Education Project in San Antonio, Texas. When the project became a separate entity, Velásquez was appointed its executive director. This organization was critical in increasing Hispanic voter registration nationwide and increasing the number of Hispanic elected officials from approximately five hundred to more than three thousand.

Velázquez, Juan Ramon (1865—1899): Santero artisan and painter. Velázquez, a Mexican American, was from the southwestern United States. He was a santero, an artisan who carved and painted representations of holy persons, not exclusively restricted to saints of the Roman Catholic church. Most santeros are anonymous. Velázquez is among the few santeros of the late nineteenth century who is known by name. (*See* SANTOS AND SANTO ART.)

Velázquez, Loreta Janeta (June 26, 1842, Havana, Cuba—?): Confederate soldier. Born into an aristocratic Spanish family, Velázquez was educated in a New Orleans, Louisiana, convent. Betrothed to a young Spaniard by her parents, Velázquez broke her engagement and in 1856 secretly married an American army officer who had been courting one of her schoolmates.

Velázquez and her husband were stationed at Fort Leavenworth, Kansas, when the U.S. Civil War began, and her husband joined the Confederate army. Velázquez had fantasized about the idea of being a man and achieving military glory since her early childhood. She raised a volunteer battalion and marched it to her husband's camp, passing herself off as Lieutenant Harry T. Buford. The deception proved successful, and she temporarily commanded that unit under General Barnard E. Bee at First Bull Run in July, 1861.

Velázquez fought again at Ball's Bluff in October, 1861, and at Shiloh in April, 1862. Her husband died in a firearms accident, and she stayed in the army until she was discovered in 1863. Velázquez then became a secret agent who operated in Washington, D.C., and Canada. After the war she remarried, traveled widely in South America, and published her memoirs, which have been characterized as lacking credibility.

Velázquez de Cuéllar, Diego (c. 1465, Cuéllar, Spain—June 11, 1524, Santiago de Cuba, Cuba): Colonist. Velázquez de Cuéllar was a wealthy colonizer of the island of Hispaniola who had traveled to Hispaniola with Christopher Columbus in 1493. When reports that gold was plentiful on the island of Cuba reached Hispaniola, the Spanish Crown decided to colonize Cuba. The Crown needed a leader with military skill, administrative talents, and loyalty to both the Crown and Diego Columbus, the governor of Hispaniola. Velázquez met the requirements. He was educated and had served as a lieutenant in Nicolás Ovando's army, which had appeased the natives of Hispaniola.

Velázquez went to Cuba in 1511 and landed near Baracoa. The natives resisted bitterly. It was only through use of brutal tactics by some of his soldiers, such as Pánfilo de NARVÁEZ, that he managed to occupy the island. Velázquez became governor of Cuba in 1511 and established several towns, including Santiago de Cuba, La Habana, and Bayamo.

While Velázquez was governor, news of a rich civilization to the west reached Cuba. Velázquez sent Hernán CORTÉS to explore in his name. Cortés achieved fame for himself, conquering the Aztec state and separating the new colony from Cuba and Velázquez. Velázquez ordered Cortés to return in 1520, and when Cortés did not heed the order, Velázquez sent a party under Narváez to arrest him. Cortés captured Narváez instead. Velázquez died in 1524 while still governor of Cuba.

Velez, Eddie (b. June 4, 1958, New York, N.Y.): Actor. Velez attended the School of Visual Arts in New York City and served in the U.S. Air Force. He has worked extensively in Los Angeles and San Francisco theaters, performing in such plays as *Steambath, Balm in Gilead, The Threepenny Opera, Barefoot in the Park, Count Dracula, The Odd Couple*, and *Bell, Book, and Candle*.

Velez made his television debut in *For Love and Honor* in 1983. His other television credits include roles in *Summer Fantasy* (1984), *Children of the Night* (1985), *C.A.T. Squad* (1986), *From the Files of Joseph Wambaugh: Jury of One* (1992), and *To Grandmother's House We Go* (1992). He has also made numerous appearances on such series as *Hill Street Blues, Cagney and Lacey, Bay City Blues*, and *The A-Team*. In 1988, he starred as a Puerto Rican lawyer opposite comedian Paul RODRÍGUEZ in the short-lived series *Trial and Error*.

Velez made his major film debut in 1984 in *Repo Man* and has also appeared in *Doin' Time* (1985), *Ex-tremities* (1986), *The Women's Club* (1987), *Rooftops* (1989), and *Romero* (1989). Velez also has performed stand-up comedy and has written, directed, and produced works for West Coast theaters.

Velez, Lupe (María Guadalupe Velez de Villalobos; July 18, 1908, San Luis Potosí, Mexico—Dec. 14, 1944, Beverly Hills, Calif.): Actress. Reared in a convent in San Antonio, Texas, Velez rose to fame in silent films and continued her career in the talkies. She made her debut in two short films in 1927 and performed with Douglas Fairbanks in *The Gaucho* (1928) and under the direction of D. W. Griffith in *Lady of the Pavements* (1929). With her deep but whimsical voice, she became a classic screen temptress who could play a variety of ethnic types. Her films include *The Squaw Man* (1931), *Kongo* (1932), *Hot Peppers* (1933), *Strictly Dynamite* (1934), *The Morals of Marcus* (1935), and *He Loved an Actress* (1937).

Beginning with *The Girl from Mexico* in 1939, Velez performed in a string of features that established her as Carmelita, the "Mexican Spitfire," a loud, physical, sensual, and strongly comic persona. The series included *The Mexican Spitfire's Party* (1941), *The Mexican Spitfire's Elephant* (1942), and *The Mexican Spitfire's Blessed Event* (1943). Velez also appeared in a number of Spanish-language films made in Mexico. Tempestuous off the screen as well as on, Velez was married to actor Johnny Weissmuller and was rumored to have had affairs with some of her leading men. She died of a drug overdose at the age of thirty-six, allegedly after a failed affair and unwanted pregnancy.

Velez, Ramón S. (b. 1933, Mayagüez, Puerto Rico): Administrator of nonprofit programs. Although he held elected office only briefly, Velez has ruled as a political power broker of the South Bronx by virtue of his network of nonprofit organizations and antipoverty programs. Velez served on the New York City Council for several years, but his strength comes from the integration of his business relations, kindred political spirits, and a network of allies and family members.

This unique arrangement has subjected Velez to numerous investigations into his dealings with city, state, and federal governmental agencies. It has also allowed him to wield political power and influence. Velez grew up as a farmer's son, moving to New York at the age of twenty-eight. He was a social worker and used his organizing skills to take control of money that followed the Great Society programs in the 1960's. He

Lupe Velez in a costume from the film Playmates *(1941).* (AP/Wide World Photos)

became president of several nonprofit organizations and held business interests in several commercial concerns.

Vélez-Ibañez, Carlos G. (b. Oct. 27, 1936, Nogales, Ariz.): Anthropologist. Among Vélez-Ibañez's publications are *Rituals of Marginality: Politics, Process, and Culture Change in Urban Central Mexico* (1983) and *Bonds of Mutual Trust: The Cultural Systems of Rotating Credit Associations Among Urban Mexicans and Chicanos* (1983). He holds a B.A. in political science (1961) and an M.A. in English (1968) from the University of Arizona as well as an M.A. (1972) and Ph.D. (1975) in anthropology from the University of California, San Diego.

Vélez-Ibañez taught high school in Coolidge, Arizona, from 1961 to 1963 and in Tucson, Arizona, from 1964 to 1968. From 1968 to 1971, he was an assistant professor of Mexican American studies at San Diego Junior College. He joined the faculty of the University of California, Los Angeles (UCLA), in 1976. From 1982 to 1987, he was an adjunct associate professor at UCLA. Vélez-Ibañez worked at the University of Arizona beginning in 1982, as an associate professor of anthropology from 1982 to 1984, as an associate dean from 1984 to 1986, and then as a professor of anthropology. He was named director of the Bureau of Applied Research in Anthropology in 1982.

Vendido: Person who does not support his or her own culture. *Vendido* (literally, "sellout") refers to a Latino who has given up cultural roots in favor of an assimilated lifestyle. The term is derogatory and implies that the person has succumbed to the dominant ANGLO culture, perhaps because of desire for personal gain or embarrassment about cultural roots. A *vendido* would not protect community rights and goals and would be most concerned with furthering his or her own goals, which may be independent of those of the cultural community.

Venegas, Daniel (b. c. 1900, Mexico): Writer. Very little is known of Venegas' life. He emigrated from Mexico as a laborer, traveling through Juárez, Mexico, and El Paso, Texas. He made his way to Los Angeles by working on the Santa Fe Railroad, and despite his becoming part of the Latino cultural elite of Los Angeles, he was proud of and identified with his working-class origins.

Venegas founded the weekly satirical Los Angeles newspaper *El Malcriado* in 1924 and edited it into

the 1930's. Prior to this, he was a journalist for the newspaper *El Pueblo* in Los Angeles. He was also a playwright and novelist and founded a theatrical company.

All of Venegas' theatrical works have been lost; only newspaper reviews remain. Some of his major plays and their production dates are *Nuestro egoísmo* (1926?), *Esclavos* (1930), *El maldito jazz* (1930?), *El con-su-lado* (1932), and *El establo de Arizmendi* (1933). His novel *Las aventuras de Don Chipote; O, Cuando los pericos mamen* (1928) focuses on Mexican immigrant workers and their culture. Venegas' work is a precursor of contemporary Chicano literature, not only in openly proclaiming a Chicano identity but also in generating a style and literary attitude that would come to typify the Chicano novels of the late 1960's and the 1970's (*see* LITERATURE, MEXICAN AMERICAN).

Verdugo, Elena (b. Apr. 20, 1926, Hollywood, Calif.): Actress. Verdugo, a Mexican American who began her career as a dancer, made her first film appearance in 1940 in *The Mark of Zorro*. Her other film credits include *Down Argentine Way* (1940), *Belle Starr* (1941), *The Moon and Sixpence* (1942), *Rainbow Island* (1944), *The House of Frankenstein* (1945), *The Frozen Ghost* (1945), *Little Giant* (1946), *Song of Scheherazade* (1947), *Tuna Clipper* (1949), *The Big Sombrero* (1949), *The Lost Volcano* (1950), *Cyrano de Bergerac* (1950), *Thief of Damascus* (1952), *The Pathfinder* (1952), *Knights of the Round Table* (1954), *Panama Sal* (1957), *Day of the Nightmare* (1965), *How Sweet It Is* (1968), and *Angel in My Pocket* (1969).

On television, Verdugo starred as an all-American girl in the 1952 comedy series *Meet Millie*, and she was featured in *The New Phil Silvers Show* during the early 1960's. In the 1970's, Verdugo became well known for her performance as Nurse Consuelo in the dramatic series *Marcus Welby, M.D.*

Versalles, Zoilo (Zoilo Casanova Versalles Y Rodriguez; Dec. 18, 1939, Havana, Cuba—June 9, 1995, Bloomington, Minn.): Baseball player. Versalles made his major league debut with the Washington Senators in 1959 and emerged as the team's starting shortstop after the franchise became the Minnesota Twins in 1961. A quick, smooth-fielding shortstop with a solid bat, he enjoyed his finest season in 1965, when he led the American League in doubles, triples, and runs scored, helped the Twins to the pennant, and won the league's Most Valuable Player Award, the first Latino to do so.

Elena Verdugo's role as Nurse Consuelo in Marcus Welby, M.D., *expanded her popularity among television audiences.* (AP/Wide World Photos)

Zoilo Versalles. (AP/Wide World Photos)

Versalles won Gold Glove Awards in 1963 and 1965 and also led the American League in triples in 1963 and 1964. He was traded to the Los Angeles Dodgers after the 1967 season and played briefly for the Cleveland Indians, the expansion Washington Senators, and the Atlanta Braves before retiring in 1971.

Vial, Pedro (1746, Lyons, France—1814, Santa Fe, N.Mex.): Cleric and explorer. Vial goes unmentioned in recorded history until about 1780, when he lived with the Comanches of the Spanish Southwest and repaired their rifles. In 1786, he was commissioned by Texas governor Domingo Cabello to find a direct route from San Antonio, the most important settlement in Texas, to Santa Fe. Vial identified such a route. In 1787, Cabello sent Vial to find a route to Natchitoches and return via San Antonio. Vial succeeded and was then entrusted with finding a useful route from Santa Fe to St. Louis. He did this from 1792 to 1793, opening what later became the SANTA FE TRAIL. During that expedition, Vial was captured by Kansa Indians but escaped. His diaries, beginning in 1792, provided an important source of information about the trail.

Vial next explored Indian country for New Mexico governor Jacobo Ugarte, dealing with Wichita, Comanche, Apache, Pawnee, Osage, and Kansa tribes in the process. Vial apparently liked Indian life; in 1797, he again chose to live with the Comanches, staying with them for five years. In 1803, Vial returned to Santa Fe, then carried out expeditions that explored the Missouri River for Spain. Over the next ten years, Vial was a trader in Santa Fe. Taken ill in 1814, he died suddenly, leaving his possessions to Maria Manuella Martin, the rumored mother of his children, to whom he was not married.

Villa, Francisco "Pancho" (Doroteo Arango; June 5, 1878, San Juan del Río, Mexico—July 20, 1923, near Parral, Chihuahua, Mexico): General in the Mexican Revolution. Villa was born to Indian parents on a hacienda sixty-five miles north of Durango, Mexico. Both his father (Agustín Arango) and his mother (Micaela

Pancho Villa (left), next to General John J. Pershing, at a friendly meeting early in 1916. (AP/Wide World Photos)

Arámbula) worked as common laborers for wealthy ranchers. Villa grew to young manhood in a Mexico controlled by the dictatorship of Porfirio Díaz. He was caught in a cycle of poverty from which there was little chance of escape. His father died when Villa was twelve years old, leaving him as the head of the household. As a ranch hand, he became a skilled horseman, working in some of the most rugged, mountainous terrain in Mexico.

In 1894, Villa fled the Rio Grande hacienda of his youth after wounding landowner Agustín López Negrete in the defense of his sister. At this time, he adopted the name of Pancho Villa, a notorious early nineteenth century bandit. Villa then joined a bandit group led by Ignacio Parra. After Parra's death, Villa became the group's leader. He soon gained a reputation as a Mexican Robin Hood who took from the rich and gave to the poor CAMPESINO. Even though Villa never had the opportunity to attend school, as an adult he taught himself to read and write. As a young man, Villa worked in the United States. He served as a soldier in the United States Army during the Spanish-American War.

When Francisco Madero visited Chihuahua during his 1910 presidential campaign, Villa was engaged in the livestock business there. Shortly thereafter, he fled after killing a man. In November, 1910, he joined the Mexican Revolution as the leader of a band of fifteen men. Soon he led a well-armed force of four hundred irregular cavalry.

After Madero's murder by Victoriano Huerta, Villa joined and fought with Venustiano Carranza. After Huerta's defeat and under Villa's leadership, the northern army separated from Carranza's movement in the hope of securing national recognition for Villa's own revolutionary agenda. Villa's separation from Carranza led to a series of armed confrontations, including decisive defeats at Celaya in 1915, that effectively ended his strategic importance to the 1910 revolution. The high point of Villa's success was in 1914, when for almost six months he and Emiliano Zapata militarily occupied Mexico City.

On January 10, 1916, Villa's followers murdered seventeen Americans near Santa Ysabel, Sonora. In an effort to bring discredit to Carranza, Villa raided Columbus, New Mexico, on March 9, 1916, killing sixteen Americans. U.S. General John J. Pershing pursued Villa's northern army for a year (*see* PERSHING EXPEDITION). In 1920, as an enticement to retire, Villa was given a large ranch in Durango and a small fortune in gold pesos.

The only peaceful years of Villa's life were from 1920 to 1923. On July 18, 1923, on his return home from a fiesta in Parral, near Durango, a group of assassins ambushed Villa, riddling him with at least fifty bullets.

Pancho Villa galvanized the disenfranchised *campesinos* of Mexico into widespread resistance against Porfirio Díaz. As commander of revolutionary forces in Chihuahua, Villa instituted many of the changes advocated by Zapata's agrarian reform plan. Villa was a highly respected and visible leader of the poorest elements of revolutionary Mexico.

Villagrá, Gaspar Pérez de (1555, Puebla de Los Angeles, New Spain—1620): Historian and poet. Villagrá, the son of Spanish immigrants to the Americas, studied in Spain at the University of Salamanca. After returning to the Americas, he joined Juan de OÑATE's 1596 colonizing expedition into the northern region of New Spain, now the state of New Mexico. He was made a captain and legal officer of the expedition and later its ecclesiastical counsel. Between 1601 and 1603, he served as *alcalde mayor* at the mines of Guanacevi and Nuestra Señora de Alancón in Nueva Vizcaya.

It is likely that Villagrá returned to Spain in 1608 or 1609, possibly to petition the crown for payment for his services in New Spain. In 1610, he produced his epic poem, *Historia de la Nueva Mexico*, recounting the experiences of the Oñate expedition. The poem was the first published history of New Mexico. Some of the events the poem details were in turn the subject of a 1612 investigation into charges of improper actions by Oñate and his officers. Villagrá, who was still in Spain, was found guilty of killing two deserters and was banished from New Mexico for six years. In 1620, he died en route to a new post in Zapotitlán, Guatemala.

Villalongín, Carlos: Actor and director. Villalongín was born into a family with a long tradition of involvement in the theater. As early as 1849, the Hernandez-Villalongín troupe was touring through northern Mexico and the southwestern United States. By 1900, the company's repertoire numbered at least a dozen plays, including melodramas, heroic epics, and patriotic works.

In 1910, the company fled the Mexican Revolution and took up residence in San Antonio, Texas, performing during the ensuing decade in such venues as the Carpa Sanabia, a traditional performance tent theater.

Villalongín, along with his actress wife, María, led the Gran Compañía Lirico Dramatica de Carlos Villalongín. Focused on serious dramatic works, the Villalongíns eschewed traditional Latino forms that depended on music and comedy, such as the ZARZUELA and REVISTA.

During the Depression, Villalongín's company was forced to play in church halls and neighborhood centers and to seek expanded audiences by touring to Austin, Dallas, Houston, Laredo, and other cities in the Southwest. Villalongín remained a fixture of the San Antonio theater through the 1950's, performing and leading companies at the city's major theatrical houses.

Villalpando, Catalina Vasquez (b. Apr. 1, 1940, San Marcos, Tex.): U.S. treasurer. Villalpando, a Mexican American, attended five colleges and universities, including Southern Methodist and Southwest Texas State. She went to work for Communications International and eventually became a senior vice president. Villalpando directed the public relations and marketing for the northeast region, based in Washington, D.C.

From 1983 to 1985, Villalpando served as a special assistant for public liaison to President Ronald Reagan. Prior to her White House duties, she also served as liaison director for the Republican Party of Texas.

In 1989, President George Bush appointed Villalpando to the largely ceremonial post of U.S. treasurer. She oversaw the operations of the U.S. Mint, the Bureau of Engraving and Printing, and the United States Savings Bond Division. Before the end of her term of service, Villalpando was indicted for accepting

Treasury Secretary Nicholas Brady presents Catalina Vasquez Villalpando with a replica dollar bill bearing her signature. (AP/Wide World Photos)

Danny Villanueva. (AP/Wide World Photos)

payments from Communications International while she served in government, in violation of the law.

Villanueva, Daniel "Danny" (b. 1937, Tucumcari, N.Mex.): Football player and broadcaster. Villanueva, a Mexican American, played in the National Football League from 1960 to 1967 as a punter and kicker for the Los Angeles Rams and Dallas Cowboys. In 1969, he became station manager of the Spanish-language television station KMEX-TV in Los Angeles. Villanueva eventually rose to the position of president of KMEX; he also organized the Spanish International Network-West (SIN-West), served on various local and state government committees, acted as boxing commissioner for the 1984 Los Angeles Olympics, and helped to raise money for numerous charitable causes.

Villanueva, Tino (b. Dec. 11, 1941, San Marcos, Tex.): Poet. After World War II and the WORKS PROGRESS ADMINISTRATION programs ended, Villanueva's parents were obliged to return to their previous occupation as migrant field workers. Consequently, he attended a variety of schools. After graduation from high school, he worked in a furniture factory for three years, during which time he began to make up for the gaps in his education.

Villanueva was drafted into the Army in 1963 and spent two years in the Panama Canal Zone, where he was brought into closer contact with Latino culture. After receiving his B.A. in English from Southwest Texas State University in 1969, Villanueva began publishing his poetry in the *San Antonio Express/Evening News*. He obtained his M.A. from the State University of New York-Buffalo in 1971 and then his Ph.D. in Spanish from Boston University in 1981. He taught at Wellesley College in Massachusetts for a number of years.

Villanueva's major collections of poetry include *Hay otra voz: Poems, 1968-1971* (1972), *Shaking Off the Dark* (1984), *Scene from the Movie Giant* (1993), and *Crónica de mis años peores* (1987; *Chronicle of My Worst Years*, 1994). He also edited an anthology of Chicano literature titled *Chicanos: Antología histórica y literaria* (1980). The power of Villanueva's poetry lies in its grappling with critical questions of Chicano cultural identity.

Villarreal, José Antonio (b. July 30, 1924, Los Angeles, Calif.): Novelist. Born to Mexican parents, Villarreal grew up in Santa Clara, California. In 1950, he earned a B.A. degree at the University of California,

Berkeley. After undertaking graduate studies at the University of California, Los Angeles, he held various teaching and editorial positions. In the early 1970's, Villarreal moved to Mexico and became a citizen of the country of his ancestors. Later he returned to the United States to take visiting teaching positions at various universities.

The significance of Villarreal's narrative, consisting primarily of two novels, *Pocho* (1959) and *The Fifth Horseman* (1974), can be determined when his work is compared to other Chicano works of literature and studied within its historical context of the period between the beginning of the Mexican Revolution and World War II. *Pocho* remains a landmark novel of identity crisis, rivaled only by Rudolfo A. ANAYA's *Bless Me, Ultima* (1972). *Pocho* shows the conflicts and dilemmas of a Mexican family residing in the United States. Critics have remarked that while *Bless Me, Ultima* finds its truth in the 1970's, *Pocho* will continue to have underground admirers who accept silence, exile, and cunning as the only possible means of individual action in an age of social contradictions and unrest.

Villarreal family: Leaders of the 1910 Mexican Revolution. The Villarreals excelled both intellectually and as leaders at a young age. Antonio and Felicitás, both born in 1875, were the children of poor parents in Monterrey, in the central Mexican state of Nuevo Leon. They and their brothers Marcelimo and Leonardo were mentored in their youth by wealthy estate owners who sponsored their education and employment. The Villarreals' exposure to the wealthy upper classes, contrasted with their humble beginnings, embittered them as well as convincing them that a complete restructuring of the Mexican political system was necessary to achieve economic and social equity.

In prerevolutionary Mexico, Antonio became a schoolteacher, Felicitás a financial expert, and Marcelimo and Leonardo successful trans-border businessmen. In 1906, Antonio was elected secretary of the organizational junta of the Mexican Liberal Party. This was the first of the Mexican political movements to formulate and publish a blueprint for the coming revolution. Many aspects of this plan, such as land reform and individual freedoms, are reflected in the 1917 Mexican Constitution, the cornerstone of modern Mexico.

Moving to the United States in 1906 to escape political violence and opposition, the Villarreals remained active in attempts to topple the regime of Porfirio Díaz. In Los Angeles, California, on August 23, 1907, Antonio was arrested (with evidence provided by the Díaz government) for violating United States neutrality laws. He was sentenced to eighteen months in federal prison. In 1910, the Villarreals, led by Antonio, joined Francisco Madero in his attempt to overthrow the Díaz government. In 1911, in an attempt to overcome the revolution's shortage of artillery, Antonio stole a cannon from an El Paso, Texas, city park.

The Villarreals were committed to changing the despotic Mexican political system of the early twentieth century. Antonio was an associate of Ricardo FLORES MAGÓN, one of the architects of the 1910 Mexican Revolution. Later, the Villarreals became close advisers to key leaders of the revolution, including Francisco Madero, an initiator of the 1910 revolution; and Venustiano Carranza, the first leader of the constitutionalist movement and president of Mexico from 1917 to 1920 after serving as provisional president from 1915 to 1917.

Antonio's prowess in planning and executing complicated military operations was respected by many, including Pancho VILLA, who viewed him as a dangerous opponent. Antonio was a major contributor to the idea that the federal army be completely destroyed and that Villa must play an integral role in the government of postrevolutionary Mexico. He supported the confiscation of church property and removal of religion from Mexican politics.

Between 1906 and 1909, the Villarreal sisters, Andrea and Teresa, with their father Próspero, led a nationwide campaign on behalf of Mexican revolutionaries imprisoned in the United States. The campaign stated that "to deport is to execute." In 1910, they published and ran the militant *La Mujer Moderna*, a prorevolution newspaper in San Antonio, Texas. Teresa went on to found *El Obrero*, a widely read socialist publication of the American Latino community.

The Villarreal family was responsible for the effective coordination of the desperate elements of the 1910 revolutionary movement. Antonio supported and initially achieved joint programs of leadership and administration with Emiliano Zapata's agrarian revolt in southern Mexico. He served as president pro tem of the 1914 constitutional convention and worked to end the civil war. He died in 1944 in Mexico City, Mexico. Felicitás was a cabinet member and finance minister of the Military Convention of Aguascalientes. He died in 1917 in Mexico City.

Throughout the 1910-1920 period, Marcelimo and Leonardo Villarreal were pivotal leaders of prorevolu-

tionary movements in the states of Arizona and Texas as well as in Sonora, Mexico. The Villarreal sisters are credited for using the Spanish-language press to awaken the United States to the plight of Mexican freedom fighters there.

Villaseñor, Victor Edmundo (b. May 11, 1940, Carlsbad, Calif.): Writer. The son of a Mexican rancher who immigrated to the United States during the Mexican Revolution and of a woman native to the state of Chihuahua, Mexico, Villaseñor was brought up near Riverside, California. The dissolution and many problems caused by the Mexican Revolution, especially among the peasants, provide the social and cultural backdrop to his novel *Macho!* (1973), a didactic novel about the conflict between two generations. Villaseñor also published a nonfiction work entitled *Jury: The People versus Juan Corona* (1977). *Rain of Gold* (1991) is the saga of several generations of Villaseñor's family, telling how they experienced the Mexican Revolution and became established in California.

Reared in an environment in which Spanish was the only language spoken, Villaseñor made his first trip to Mexico at the age of twenty to become more familiar with his ethnic heritage. He read avidly during this period and was determined to finish high school. After graduation, he enrolled at the University of San Diego to study philosophy. His flair for writing soon became evident. Richard Vásquez's novel *Chicano* (1970) and Villaseñor's book were among the first contemporary Chicano novels issued by a mainstream publisher. Both attempted to exploit the new taste for Chicano themes that developed in the early 1970's.

Viramontes, Helena María (b. Feb. 26, 1954, East Los Angeles, Calif.): Short-story writer. The daughter of working-class parents, Viramontes was reared in East Los Angeles. Her father was a construction worker, and her mother was a traditional Chicana who raised nine children.

Viramontes received her B.A. in English from Immaculate Heart College in 1975. She also attended the creative writing program at the University of California, Irvine, in 1981. She has been coordinator of the Los Angeles Writers Association, literary editor of *Xhisme Arte Magazine*, and a fellow of the National Endowment for the Arts.

Viramontes made the overall purpose of her writing evident in her 1985 collection *The Moths and Other Stories*. Each of her tales exhibits an acute sense of political and sociological awareness, some by challenging the prejudices of the dominant society and some by committing the author to global solidarity with people who are immigrants to the United States. She also coedited *Chicana Creativity and Criticism: Charting New Frontiers in American Literature* (1988). Groundbreaking narrative strategies, combined with sociopolitical focus, situate Viramontes at the forefront of an emerging Chicana literary tradition that redefines Chicano literature and feminist theory.

Virgin Mary: During the Roman occupation of the lands of present-day Israel, a young Jewish girl, Mary, gave birth to a child, Jesus, considered to be the Christ child. The circumstances surrounding the conception and birth of the child fulfilled the prophecies of the Old Testament concerning a messiah. Mary reared Jesus, witnessed many of the major, miraculous events of his public life, and was present at his crucifixion.

Latinos have a special reverence for the Virgin Mary because she is believed to be the Mother of God, and motherhood is the most important and protected role for women in the Latino culture. Through prayer, Latinos ask the Virgin Mary for assistance with life's problems, illnesses, and expectations, because it is believed that she can petition her son Jesus on behalf of the sorrowful and needy. Many worshipers light candles and leave flowers at altars of the Virgin in their local churches. At her wedding, a Latina bride will often leave her bridal bouquet at Mary's altar; this is also a custom at girls' fifteenth birthday celebrations (the QUINCEAÑERA). In some locations, devoted Latinos will also leave coins at the foot of the altar statues.

When asking for answers to special prayers, believers make promises to the Virgin, including pledges to visit holy shrines, attend weekday Masses, and recite the Rosary (a series of devotional prayers dedicated to the Virgin). Other promises or vows may extend to naming the family's first daughter for the Virgin. Variations on the name of Mary in the Latino world are numerous and often include one of Mary's special titles, such as María Luz (Mary who brings light), Marisol (Mary who brings Sun), María Nieves (Mary

A nativity drama, reenacting events surrounding the Virgin Mary giving birth to Jesus. (Odette Lupis)

of the Snows), and María del Rosario (Mary of the Rosary). Other names such as Inmaculada (Mary Immaculate without sin) or Beatriz (Mary the Blessed One) celebrate characteristics of the Virgin.

In traditional Latino homes, it is not uncommon to find a small altar devoted to Mary on a fireplace mantel or a corner shelf. Home altars typically contain small statues of the Virgin and numerous candles. Fresh flowers and food offerings are also placed on these home altars.

The Roman Catholic church celebrates important events in the story of Mary and Jesus with Masses and other religious devotions. The month of May is dedicated to Mary, as is the first Friday of every month. Latinos attend these services in large numbers. Other religious celebrations include the Annunciation, the Assumption, and, most important, the Immaculate Conception. The Immaculate Conception is celebrated on December 8, which is the same date chosen to honor the Virgin of Guadalupe, patroness of Mexico and of Latinos of Mexican ancestry.

Visas: Official government endorsements on a passport. Visitors to a country are requested to show visas when entering.

To obtain a visa to enter the United States, individuals generally are required to make a personal appearance at an American embassy or consulate in their home country. In addition to the application form (Form OF-156), an applicant may be asked to provide other documents, such as proof of status as a student, exchange visitor, temporary worker, or trainee. These documents may provide evidence that the applicant is eligible for nonimmigrant status. Consular officers may also request that the applicant show evidence of financial resources, educational background, or English language proficiency.

Examples of common types of visas for the United States include H-1 (temporary worker of distinguished merit and ability); H-2A (temporary agricultural worker); H-2B (temporary worker performing services unavailable in the United States); H-3 (trainee); H-4 (spouse or child of alien classified H-1, H-2, or H-3); I (representative of foreign information media, along with spouse and children); J-1 (exchange visitor); J-2 (spouse or child of exchange visitor); K-1 (fiancée or fiancé of U.S. citizen); K-2 (child of fiancée or fiancé of U.S. citizen); L-1 (intracompany transfer); L-2 (spouse or child of alien classified L-1); M-1 (student in a vocational or other recognized nonacademic institution); M-2 (spouse or child of a person in a voca-

tional or other recognized nonacademic institution); N-8 (parent of an alien child accorded special immigrant status); and N-9 (child of an alien parent accorded special immigrant status).

Some Latinos who entered the United States on visas overstayed the time period specified for their stay, thus becoming illegal residents. Many of them later were granted AMNESTY by the U.S. government and were given residency status.

U.S. consular officers must follow standardized guidelines written by the Department of State. If, however, they have reason to suspect that an applicant intends to become an immigrant rather than visiting temporarily, they may deny a visa. The applicant bears the burden of proving eligibility.

Visitador: Political emissary of the viceroy in colonial Spanish America. A *visitador* (visitor) was a judge/inspector on a colonial *visita* (visit). *Visitas* were tours of inspection, ordered by the viceroy, of remote areas. *Visitas* were the only mechanism for viceroys to discover and decide about irregularities occurring in the interiors of their colonies. The *visitador* represented the viceroy. His role was to investigate problems and decide on solutions. Because some colonial regions were very remote, the *visitador* was the strongest authority figure with power to shape colonial society.

Viva Kennedy clubs: These clubs were created in 1960 to generate support among Latinos, particularly Mexican Americans, for John F. Kennedy's presidential campaign. Kennedy was the first U.S. presidential candidate to take seriously the Mexican American electorate. He offered a political program that addressed issues of discrimination and minority economic development, and he made the first statement on migrant farmworkers' rights in the history of the Democratic Party.

Some historians argue that Kennedy's attention to these issues was the result of an antagonistic Democratic Party in Texas and the influence of Kennedy's vice presidential candidate from Texas, Lyndon B. Johnson. Targeting Mexican American voters was consistent with the need to gain blocs of voters in large states to secure a majority of electoral college votes.

The Viva Kennedy clubs were created by Mexican Americans who took the idea to the Kennedy campaign for official sanction. Henry B. GONZÁLEZ, Héctor Pérez GARCÍA, and Alberto Peña, Jr., from Texas; Edward Roybal (*see* ROYBAL FAMILY) and Henry López of California; José Alvarado of Illinois; and

Viva Kennedy clubs rallied the support of Mexican Americans and other Latinos to help elect John F. Kennedy as president.
(AP/Wide World Photos)

Senator Dennis CHÁVEZ of New Mexico were involved in the early development of the clubs. Organizations such as the AMERICAN G.I. FORUM, the LEAGUE OF UNITED LATIN AMERICAN CITIZENS, the MEXICAN AMERICAN POLITICAL ASSOCIATION, and the ALIANZA HISPANO-AMERICANA were also supportive. College students played important roles in the clubs.

Viva Kennedy clubs, which numbered in the thousands, mobilized an unprecedented number of Mexican Americans in the Southwest, registering many to vote for the first time. In Texas, for example, Kennedy won 91 percent of the Mexican American vote, estimated at 200,000. These votes helped him to win the state, which carried a large number of votes in the electoral college. In New Mexico, 70 percent of the Mexican American vote went to Kennedy. Although he did not receive the majority of Anglo votes, he carried the state by two thousand votes. Significant support for Kennedy was also clear in California, Arizona, and Colorado but was hampered by low numbers of Mexican Americans registered to vote. The voter returns made politicians realize, perhaps for the first time, the potential impact of the Mexican American vote.

The establishment of the Viva Kennedy clubs marked the entry of the Mexican American middle class and professional leaders into national politics. Those who hoped for political appointments after Kennedy's election were disappointed. In 1961, a conference of Viva Kennedy club leaders expressed a sense of betrayal and outrage that the one Mexican American Kennedy had appointed to a significant post was a Republican. Héctor Pérez García and Henry González had both been offered appointments but had other commitments. Disappointment with Kennedy's actions led to the creation of the POLITICAL ASSOCIATION OF SPANISH SPEAKING ORGANIZATIONS, with a goal of making Latinos independent from the Democratic Party.

Vivó, Paquita (b. San Juan, Puerto Rico): Cultural affairs administrator. After studying at the University of Puerto Rico from 1953 to 1955, Vivó became assistant to the undersecretary in the Commonwealth Department of State, a position she held from 1955 to 1960. From 1960 to 1962, she was a staff writer and researcher for the Puerto Rico News Service. In 1962, she became a public affairs officer for the Organization of American States, holding that position until 1980. From 1980 to 1990, she was president of ISLA, Inc. She became president of the Institute for Puerto Rican Affairs in 1988. As a member of the National Conference of Puerto Rican Women from 1972 to 1989, she served as president, secretary, and treasurer in local and national chapters. She has also served on the boards of directors of the National Urban Coalition (1986-1991) and the National Puerto Rican Coalition (1976-1979). Vivó is the author of *The Puerto Ricans: An Annotated Bibliography* (1973) and several other bibliographies.

Vodun: Caribbean religion practiced in Haiti. Vodun combines elements of several religions and is prac-

ticed predominantly in Haiti, where it originated. Vodun, which means "spirit" in the Dahomey (West African) language, is also referred to as voodoo. It was created by black slaves brought from West Africa to Haiti by the French, beginning in the seventeenth century. These slaves practiced their traditional religion in secret. The surrounding influences of Roman Catholicism and indigenous West Indian religion made their mark on the slaves' traditional practices, and the religion expanded to reflect these influences. After the abolition of slavery, the various groups of people practicing vodun merged to form one group. Vodun is characterized by a supreme deity as well as lesser gods called *loa*, who are known by African names and Catholic saints' names. The *loa* may be spirits of natural forces (wind, fire, and water) or spirits of dead ancestors. They act as protectors and guides and are invoked during ceremonies presided over by a priest or priestess. Vodun is similar to SANTERÍA.

Volunteers in Service to America (VISTA): Federal agency. VISTA was created by President Lyndon B. Johnson as part of his War on Poverty program. The

A vodun ceremony at the 1989 Festival of American Folklife. (Smithsonian Institution)

Economic Opportunity Act of 1964 provided for funding of VISTA, an organization that closely resembled the Peace Corps established by President John F. Kennedy. Much as the Peace Corps was entrusted with a mission to improve the conditions of people in foreign countries, VISTA was designed to improve the social and economic conditions of underprivileged citizens of the United States. VISTA provided particular assistance to Mexican Americans and other Latinos struggling to create better lives for themselves. Some VISTA programs were targeted at improving conditions in migrant worker camps, barrios, inner-city schools, and other places important to Latinos.

Voting rights: Fundamental rights allowing citizens to participate in government and to choose representatives. In both the United States and Canada, there has been a continuing enlargement of the voting franchise to include minorities and women in the twentieth century. It was not until 1975, however, that significant protections were extended to U.S. Latinos as a "language minority." Although bilingual ballots and registration drives have made it easier for Latinos to vote, many qualified Latinos do not exercise their voting rights.

U.S. Historical Background. Patriots of the American Revolution emphasized the theme of representation based on free elections. After 1776, the states adopted constitutions that relaxed but did not abolish the existing property and religious requirements for the ballot. The Constitution of 1787 did not guarantee a right to vote and left it to the states to determine voter qualifications.

With the gradual end of property tests as a qualification for voting early in the nineteenth century, most white male citizens over the age of twenty-one became eligible to vote. It was standard practice, however, to deny the ballot to women, Native Americans, and slaves, and often to free blacks in the North. The Seneca Falls Convention of 1848 was denounced as radical when its Declaration of Principles, written by Elizabeth Stanton, urged women to secure "their sacred right to the elective franchise."

With the end of slavery, the FOURTEENTH AMENDMENT (1868) required states to provide "equal protection of the laws" and reduced the number of representatives for states that did not allow all male citizens to vote. The Fifteenth Amendment (1870) mandated that the right to vote not be denied "on account of race, color, or previous condition of servitude," and it authorized Congress to enforce the amendment with appropriate legislation. With the coming of the Jim Crow system after 1877, however, southern states prevented African Americans from voting through a combination of literacy tests, character tests, poll taxes, and intimidation. Some states even passed so-called "grandfather clauses," which exempted those whose ancestors could vote before the Fifteenth Amendment (that is, whites) from taking literacy tests, while requiring African Americans to prove literacy to the satisfaction of white officials.

Before the Civil Rights movement of the 1950's and 1960's, most African Americans in the South were routinely denied the right to vote, and neither Congress nor the federal courts acted to enforce the Fifteenth Amendment or to apply the penalties of the Fourteenth Amendment. Outside the South, subtle means were used to discourage minorities from voting, and everywhere, those who did not speak English were disenfranchised.

Women's Suffrage. The first victory for women's suffrage occurred in 1870, when the Wyoming territorial legislature enacted a law allowing citizens of both sexes to vote. Further progress at the state level, however, was slow. In 1872, Susan Anthony was arrested, convicted, and fined for disobeying a law that made it illegal for women to register to vote. When the Supreme Court ruled in *Minor v. Harpersett* (1875) that the franchise was not guaranteed to all citizens by the Fourteenth Amendment, feminists resolved to win the ballot nationally by amending the Constitution. In 1912, the Progressive Party, led by Theodore Roosevelt, was the first party to endorse such an amendment in its platform. At the state level, women scored a number of successes after 1910. By the election of 1916, they could vote in twelve states, gaining clout that politicians noticed.

During World War I, pressure for a women's suffrage amendment increased. Alice Paul's militant suffragists picketed the White House, while Carrie Catt's more moderate organization held huge parades and established alliances. After Woodrow Wilson finally endorsed the Nineteenth Amendment, Congress voted affirmatively, and the amendment was ratified in 1920. Since then, it has been unconstitutional to deny a citizen the right to vote "on account of sex." The Nineteenth Amendment was popular, and there were no serious efforts to circumvent its application.

African Americans. The realization of Fifteenth Amendment rights for African Americans and other minorities continued to be much more difficult. In 1915, African Americans gained one of their first victories when the Supreme Court ruled in *Guinn v.*

United States that Oklahoma's "grandfather clause" was unconstitutional. This decision, however, had limited impact because southern states, with their single-party systems, discovered that it was easy to disfranchise blacks with the tool of the whites-only primary. Southerners argued that political parties were private organizations whose primaries were not covered by the Fifteenth Amendment. In 1935, the Supreme Court agreed, but nine years later, in the landmark case of *Smith v. Allwright*, the Court reversed itself and ruled that because primaries were an integral part of the elective process, they were subject to the requirements of the amendment.

The Civil Rights movement brought more rapid change. The Civil Rights Act of 1957, among other provisions, allowed for limited federal protection of voters in the South. The Twenty-Fourth Amendment, ratified in 1964, made it illegal to use the poll tax as a requirement for voting. Two years later, the Supreme Court ruled that it was unconstitutional for states to use a poll tax as a condition to vote in state and local elections.

In 1965, after Martin Luther King, Jr., stirred the nation's conscience with the Selma-Montgomery march, President Lyndon B. Johnson asked for strong federal legislation. Congress responded with the landmark VOTING RIGHTS ACT OF 1965, which prohibited literacy tests for five years and authorized federal supervision of elections in states where less than 50 percent of qualified voters were registered (meaning the South). This 1965 law is generally considered the most successful of the civil rights statutes. Within ten years of its passage, elected black officials increased from fewer than 100 to 1,398. The law meant that southern elected officials and candidates no longer could ignore the views of African Americans.

Latinos and Other Minorities. After 1965, the voting rights movement began to have an effect on the Latino community. The Voting Rights Act included a provision designed for Puerto Rico-educated citizens who lived in New York, where they were being denied the right to vote because of an inability to read or write English, even though they were often well informed about public affairs. The relevant section provided that

Beginning in the 1960's, the United States passed numerous laws securing or expanding Latinos' voting rights. (Frances M. Roberts)

Gloria Molina won election to the Los Angeles County Board of Supervisors after disputes concerning district boundaries and accusations of gerrymandering. (AP/Wide World Photos)

persons having a sixth-grade education in an American-flag school, taught in a non-English language, could not be disenfranchised because of any literacy test in English. The Supreme Court recognized the power of Congress to make this provision in *Katzenbach v. Morgan* (1966). After the Commission on Civil Rights concluded that literacy tests had an especially negative impact on African Americans and "persons of Spanish surnames," Congress amended the Voting Rights Act in 1970 to ban literacy tests throughout the nation for five years (*see* Voting Rights Act of 1970). An amendment of 1975 made the ban permanent. The 1975 amendment was of special significance to Latinos because it specified that federal protection applied to "language minorities" as well as to minority races. It also required that bilingual ballots be provided in areas in which language minorities composed at least 5 percent of the population. (*See* Voting Rights Acts of 1975 and 1982.)

The twentieth century expansion of voting rights involved many issues and numerous minorities. The Twenty-third Amendment (1961) allowed citizens in the District of Columbia to vote in presidential elections, and the Twenty-sixth Amendment (1971) stipulated that a citizen eighteen years of age or older could not be denied the vote because of age. Beginning with the watershed case of *Baker v. Carr* (1962), the Supreme Court made a number of legislative reapportionment decisions requiring that state legislatures and other jurisdictions be represented on the basis of "one person, one vote." By the 1980's, the most controversial issue in U.S. voting rights was the dilution of minorities' votes because of the gerrymandering of district lines to favor a certain party or population, as well as the use of at-large voting systems. The Voting Rights Amendment of 1982 prohibited any practice or law that has the result of abridging voter rights, regardless of motive. Based on this law, Court of Appeals Judge Reynaldo Garza ruled in *Velásquez v. City of Abilene* (1984) that a city's at-large voting system diluted the vote of Mexican Americans and African Americans and was an illegal form of discrimination.

Although by the 1990's the right to vote was almost universal, fewer Americans exercised this right than in many democratic countries. This was essentially true of Latinos, who continued to have the lowest rates of voter registration and turnout. In the presidential election of 1988, for example, 59 percent of qualified whites and 52 percent of qualified blacks voted, while only 29 percent of qualified Latinos went to the polls. A number of organizations, such as the Southwest Voter Registration Education Project, continue to address the complex issues involved in low rates of Latino exercise of voting rights. Nevertheless, Latinos were one of the fastest growing groups of elected officials in the late twentieth century. In 1990, thirteen Latinos were elected to Congress, and four thousand other elected officials were Latinos.

Canadian History. In the Canadian system of government, there was no constitutional right to vote until the constitutional reforms of 1982. Until then, each legislative body had discretion in deciding qualifications and was free to exclude classes of citizens.

Property qualifications at both the federal and provincial levels continued until the mid-1880's. Native Americans and citizens of Asian ancestry were the largest ethnic class to experience disenfranchisement. In the first half of the twentieth century, anti-Asian sentiment was especially widespread in British Columbia, and a 1898 law stated that "no Chinaman, Japanese, or Indian" could register to vote. The courts in 1903 upheld this law in *Cunningham v. Tomey Homma*, and citizens of Japanese ancestry were not enfranchised in British Columbia until 1949. The federal government extended the vote to the Inuit in 1950 and to status Indians in 1960. The province of Quebec did not allow nonstatus Indians to vote until 1969.

The feminist struggle for the right to vote in Canada was often parallel to that in the United States. In the latter part of the nineteenth century, there were many suffragist organizations, especially in Toronto, that were in close communication with sister groups in Great Britain and the United States. Nellie McClung was the most famous of the Canadian leaders. Manitoba in 1916 became the first province to enfranchise women, and by 1922 all but two provinces had followed this example. Quebec did not enfranchise women until 1940. In 1918, the Federal Woman's Franchise Act guaranteed women the right to vote in federal elections.

The Canadian Charter of Rights and Freedoms of 1982 proclaims that "every citizen has the right to vote" in both federal and provincial legislatures, but it allows for exceptions that are reasonable and consistent with democratic principles. The few exceptions include those under eighteen years of age and those serving prison terms. With a relatively small Latino population, Canada has not had particular policies directed at their voting rights.

In Canada, a higher percentage of citizens usually exercises voting rights than is true in the United States. In the elections of 1984, for example, 76 percent of qualified voters went to the polls in Canada, while in the United States the comparable figure was only 54 percent.   —*Thomas T. Lewis*

SUGGESTED READINGS:

• Chute, Marchette. *First Liberty: A History of the Right to Vote in America, 1619-1850.* New York: Dutton, 1969. A well-written survey of the legal restraints on voting.

• Claude, Richard. *The Supreme Court and the Electoral Process.* Baltimore: The Johns Hopkins University Press, 1970. Detailed accounts of major Supreme Court decisions. For advanced students.

• Coolidge, Oliva. *Women's Rights: The Suffrage Movement in America.* New York: E. P. Dutton, 1966. An interesting introduction for the middle-school or high-school student.

• Flexner, Eleanor. *Century of Struggle: The Woman's Rights Movement in the United States.* Rev. ed. Cambridge: Harvard University Press, 1975. A scholarly and detailed account of major personalities and organizations, from the efforts of Susan Anthony to the passage of the Nineteenth Amendment.

• Hogg, Peter. *Constitutional Law of Canada.* 3d ed. Scarborough, Ontario, Canada: Carswell, 1992. Useful synthesis of the political system, with a summary of the history of the franchise.

• Kanellos, Nicolás, ed. *The Hispanic-American Almanac.* Detroit: Gale Research, 1993. Includes much material on the political participation of Latinos, with an incisive discussion of the voting issue.

• Lawson, Steven. *Black Ballots: Voting Rights in the South, 1944-1969.* New York: Columbia University Press, 1976. Scholarly study of Jim Crow as it affected the vote, with detailed accounts of the passage of the Civil Rights laws of 1957, 1960, and 1965.

Voting Rights Act of 1965: Civil rights legislation. This landmark federal legislation was designed primarily to ensure that African Americans would be allowed to vote in the South, where discriminatory practices violated their constitutional right to vote. The provisions of this act eventually were extended to help protect the voting rights of Latinos in the United States.

Voting Rights Act of 1970: Amendments to the VOT-ING RIGHTS ACT OF 1965. These amendments helped protect the constitutional right to vote of minority groups. Among other provisions, these amendments eliminated redistricting practices that would dilute the voting strength of Mexican American voters and prevent them from electing representatives from their own communities.

Voting Rights Acts of 1975 and 1982: These two acts extended and strengthened the VOTING RIGHTS ACT OF 1965 following its five-year extension in 1970. The Voting Rights Act of 1965, signed into law by President Lyndon B. Johnson on August 4, 1965, was drafted primarily to ensure the voting rights of African Americans throughout the United States, but particularly in the Deep South, where many of them had been disenfranchised. A major element in Johnson's civil rights program and in his vision for the GREAT SOCIETY, the bill came up for extension in 1970, when it was again passed. It was still aimed essentially at black voters. Important in the original bill was the abolition of poll taxes that kept many impoverished people in the South from voting.

The Voting Rights Act of 1975 not only extended the earlier acts but also added provisions important to non-English speakers, particularly Spanish speakers. The bill reiterated its support of continuing black voting rights in the South and in parts of some other states. It specifically added Texas, because of its large Hispanic population, and Alaska, because of its large Native American population, to its list of states to be directly affected by the bill's provisions.

Further, it added parts of California and Colorado to the states to be carefully monitored, citing large concentrations of non-English-speaking minorities in these states. It provided the mechanism for individual citizens to bring suit against local jurisdictions if their rights were violated. If they prevailed in these suits, the government would pay their legal fees. Finally, it mandated bilingual ballots in areas with large concentrations of voters who communicated primarily in a language other than English, as well as aural assistance for those whose major tongue has no written form.

The 1982 bill was signed into law by President Ronald Reagan on June 29, 1982, and extended the original bill for an additional twenty-five years. Its permanent section abolished such discriminatory practices as literacy tests in all fifty states. The temporary section of the bill required all or parts of twenty-two states to present the federal government with documentary proof of changes in their election policies that would put them in compliance with operative federal voting rights laws.

The thrust of voting rights legislation has been to extend the franchise to every adult citizen of the United States. The first bill in 1965 and the one that followed in 1970 were written with black citizens foremost in mind. The 1975 and 1982 bills, however, are much more inclusive and contain language that specifically includes Hispanic, Asian, Native American, and other non-English-speaking communities.

W

Wage levels. *See* **Income and wage levels**

Wards Cove Packing Co. Inc. v. Atonio (June 5, 1989): Case alleging employment discrimination. This Supreme Court case (490 U.S. 642), decided by Justice Byron White, involved a plaintiff employer who had been sued by former salmon cannery workers. The cannery workers contended without success that the concentration of minority workers in low-skilled jobs proved discrimination under Title VII of the 1964 Civil Rights Act.

The plaintiff owned salmon canneries in Alaska that hired mostly seasonal workers. Minority workers were concentrated in unskilled labor jobs on the cannery lines, while most skilled labor jobs were filled by white workers.

During the salmon season, workers lived on site at the company's Alaska cannery. The company offered separate housing and living arrangements to its unskilled and skilled workers. There was little or no mobility from unskilled labor positions at the company to skilled labor positions.

Based on these facts, minority workers found evidence that company policy had a disparate impact on them. The Court, however, did not consider mere racial imbalance between a group of skilled workers and a group of unskilled workers evidence of disparate impact. The Court recognized that the pool of available workers and its composition had to be considered.

Justice White set difficult standards for the minority employees to meet. He held that even if minority workers successfully proved disparate impact, the company could defeat their claims by a business necessity defense. In order to defeat employer claims of business necessity for practices challenged as having a disparate impact on minorities, workers had to consider the rationale the employer offered to defend challenged policies and prove the reasonable availability of alternative practices to achieve the same business ends with less racial impact.

Justice White, known for his relatively conservative approach to judicial activism, contended that the judiciary should proceed with caution before ordering an employer to adopt the selection or hiring practices proposed by plaintiffs in an AFFIRMATIVE ACTION lawsuit based on Title VII. Although he remanded the case to lower courts for further consideration and left some openings for affirmative action advocates to seek redress against Wards Cove Packing Company, Justice White handed the company a significant victory in this case.

The more liberal members of the Court issued a vigorous dissent. Justices Harry Blackmun, William Brennan, and Thurgood Marshall showed alarm at what they saw as Justice White's retreat from established civil rights principles in this case. They complained that Justice White had upset "the longstanding distribution of burdens of proof in Title VII disparate impact cases." Justice John Paul Stevens also issued a lengthy dissent that stressed that the case had changed the burden of proof and the weight of the parties' burdens in disparate impact affirmative action cases.

This case represented a significant defeat for proponents of affirmative action in disparate impact cases falling under Title VII of the CIVIL RIGHTS ACT OF 1964. The Civil Rights Act of 1991 shifted the burden of proof back to employers, who had to defend any business practices alleged to be discriminatory. The act made it easier for employees to win discrimination suits.

Washington, D.C. (incorporated 1802): Capital city of the United States. The Latino population in Washington, D.C., increased by 85 percent between 1980 and 1990, according to census data. The 1990 figure for the metropolitan statistical area including the city was 224,786.

The Latino community in the United States' capital grew steadily after 1980. Officially, the 1990 census recognized approximately thirty-three thousand Latinos in Washington, D.C. The Mayor's Office on Latino Affairs, however, used a higher estimate of sixty-five thousand. The larger estimate was based on such figures as school enrollment. Unlike the national Hispanic population, which was dominated numerically by Mexicans, Puerto Ricans, and Cubans, approximately 80 percent of Washington's Latinos were Central Americans.

The political turmoil in El Salvador throughout the 1980's caused the northward migration of countless Salvadorans (*see* SALVADORAN AMERICANS). At the same time, Washington, D.C., saw a period of economic growth. A flourishing construction industry, as well as employment opportunities in hotels, restaurants, and office building maintenance, attracted a growing number of Salvadorans. The Latino community was concentrated primarily in the neighborhoods of Mount Pleasant, Adams-Morgan, and Columbia Heights.

The Census Bureau generally did not track specific countries of origin for Washington's Latino community, but data from the U.S. IMMIGRATION AND NATURALIZATION SERVICE (INS) showed that in 1990 Salvadorans dominated Latino immigration to that city. The next largest groups reported that year were Dominicans, Guatemalans, and Nicaraguans.

Immigration legislation passed in 1986 and 1990 had a major impact on Washington's Latinos. The IMMIGRATION REFORM AND CONTROL ACT OF 1986 awarded legal status to many undocumented immigrants who could prove they had entered the United States before 1982 and maintained residence. It also imposed sanctions on any employer who knowingly hired an undocumented immigrant. In 1990, Section 303 of the Immigration Act created temporary protected status for refugees from El Salvador for an eighteen-month period. The INS reported that by mid-1991, the Washington, D.C., metropolitan area had one of the highest concentrations of those registering under Section 303.

LATINO POPULATION OF WASHINGTON, D.C., 1990

Total number of Latinos = 224,786; 5.7% of population

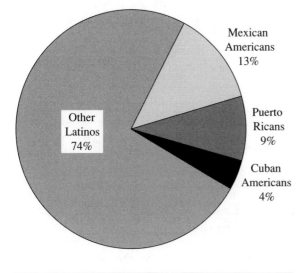

Other Latinos 74%

Mexican Americans 13%

Puerto Ricans 9%

Cuban Americans 4%

Source: Data are from Marlita A. Reddy, ed., *Statistical Record of Hispanic Americans* (Detroit: Gale Research, 1993), Table 111.
Note: Figures represent the population of the Metropolitan Statistical Area as delineated by the U.S. Bureau of the Census.

In May, 1991, civil disturbances later called the MOUNT PLEASANT RIOTS broke out in the Washington Latino community. The D.C. Latino Civil Rights Task Force was organized in response to the unrest. It reported that the arrest and subsequent shooting of a Latino by a district police officer in Mount Pleasant had sparked the rioting. The symptoms of growing frustration, however, had been reported as early as 1985. Latino community leaders formed an ad hoc coalition and presented "The Latino Community Agenda" to local government officials. Specific recommendations to rectify socioeconomic problems were acknowledged but not fully addressed.

In January, 1993, after three days of public hearings, the U.S. Commission on Civil Rights issued its findings on civil rights issues underlying the May, 1991, disturbances. The commission concluded that a pattern of police misconduct had existed in the Latino neighborhoods and that the lack of Latinos in city government had resulted in less city services for that community.

Washington's Latinos were hit hard by the economic recession of the late 1980's. City officials reported that the poverty rate for district Latinos in the early 1990's was 35 percent and that Latinos were more likely to be poor than members of any other racial or ethnic group in Washington. The success of Latino activists in conveying the urgency of the community's concerns with city government to the U.S. Civil Rights Commission revealed a growing sophistication within their community.

Welch, Raquel (Raquel Tejada; b. Sept. 5, 1940, Chicago, Ill.): Actress. The daughter of a Bolivian American father and an English mother, Welch studied ballet as a child and was a teenage beauty queen. She married James Welch at the age of eighteen and had two children before leaving the marriage to attend San Diego State University and pursue a film career in Los Angeles.

As the result of a 1963 publicity tour that she devised with her manager and second husband, Patrick Curtis, Welch became a popular entertainment figure before she had given a major film performance. In the following years, her sensuous performances in *A Swingin' Summer* (1965), *Fantastic Voyage* (1966), and *One Million Years B.C.* (1966) helped to establish her as a leading film personality and legendary sex symbol. Welch's numerous other film credits include *Bandolero!* (1968), *The Biggest Bundle of Them All* (1968), *One Hundred Rifles* (1969), *Myra Breckenridge* (1970), *Bluebeard* (1972), *Fuzz* (1972), *Kansas*

Raquel Welch. (AP/Wide World Photos)

City Bomber (1972), *The Three Musketeers* (1974), *The Wild Party* (1974), *Mother, Jugs, and Speed* (1977), and *The Prince and the Pauper* (1977). Welch has also appeared on numerous television programs and has hosted her own television specials. In 1981, she made her Broadway debut in the title role of *Woman of the Year*.

Wetback: Derogatory term for Mexican immigrants. The term refers to someone who crosses the border from Mexico to the United States without going through the proper legal procedures. The literal meaning of the term derives from the experience of many Mexican immigrants who crossed the Rio Grande to avoid the monitored points of entry into the United States. Many Americans came to use the derogatory term in reference to all Mexican people who had recently arrived or who retained some of the customs of Mexico. The United States government made it an official part of the American lexicon in the late 1940's

and early 1950's, most obviously with implementation of "OPERATION WETBACK" in 1954. This was an IMMIGRATION AND NATURALIZATION SERVICE program that aimed to separate "legal," temporary Mexican immigrant workers from "illegal aliens."

White card: Form I-186, issued by the IMMIGRATION AND NATURALIZATION SERVICE. This form allows a foreigner into the United States for a maximum of three days for business or recreation. Holders of white cards must remain within twenty-five miles of the border. Despite the fact that employment violates the regulations associated with Form I-186, many Latinos use the form to aid in commuting from Mexico to jobs in the United States.

White House Conference on Hispanic Affairs (August, 1977): Conference of Hispanic leaders regarding immigration laws. President Jimmy Carter met in Washington, D.C., with leaders of Latino civil rights groups to discuss proposals for solving problems associated with undocumented workers, particularly the estimated five to six million Mexicans working in the United States without proper authorization. Carter proposed AMNESTY for all illegal residents. Conference delegates supported the president's call for severe penalties against employers who knowingly hired undocumented workers.

Economic assistance to the Mexican government was also discussed and approved at the meeting. The money would be used for job training programs in Mexico and for economic development as a means of easing the flow of unemployed, impoverished, and uneducated Mexican agricultural laborers across the border into the United States. Carter presented these proposals to Congress, but legislation putting these ideas into effect was not passed until the IMMIGRATION REFORM AND CONTROL ACT OF 1986.

Wickersham Commission Report: The published results of a two-year federal investigation into crime and the effectiveness of law enforcement in the United States. In 1929, President Herbert Hoover appointed former U.S. attorney general George Woodward Wickersham to the chair of the National Commission on Law Observance and Enforcement, widely known as the Wickersham Commission. Over a two-year period (1929-1931), the commission issued fourteen separate reports, each one providing an in-depth analysis of the commission of crime and the effectiveness of law enforcement.

The term "wetback" refers most specifically to Mexicans who cross the U.S.-Mexico border without proper authorization.
(AP/Wide World Photos)

The final report, issued by the commission in 1931, studied the involvement of foreign-born Americans in criminal activity. The report found that contrary to popular opinion, the foreign-born, in proportion to their respective numbers, committed significantly fewer crimes than the native-born. This finding was an important victory for foreign-born people residing in the United States.

At the heart of the report was a detailed statistical table, broken down by country of birth, showing the number of adult persons per 100,000 arrested in the state of New York in 1929 for a criminal offense. The analysis led to three conclusions: in proportion to their numbers, the foreign-born committed considerably fewer crimes than the native-born; the foreign-born approached the rate of the native-born in the commission of crimes involving personal violence; and in crimes of gain, such as theft, the native-born were overwhelmingly the perpetrators.

The report also found that the erroneous and widespread belief that foreign-born people were responsible for the preponderance of crime in America was a misconception almost as old as the country itself. Language barriers and cultural differences contributed to the problem, as each new wave of immigrants was accused of criminal wrongdoing by the preceding generations of immigrants.

Appended to the report were detailed studies on crime and criminal justice with respect to Mexican immigrants in the United States, as well as community studies of crime and the foreign-born in New Orleans. Both studies led to the same conclusion: The foreign-born had been unjustly charged with a disproportionate share of crime. The study of Mexican immigrants found that the statistical record of law violations was influenced by racial antipathy. This factor, along with the political and economic helplessness of Mexican immigrants, largely accounted for the fact that Mexicans were arrested far more often for trivial crimes and were detained in jail for longer periods than were native-born whites. Once in court, Mexicans routinely appeared without appropriate counsel, interpreters, or witnesses.

The report exonerated foreign-born Americans who previously had been identified in the public's mind with excessive criminality. It brought the plight of Mexican immigrants to the public's attention, exposing the racism and lack of due legal process to which they had been systematically subjected. Perhaps most significant, it quelled a longstanding, contentious debate over immigration policy in the United States. No longer could opponents of immigration policy cite an increase in criminal activity as a reason to keep immigrants out of the United States. Future policy would have to be determined by more general social and economic conditions.

Widowhood: Status of women whose husbands have died and who have not remarried. Few written accounts exist regarding Latina widows. Oral histories, census records, and cross-cultural comparisons have been used to piece together their history in the United States. Some data are available about women who emigrated north from Mexico in the nineteenth century, and their experiences may be in some ways generalizable to other Latina groups.

The role of widows in the Latino culture is affected by GENDER ROLES and such cultural scripts as familism (the central and strong role of family in Latino life) and respect for elders. A Latina's role as the center of her family continues throughout her life, and the respect that younger family members owe elders within a closely knit, interdependent family system provides a clear place for widows. In the early part of the twentieth century, it was usual that when the husband died, a Latina widow would assume headship of her family, and she seldom remarried. As did many families in the Southwest, Mexican American families usually had small "truck farms" and regularly canned and dried produce for their families. Women did most of the nonfield work; widows simply continued to care for their families in this manner. As a result of economic necessity, however, many of them were forced to obtain additional jobs as launderers, seamstresses, and domestic workers.

The Catholic church offered spiritual support for widows, aiding the natural process of grieving and loss. Many rituals and customs were attached to widowhood. For example, a woman was required to wear black for a year after her husband's death. Latina widows were not supposed to socialize overtly, attend parties, or dance for a year, though they could visit family members, friends, and neighbors. The husband's funeral was of special importance to the widow, who found solace in the quality of the relationships surrounding the event. The widow was not alone but instead part of a strong network of family, friends, and clergy. If a widow and her family were left in difficult financial circumstances, the *COMPADRES* (children's godparents) were often a source of aid and support for the godchild. Widowed Latinas often lived near their children and grandchildren, and the interdependence of the extended family provided a continued function

The extended family structure maintains a place for Latinas who become widows. (James Shaffer)

and role for elderly widows. Among younger widows with children to support, the woman's burden became greater at the death of her husband. Despite the support offered by the extended family, many young widows were forced to seek work or find ways to add to the family income. Thus cultural values, customs, experience, and socially defined roles provided personal resources, and the extended family played a central role in widows' support network.

Traditional rural support systems have become weaker as Latinos have migrated into cities. Widows still often live with family members and provide emotional and practical support to younger relatives. Urban Latina widows, however, are faced with many of the problems confronted by urban elders of any ethnic group, including fixed incomes, limited access to resources and services, and health problems. In many cases, as a result of their minority-group status and incomplete acculturation to U.S. society, Latina widows face additional challenges of living in communities in which their values and customs are neither understood nor appreciated.

Witches and witchcraft: The practitioners and practice of magic and sorcery. Traditionally, most witches have been women. Frequently they are believed to have supernatural powers and to be aided by spirits. In Latino communities, they are referred to as BRUJOS (male) and *brujas* (female) or as *hechiceros* and *hechiceras*.

Almost all cultures have references to witches and witchcraft. This practice is often related to healing, particularly the dark side of healing. Witchcraft in Latino communities within the United States has roots in traditions from both Europe and the Americas. In Spain and Latin America, *brujos* or *brujas* have been those who could bewitch or enchant. Often they were also native folk health practitioners (empirics or *curanderos*). They were considered to be magical healers, including astrologers and necromantic conjurers who used magico-religious cures or were familiar with the occult or so-called "black arts." Practitioners of *brujería* were persecuted by the Catholic church for what it considered to be heretical practices.

In many Latino communities, *brujos* or *brujas* are believed to have the ability to cause physical sickness. A *curandero* who does evil is often considered to be a *brujo*. *Brujos* are purported to use their knowledge to harm others or bring about evil consequences such as impotency or infertility. They are said to be able to cause such folk illnesses as *mal de ojo* (evil eye); cause people to do things that they would not normally do,

such as fall in love and leave their spouses and families; and inflict possession by the devil or other evil spirits. In some Latino traditions of curing, bewitchment was believed to be the only reason a patient did not improve after a *curandero*'s treatment.

Historically, *brujas* have also been accused of kidnapping and harming children and of killing animals. In order to be cured of evil or physical illness caused by a spell, one must go to a *curandero* who can remove the spell. There are as many ways of treating the effects of bewitchment as there are ways to bewitch. *Brujos* or *brujas* use herbal treatments, amulets, potions, oils, religious objects, and charms in their practices. Many of the tools of their trade can be found in *yerberías* or BOTÁNICAS (Latino herb shops), which also sell other magico-religious products. According to some Hispanic beliefs, most *brujas* take up witchcraft voluntarily.

Witches and witchcraft persist in Latino communities because they are part of a related folk complex associated with CURANDERISMO and because they serve various societal functions. They relieve individuals of responsibility for some illnesses, and they create the belief that something can be done about mysterious and unexplained illness.

Women's suffrage: Right of women to vote in elections. Despite their current and past participation in many aspects of society and their role as rulers of some countries, women historically were excluded from the voting process. In the United States, some women who were taxpayers and "free-born" had VOTING RIGHTS under colonial law, but this right was revoked in all colonies by 1807. Changing social conditions during the 1830's, including the antislavery and temperance movements, served as vehicles through which women began to demand their right to vote.

The first woman suffrage convention met in Seneca Falls, New York, in 1848. In the following decades, women organized into suffrage associations in an effort to persuade individual states to grant the vote to women. In 1869, the territorial legislature of Wyoming was the first to grant women the right to vote. Beginning in the 1890's, several states followed suit, and in 1920 the Nineteenth Amendment was added to the U.S. Constitution, giving women the right to vote.

Several countries had given women the vote before World War I, and many others did so immediately after the war. In the 1930's several more countries (including Cuba) had woman suffrage, and by 1975 only eight nations in the world did not allow women to vote.

Increasing participation by women in the electoral process has helped women gain election to office. (AP/Wide World Photos)

With the exception of Puerto Rican women, who are U.S. citizens, Latinas' suffrage, like that of their male Latino counterparts, is directly affected by citizenship status, as only United States citizens have the right to vote. For immigrants, gaining U.S. citizenship means giving up the citizenship of birth, something that carries both functional and psychological effects. Once Latinas gain U.S. citizenship (usually as the second generation of immigrants, or children of immigrants), they often enter the electoral process through school board elections. It appears that women's traditional interest in the well-being of their family translates into POLITICAL ACTIVISM to improve children's educational opportunities.

Latinos as a whole vote to a lesser extent than either non-Latino whites or African Americans. Latinas, however, have consistently voted in higher numbers than Latino men. This is perhaps a reflection of Latinas' efforts at the forefront of their communities' activities to secure better living conditions, access to services, and other social goods. In the traditional Latino family structure, the man's role as sole financial provider for

his family has at times freed the woman to engage in activities that will ultimately affect the family and community.

A natural extension of the right to vote is the right to run for public office. Latinas are slowly making inroads as elected officials at different levels of government, particularly in states in which there are large concentrations of Latinos, such as California, Texas, Florida, and New Jersey. Latina political candidates have often had to contend with traditional views regarding gender roles as well as the perception that a woman's political activity will detract from what should be her most important focus: the family. Furthermore, Latino society still sees political leadership as something appropriate for men rather than women. It remains to be seen if Latinas' higher rates of voting will have an impact on the number of Latinas elected to public office.

Works Progress Administration (WPA): U.S. national project to provide employment during the Depression. When the Great DEPRESSION ravaged the United States in the early 1930's, Congress created the WPA as a means to provide jobs to destitute citizens. In 1937, Congress removed noncitizens from eligibility for WPA programs. This decision had a disproportionate impact on Latinos.

The WPA funded public works programs, providing jobs for construction workers, as well as arts programs. The CENTRO ASTURIANO, a mutual aid society with a theater group, joined the WPA's theater project as its only Hispanic unit.

X

Ximenes, Vicente Treviño (b. Dec. 5, 1919, Floresville, Tex.): Government official. Ximenes attended the University of Texas at Austin and was graduated from the University of New Mexico in 1950. He earned his master's degree two years later.

Ximenes began his career in 1939 as a clerk for the Civil Conservation Corps. He worked for the University of New Mexico from 1952 to 1960. With President John F. Kennedy's New Frontier, Ximenes went to work for the United States Agency for International Development, as an economist, in Ecuador from 1961 to 1964. He began a period of political organizing in 1964 by working for the Democratic National Committee as the Viva Johnson campaign director. In 1965, Ximenes returned to the Agency for International Development as the deputy director in Panama. He served as President Lyndon B. Johnson's cabinet committee chairman for Mexican American affairs in 1967 and 1968. Ximenes also served as a commissioner on the Equal Employment Opportunity Commission from 1967 to 1977. He was the first Mexican American on that commission.

Y

Yakima Valley, Washington: The Yakima Valley, in south-central Washington, has a strong economic base in agriculture. Agricultural work attracted a large Latino population.

The history of the Yakima Valley follows that of much of the northwestern United States, and the history of the Latino population is the history of field workers. Before 1943, a small number of Mexican laborers traveled into the valley each year to harvest crops. They were encouraged to come to the area by Washington labor contractors working in the Southwest.

The valley was attractive to workers because of the diversity of crops, nourished by irrigation. The valley offered work from the first spring pickings of asparagus, through the various fruits and vegetables of summer, and into the fall harvest of hops, grapes, and apples. Many of the crops of the valley, such as grapes and hops, require much hand labor in both cultivation and harvest.

With the onset of World War II came internment of the local Japanese population, many of whom had been field laborers. The shortage of field workers in the valley was crippling. The BRACERO PROGRAM, devised by the United States government in cooperation with the nation of Mexico, allowed families of workers from Mexico to legally come to the valley for seasonal work. In the early 1980's, long after the end of the Bracero Program, the Utah and Idaho sugar plant came to the valley, adding to the need for field workers.

Because of the long seasons of work, some migrant workers eventually settled. Others continued to work the migrant circuit. Among those who settled, some eventually became landowners and merchants. A more stable lifestyle enabled the children to attend school regularly, leading them out of field work as an occupation.

Yakima Valley is defined roughly as beginning to the north of the city of Yakima, following the Yakima

LATINO POPULATION OF YAKIMA, WASHINGTON, 1990

Total number of Latinos = 45,114; 24% of population

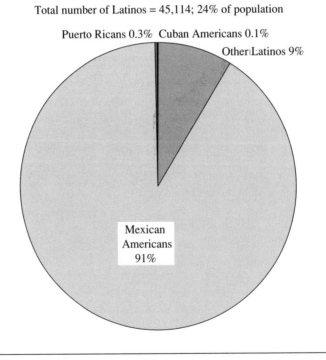

Puerto Ricans 0.3% Cuban Americans 0.1%

Other Latinos 9%

Mexican Americans 91%

Source: Data are from Marlita A. Reddy, ed., *Statistical Record of Hispanic Americans* (Detroit: Gale Research, 1993), Table 111.

Note: Figures represent the population of the Metropolitan Statistical Area as delineated by the U.S. Bureau of the Census. Percentages are rounded to the nearest whole number except for Cuban Americans and Puerto Ricans, for whom rounding is to the nearest 0.1%.

River down through Toppenish and Granger to its lower end around Grandview and Mabton. Most of the valley's Latino population in the early 1990's was located in the Lower Valley, south of the cities of Yakima and Union Gap. Even in the Lower Valley, variation occurred. For example, the towns of Sunnyside and Grandview were predominantly Latino, but the town of Zillah was more than 90 percent of Anglo descent. Mabton was 90 percent Latino. During the 1960's, Yakima Valley received an influx of refugees from Cuba, adding a new dimension to the Latino population.

Many dialects of the Spanish language are common in the valley, and these are spoken as frequently in everyday society as is English. A number of Latino festivals, especially those with Mexican origins, are held in towns throughout the valley. CINCO DE MAYO is a popular festival among both the Latino and Anglo populations. The town of Granger annually celebrates Charro Days, observing Mexico's independence from Spain.

Yañez, Agustín (May 4, 1904, Guadalajara, Mexico—Jan. 17, 1980, Mexico City, Mexico): Writer. The son of Elpidio Yañez and Maria Santos Delgadillo, Yañez learned to read before he enrolled in the second grade. In the third grade, he became a voracious reader. When he was almost nine years old, Yañez created a newspaper on notebook paper and issued it monthly.

In 1929, Yañez was graduated from the Law School of Guadalajara. During his lifetime, he held many positions in the fields of education, government, and publishing. He was the government's secretary of public education and from 1953 to 1959 served as governor of the state of Jalisco. He also served as editor of various journals of literature, philosophy, and history.

His major publications include *Genio y figuras de Guadalajara* (1941) and *Flor de juegos antiguos* (1941), two short narratives about Guadalajara; *Archipiélago de mujeres* (1943), a collection of short stories; and *Al filo del agua* (1947; *The Edge of the Storm*, 1963), a novel set against the backdrop of the MEXICAN REVOLUTION. Yañez's ultimate desire was to create a portrait of Mexico's problems in a musical prose that some have called baroque.

Ybor City, Florida: Ybor City, a unique community northwest of downtown TAMPA, FLORIDA, was the brainchild of Don Vicente MARTÍNEZ YBOR, a Cuban expatriate and prominent cigar manufacturer. Near the end of the nineteenth century, Martínez Ybor selected a site along the insect-infested land on the Gulf Coast and built a company town that would eventually attract thousands of workers and residents.

Martínez Ybor's search for an undeveloped site had taken him far afield. Key West was ruled out because of the presence of labor unions. Other U.S. cities lacked a warm climate and were too far away from shipping or other transportation facilities to be practical. Eventually, two of Martínez Ybor's friends stumbled on a suitable location as they searched unsuccessfully for guava groves in the undeveloped land north of Tampa. Martínez Ybor purchased forty acres from the city of Tampa and began building in 1885.

In 1886, Ybor City was complete, and the first cigar factory opened. This facility, the largest of its kind in the world, employed more than four thousand people at the peak of its production. Other factories followed, most of them smaller, independent enterprises hoping to mimic Martínez Ybor's operation. None matched his success. (*See* CIGAR MANUFACTURING.)

Hand-rolled cigars were extremely popular in the late 1800's. They were expensive to buy and extremely profitable to produce. Martínez Ybor and his associates could afford to pay good wages, and the company town and its multiethnic residents prospered.

The face of Ybor City was primarily Hispanic, but non-Hispanics such as Italians, Germans, and Jews from Eastern and Central Europe would ultimately settle there as well. They were attracted by good jobs, the pleasant climate, and the city's quirky, independent personality. Newspapers were available in Spanish, English, Italian, and German. Hospitals, restaurants, social clubs, and mutual aid societies catered to the physical and emotional needs of the new arrivals. Hospitals were among the first in the United States to be run as cooperatives.

As the factories increased production, Tampa became the cigar capital of the world. Seven hundred million cigars were produced annually. The people who made the cigars called themselves TABAQUEROS. They were not exclusively of Cuban descent; many were Spanish or Italian. They shared proficiency in the craft of cigar making and a unique subculture. Most were marginally literate but politically conversant despite a lack of formal education. The factories took a special interest in educating their personnel. Employees known as *lectores* read aloud to other workers, enhancing basic understanding of international affairs, classical philosophy, and literature.

The heart of *tabaquero* culture was Seventh Avenue, also known as La Septima Avenida. Along it could be found the shops, clubhouses, ballrooms, casinos, and speakeasies that for many visitors characterized this distinctive community. La Septima Avenida's carnival atmosphere peaked in the 1920's. The area's vitality persisted even after most of the cigar factories closed in the 1930's and did not fully decline until the 1950's.

Yerbero: Healer who specializes in curative plants and practices used in spiritual healing. A *yerbero* (herbalist) has knowledge of the use of herbs for curative and spiritual healing. Herbal remedies are usually administered in the form of baths, perfumes, or poultices, or through magical rites and practices. The *yerbero* is a key member of communities whose religious practices derive from African and indigenous sources. In the Mexican American, Caribbean, and Latin American communities of the United States, the *yerbero* usually works from a BOTÁNICA, a store where one finds herbs as well as amulets, prayers, saint figurines, candles, and other magical and SANTERÍA objects.

Young Lords: Puerto Rican young people's political organization. The Young Lords formed in 1970, primarily in response to police harassment. The New York chapter subsequently formed the Young Lords Party, which sought to unify the Puerto Rican community in the continental United States by bringing attention to and helping to remedy local problems.

In the late 1960's, a Puerto Rican street gang in Chicago called the Young Lords organized to combat police harassment. The Young Lords Organization elected a chairperson, Cha Cha Jiménez, and a central committee. The organization set up an office to redress community grievances. Its activities included gang warfare mediation, political education, Puerto Rican history instruction, breakfast and health programs, and a newspaper.

In New York City, several groups, such as Sociedad Albizu Campos and Puerto Rican college student organizations, agreed to merge under the Young Lords Organization. The leadership consisted of Felipe Luciano, Pablo "Yoruba" Guzmán, Juan GONZÁLEZ,

A botánica *will stock various objects used in religious practices as well as some of the herbs employed by* yerberos. (Impact Visuals, Allan Clear)

David Pérez, and Juan "Fi" Ortíz. They set up an office on 112th Street and Madison Avenue in El Barrio.

One of the Young Lords Organization's first projects in New York in 1969 was the Garbage Offensive. Members built road blockades with piled-up garbage and disrupted traffic to force the city to attend to the poor sanitary conditions of the community. They had physical confrontations with the police but adhered to a no-guns policy.

The second offensive occurred in January of 1970, when the group occupied the First Spanish Methodist Church for eleven days and declared it as the People's Church. They set up food programs, collected clothing, offered classes, and provided poetry readings, music, and films. Community people set up all-night vigils to keep the police from arresting the Young Lords Organization members. Three thousand people participated in the programs.

The third offensive involved the occupation of an abandoned building of Lincoln Hospital in the Bronx in July of 1970. The Young Lords Organization offered tests for tuberculosis and lead poisoning and set up a day care center.

By this time, the New York Young Lords Organization had its own radio program on WBAI-FM and a biweekly newspaper, both titled *Palante* (forward). Meanwhile, the New York-East Coast Young Lords Organization broke from the Chicago organization to form its own party with a political platform advocating self-determination for Puerto Rico.

A turning point for the Young Lords Party came when a member, Julio Roldán, was arrested for burning garbage, was taken to the Manhattan Men's Prison, and died of strangulation in what the police stated was a suicide. The community believed otherwise. A funeral march of eight thousand people was organized, and the party declared a second People's Church, this time announcing intent to bear arms in defense.

By 1973, the Young Lords Party had become the Puerto Rican Revolutionary Workers Organization. Its members stirred up a sense of nationalism and pride among mainland Puerto Ricans and strengthened ties between the island and mainland communities.

Youth: Adolescence is a time of excitement and anxiety, of discovery and bewilderment, and of breaks with the past and continuations of childhood behavior. It can be a confusing time for the young people experiencing this phase of life as well as for their parents and other adults charged with enhancing youth development, such as teachers or counselors.

Latino youth can be especially troubled by adolescence because of the survival challenges faced by many of their families, the tensions between their families' values and those of the mainstream society, and the lack of strong social institutions and role models to help them through this difficult phase.

Youth at Risk. Throughout the world, the 1980's was a period of increasing risk for young people. In the United States, the phasing out of many social programs, the rise of single-parent families, and the spread of homelessness contributed to a startling new statistic: People under the age of eighteen had become 40 percent of the nation's poor by 1990. About 26 percent of school-age Latinos were poor in 1989, compared to 13 percent of non-Latinos.

This shift was accompanied by changes in youth behavior. Although American young people were not generally exceeding previous levels of substance abuse, they were using more cocaine, a drug strongly associated with street crime in inner-city areas. GANGS, which have long been a characteristic of barrio communities, were becoming more widespread and more violent, with younger recruits. In the state of California, Latinos accounted for one-third of all youth homicides in 1987. Teenage pregnancy was also on the rise among Latinas.

Education is perhaps the clearest area of risk in the lives of young Latinos, who remain the least educated Americans (*see* DROPOUTS AND DROPOUT RATES; EDUCATION AND ACADEMIC ACHIEVEMENT). Rates of high school completion for Latinos improved overall in the period between 1970 and 1990. In 1970, only three in ten Latino adults twenty-five years old or older had completed four years of high school. In 1980, this figure had risen to four in ten, and in 1990, it was nearly five in ten. Despite these advances, the Latino dropout rate of 35 percent in 1991 was high when compared to those of other American racial and ethnic groups. This fact creates the perception that mainstream social institutions have "given up" on Latino youth.

A 1988 U.S. Department of Education study of educational risk factors for eighth graders is suggestive of the problems faced by Latino youth. About one-fourth of Latino eighth graders lived with single parents, and one-third of their parents lacked high school diplomas. Of the students surveyed, 38 percent came from families with incomes of less than $15,000. Nine percent spoke only limited English, and 16 percent had brothers or sisters who had dropped out of school. Although 30 percent of the Latino students sampled had none of these risk factors that might inhibit their educational

Gangs pose an increasing threat to Latino youth. (AP/Wide World Photos)

success, by comparison 53 percent of all students were risk-free. About 23 percent of Latino students had two risk factors, and 16 percent had three or more, compared to 14 percent and 7 percent, respectively, among all students and 26 percent and 17 percent, respectively, for African American students.

The Family. In most Latino communities, the family is the main social institution influencing the social, emotional, and identity development of adolescents. The family, however, is losing some of its traditional influence as generations of Latinos acculturate to the dominant American culture and undergo continued socioeconomic stress. For example, Latinos influenced by American youth culture are more likely to want some independence from, rather than having respect for, the authority of their elders. Young Latinas in particular may expect more freedom in dating and decision making than their traditional parents are willing to allow.

Many Latino youth feel caught between the expectations of two cultures. Although 70 percent of those between the ages of fifteen and nineteen in 1990 were native-born, 72 percent of those who were foreign-born had immigrated between 1980 and 1990. These new immigrants and those reared in traditional immigrant families are generally far more exposed to the dominant culture in the United States than their parents, yet they are still expected to abide by traditional norms at home. They have to reconcile their love for family with their ambitions to take their place in the larger society. Some also take on the role of intermediary for their relatives who are less fluent in English or less familiar with American systems. This is all part of the unique struggle of Latino youth to form their own identities.

Identity Issues. Adolescence can be a time of life with mixed blessings. It is a period when excessive social problems surface, but young people are resilient and most of them can successfully meet the challenges of this transition period. They can understand and integrate the biological, cognitive, emotional, and social changes they are experiencing and form a useful (if sometimes temporary) self-definition. This sense of self, or identity, allows young people to make decisions about and commitments to educational paths, careers, and other people.

A major task of the adolescent years is this formation of individual identity. For minority adolescents, this period of life may be especially difficult and confusing. Researchers note that minority adolescents are faced with, and presumably are conscious of, prejudicial attitudes and discriminatory practices directed against themselves, their peers, and their families. Some Latino youth may engage in risk behaviors such as drug or alcohol use, early sexual activity, or delinquent activities as a way of acting out their struggles to overcome their issues of individuality. They may see such behavior as the only way to survive in tough barrios.

Latino adolescents receive conflicting messages about themselves, their families, their cultures, and their chances for success. The mainstream society implies that they cannot succeed unless they abandon their traditional values, beliefs, and attitudes. Family and cultural norms encourage achievement in terms of helping the family rather than individual achievement per se. Schools often perpetuate youths' low self-esteem with low expectations of them or contribute to identity confusion in their efforts to help Latino youth "move beyond" their current abilities and background. The film *Stand and Deliver* (1988), based on real events in a Los Angeles high school, showed the difference that the caring, confidence, and high standards of a Jaime ESCALANTE, a dedicated Latino teacher, made in the achievement of his students.

Reducing the inequality between Latinos and non-Latinos is vital to the health of American society, particularly because Latinos are a growing proportion of the U.S. population. In order for Latino youth to take

Latino youth face pressures to conform to traditional roles rather than finding their own identities. (James Shaffer)

their responsible places in society, a holistic approach is needed. Effective programs must be based on a clear understanding of Latino adolescents' unique place in modern American society, including their history and their socioeconomic, cultural, and linguistic needs.

—Francisco A. Villarruel, Manuel Chavez,
and Gloria Gonzalez-Kruger

SUGGESTED READINGS: • Hernandez, Donald J. *America's Children: Resources from Family, Government, and the Economy*. New York: Russell Sage Foundation, 1993. • Martinez, Ruben, and R. L. Dukes. "Race, Gender, and Self-Esteem Among Youth." *Hispanic Journal of Behavioral Sciences* 9 (December, 1987): 427-443. • Moll, Luis C., ed. *Vygotsky and Education*. Cambridge, England: Cambridge University Press, 1990. • Moll, Luis C., and J. Greenberg. "Creating Zones of Possibilities: Combining Social Contests for Instruction." In *Vygotsky and Education*, edited by Luis C. Moll. Cambridge, England: Cambridge University Press, 1990. • Spencer, Margaret B., and Carol Markstrom-Adams. "Identity Processes Among Racial and Ethnic Minority Children in America." *Child Development* 61 (April, 1990): 290-310. • Spencer, M. B. "Identity, Minority Development of." In *Encyclopedia of Adolescence*, edited by Richard Lerner, Anne C. Peterson, and Jeanne Brooks-Gunn. New York: Garland, 1991. • Spencer, M. B., and S. Dornbusch. "Challenges in Studying Minority Adolescents." In *At the Threshold: The Developing Adolescent*, edited by Shirley Feldman and Glen R. Elliott. Cambridge, Mass.: Harvard University Press, 1990. • U.S. Bureau of the Census. *Hispanic Americans Today*. Washington, D.C.: Government Printing Office, 1993.

Z

Zambos: People of mixed African and indigenous blood. In early Spanish colonial times, a zambo was the offspring of one indigenous and one black parent. Zambos were on the bottom of the social hierarchy. Some were slaves; others were considered free but were forced to live with an employer and pay him, with violation punished by forced labor in public works or mines.

Zambrano, Sergio: Artist. Zambrano is a Mexican American muralist working from Chicago, Illinois. He worked on the mile-long mural story on the walls on West Hubbard Street in Chicago. He also painted with José G. González, José Maldonado, Nancy Marrero, Gloria SOLÍS, and seven assistants on the first eight panels of the thirty-two-panel work *La Raza de Oro*. The panels honor pre-Columbian cultures.

Zampoña: Bagpipe of the Balearic Islands, Spain. The *zampoña* is synonymous with the *gaita*, or mouth-blown bagpipe. It differs from the Scottish Highland pipe in that it has only one long drone, which hangs in front of the sheepskin bag, where it is held in a stock together with two other small drones. It has eight holes including the thumb-hole and is usually on a C-major scale, although B-flat and D *zampoñas* also exist. Players wear *zampoñas* on their shoulders. The *zampoña* is played in the Balearic Islands, Asturias, and Galicia.

Zapata, Carmen (b. July 15, 1927, New York, N.Y.): Actress and director. Zapata, a Mexican American who was reared in New York City, received her education at the University of California, Los Angeles, and New York University. She went to Los Angeles in 1965 and soon established herself as a character actress in film and television. In 1973, she won an Emmy Award. That same year, she teamed with Margarita Galban and Estela Scarlata to found the BILINGUAL FOUNDATION FOR THE ARTS. She has served the organization as president, producing director, stage director, and acting coach. The organization hires dozens of Latino performers and helps to introduce them to the film industry.

In 1983, Zapata received both the Ruben Salazar Award of the NATIONAL COUNCIL OF LA RAZA and the Women in Film Humanitarian Award. In 1985, she was chosen Woman of the Year by the Hispanic Women's Council, and in 1986 she received a Dramalogue Award for Best Actress. Zapata is also a published translator of the plays of Federico García Lorca.

Zapata, Emiliano (Aug. 8, 1879, Anenecuilco, Morelos, Mexico—Apr. 10, 1919, Chinameca, Morelos, Mexico): Leader and symbol of the agrarian revolt. Zapata was a man driven by hope in his struggle to free Indians from the yoke of serfdom. By the time of his assassination, Zapata was the leader of the agrarian revolt in Mexico.

Born in the southern Mexican state of Morelos and reared under a political system dominated by rich landowners, Zapata overcame humble socioeconomic circumstances through his focused effort and the benefit of an elementary education. Orphaned at the age of fifteen, he inherited a ranch with his brother Eufemio. Zapata worked the land after his brother left, sharecropped local hacienda acreage, and bought and sold livestock, eventually developing a national reputation as a respected horseman and horse trainer. The positive characteristics of the Morelos Indian were reflected by Zapata to his last days: He was quiet, honest, gentle, and courteous, but he distrusted outsiders and non-Indians. He, as did many Indians, saw land and its resources as belonging communally to the people who lived and worked on it, not to individuals.

When, at the end of the nineteenth century, wealthy Morelos landowners began expanding their holdings at the expense of small Indian claims and of village common lands, Zapata became a revolutionary leader. He began with a local constituency. His early years working as a stable hand for wealthy ranchers, serving in the army, and laboring as a tenant farmer and landowner provoked Zapata to exclaim, "I join the revolution not out of poverty, but to free Mexican people from the yoke of tyranny."

Zapata was the undisputed leader of the Morelos-based revolutionary movement that advocated the return of all land to Indians. President Francisco Modero's failure to return lands to disfranchised peasants moved Zapata to rise in revolt with his agrarian reform platform in 1911. He succeeded in getting his PLAN DE AYALA incorporated into the revolutionary goals of the Aguascalientes Convention of 1914.

Zapata and Francisco "Pancho" VILLA captured Mexico City in 1914 and shared the presidential chair. At one time during the revolution, Zapata controlled

Emiliano Zapata. (AP/Wide World Photos)

most of southern Mexico. He was assassinated by representatives of Venustiano Carranza. Modern Mexico considers him to be one of the greatest heroes of the MEXICAN REVOLUTION. A statue in his memory was placed on the Calzada de Tlalpan in Mexico City.

Both before and after death, Zapata was a hero of legends and songs of the Mexican Indians. His name is often invoked in whispers, as he has become almost divine, a living spirit of the Morelos Indian. Zapata is a spiritual symbol to Latino people in their efforts to achieve equality.

Zapote: Fruit of the chicle tree. Often called *sapo-dilla*, the *zapote* is a rough-skinned, roundish fruit with cream-colored skin. It grows wild and is also cultivated in Mexico, Central America, and the Caribbean. It is produced by the chicle tree, the sap of which is used to make chewing gum. Allowed to ripen on the tree, the fruit is bitter and inedible, but ripening it further after removal from the tree will produce a sweet, very soft fruit, suitable for eating raw or making into puddings or preserves. The *zapotes* of Chile and Peru and the white *zapote* of western Mexico are unrelated. All these fruits are united by their need to ripen until nearly rotted before they become edible.

Zarzuela: Spanish theatrical genre combining music, dance, and dialogue. Zarzuelas originated in the royal hunting lodge known as La Zarzuela, outside of Madrid, Spain. Professional entertainers performed them to liven up the Spanish court. Zarzuelas were established by the Spanish playwright Pedro Calderón de la Barca (1600-1681). Later, the lyricist Ramón de la Cruz (1731-1794) substituted local customs for the mythological themes of early zarzuelas. After being temporarily eclipsed by the success of the *tonadilla*, the zarzuela was revived after fifty years by the prolific Francisco Asenjo Barbieri (1823-1894), who composed no fewer than seventy zarzuelas.

Zavala, Lorenzo de (Oct. 3, 1788, Mérida, Yucatán, Mexico—Nov. 16, 1836, Texas Point, Tex.): Politician. Zavala, who became one of the most distinguished liberal and republican statesmen of early nineteenth century Mexico, grew up in Mérida. He was jailed by Spanish authorities between 1814 and 1817 for championing the cause of Mexican independence. Upon his release, Zavala practiced medicine to support himself and his family.

Zavala played an active role in Mexican domestic politics. He helped draft the 1824 federal constitution

and assisted in the creation of York Rite masonic lodges. Zavala also served as governor of the state of Mexico and as minister to France. He advocated radical policies such as the redistribution of wealth and relatively unrestricted suffrage. Zavala was also a prolific writer best known for his *Ensayo político de las revoluciones*, an account of the years 1808-1830 that portrayed the independence movement as a struggle against three hundred years of Spanish tyranny.

In 1835, when General Antonio López de Santa Anna established a centralist regime in Mexico, Zavala helped the Texas colonists achieve their independence. He was chosen as vice president of the new Lone Star Republic when an interim Texas government was organized in March, 1836. Zavala resigned this post because of ill health seven months later. He contracted pneumonia and died shortly thereafter.

Zavella, Patricia (b. Nov. 28, 1949, near Tampa, Fla.): Anthropologist. Zavella's work has focused on the role of gender in the workplace and the relationship between women's paid employment and their family roles. She is the author of such works as *Women's Work and Chicano Families: Cannery Workers of the Santa Clara Valley* (1987) and *Sunbelt Working Mothers: Reconciling Family and Factory* (1993).

As a young child, she moved frequently with her family, and as a result she never spent a full year at any school until the sixth grade. She found that teachers expected less of her because of her Mexican American background, but she surprised them with her ability. She earned her A.A. (1971) from Chaffey College and her bachelor's degree in anthropology (1973) from Pitzer College, both in California. While earning her undergraduate degrees, she became involved in Hispanic activist organizations. She earned her M.A. (1975) and Ph.D. (1982) from the University of California, Berkeley. Her dissertation research involved a discrimination suit filed by cannery workers. Zavella decided to study how Chicana workers were tracked into particular job categories.

Zavella began teaching at the University of California, Santa Cruz, in 1983, becoming an associate professor in 1989. She remained committed to the Chicana movement and served as a consultant to various family studies projects.

Zeno Gandía, Manuel (Jan. 10, 1855, Arecibo, Puerto Rico—Jan. 30, 1930, San Juan, Puerto Rico): Writer. After local schooling, Zeno Gandía moved to Barcelona, Spain, for his high school studies and to Madrid for his university degree in medicine and surgery, which he obtained from the University of San Carlo in 1875. He later studied internal medicine and worked at the Hospital San Andrés in Burdeos, Spain, and then at various hospitals in Paris.

In France, Zeno Gandía became familiar with the works of contemporary French novelists. While completing his medical studies in Madrid, he had begun to submit articles and stories to local reviews, and after his return to Puerto Rico in 1876 he was active in literature, medicine, journalism, and politics. His major work of fiction is the tetralogy *Crónicas de un mundo enfermo* (1894-1925), beginning with what is considered his finest work, *La charca* (1894; English translation, 1982). That mildly naturalistic novel offers a scrutiny of humanity's troubles in a world in which God does exist. Zeno Gandía's work has been referred to as offering some of the best portraits of Puerto Rican society in one of the most decisive and interesting periods of Puerto Rico's history.

Broadcast Media

The following lists include radio and television stations that indicated that some of their programming is oriented to a Latino audience, though not necessarily broadcast in Spanish. Stations, identified by their call letters and followed by their broadcast frequencies or channels, are listed alphabetically by city within their states; many, however, reach audiences in broad regions. Most radio stations listed broadcast five or more hours of Latino-oriented programming per week; all broadcast at a power greater than one kilowatt. Broadcast frequencies listed are in kilohertz for AM stations and megahertz for FM stations. Television stations listed indicated that they broadcast some Latino-oriented programming.

Data come primarily from *Burrelle's 1992 Black/Hispanic Media Directory* (Burrelle's Media Directories, Livingston, N.J., 1992).

Radio Stations

ALASKA

City	Call	Freq.
Anchorage	KSKA-FM	91.1

ARIZONA

City	Call	Freq.
Phoenix	KPHX-AM	1480
Phoenix	KASA-AM	1540
Phoenix	KVVA-FM	107.1
Tucson	KQTL-AM	1210
Tucson	KTUC-AM	1400
Tucson	KUAT-AM	1550
Tucson	KXCI-FM	91.3
Tucson	KRKN-FM	97.5
Tucson	KXMG-FM	98.3

ARKANSAS

City	Call	Freq.
Little Rock	KABF-FM	88.3
Warren	KWRF-FM	105.5

CALIFORNIA

City	Call	Freq.
Bakersfield	KCHJ-AM	1010
Bakersfield	KTQX-FM	90.1
Bakersfield	KSUV-FM	102.9
Barstow	KDUC-FM	94.3
Berkeley	KPFA-FM	94.1
Blythe	KJMB-FM	100.3
Calexico	KQVO-FM	97.7
Camarillo	KMRO-FM	90.3
Chico	KCHO-FM	91.7
Chula Vista	XHKY-FM	95.7
Chula Vista	XLTN-FM	104.5
Corona	KWRM-AM	1370
Davis	KDVS-FM	90.3
Delano	KDNO-FM	98.5
East Highlands	KCAL-AM	1410
El Cajon	KECR-FM	93.3
El Centro	KUBO-FM	88.7
El Centro	KGBA-FM	100.1
Fresno	KYNO-AM	1300
Fresno	KXEX-AM	1550
Fresno	KGST-AM	1600
Fresno	KFCF-FM	88.1
Fresno	KSJV-FM	91.5
Fresno	KXMX-FM	92.1
Hollister	KMPG-AM	1520
Hollywood	KKHJ-AM	930
Hollywood	KTNQ-AM	1020
Hollywood	KWKW-AM	1330
Hollywood	KALI-AM	1430
Hollywood	KLVE-FM	107.5
Indio	KCLB-AM	970
Lakeport	KXBX-FM	98.3
Livingston	KNTO-FM	95.9
Long Beach	KGER-AM	1390
Los Angeles	KSKQ-AM	1540
Los Angeles	KXLU-FM	88.9
Los Angeles	KSKQ-FM	97.9
Los Angeles	KBOB-FM	98.3
Los Angeles	KRTH-FM	101.1
Los Banos	KLBS-AM	1330
Modesto	KMPO-FM	88.7
Napa	KVON-AM	1440
National City	XHRM-FM	92.5
North Hollywood	KPFK-FM	90.7
Oxnard	KOXR-AM	910
Oxnard	KTRO-AM	1520
Pasadena	KMAX-FM	107.1
Porterville	KIOO-FM	99.7
Rancho Cucamonga	KNSE-AM	1510
Riverside	KUCR-FM	88.1
Riverside	KGGI-FM	99.1
Roseville	KRCX-AM	1110
Sacramento	KSFM-FM	102.5
Salinas	KTGE-AM	1570
Salinas	KHDC-FM	90.9
Salinas	KLFA-FM	93.9
Salinas	KRAY-FM	103.5
San Francisco	KIQI-AM	1010
San Jose	KLOK-AM	1170
San Jose	KAZA-AM	1290
San Jose	KBRG-FM	104.9
San Luis Obispo	KCPR-FM	91.3
Santa Ana	KWIZ-AM	1480
Santa Cruz	KZSC-FM	88.1
Santa Cruz	KUSP-FM	88.9
Stockton	KUOP-FM	91.3
Stockton	KSTN-FM	107.3
Wasco	KERI-AM	1180

COLORADO

City	Call	Freq.
Alamosa	KRZA-FM	88.7
Boulder	KGNU-FM	88.5
Denver	KDKO-AM	1510
Denver	KUVO-FM	89.3
Fort Collins	KCSU-FM	90.5
Greeley	KFKA-AM	1310
Lamar	KVAY-FM	105.7
Rocky Ford	KAVI-FM	95.9
Telluride	KOTO-FM	91.7
Yuma	KJCO-FM	100.9

CONNECTICUT

City	Call	Freq.
Bridgeport	WPKN-FM	89.5
Middletown	WESU-FM	88.1
Milford	WFIF-AM	1500
Storrs	WHUS-FM	91.7
West Haven	WNHU-FM	88.7

DISTRICT OF COLUMBIA

City	Call	Freq.
Washington, D.C.	WPFW-FM	89.3

FLORIDA

City	Call	Freq.
Cape Coral	WDCQ-AM	1200
Clewiston	WAFC-AM	590
Fort Lauderdale	WEXY-AM	1520
Jacksonville	WROS-AM	1050
Jupiter	WTRU-FM	99.5
Miami	WAQI-AM	710
Miami	WQBA-AM	1140
Miami	WCMQ-AM	1210
Miami	WSUA-AM	1260
Miami	WRHC-AM	1550
Miami	WLRN-FM	91.3
Miami	WCMQ-FM	92.3
Miami	WXDJ-FM	95.7
Miami	WRTO-FM	98.3
Miami	WQBA-FM	107.5

City	Station	Freq.
North Miami	WKAT-AM	1360
Orlando	WONQ-AM	1030
Orlando	WXXU-AM	1300
Orlando	WXTO-AM	1600
Tampa	WQBN-AM	1300
Tampa	WAMA-AM	1550
Wauchula	WAUC-AM	1310

GEORGIA

City	Station	Freq.
Atlanta	WAEC-AM	860
Atlanta	WRFG-FM	89.3
Austell	WXEM-AM	1460
Austell	WAOS-AM	1600

IDAHO

City	Station	Freq.
Caldwell	KBGN-AM	1060

ILLINOIS

City	Station	Freq.
Chicago	WIND-AM	560
Chicago	WMBI-AM	1110
Chicago	WOJO-FM	105.1
Chicago Heights	WTAS-FM	102.3
Evanston	WONX-AM	1590
Highland Park	WVVX-FM	103.1
La Grange	WTAQ-AM	1300
Loves Park	WLUV-FM	96.7

INDIANA

City	Station	Freq.
Goshen	WGCS-FM	91.1
Pendleton	WEEM-FM	91.7
Portage	WNDZ-AM	750

KANSAS

City	Station	Freq.
Dodge City	KINF-FM	91.9
Kansas City	KCNW-AM	1380
Liberal	KSLS-FM	101.5
Manhattan	KSDB-FM	91.9
Wichita	KMUW-FM	89.1

KENTUCKY

City	Station	Freq.
London	WWEL-FM	103.9

LOUISIANA

City	Station	Freq.
Leesville	KVVP-FM	105.5
Shreveport	KDAQ-FM	89.9

MAINE

City	Station	Freq.
Portland	WMPG-FM	90.9

MARYLAND

City	Station	Freq.
Silver Spring	WMDO-AM	1540

MASSACHUSETTS

City	Station	Freq.
Amherst	WFCR-FM	88.5
Boston	WUNR-AM	1600
Boston	WERS-FM	88.9
Boston	WBUR-FM	90.9
Brockton	WBET-AM	1460
Cambridge	WHRB-FM	95.3
Chicopee	WACE-AM	730
Lowell	WLLH-AM	1400
Lowell	WJUL-FM	91.5
Medford	WMFO-FM	91.5
New Bedford	WJFD-FM	97.3
Newton	WNTN-AM	1550
Somerset	WSAR-AM	1480
Springfield	WTCC-FM	90.7
Woburn	WSSH-AM	1510

MICHIGAN

City	Station	Freq.
Battle Creek	WBCK-AM	930
Detroit	WDTR-FM	90.9
East Lansing	WKAR-AM	870
Grand Rapids	WBYW-FM	89.9

MINNESOTA

City	Station	Freq.
Saint Cloud	KVSC-FM	88.1

MISSISSIPPI

City	Station	Freq.
Lorman	WPRL-FM	91.7

MISSOURI

City	Station	Freq.
Columbia	KOPN-FM	89.5
Kansas City	KCMO-AM	810
St. Louis	KDHX-FM	88.1

NEBRASKA

City	Station	Freq.
Lincoln	KZUM-FM	89.3

NEW HAMPSHIRE

City	Station	Freq.
Salem	WNNW-AM	1110

NEW JERSEY

City	Station	Freq.
Hillside	WNJR-AM	1430
New Brunswick	WRSU-FM	88.7
Paterson	WWRV-AM	1330
Trenton	WTSR-FM	91.3

NEW MEXICO

City	Station	Freq.
Albuquerque	KXKS-AM	1190
Albuquerque	KABQ-AM	1350
Albuquerque	KANW-FM	89.1
Albuquerque	KUNM-FM	89.9
Deming	KDEM-FM	94.3
Espanola	KDCE-AM	950
Hobbs	KYKK-AM	1110
Las Cruces	KRWG-FM	90.7
Las Vegas	KNMX-AM	540
Lovington	KLEA-FM	101.7
Roswell	KCRX-AM	1430
Tucumcari	KQAY-FM	92.7

NEW YORK

City	Station	Freq.
Binghamton	WHRW-FM	90.5
Bronx	WFUV-FM	90.7
Brooklyn	WNYE-FM	91.5
Geneva	WEOS-FM	89.7
Grand Island	WHLD-AM	1270
Hamilton	WRCU-FM	90.1
Ithaca	WVBR-FM	93.5
Loudonville	WVCR-FM	88.3
New Rochelle	WRTN-FM	93.5
New York	WSKQ-AM	620
New York	WADO-AM	1280
New York	WKDM-AM	1380
New York	WSKQ-FM	97.9
New York	WCBS-FM	101.1
North Greece	WGMC-FM	90.1
Penfield	WBER-FM	90.5
Rochester	WWWG-AM	1460
Rochester	WRUR-FM	88.5
Schenectady	WVKZ-AM	1240

OHIO

City	Station	Freq.
Berlin Heights	WNZN-FM	89.1
Bowling Green	WBGU-FM	88.1
Cincinnati	WAIF-FM	88.3
Conneaut	WGOJ-FM	105.5
Lorain	WZLE-FM	104.9

OREGON

City	Station	Freq.
Eugene	KLCC-FM	89.7
Hillsboro	KUIK-AM	1360
Klamath Falls	KAGO-FM	99.5
Portland	KBOO-FM	90.7
Woodburn	KWBY-AM	940

PENNSYLVANIA

City	Station	Freq.
Erie	WERG-FM	89.9
Indiana	WIUP-FM	90.1
Lehighton	WYNS-AM	1160
Philadelphia	WTEL-AM	860
Philadelphia	WRTI-FM	90.1
Washington Crossing	WIMG-AM	1300

RHODE ISLAND

City	Station	Freq.
North Providence	WRCP-AM	1290
Providence	WALE-AM	990

SOUTH CAROLINA

City	Station	Freq.
Gaffney	WFGN-AM	1180
Greenville	WMUU-AM	1260

TENNESSEE

City	Station	Freq.
Clarksville	WAPX-FM	91.7
Memphis	WEVL-FM	89.9

TEXAS

City	Station	Freq.
Alice	KBIC-FM	102.3
Amarillo	KPUR-AM	1440
Arlington	KSGB-AM	1540
Austin	KTXZ-AM	1560
Austin	KRGT-FM	92.1
Beaumont	KVLU-FM	91.3

Bishop	KFLZ-FM	107.1	Houston	KEYH-AM	850	San Antonio	KEDA-AM	1540
Brownsville	KBNR-FM	88.3	Houston	KLAT-AM	1010	San Antonio	KSYM-FM	90.1
Coleman	KSTA-FM	107.1	Houston	KGOL-AM	1180	San Antonio	KXTN-FM	107.5
Corpus Christi	KBNJ-FM	91.7	Houston	KPFT-FM	90.1	Spearman	KRDF-FM	98.3
Corpus Christi	KSAB-FM	99.9	Houston	KHCB-FM	105.7	Waco	KBBW-AM	1010
Crystal City	KHER-FM	94.3	Houston	KQQK-FM	106.5	Wichita Falls	KWFT-AM	620
Dallas	KRLD-AM	1080	Houston	KNGV-FM	92.7	Wichita Falls	KLLF-AM	1290
Dallas	KESS-AM	1270	Kingsville	KVOZ-AM	890	Wichita Falls	KWFS-FM	103.3
Dallas	KSVZ-AM	1540	Laredo	KHOY-FM	88.1			
Dallas	KSSA-AM	1600	Laredo	KBNL-FM	89.9	**UTAH**		
Dallas	KNON-FM	89.3	Laredo	KJBZ-FM	92.7	Ogden	KWCR-FM	88.1
Dallas	KSSA-FM	106.9	Laredo	KOYE-FM	94.9	Salt Lake City	KRCL-FM	90.9
Del Rio	KTDR-FM	96.3	Laredo	KLVT-FM	105.5	West Valley City	KZQQ-AM	1550
Denton	KNTU-FM	88.1	Levelland	KXTQ-AM	950			
Dumas	KMRE-FM	95.3	Lubbock	KCLR-AM	1530	**VIRGINIA**		
Eagle Pass	KINL-FM	92.7	Lubbock	KKIK-FM	93.7	Falls Church	WFAX-AM	1220
Edinburg	KRIO-AM	910	Lubbock	KQXX-FM	98.5	Hampton	WHOV-FM	88.3
Edinburg	KOIR-FM	88.5	McAllen	KLSR-FM	105.3	Onley	WESR-AM	1330
El Paso	KAMA-AM	750	Memphis	KWEL-AM	1070			
El Paso	KELP-AM	1590	Midland	KXYZ-AM	1320	**WASHINGTON**		
El Paso	KTEP-FM	88.5	Pasadena	KVWG-FM	95.3	Granger	KDNA-FM	91.9
El Paso	KBNA-FM	97.5	Pearsall	KMFM-FM	104.9	Moses Lake	KBSN-AM	1470
El Paso	KPAS-FM	103.1	Premont	KCTM-FM	103.1	Olympia	KAOS-FM	89.3
Floresville	KWCB-FM	89.7	Rio Grande City	KFRD-FM	104.9	Prosser	KARY-AM	1310
Fort Stockton	KFST-FM	94.3	Rosenberg	KSJT-FM	107.5	Prosser	KARY-FM	100.9
Gonzales	KPJN-FM	106.3	San Angelo	KSLR-AM	630	Seattle	KKFX-AM	1250
Harlingen	KGBT-AM	1530	San Antonio	KSAH-AM	720	Sunnyside	KREW-AM	1210
Harlingen	KIWW-FM	96.1	San Antonio	KVAR-AM	1160	Sunnyside	KREW-FM	96.7
Hearne	KHRN-FM	94.3	San Antonio	KXTN-AM	1310	Tacoma	KKMO-AM	1360
Hereford	KPAN-FM	106.3	San Antonio	KCOR-AM	1350	Wenatchee	KPQ-AM	560

Television Stations

ALABAMA			Palm Springs	KESQ-TV	42	Grand Junction	KREX-TV	5
Muscle Shoals	WTRT-TV	26	Redding	KIXE-TV	9	Grand Junction	KREZ-TV	6
			Rohnert Park	KRCB-TV	22	Grand Junction	KREY-TV	10
ARIZONA			San Bernardino	KVCR-TV	24	Pueblo	KTSC-TV	8
Flagstaff	KMOH-TV	6	San Diego	KPBS-TV	15			
Phoenix	KPHO-TV	5	San Francisco	KDTV-TV	14	**CONNECTICUT**		
Phoenix	KTVW-TV	33	San Jose	KNTV-TV	11	Hartford	W13BF-TV	13
Tucson	KUAT-TV	6	San Jose	KSTS-TV	48	Hartford	WTIC-TV	61
Yuma	KSWT-TV	13	San Jose	KTEH-TV	54	New London	WTWS-TV	26
			San Jose	KLXV-TV	65			
CALIFORNIA			San Leandro	KFTL-TV	64	**DISTRICT OF COLUMBIA**		
Clovis	KAIL-TV	53	San Mateo	KCSM-TV	60	Washington, D.C.	WJLA-TV	7
Concord	KFCB-TV	42	Santa Barbara	KEYT-TV	3	Washington, D.C.	WHMM-TV	32
El Centro	KECY-TV	9	Santa Maria	K07TA-TV	7			
Fresno	KVPT-TV	18	West Sacramento	KOVR-TV	13	**FLORIDA**		
Fresno	KFTV-TV	21				Clearwater	WCLF-TV	22
Fresno	KNXT-TV	49	**COLORADO**			Hialeah	WSCV-TV	51
Fresno	KMSG-TV	59	Colorado Springs	KKTV-TV	11	Miami	WLTV-TV	23
Glendale	KVEA-TV	52	Denver	KRMA-TV	6	Orlando	WTGL-TV	52
Los Angeles	KWHY-TV	22	Denver	KMGH-TV	7	Pembroke Park	WHFT-TV	45
Los Angeles	KMEX-TV	34	Evergreen	K11SF-TV	11	Tampa	W57BA-TV	57
Los Angeles	KLCS-TV	58	Evergreen	K49AY-TV	49			
Modesto	KCSO-TV	19	Evergreen	K54CQ-TV	54	**ILLINOIS**		
Monterey	KSMS-TV	67	Grand Junction	KREG-TV	3	Chicago	WCIU-TV	26

Chicago	WCFC-TV	38
Chicago	WSNS-TV	44
Dundas	WUSI-TV	16
Quincy	WTJR-TV	16

INDIANA

Indianapolis	WFYI-TV	20

KANSAS

Bunker Hill	KOOD-TV	9
Shawnee Mission	KYFC-TV	50

KENTUCKY

Ashland	WTSF-TV	61
Louisville	WKPC-TV	15

LOUISIANA

New Orleans	WLAE-TV	32

MARYLAND

Silver Spring	W48AW	48

MASSACHUSETTS

Boston	WGBH-TV	2
Boston	WGBX-TV	44
Brighton	WQTV-TV	64
Dorchester	W19AH-TV	19
Shrewsbury	WHLL-TV	27

MICHIGAN

Flint	WJRT-TV	12
Flint	WFUM-TV	28
Grand Rapids	WGVU-TV	35
Grand Rapids	WGVK-TV	52

MINNESOTA

Minneapolis	KARE-TV	11

MISSOURI

Warrensburg	KMOS-TV	6

MONTANA

Bozeman	KUSM-TV	9

NEVADA

Reno	KOLO-TV	8
Reno	KREN-TV	27

NEW JERSEY

Secaucus	WXTV-TV	41
Teterboro	WNJU-TV	47

NEW MEXICO

Albuquerque	KAZQ-TV	32
Albuquerque	KLUZ-TV	41
Albuquerque	KDB59-TV	59
Las Cruces	KRWG-TV	22

NEW YORK

Albany	WTEN-TV	10
New York	WNBC-TV	4
New York	WNYW-TV	5
New York	WABC-TV	7
Rochester	WHEC-TV	10
Syracuse	WSTM-TV	3
Utica	WKTV-TV	2

OHIO

Bowling Green	WBGU-TV	27
Toledo	WTOL-TV	11

OKLAHOMA

Broken Arrow	KDOR-TV	17
Claremore	KXON-TV	35

PENNSYLVANIA

Erie	WSEE-TV	35
Harrisburg	WITF-TV	33
Philadelphia	WTGI-TV	61

TEXAS

Amarillo	KACV-TV	2
Brownsville	KVEO-TV	23
Corpus Christi	KIII-TV	3
Corpus Christi	KORO-TV	28
Dallas	KDTN-TV	2
Dallas	KDFI-TV	27
El Paso	KDBC-TV	4
El Paso	KCOS-TV	13
El Paso	KINT-TV	26
Garland	KUVN-TV	23
Harlingen	KGBT-TV	4
Harlingen	KMBH-TV	60
Houston	KUHT-TV	8
Houston	KTRK-TV	13
Houston	KHTV-TV	39
Houston	KXLN-TV	45
Houston	KTMD-TV	48
Irving	KFWD-TV	52
Laredo	KVTV-TV	13
Lubbock	KTXT-TV	5
Lubbock	KCBD-TV	11
Lubbock	KLBK-TV	13
Lubbock	KAMC-TV	28
Lubbock	KJTV-TV	34
Lufkin	KTRE-TV	9
Midland	KMID-TV	2
Pasadena	KLTJ-TV	22
Pasadena	KRTW-TV	57
San Antonio	KLRN-TV	9
San Antonio	KWEX-TV	41
Temple	KCEN-TV	6
Tyler	KLTV-TV	7
Weslaco	KRGV-TV	5

UTAH

Salt Lake City	KUED-TV	7

WASHINGTON

Yakima	KYVE-TV	47

WISCONSIN

Milwaukee	WVTV-TV	18
Milwaukee	WMVT-TV	36

Businesses Owned by Latinos, 1993

Hispanic Business, a U.S. business magazine, annually ranks Latino-owned businesses according to their sales volume. The magazine compiles information on sales volume, name of the chief executive, number of employees, and year of establishment. Companies on the list that follows are headquartered in the United States, and each has more than half of its ownership in the hands of Latinos who are citizens of the United States. The names of these companies were published in the June, 1993, issue of *Hispanic Business*.

The list below consists of the names of 105 companies, listed alphabetically, with sales of more than $20 million in 1993. The list also provides data on each company, including address, telephone number, date of establishment, chief executive, number of employees, and type of business as categorized by the Standard Industrial Classification (SIC) code. The SIC code was established by the Executive Office of the President, Office of Management and Budget. It was developed for use in classifying establishments by type of activity, primarily for purposes of collecting statistics and data. The SIC is meant to cover all the fields of economic activity in the United States. Most major business reference sources arrange the names of companies by SIC code. The last line in each entry provides 1993 sales volume (in millions of dollars), with the ranking among the 105 businesses in parentheses.

A quick review of the listing reveals that the three states with the most large Latino businesses are California, Florida, and Texas. These are coastal and border states with large Latino populations. A large proportion of the companies fall in the manufacturing, retail, and service areas of business. Car dealerships appear to be promising enterprises. A new area that shows growth is the computer service industry, with many companies providing software design and consulting services.

Addresses, telephone numbers, and SIC codes were researched in various business reference sources that are updated annually. These included *Million Dollar Directory* (Dun's Marketing Services), *Register of Corporations* (Standard & Poor), *Try Us* (National Minority Business Campaign), and *Ward's Business Directory of U.S. Private and Public Companies* (Gale Research).

Several businesses were not listed in any of these sources, so information had to be retrieved from telephone directories. The annual list compiled by *Hispanic Business* includes the top 500 Latino-owned corporations, but for purposes of this publication only the top 105 businesses, with annual sales volumes of more than $20 million, were included. Additional Latino businesses can be found in the above-cited reference books.   —*Rafaela Castro*

Advanced Data Concepts Inc.
700 N.E. Multnomah Street
Portland, OR 97232
503-233-1220
Established 1979
Chief Executive: Frank E.
  Rivera, Sr.
Employees: 520
Business: Computer software
  engineering systems (SIC 7371)
Sales and rank: 20.22 (103)

Advanced Sciences Inc.
6739 Academy Road, NE
Albuquerque, NM 87109-3345
505-828-0959
Established 1977
Chief Executive: Ed L. Romero
Employees: 500
Business: Engineering services
  (SIC 8711)
Sales and rank: 66.59 (30)

AIB Financial Group Inc.
3830 W. Flagler
Miami, FL 33134
305-445-0045
Established 1984
Chief Executive: Jose M. Alvarez
Employees: 250
Business: Insurance agents,
  brokers, and services (SIC 6411)
Sales and rank: 55.16 (39)

All American Containers Inc.
11825 NW 100th Road
Miami, FL 33178
305-887-0797
Established 1991
Chief Executive: Remedios
  Diaz-Oliver
Employees: 27
Business: Glass, plastic, metal
  containers (SIC 5199)
Sales and rank: 20.19 (104)

Alrod International Inc.
880 Stanton Road
Burlingame, CA 94010
415-692-3862
Established 1978
Chief Executive: Alberto M.
  Rodriguez
Employees: 100
Business: Freight forwarding
  (SIC 4731)
Sales and rank: 34.97 (63)

Ancira Enterprises Inc.
6111 Bandera Road
San Antonio, TX 78238
512-681-4900
Established 1983
Chief Executive: Ernesto Ancira, Jr.
Employees: 300
Business: Automotive sales and
  service (SIC 5511)
Sales and rank: 168.00 (6)

Aucoin & Miller Electric Supply Co.
1719 Live Oak Street
P.O. Box 53122
Houston, TX 77052
713-234-2400
Established 1967
Chief Executive: B. Tom Miller
Employees: 47
Business: Electrical supplies, services (SIC 5063)
Sales and rank: 22.00 (91)

Avanti Press Inc.
13449 NW 42nd Avenue
Miami, FL 33054
305-685-7381
Established 1965
Chief Executive: Joe Arriola
Employees: 400
Business: Web offset printing services; Sales catalogs (SIC 2759)
Sales and rank: 60.80 (35)

Bared and Company
7841 NW 56th Street
Miami, FL 33166
305-592-4710
Established 1977
Chief Executive: Jose P. Bared
Employees: 90
Business: Mechanical contractor (SIC 1711)
Sales and rank: 55.00 (40)

Burt on Broadway (Burt Chevrolet, Inc.)
5200 S. Broadway
Englewoods, CO 80110
303-761-0333
Established 1939
Chief Executive: Lloyd G. Chavez
Employees: 600
Business: Automotive sales and service (SIC 5511)
Sales and rank: 422.76 (2)

Business Men's Insurance Corp
2620 SW 27th Avenue
Miami, FL 33140
Established 1975
Chief Executive: Antonio M. Sierra

Employees: 50
Business: Life and health insurance (SIC 6411)
Sales and rank: 52.60 (43)

C & F Foods Inc.
18825 Railroad Street
City of Industry, CA 91748
818-964-2496
Established 1975
Chief Executive: Manuel G. Fernandez
Employees: 72
Business: Packaging, agricultural commodities distribution (SIC 0723)
Sales and rank: 25.14 (84)

Cacique Inc.
14940 Proctor Avenue
City of Industry, CA 91746
818-961-3399
Established 1973
Chief Executive: Gilbert L. de Cardenas
Employees: 260
Business: Meat and cheese manufacturing (SIC 2022)
Sales and rank: 54.10 (42)

Cal-State Lumber Sales Inc.
10145 Via de La Amistad
San Ysidro, CA 92173
619-661-6599
Established 1984
Chief Executive: Benjamin Acevedo
Employees: 98
Business: Lumber and molding products, broker (SIC 5031)
Sales and rank: 169.64 (5)

Camino Real Chevrolet
2401 S. Atlantic Blvd.
Monterey Park, CA 91754-6807
213-264-3050
Established 1976
Chief Executive: Mike A. Hernandez, Sr.
Employees: 87
Business: Automotive sales and service (SIC 5511)
Sales and rank: 28.00 (77)

Candy's Tortilla Factory Inc.
2110 Santa Fe Drive
Pueblo, CO 81006
719-543-4350
Established 1957
Chief Executive: Anthony J. Estrada
Employees: 430
Business: Mexican food products (SIC 2099)
Sales and rank: 39.09 (56)

Capital Bancorpation
1221 Brickell Avenue
Miami, FL 33131
305-536-1500
Established 1974
Chief Executive: Abel Holtz
Employees: 700
Business: Financial services; Banking (SIC 6022)
Sales and rank: 114.17 (14)

CareFlorida Inc.
7950 NW 53rd Street
Miami, FL 33172
305-591-3311
Established 1986
Chief Executive: Paul L. Cejas
Employees: 194
Business: Health care services (SIC 8099)
Sales and rank: 110.60 (17)

Carfel Inc.
7495 NW 48th Street
Miami, FL 33134
305-592-2760
Established 1961
Chief Executive: George Feldenkreis
Employees: 90
Business: Aftermarket transmission parts (SIC 5541)
Sales and rank: 20.30 (101)

Casey Luna Ford-Mercury
19381 N Highway #85
Belen, NM 87002
505-865-9626
Established 1981
Chief Executive: Casey Luna
Employees: 63

Business: Automobile sales and service (SIC 5511)
Sales and rank: 20.40 (100)

COLSA Corp.
6726 Odyssey Drive DW
Huntsville, AL 35806
205-922-1512
Established 1980
Chief Executive: Francisco J. Collazo
Employees: 700
Business: Computer systems analysis and design (SIC 7373)
Sales and rank: 112.00 (15)

Community Asphalt Corporation
10011 Pines Blvd., Suite 203
Hollywood, FL 33024-6167
305-432-0804
Established 1980
Chief Executive: Jose Luis Fernandez
Employees: 200
Business: Concrete asphalt; Highway paving (SIC 2951)
Sales and rank: 35.89 (59)

Comprehensive Technologies International Inc.
14500 Avion Parkway, Suite 250
Chantilly, VA 22021
703-263-1000
Established 1980
Chief Executive: Celestino M. Beltran
Employees: 490
Business: Software development, integrated systems (SIC 7373)
Sales and rank: 39.23 (55)

Condal Distributors Inc.
2300 Randall Avenue
Bronx, NY 10473
212-824-9000
Established 1968
Chief Executive: Nelson Fernandez
Employees: 250
Business: Groceries; Food distributor (SIC 5141)
Sales and rank: 95.00 (21)

Condor Communications Inc.
1933 NW 21st Terrace
Miami, FL 33145
305-324-0123
Established 1980
Chief Executive: Rogelio R. Betancourt
Employees: 24
Business: Radio communication sales and service (SIC 4899)
Sales and rank: 21.58 (95)

CTA Inc.
6116 Executive Blvd., Suite 800
Rockville, MD 20850
301-816-1200
Established 1979
Chief Executive: C. E. Tom Velez
Employees: 1,280
Business: Computer systems analysis; Defense systems (SIC 7373)
Sales and rank: 115.94 (13)

De La Fuente Auto Group
1385 E. Main Street
El Cajon, CA 92021
619-440-2400
Established 1980
Chief Executive: Roque De La Fuente
Employees: 80
Business: Automotive sales and service (SIC 5511)
Sales and rank: 36.67 (58)

De Lara Travel Consultants
Coral Gables, FL
Established 1974
Chief Executive: Hector G. De Lara, Jr.
Employees: 35
Business: Corporate travel services (SIC 4724)
Sales and rank: 23.00 (90)

Delta Shoe Group Inc.
501 SW 37th Avenue
Miami, FL 33135-2538
305-446-6263
Established 1975
Chief Executive: Homero R. de la Torre

Employees: 15
Business: Footwear importing (SIC 5139)
Sales and rank: 20.54 (98)

Development Associates Inc.
1730 N. Lynn Street
Arlington, VA 22209
703-276-0677
Established 1969
Chief Executive: Leveo V. Sanchez
Employees: 250
Business: Management services; Government consulting (SIC 8748)
Sales and rank: 25.24 (83)

Dial-A-Mattress
3110 48th Avenue
Long Island City, NY 11101
718-472-1200
Established 1977
Chief Executive: Napoleon Barragan
Employees: 180
Business: Mattress sales (SIC 5712)
Sales and rank: 28.20 (75)

Eagle Brands Inc.
3201 NW 72nd Avenue
Miami, FL 33122
305-599-2337
Established 1984
Chief Executive: Carlos M. de la Cruz, Sr.
Employees: 200
Business: Beer distributor (SIC 5181)
Sales and rank: 97.95 (19)

El Dorado Furniture Corp.
1260 NW 72nd Avenue
Miami, FL 33126
305-572-1121
Established 1967
Chief Executive: Manuel Capo
Employees: 292
Business: Furniture sales (SIC 5712)
Sales and rank: 32.27 (67)

Electropolis Corp.
1905 NW 93rd Avenue
Miami, FL 33172
305-477-4545
Established 1988
Chief Executive: Alejandro
    Gerendas
Employees: 20
Business: Consumer electronics
    distribution (SIC 5064)
Sales and rank: 20.79 (97)

Essco of Arizona
1811 Industrial Blvd.
Lake Havasu, AZ 86403
602-855-8131
Established 1976
Chief Executive: Timothy D. Tapia
Employees: 85
Business: Electrical supplies
    distribution (SIC 5063)
Sales and rank: 20.00 (105)

F. Gavina & Sons Inc.
2369 E. 51st Street
Los Angeles, CA 90058
213-582-0671
Established 1967
Chief Executive: Pedro L. Gavina
Employees: 140
Business: Specialty coffee roasting
    (SIC 2095)
Sales and rank: 27.50 (80)

Film Roman Inc.
12020 Chandler Blvd. S
North Hollywood, CA 91617
818-761-2544
Established 1984
Chief Executive: Phil Roman
Employees: 210
Business: TV, theater animation
    entertainment (SIC 7812)
Sales and rank: 25.00 (86)

Frank Parra Autoplex
1000 E. Airport Freeway
Irving, TX 75062
214-721-4300
Established 1971
Chief Executives: Tim and Mike
    Parra
Employees: 284

Business: Automotive sales and
    services (SIC 5511)
Sales and rank: 146.60 (9)

**Frederick Chevrolet Cadillac
    Buick Inc.**
1505 Quentin Road
Lebanon, PA 17042
717-274-1461
Established 1984
Chief Executive: Frederick C.
    Laurenzo
Employees: 110
Business: Automotive sales and
    service (SIC 5511)
Sales and rank: 42.22 (51)

Fullerton Dodge Inc.
1110 W. Orangethorpe Avenue
Fullerton, CA 92633
714-879-6880
Established 1991
Chief Executive: Steven R. Rojas
Employees: 48
Business: Automotive sales and
    service (SIC 5511)
Sales and rank: 35.81 (60)

Galeana's Van Dyke Dodge Inc.
P.O. Box 1539
Warren, MI 48090
313-573-4000
Established 1977
Chief Executive: Frank Galeana
Employees: 334
Business: Automotive sales and
    service (SIC 5511)
Sales and rank: 186.30 (4)

Gaseteria Oil Corp.
364 Maspeth Avenue
Brooklyn, NY 11211
718-782-4200
Established 1972
Chief Executive: Oscar Porcelli
Employees: 450
Business: Gasoline stations
    (SIC 5541)
Sales and rank: 108.00 (18)

Gato Distributors
3505 NW 107th Street
Miami, FL 33172

Established 1986
Chief Executive: Juan A. Galan, Jr.
Employees: 137
Business: Beer distribution
    (SIC 5181)
Sales and rank: 44.00 (50)

Gator Industries Inc.
1000 S.E. 8th Street
Hialeah, FL 33010
305-888-5000
Established 1970
Chief Executive: Guillermo
    Miranda, Jr.
Employees: 989
Business: Shoe manufacturing
    (SIC 5139)
Sales and rank: 65.00 (32)

**Government Micro Resources
    Inc.**
14121 Parke-Long Ct.
Chantilly, VA 22021
703-263-9146
Chief Executive: Humberto A.
    Pujals
Business: Microcomputer,
    network systems (SIC 7373)
Sales and rank: 50.50 (46)

Goya Foods
100 Seaview Drive
Secaucus, NJ 07096
201-348-4900
Established 1936
Chief Executive: Joseph A. Unanue
Employees: 1,600
Business: Food manufacturing;
    Marketing (SIC 2032)
Sales and rank: 453.00 (1)

Graphic Productions Corp.
5600 N.W. 32nd Avenue
Miami, FL 33142
305-635-4895
Established 1974
Chief Executive: Noel Hernandez
Employees: 230
Business: Communication web
    offset printing (SIC 2759)
Sales and rank: 31.00 (70)

Gus Machado Ford Inc.
1200 W. 49th Street
Hialeah, FL 33013
305-822-3211
Established 1984
Chief Executive: Gus Machado
Employees: 146
Business: Automotive sales and
service (SIC 5511)
Sales and rank: 60.42 (36)

H & H Meat Products Co. Inc.
P.O. Box 358
Mercedes, TX 78570
512-565-6363
Established 1947
Chief Executive: Liborio E.
Hinojosa
Employees: 88
Business: Meat packing
distribution (SIC 2011)
Sales and rank: 68.79 (29)

Handy Andy Supermarkets
2001 S. Laredo Street
San Antonio, TX 78207
210-227-8755
Established 1983
Chief Executive: A. Jimmy
Jimenez
Employees: 1,705
Business: Supermarket chain
(SIC 5411)
Sales and rank: 148.00 (8)

**Havana Potatoes of New York
Corp**
449-461 New York
Bronx, NY 10474
212-378-5400
Established 1975
Chief Executive: Pedro Perez
Employees: 50
Business: Tropical fruit, fresh
vegetables (SIC 5148)
Sales and rank: 32.00 (68)

Infotec Development Inc.
3505 Cadillac Avenue, Bldg. M
Costa Mesa, CA 92626
714-241-8254
Established 1978

Chief Executive: J. Fernando
Niebla
Employees: 600
Business: Software systems
integration; Management
services (SIC 7373)
Sales and rank: 126.03 (12)

International Bancshares Corp.
1200 San Bernardino Avenue
Laredo, TX 78042
512-722-7611
Established 1979
Chief Executive: Dennis E. Nixon
Employees: 650
Business: Financial services;
Banking (SIC 6712)
Sales and rank: 160.70 (7)

JAK Construction Inc.
102 W. Jefferson Street
Falls Church, VA 22046
703-241-0341
Established 1982
Chief Executive: Jorge A. Kfoury
Employees: 35
Business: General contracting
(SIC 1542)
Sales and rank: 23.65 (88)

J. T. Slocomb Company
65 Matson Hill Road
South Glastonbury, CT 06073
Established 1891
Chief Executive: E. John Gregory
Employees: 260
Business: Aircraft engine
components (SIC 3541)
Sales and rank: 28.00 (78)

La Reina Inc.
316 N. Ford Blvd.
Los Angeles, CA 90022
213-268-2791, 800-367-7522
Established 1958
Chief Executive: Mauro P. Robles
Employees: 300
Business: Mexican food
manufacturing (SIC 2099)
Sales and rank: 45.00 (48)

Lloyd A. Wise Inc.
10550 E. 14th Street

Oakland, CA 94603
510-638-4000
Established 1914
Chief Executive: A. A. Batarse, Jr.
Employees: 291
Business: Automotive sales and
service (SIC 5511)
Sales and rank: 137.21 (11)

McBride and Associates Inc.
6013 Signal Road N.E.
Albuquerque, NM 87113
505-825-9211
Established 1985
Chief Executive: Teresa McBride
Employees: 49
Business: Computer products,
services (SIC 5734)
Sales and rank: 23.43 (89)

Magnet Industrial Group Inc.
25 High Street
Milford, CT 06460-4733
203-877-2034
Established 1984
Chief Executive: John Soto
Employees: 165
Business: Investment holding
company; Aircraft parts
(SIC 6719, 3724)
Sales and rank: 29.00 (73)

Malaco International Inc.
564 Market Street, Suite 705
San Francisco, CA 94104
415-398-3006
Established 1977
Chief Executive: Manuel Llama
Employees: 6
Business: Petroleum products,
chemical distribution (SIC 5063)
Sales and rank: 22.00 (92)

Marman USA Inc.
5401 W. Kennedy Blvd.
Tampa, FL 33609
813-286-2503
Established 1982
Chief Executive: Frank G. Cisneros
Employees: 11
Business: Chemical manufacturing,
distribution (SIC 5191)
Sales and rank: 27.00 (82)

Mason Distributors Inc.
5105 NW 159th Street
Hialeah, FL 33014
305-624-5557
Established 1967
Chief Executive: Carlos J.
Rodriguez
Employees: 180
Business: Vitamins, health care
products (SIC 5122)
Sales and rank: 35.50 (61)

Matlyn-Stofel Foods Inc.
102 Montague Street
Brooklyn, NY 11201
Established 1982
Chief Executive: Roberto Arguello
Employees: 160
Business: Supermarket chain
(SIC 5411)
Sales and rank: 21.20 (96)

Mendez Dairy/Tropical Cheese Inc.
452 Fayette Street
Perth Amboy, NJ 08861
908-442-6337
Established 1974
Chief Executive: Rafael Mendez
Employees: 100
Business: Dairy, cheese
manufacturing (SIC 2022)
Sales and rank: 32.00 (69)

Metro Ford Inc.
9000 NW 7th Avenue
Miami, FL 33150
305-751-9711
Established 1983
Chief Executive: Lombardo Perez
Employees: 99
Business: Automotive sales and
service (SIC 5511)
Sales and rank: 44.09 (49)

Mexican Industries in Michigan Inc.
1616 Howard Street
Detroit, MI 48216
313-963-6114
Established 1979
Chief Executive: Henry J. Aguirre
Employees: 800

Business: Automotive trimmings
(SIC 2396)
Sales and rank: 87.50 (24)

Miami Honda and Central Hyundai (Bengal Motor)
3100 NW 36th Street
Miami, FL 33134
305-638-4800
Established 1990
Chief Executive: Carlos M. de la
Cruz, Sr.
Employees: 145
Business: Automotive sales and
service (SIC 5511)
Sales and rank: 66.38 (31)

Microretailing Inc.
13001 S. Dixie Highway
Miami, FL 33100
305-233-8938
Established 1983
Chief Executive: Francisco Victoria
Employees: 92
Business: Microcomputer services
(SIC 7373)
Sales and rank: 55.00 (41)

MVM Inc.
5113 Leesburg Pike, #700
Falls Church, VA 22041
Established 1979
Chief Executive: Dario O.
Marquez, Jr.
Employees: 1,152
Business: Investigation, security
systems (SIC 7381)
Sales and rank: 24.45 (87)

National Systems and Research Co.
5475 Mark Dabling Blvd.,
Suite 200
Colorado Springs, CO 80918
719-590-8880
Established 1980
Chief Executive: Celestino E.
Archuleta
Employees: 481
Business: Computer integrated
systems design (SIC 7373)
Sales and rank: 41.61 (53)

Normac Foods Inc.
(Subsidiary of Wilson Foods
Corp.)
9500 NW 4th Street
Oklahoma City, OK 73108
405-789-7500
Established 1970
Chief Executive: John C. Lopez
Employees: 255
Business: Prepared beef products
(SIC 2013)
Sales and rank: 142.73 (10)

1 Day Paint & Body Centers Inc.
21801 Southwestern Avenue
Torrance, CA 90510
310-328-8900
Established 1967
Chief Executive: Javier R. Uribe,
Sr.
Employees: 580
Business: Auto painting;
Bodywork (SIC 7532)
Sales and rank: 25.00 (85)

Pacifica Services Inc.
106 S. Mentor Avenue,
Suite 200
Pasadena, CA 91106
818-405-0131
Established 1979
Chief Executive: Ernest M.
Camacho
Employees: 675
Business: Engineering services
(SIC 8711)
Sales and rank: 57.45 (37)

Pan American Hospital
5959 NW 7th Street
Miami, FL 33130
305-264-1000
Established 1963
Chief Executive: Carolina Calderin
Employees: 600
Business: Health care services
(SIC 8099)
Sales and rank: 76.00 (28)

Paul Young Auto Mall
3701 E. Saunders Street
Laredo, TX 78041
210-727-1192

Established 1941
Chief Executive: Paul H. Young, Jr.
Employees: 115
Business: Automotive sales and
service (SIC 5511)
Sales and rank: 29.52 (72)

Pharmed Group
7352 NW 35th Terrace
Miami, FL 33122
305-592-2324
Established 1981
Chief Executive: Carlos M.
De Cespedes
Employees: 87
Business: Medical supplies
distribution (SIC 5047)
Sales and rank: 32.46 (66)

Popular Ford Sales Inc.
2505 Coney Island Avenue
Brooklyn, NY 11223
718-376-5600
Established 1980
Chief Executive: Harry F. Risso
Employees: 74
Business: Automotive sales and
service (SIC 5511)
Sales and rank: 38.49 (57)

Precision Trading Corp.
1401 NW 88th Avenue
Miami, FL 33172
305-592-4500
Established 1979
Chief Executive: Israel Lapciuc
Employees: 35
Business: Consumer electronics;
Electrical appliances (SIC 5064)
Sales and rank: 96.00 (20)

Ramos Oil Co. Inc.
1515 S. River Road
West Sacramento, CA 95691
Established 1951
Chief Executive: William Ramos
Employees: 135
Business: Petroleum products
distribution (SIC 1382)
Sales and rank: 61.29 (34)

Ready State Bank
7900 W. Flagler Street

Hialeah, FL 33134
305-266-8333
Established 1983
Chief Executive: Enrique O. Ortiz
Employees: 212
Business: Commercial banking
(SIC 6022)
Sales and rank: 21.98 (94)

Refricenter of Miami Inc.
3701 NW 51st Street
Miami, FL 33142
305-633-1536
Established 1971
Chief Executive: Cirilo Hernandez
Employees: 102
Business: Air conditioning and
refrigeration distributor
(SIC 5075)
Sales and rank: 50.68 (45)

RioStar Corp.
214 N. Nagle Street
Houston, TX 77003
713-228-6906
Established 1973
Chief Executive: Roland D.
Laurenzo
Employees: 1,650
Business: Tex-Mex specialty
restaurant chain (SIC 5812)
Sales and rank: 32.69 (65)

RJO Enterprises Inc.
4500 Forbes Blvd.
Lanham Seabrook, MD 20706
301-731-3600
Established 1979
Chief Executive: Richard J. Otero
Employees: 500
Business: Electronic computers;
Telecommunications (SIC 3511)
Sales and rank: 56.83 (38)

Rosendin Electric Inc.
880 Mabury Road
San Jose, CA 95133
408-286-2800
Established 1919
Chief Executive: Raymond J.
Rosendin
Employees: 650

Business: Electrical contracting
(SIC 1731)
Sales and rank: 91.00 (23)

Ruiz Food Products Inc.
501 S. Alta Avenue
Dinuba, CA 93618
209-591-5510
Established 1964
Chief Executive: Frederick R. Ruiz
Employees: 1,123
Business: Frozen Mexican food
(SIC 2038)
Sales and rank: 83.26 (26)

San Diego Wholesale Electric
9275 Carroll Park Drive
San Diego, CA 92121
619-452-9001
Established 1983
Chief Executive: Robert S.
Zamarripa, Jr.
Employees: 52
Business: Electrical supplies
distribution (SIC 5063)
Sales and rank: 22.00 (93)

**Sanchez-O'Brien Oil & Gas
Corp.**
1920 Sandman Street
Laredo, TX 78041
210-722-8092
Established 1973
Chief Executive: Antonio R.
Sanchez, Jr.
Employees: 80
Business: Oil, gas exploration
and development (SIC 1382)
Sales and rank: 27.50 (81)

SaniServ Inc.
P.O. Box 41240
2020 Production Drive
Indianapolis, IN 46241
317-246-0460
Established 1977
Chief Executive: Gabriel E.
Aguirre
Employees: 96
Business: Ice cream, yogurt
machine manufacturing
(SIC 3556)
Sales and rank: 28.00 (79)

Scientech Inc.
1690 International Way
Idaho Falls, ID 83402
208-523-2077
Established 1983
Chief Executive: Larry J.
    Ybarrondo
Employees: 257
Business: Consulting engineer;
    Environmental safety (SIC 8711)
Sales and rank: 20.43 (99)

Sedano's Supermarkets Inc.
3925 Palm Avenue
Hialeah, FL 33012
305-825-1243
Established 1962
Chief Executive: Manuel A. Herran
Employees: 1,500
Business: Supermarket chain
    (SIC 5411)
Sales and rank: 224.56 (3)

**Shadrock Petroleum Products
    Inc.**
2830 S.W. White Road
San Antonio, TX 78222
Established 1946
210-359-6633
Chief Executive: Richard Villareal
Employees: 9
Business: Petroleum and natural
    gas products (SIC 5172)
Sales and rank: 41.67 (52)

Solvents and Chemicals Inc.
P.O. Box 490
Dearland, TX 77588
713-485-5377
Established 1971
Chief Executive: Gabriel Baizan
Employees: 80
Business: Solvents, chemicals,
    packaging distribution
    (SIC 5191)
Sales and rank: 28.17 (76)

Spanish Broadcasting System
27 W. 56th Street
New York, NY 10019
212-541-9200
Established 1983

Chief Executive: Raul Alarcon, Jr.
Employees: 150
Business: Radio stations (SIC
    4832)
Sales and rank: 29.00 (74)

**Superior Tomato & Avocado
    Co. Inc.**
750 Merida Street
San Antonio, TX 78207
210-434-4121
Established 1988
Chief Executive: Bertha Caballero
Employees: 175
Business: Fresh vegetables, fruit
    distribution (SIC 5148)
Sales and rank: 30.10 (71)

Supreme International Corp.
7495 N.W. 48th Street
Miami, FL 33166
305-592-2760
Established 1961
Chief Executive: George
    Feldenkreis
Employees: 44
Business: Men's apparel
    (SIC 2321)
Sales and rank: 34.20 (64)

Suram Trading Corp
2655 S. Le Jeune Road
Coral Gables, FL 33134
305-448-7165
Established 1983
Chief Executive: Guido M. Adler
Employees: 7
Business: Seafood importing
    (SIC 5146)
Sales and rank: 52.00 (44)

Tamiami Automotive Group
8250 SW 8th Street
Miami, FL 33144
305-266-5500
Established 1989
Chief Executive: Carlos Planas
Employees: 105
Business: Automotive sales
    and service (SIC 5511)
Sales and rank: 41.10 (54)

**TAMSCO Technology and
    Management Services Corp.**
4041 Powder Mill Road, Suite 5
Beltsville, MD 20705
301-595-0710
Established 1982
Chief Executive: Nicholas R.
    Innerbichler
Employees: 491
Business: Electronics
    manufacturing and
    telecommunications
    (SIC 8711)
Sales and rank: 35.00 (62)

TELACU Industries
5400 E. Olympic Blvd. #300
Los Angeles, CA 90022
213-721-1655
Established 1968
Chief Executive: David C.
    Lizarraga
Employees: 600
Business: Economic development;
    Financial services (SIC 6141)
Sales and rank: 93.00 (22)

Troy Motors Inc.
777 John R. Road
Troy, MI 40808
313-585-4000
Established 1967
Chief Executive: Irma B. Elder
Employees: 115
Business: Automotive sales and
    service (SIC 5511)
Sales and rank: 111.09 (16)

**United Poultry Corp/Belca
    Foodservice**
1517 Johnson Ferry Road
Marietta, GA 30062
404-944-6499
Established 1976
Chief Executive: Alfredo Caceres
Employees: 108
Business: Food service
    distribution; Poultry products
    (SIC 5141)
Sales and rank: 78.22 (27)

Vega Enterprises Inc.
100 W. Carey Avenue

North Las Vegas, NV 89030-4144
702-384-3111
Established 1978
Chief Executive: Rafael E. Vega
Employees: 133
Business: Variety store products;
Tobacco products (SIC 5194)
Sales and rank: 63.76 (33)

The Vincam Group Inc.
9040 Sunset Drive, Suite 70
Miami, FL 33173
305-271-9920
Established 1985

Chief Executive: Carlos A.
Saladrigas
Employees: 6,500
Business: Employee leasing
(SIC 7363)
Sales and rank: 85.30 (25)

Washington Consulting Group
11 Dupont Circle
Washington, DC 20036
202-797-7800
Established 1979
Chief Executive: Armando C.
Chapelli, Jr.
Employees: 350

Business: Aviation, computer
systems and services (SIC 7379)
Sales and rank: 20.30 (102)

World Travel and Incentives Inc.
701 Fourth Avenue S, Suite 1500
Minneapolis, MN 55415
612-333-0920
Established 1975
Chief Executive: Robert de
LaFayette Cox
Employees: 160
Business: Travel services
(SIC 4724)
Sales and rank: 47.38 (47)

Educational Institutions and Programs

There are literally thousands of institutions and programs devoted to disseminating information about the Latino experience or otherwise of use to Latinos. The following is a very selective list of Latino organizations, arranged by general areas of information provided. The goal was to be representative rather than exhaustive.

—*Richard Chabrán*

BUSINESS

Hispanic-American Contractors Association
1350 U St. NW, 2nd Floor
Washington, DC 20009
(202) 265-5971

Hispanic Public Relations Association
5400 E. Olympic Blvd. #250
Los Angeles, CA 90022
(213) 726-7690
(213) 726-3126 (fax)

Latin Business Association
5400 E. Olympic Blvd. #237
Los Angeles, CA 90022
(213) 721-4000

Mexican American Chamber of Commerce
P.O. Box 65765
Los Angeles, CA 60065
(213) 221-8044

Mexican American Growers Association
405 North San Fernando Road
Los Angeles, CA 90031
(213) 227-1565

National Hispanic Corporate Council
1112 East Buckeye, Suite 2
Phoenix, AZ 85034
(602) 257-5515

National Society of Hispanic MBAs
P.O. Box 2903
Chicago, IL 60690
(312) 782-5800
(312) 782-4339 (fax)

United States Hispanic Chamber of Commerce
2000 M St. NW #860
Washington, DC 20036
(202) 862-3939
(202) 862-3947 (fax)

CULTURAL

Association for Puerto Rican-Hispanic Culture
83 Park Terrace, W.
New York, NY 10034
(212) 942-2338

Association of Hispanic Arts
173 E. 116th St., 2nd Floor
New York, NY 10029
(212) 860-5445
(212) 427-2787 (fax)

Bilingual Foundation for the Arts
421 Avenue 19
Los Angeles, CA 90031
(213) 225-4044

Casa Aztlan
1831 S. Racine Ave.
Chicago, IL 60608
(312) 666-5508

Centro Cultural de la Mision
2868 Mission
San Francisco, CA 94110
(415) 821-1155

Centro Cultural de la Raza
2125 Park Blvd.
San Diego, CA 92101
(619) 235-6135

Guadalupe Cultural Center
1300 Guadalupe Street
San Antonio, TX 78207
(512) 271-3151

Hispanic Academy of Media Arts & Science
22049 Century Park East, Suite 4100
Los Angeles, CA, 90067
(310) 201-9251

Hispanic Heritage
4011 W. Flager Street, Suite 505
Miami, FL 44134
(305) 541-5223

Instituto de Arte y Cultura
3501 Chicago Ave.
Minneapolis, MN 55407
(612) 824-0708

Latino Chicago Theater Company
1625 N. Damen
Chicago, IL 60647
(312) 486-5120

Mexican-American Cultural Center
3019 W. French Pl.
San Antonio, TX 78228
(512) 732-2156

Michigan Hispanic Cultural Arts Association
P.O. Box 17112
Lansing, MI 48901
(517) 373-8339

Movimiento Artistico Chicano
221 S. Clark Street
P.O. Box 2890
Chicago, IL 60690

La Pena Cultural Center
3105 Shattuck Ave.
Berkeley, CA 94705
(510) 849-2572

Plaza de la Raza
3540 N. Mission Road
Los Angeles, CA 90031
(213) 223-2475

Puerto Rican Cultural Center
1671 N. Claremont
Chicago, IL 60647
(312) 342-8023

La Raza Graphic Center
74 O Street
San Francisco, CA 95814
(415) 648-0930

Self-Help Graphics
3802 Brooklyn Ave.
Los Angeles, CA 90063
(213) 264-1259

**Social and Public Art Resource
Center**
685 Venice Blvd.
Venice, CA 90291
(310) 463-5356

El Teatro Campesino
P.O. Box 1240
San Juan Bautista, CA 95045
(408) 623-2444

EDUCATIONAL

**American Association for
Higher Education-Hispanic
Caucus**
University of Texas
San Antonio, TX 88285
(512) 691-4110

ASPIRA Association
1112 16th St. NW, Suite 340
Washington, DC 20036
(202) 835-3600
(202) 223-1253 (fax)

**Association of Hispanic Affairs
in Private Colleges and
Universities**
817 W. 34th St.
Los Angeles, CA 90089
(213) 743-5374

**Association of Mexican-
American Educators**
P.O. Box 1155
Pico Rivera, CA 90660
(213) 942-1500

Boricua College
3755 Broadway
New York, NY 10032
(202) 694-1000

**Hispanic Association of Colleges
and Universities**
411 SW 24th St.
San Antonio, TX 78207
(512) 433-1501

**Latin American Educational
Foundation**
303 W. Colfax Ave. #825
Denver, CO 80204
(303) 893-0656

**National Association for
Bilingual Education**
Union Center Plaza
810 1st Street NE, 3rd Floor
Washington, DC 20002
(202) 898-1829
(202) 789-2866 (fax)

**National Association for
Chicano Studies**
Department of Modern Languages
University of New Mexico
Albuquerque, NM 87131
(505) 277-5907

**National Hispanic Scholarship
Fund**
1400 Grant Ave.
Novato, CA 94945
(415) 892-9971
(415) 289-6673 (fax)

National Hispanic University
262 Grand Ave.
Oakland, CA 94610
(510) 451-0511
(510) 451-4648 (fax)

LAW

**Cuban American Legal Defense
and Education Fund**
2119 S. Webster St.
Ft. Wayne, IN 46804
(219) 745-5421

**Mexican American Legal
Defense and Education Fund**
634 S. Spring St., 11th Floor
Los Angeles, CA 90014
(213) 629-2512
(213) 629-8016 (fax)

**Puerto Rican Legal Defense
and Education Fund**
99 Hudson St. #1400
New York, NY 10013
(212) 219-3360
(212) 431-4276 (fax)

LIBRARIES

**Center for Puerto Rican Studies
Library**
Hunter College, CUNY
695 Park Ave.
New York, NY 10021
(212) 772-5685

Chicano Research Collection
Special Collections
Arizona State University
Tempe, AZ 85287-1006
(602) 965-3145

Chicano Resource Center
California State University,
Fullerton
P.O. Box 4150
Fullerton, CA 92634
(714) 773-2537

Chicano Studies Library
3404 Dwinelle Hall
University of California, Berkeley
Berkeley, CA 94720
(510) 642-3859

**Chicano Studies Research
Library**
54 Haines Hall

University of California, Los
Angeles
Los Angeles, CA 90024
(310) 206-6052

Coleccion Tloque Nahuaque
University Library
University of California,
Santa Barbara
Santa Barbara, CA 93106
(805) 893-2756
(805) 893-4676 (fax)

**Hispanic Division and Reading
Room**
Library of Congress
Hispanic Division
Jefferson Building, Room LJ 205
Washington, D.C. 20540
(202) 707-5400
(202) 707-2005 (fax)

Mexican American Archives
Special Collections
Cecil H. Green Library
Stanford University
Stanford, CA 94305
(415) 725-1022
(415) 725-6748 (fax)

**Mexican American Library
Program**
Nettie Lee Benson Latin American
Collection
SRH, 1.109
University of Texas
Austin, TX 78712
(512) 495-4520

**New Mexico State Records
Center and Archives**
404 Montezuma Street
Santa Fe, NM 87503
(505) 827-7332
(505) 827-7331 (fax)

Special Collections
University of Texas
El Paso, TX 79968
(915) 747-5697
(915) 747-5327 (fax)

MUSEUMS

Galeria de la Raza
2851 24th Street
San Francisco, CA 94110
(415) 826-8009

**Latino Museum of History, Art,
and Culture**
634 Spring Street, 11th Floor
Los Angeles, CA 90014
(213) 629-4419

Mexican Museum
Fort Mason, Building D
Laguna and Marina Blvd.
San Francisco, CA 94123
(415) 441-0445
(415) 441-7683 (fax)

Museo del Barrio
1230 5th Ave.
New York, NY 10029
(212) 831-7272

**Museum of Contemporary
Hispanic Art**
584 Broadway
New York, NY 10029
(212) 966-6699

**Museum of International Folk
Art**
706 Camino Lejo
Santa Fe, NM 87501
(505) 827-6250
(505) 827-6349 (fax)

Museum of New Mexico
113 Lincoln Ave.
Santa Fe, NM 87501
(505) 827-6450
(505) 827-6349 (fax)

POLITICAL

**Committee 51st State for Puerto
Rico**
P.O. Box 409
Brooklyn, NY 11217
(718) 782-2515

Congressional Border Caucus
440 CHOB
Washington, DC 20515
(202) 225-4831

Congressional Hispanic Caucus
House Annex II-Room 557
Washington, DC 20515
(202) 226-3430
(202) 225-7569 (fax)

**Council for Puerto Rico-U.S.
Affairs**
14 E. 60th St. #605
New York, NY 10022
(212) 832-0935

**Democratic National Committee
Hispanic Caucus**
430 S. Capitol St. SE
Washington, DC 20003
(202) 863-8000
(202) 863-8140 (fax)

**Hispanic Political Action
Committee**
246 O'Connor St.
Providence, RI 02905
(401) 941-6831

**National Association of Latino
Elected and Appointed
Officials**
3409 Garnet
Los Angeles, CA 90023
(213) 262-8503
(213) 262-9823 (fax)

**National Federation of Cuban-
American Republican Women**
2119 S. Webster
Fort Wayne, IN 46804
(219) 745-5421

**Republican National Hispanic
Assembly of the United States**
440 First St. NW #438
Washington, DC 20001
(202) 662-1355
(202) 662-1408 (fax)

Senate Republican Conference Hispanic Affairs Task Force
SD 513, DSOB
Washington, DC 20510
(202) 224-3435

Southwest Voter Registration Education Project
403 E. Commerce St. #240
San Antonio, TX 78205
(512) 222-0224
(512) 222-8474 (fax)

White House, Office of Hispanic Liaison
Old Executive Office Building #129
Washington, DC 20500
(202) 456-7845
(202) 456-6218 (fax)

RESEARCH AND POLICY CENTERS

Center for Mexican American Studies
University of Texas at Austin
CMAS 59200
Austin, TX 78712
(512) 471-4557
(512) 471-9639 (fax)

Center for Puerto Rican Studies
Hunter College, CUNY
695 Park Ave.
New York, NY 10021
(212) 772-5689
(212) 772-4348 (fax)

Chicana/Latina Research Center
c/o Chicana/o Studies Program
3125 Hart Hall
University of California, Davis
Davis, CA 95616
(916) 752-8814
(916) 752-8882 (fax)

Chicano Studies Research Center
180 Haines Hall
University of California,
 Los Angeles
Los Angeles, CA 90024
(310) 206-6052
(310) 206-1784 (fax)

Committee on Public Policy Research on Contemporary Hispanic Issues
Social Science Research Council
605 3rd St.
New York, NY 10158
(212) 661-0280
(212) 370-7896 (fax)

Cuban Research Institute
Latin American and Caribbean
 Center
DM 363, University Park Campus
Florida International University
Miami, FL 33199
(305) 348-1991
(305) 348-3593 (fax)

Hispanic Development Project
250 Park Ave, Suite 5000A
New York, NY 10458
(212) 529-9323

Hispanic Research Center
Box 2702
Arizona State University
Tempe, AZ 85287
(602) 965-3990
(602) 965-2012 (fax)

Hispanic Research Center
Thebaud Hall
Fordham University
Bronx, NY 10458
(212) 579-2629
(212) 365-1591 (fax)

Institute for Puerto Rican Policy
286 5th Ave., Suite 804
New York, NY 10001
(212) 564-1075

Inter-University Program for Latino Research
Centro de Estudios Puertorriquenos
Hunter College, CUNY
695 Park Avenue
New York, NY 10021
(212) 772-5689

Julian Samora Research Institute
216 Erickson Hall
Michigan State University

East Lansing, MI 48824
(517) 336-1317
(517) 336-2221 (fax)

Latino Institute
228 S. Wabash, Suite 204
Chicago, IL 60604
(312) 663-3603

Latino Policy Project
2420 Bowditch Street
University of California, Berkeley
Berkeley, CA 94720
(510) 642-2088
(510) 642-3260 (fax)

Mauricio Gaston Institute for Latino Community Development and Public Policy
University of Massachusetts
Dorchester, MA 02125
(617) 287-5790

Mexican-American Studies and Research Center
University of Arizona
Douglass Bldg. 315
Tucson, AZ 85721
(602) 621-7551
(602) 621-7966 (fax)

Southwest Hispanic Research Institute
University of New Mexico
1829 Sigma Chi
Albuquerque, NM 87131
(505) 277-2965
(505) 277-3343 (fax)

Stanford Center for Chicano Research
Cypress Hall
E Wing
Stanford University
Stanford, CA 94305
(415) 723-3914
(415) 725-0353 (fax)

Tomás Rivera Policy Institute
Claremont McKenna College
710 N. College
Claremont, CA 91711
(909) 625-6607

Filmography

The following filmography consists of two sections, each arranged alphabetically by title: educational and documentary films, and feature films.

—Francis C. Poole

EDUCATIONAL AND DOCUMENTARY FILMS

La Acequia [Color. 10 min. Sound. 16mm. Bluesky (1979)]. Shows the cleaning of rural irrigation ditches in New Mexico, an annual tradition practiced since the arrival of the Spanish settlers in the sixteenth century.

Agueda Martinez: Our People, Our Country [Color. 17 min. Sound. 16mm. Moctesuma Esparza Productions (1977)]. Explores the history, life, and values of Agueda Martinez, a seventy-seven-year-old woman of Navajo-Mexican descent. Her roots are in the traditions of her ancestors and in the land that supports her life as a farmer and weaver. Her life reflects the rhythms of nature and a special harmony with herself and her surroundings.

America de los Indios [Color. 29 min. Sound. 16mm. Menyah Productions (1978)]. A musical expression of the historical experience of Chicanos in the Americas. Captures a live solo performance by Daniel Valdez, formerly of El Teatro Campesino. His performance is an example of Chicano music and its guitar rhythms.

America Tropical [Color. 30 min. Sound. 16mm. KCET (1971)]. Examines the controversy surrounding the mural *American Tropical*, painted by Mexican political artist David Alfaro Siqueiros in Los Angeles in 1932. It shows a man crucified upon a double cross under the eagle of the United States currency. Relates that, after the mural's appearance, the government refused to renew Siqueiros' visa. Within two years, the mural was covered with whitewash. Indicates that the mural has been restored and preserved.

The Americas: The Latin American and Caribbean Presence in the United States [Color. 60 min. Sound. Annenberg/CPB (1992)]. Profiles the Mexican American population of California and the Latin American and Caribbean communities of Miami and New York City, posing questions about assimilation and national identity. Final installment of a ten-part series on the Americas.

And Now Miguel [B&W. 63 min. Sound. 16mm. Inform (1953)]. Story of an American family in the Southwest that has inherited the traditions of sheep raising, through several generations, from Spanish ancestors. Portrays their family life and the fulfillment of young Miguel's dream of being accepted on an equal footing by his father and older brother.

Angie [Color. 11 min. Sound. 16mm. ROES; BFA Educational Media (1971)]. Presents the reflections of Angelita Gonzales, a teenage Mexican American, as she spends her day at home, in her neighborhood, and at school. Records the pride she has in her family and culture and expresses her thoughts that higher education is needed to raise her cultural group out of poverty. Relates her sentiments toward observed prejudice in employment.

Another American [Color. 27 min. Sound. VHS. Films Incorporated (1985)]. Projections indicate that by the end of the twentieth century, Latinos may make up the largest minority group in the United States. Interviews with Ricardo Montalbán, Rita Moreno, Anthony Quinn, Adolfo, Jose Torres, Julio Iglesias, and Tito Puente underline the individualism of Latinos.

Arturo Madrid [Color. 30 min. Sound. VHS. Public Affairs Television; PBS (1988)]. Arturo Madrid is a teacher and president of the Tomás Rivera Center, which is one of the first institutes in the United States to focus on the issues of policies affecting the Latino community. Madrid has devoted himself to challenging the stereotypes that keep Latinos outside the mainstream of American life. Part of the World of Ideas series with Bill Moyers, which features interviews with people whose ideas shape America and broaden and enhance the process of democracy.

Las Aztecas and Their Medicine [Color. 30 min. Sound. 16mm. Association for Advancement of Mexican Americans (1974)]. The Aztecs made several notable contributions to the field of medicine. Among these are aspirin, toothpaste, and skull surgery.

Ballad of an Unsung Hero [Color. 28 min. Sound. 16mm. KPBS-TV; Cinewest (1983)]. Tells the story of Pedro Gonzales, a 1920's Spanish-language radio star and singer. His use of his radio popularity to protest against Depression-era racial discrimination caused trouble with the Los Angeles district attorney. Jailed on trumped-up rape charges, he was eventually deported.

Bilingual, Bicultural Mental Health Services [Color. 25 min. Sound. VHS. University of Texas, Austin, School of Social Work]. The director of La Frontera Mental Health Center in Tucson, Arizona, discusses responsive and nonresponsive models of mental health services for Chicanos. Presents a description of programs and services of La Frontera Mental Health Center, which serves more than two thousand clients per month. The importance of therapist and community worker teams is discussed as it relates to provision of resources for relief of situational and emotional stress.

Bilingualism: Promise for Tomorrow [Color. 29 min. Sound. 16mm. Inform (1977)]. Discusses language problems of Spanish-speaking children in English-speaking schools of the United States and illustrates the need for bilingual education. Presents results of the International Bilingual Conference and court rulings that have fostered bilingual education.

Brujerias [B&W. 30 min. Sound. 16mm. El Teatro de la Esperanza (1972)]. The first attempt by any group of Chicanos to record a slice of Chicano life on film, not as a documentary, but as a screenplay. A humorous look at superstitions and how people allow superstitions to overtake them.

Career for Richie [Color. 26 min. Sound. 16mm. Brigham Young University (1973)]. Presents the need for career education, the making of choices, and the selection of paths toward goals, as opposed to vocational education for specific skills.

Celebracion del Matrimonio [Color. 30 min. Sound. VHS. Margaret Hixon: University of California Extension Media Center (1986)]. This sensitive portrait of a traditional Spanish wedding ceremony in northern New Mexico illuminates the rich heritage of Hispanic culture in the Southwest and shows the importance of traditional customs and values in contemporary life.

Chicana [Color. 22 min. Sound. 16mm. InterAmerican Pictures (1979)]. Presents the traditional image of Mexican American women as nurturing mothers who free men to work, prepare the future labor force, and preserve the culture. Gives the role of women in Mexican history and the struggle of the Chicana against exploitation and for equality.

La Chicana [Color. 23 min. Sound. 16mm. Ruiz (1979)]. Photographs and paintings are used to depict the life and work of the Mexican and Mexican American woman.

Chicano [Color. 27 min. Sound. 16mm. McGraw-Hill (1971)]. Comments of Mexican Americans who have achieved economic status are interspersed with those of demonstrators advocating "Chicano power."

Chicano [Color. 23 min. Sound. 16mm. Inform (1971)]. A statement by four San Diego Mexican Americans who proudly call themselves "Chicano" to express how they feel about their Mexican heritage and their experiences in the United States. Includes interviews with poets, teachers, and labor organizers.

Chicano from the Southwest [Color/ B&W. 14 min. Sound. 16mm. Inform (1970)]. Depicts the problems faced by a Chicano family that recently moved from Texas to Los Angeles. Compares the family's lifestyle now to that when they were migrant workers in the southwestern United States.

A Chicano Perspective [Color. 28 min. Sound. 16mm. Educational Media Corporation (1978)]. Three members of the emerging generation of Latinos who are keenly aware of the need to improve the social status and the economic and political power of the Latino community in East Los Angeles.

Chile Pequin [Color. 30 min. Sound. 16mm./VHS. University of California Extension Media Center (1982)]. The tale of Irma, a young and spirited Chicana who chooses to leave home, obtain a university education, and pursue her ambitions. Focuses on Irma's struggle to extricate herself from what she believes are the constraints of a small town, a traditional Hispanic father, and a closely knit family and community.

Chulas Fronteras [Color. 58 min. Sound. 16mm./VHS. Les Blank; Flower (1976)]. An introduction to *norteña* (northern Texas-Mexican border) musicians. The music and spirit of the people is seen embodied in their strong family life and enjoyment of domestic rituals. The film makes clear the role that music has in redeeming their lives by giving utterance to collective pain.

Los Compadres [Color. 28 min. Sound. 16mm. St. Francis Productions (1971)]. Documents the history of the Spanish American people living in northern New Mexico and southern Colorado from 1598 on.

Corrido [Color. 28 min. Sound. 16mm. Pyramid Films (1975)]. Shows the Chicano people as colonized by the imperialistic United States. Includes their experience in politics in the Southwest.

Dale Kranque—Chicano Music and Art in South Texas [Color. 29 min. Sound. U-Matic. University of Minnesota Audio Visual Library Service (1982)]. Presents Chicano music and art as unique reflections of Chicano culture. Includes the work of Estaban (Steve) Jordan (accordionist), César Martínez (painter), Valerio Longoria (father of the modern accordion sound), Roberto Rios (painter), and Jose Rivera (sculptor).

Day of the Dead [Color. 17 min. Sound. 16mm. EAMES (1963)]. Shows preparations for the November 2 celebration of the Mexican Day of the Dead, one of the most popular festivals. Demonstrates the acceptance of death through a party planned for a dead girl.

Los Desarraigados (Uprooted) [B&W. 13 min. Sound. 16mm. Ruiz Productions]. A study of immigration policies and imported labor in the Los Angeles area. Focuses on one woman, showing her family, her experiences with immigration officials, and her work environment in a factory. Spanish and English narration.

Entelequia [Color. 20 min. Sound. 16mm. Chispa Productions (1977)]. Explores the range of the Chicano experience with the intent of offering a better understanding of the mestizo mentality. Narrated in Spanish and English.

Escuela Tlatelolco [Color. 45 Min. Sound. 16mm. Crusade for Justice (1972)]. Examines and discusses the events leading up to the founding of the Escuela Tlatelolco as part of the Crusade for Justice in Denver, Colorado.

La Familia: A Celebration [Color. 22 min. Sound. 16mm. Universal Education and Visual Arts Division (1977)]. A Latino extended family is shown as Juan and Delores Venegas celebrate their sixtieth wedding anniversary. There are ten children, fifty-five grandchildren, fifteen great-grandchildren, and more than two hundred in-laws and friends.

La Familia: Cultural Diversity and Its Implications of Social Work Practice [Color. 60 min. Sound. VHS. University of Texas, Austin, School of Social Work (1978)]. Major characteristics of families are discussed as well as the influence of demographic factors on family functioning and self-definition. Presents various concepts for understanding cultural variations in *la familia*.

Los Four [Color. 28 min. Sound. 16mm. RUIZ (1974)]. Documentary of a major exhibit of contemporary Chicano art at the Los Angeles County Museum of Art.

Frank Ferree: El Amigo [Color. 30 min. Sound. 16mm. R R Filmworks (1982)]. Frank Ferree, Nobel Peace Prize nominee, worked for more than forty years on the border between Texas and Mexico helping the poor and needy. Interviews with those who were aided by him tell the story of his efforts to help wherever he was needed.

Goodnight Miss Ann [Color. 28 min. Sound. 16mm. Pyramid Films (1979)]. Documentary of the boxers who train and fight at the historic Main Street Gym and the Olympic Auditorium in Los Angeles. Highlights the training of young Mexican and Mexican American boxers in the lighter weight divisions. Includes commentary by managers, trainers, and boxers, and captures the gritty reality of the boxing world.

Healthier Place to Live [Color. 11 min. Sound. 16mm. National Audio-Visual Center (1964)]. Documents the health hazards often encountered by families that live in camps for seasonal farmworkers. Describes ways to fight health and sanitation problems in the camps.

Henry: Boy of the Barrio [B&W. 30 min. Sound. 16mm. Atlantis Productions (1968)]. Presents two years in the life of a Mexican American youth in the ghetto of a major southwestern city. Shows Henry's attitude toward school, the death of his father, his mother's alcoholism, and his gradual drift toward drugs and crime.

Hispanic America [Color. 12 min. Sound. 16mm. CBS (1980)]. Survey of the growing Latino presence in the United States. Discusses the three major groups (Cubans, Puerto Ricans, and Mexican Americans). Includes mention of efforts at increased voter registration and the pros and cons of voter registration.

Home Boys [Color. 58 min. Sound. 16mm. Focal Point Films (1978)]. Life in Cuatro Flats, a housing project in East Los Angeles, is depicted as seen by *vatos* (gang members), or "home boys," as they call themselves. Explores the negative aspects of their lives: police harrassment, low-paying jobs, and the search for cultural identity.

Huelga [Color. 53 min. Sound. 16mm. McGraw-Hill (1967)]. Documentary of the migratory farmworker's strike that began in California in 1965. Focuses on the dispute between the grape growers and the migrant workers, giving both sides. The history of labor unions is compared with the labor movement activities of the farmworkers.

I Am Joaquin [Color. 20 min. Sound. 16mm. El Teatro Campesino (1970)]. A dramatic rendering of Rodolfo "Corky" Gonzáles' historical poem of the Chicano experience, accompanied by the music of modern mariachi brass and ancient temple drums. The poem unfolds with images of pyramids, murals, and twentieth century scenes. Extends from the glory of Quetzalcóatl through the War of Independence.

In the Shadow of the Law [Color. 58 min. Sound. University of California Center for Media and Independent Learning (1987)]. Shows the economic and social conditions of undocumented Mexican Americans, along with their anxiety concerning possible discovery and deportation. Also discusses difficulties of attempting to gain legal resident status under the Immigration Reform and Control Act of 1986.

An Island in America [Color. 28 min. Sound. 16mm. Anti-Defamation League of B'nai B'rith (1972)]. Overcrowding, unemployment, delinquency, crime, and discrimination in Puerto Rican communities in the United States. Includes interviews with prominent government officials who discuss the problems of Puerto Ricans.

Latino: A Cultural Conflict [Color/ B&W. 21 min. Sound. 16mm. Inform (1971)]. Story of the problems faced by a Latino high-school boy who experiences cultural misunderstandings between Latino students and Anglo teachers. The film describes the plight of Latinos in American cities in a dramatic way.

The Lemon Grove Incident [Color. 58 min. Sound. 16mm. Cinema Guild (1985)]. Docudrama that uses archival photos, dramatic reenactments, and interviews with former students to examine a successful school desegregation suit that preceded the *Brown v. Board of Education* (1954) decision. On July 23, 1930, in Lemon Grove, Calilfornia, the school board called a special meeting to consider an urgent request by the town PTA to build a second school to segregate Mexican American students. Mexican Americans boycotted classes, and parents filed a suit that eventually won with the help of the Mexican consulate in San Diego.

Luisa Torres [Color. 46 min. Sound. 16mm. Bluesky (1980)]. An elderly Hispanic woman in northern New Mexico lives a simple life that keeps her in touch with the earth and the traditions of her ancestors.

Madre Campesina [Color. 11 min. Sound. 16mm. Mexican American Cultural Center (1980)]. Presents the hardships encountered by mothers who must work in the fields and care for their children.

Manuel from Puerto Rico [Color/ B&W. 14 min. Sound. 16mm. Encyclopedia Britannica (1968)]. When he moves from Puerto Rico to New York City with his parents, a young boy has difficulty adjusting to his new life.

Mexican-American Culture, Its Heritage [Color. 19 min. Sound. 16mm. Communication Group West (1970)]. The history of Mexico and its relationship with the United States through music, dance, and art. Narrated by Ricardo Montalbán.

A Mexican-American Family [Color. 16 min. Sound. 16mm. Atlantis Productions (1970)]. The life of a Mexican American family. Shows the warmth and love among the members, the traditions they cherish, and their adjustment to a new language and society.

The Mexican-American Heritage and Destiny [Spanish ed. Color. 29 min. Sound. 16mm. Handel Film Corporation (1977)]. Shows the unique cultural achievements of the second largest minority group in the United States. Points out the success of Mexican Americans in mainstream American society.

The Mexican American Speaks: Heritage in Bronze [Color. 19 min. Sound. 16mm. Encyclopedia Britannica (1972)]. Shows the rich history and cultural heritage of the Spanish Indians in the Southwest.

Mexican-American, the Invisible Minority [Color/B&W. 38 min. Sound. 16mm. NET (1969)]. Mexican Americans, the second largest and fastest growing ethnic minority, struggle for an identity within the protest movement. The majority of Mexican Americans live in economic poverty in the southwestern region of the United States.

Mexican Americans: Viva la Raza [B&W. 47 min. Sound. 16mm. CBS; McGraw-Hill (1972)]. Grievances of the Mexican American community in Los Angeles are discussed by political and religious leaders, the police, and Chicano leaders, both moderate and militant. A violent confrontation between the Brown Berets and the police is included.

Mexican Charro: Man of Two Worlds [Color. 12 min. Sound. 16mm. Southwest Media Services (1975)]. *La charreada* (Mexican rodeo) and the *charro* (Mexican cowboy) are shown as a part of the Mexican American community.

Minnesotanos Mexicanos [Color. 52 min. Sound. VHS. Spanish Speaking Cultural Club (1978)]. Describes the problems that Mexican Americans have encountered in Minnesota, such as discrimination, unemployment, and ineffective bilingual education and political representation. Introduced with a review of Mexican ancestry in Mesoamerica.

El Mojado [Color. 20 min. Sound. VHS. Facets (1972)]. The story of a young Mexican from Chihuahua who travels a hundred miles on foot to cross the border and find work in the United States. During his journey, he is hunted by the border patrol.

Most Hated Man in New Mexico [Color. 30 min. Sound. 16mm. Films Incorporated (1969)]. Reies López Tijerina was a migrant farmworker and itinerant preacher who worked to improve the conditions of the Mexican American people living in the rural ghetto of Rio Arriba country in northern New Mexico. A look at his efforts to help their dreams become reality. Produced by NBC.

La Mujer, el Amor y el Miedo (Women, Love and Fear) [Color. 18 min. Sound. 16mm. Bilingual Cine-Television]. Discusses the needs of battered and emotionally abused Hispanic women. Focuses on the needs of the battered woman as she struggles to regain her identity and dignity.

Murals of Aztlan [Color. 23 min. Sound. U-matic. Bronson Films (1981)]. Presents murals painted by nine Chicano street artists at the Craft and Folk Art Museum in Los Angeles while the museum was open to the public. The murals reflect a variety of themes and present a cross section of styles in the mural movement.

The Murals of East Los Angeles [Color. 37 min. Sound. 16mm. RKO (1976)]. Presents the visual and artistic revolution that has graced "El Barrio del Este de Los Angeles." How Chicano artists are changing the environment with murals that express Chicano concerns and aspirations.

Nine Months [Color. 25 min. Sound. VHS. University of California Extension Media Center (1966)]. Presents a model for developing cultural relationships between health care providers and pregnant Hispanic teenagers. Prepared especially for the education of both pregnant teenagers and health care and social work personnel. Highlights the conflict between Maria, a pregnant Hispanic teenager, and her mother's beliefs. Strong message about the need for proper prenatal care.

North from Mexico: Exploration and Heritage [Color. 20 min. Sound. 16mm. Greenwood Press (1970)]. Based on a book by Carey McWilliams, this film traces Mexican American history in the Southwest from 1540 to Chicano protest demonstrations of the 1960's. Emphasizes contributions Mexican Americans have made in architecture, irrigation, agriculture, mining, and ranching. Describes Anglo-Chicano conflicts and prejudices, and relates to the Chicano struggle for equality in higher education as well as for the rights of farmworkers.

The Other Side of the Border [Color. 60 min. Sound. Video. PBS Video (1987)]. Treats illegal entry into the United States from Mexico and discusses changes in immigration law.

Our Hispanic Heritage [Color. 60 min. Sound. 16mm. Mexican International Film (1978)]. Narrated by Orson Welles, this film attempts to tell the true story of the powerful role of the Hispanic people in the discovery, conquest, settlement, development, and destiny of the United States.

Paso a Paso con los Pinos [Color. 30 min. Sound. 16mm. Southwest Educational Lab (1971)]. Preschool Mexican and Chicano children performing traditional ethnic dances, games, and songs. Shows how awareness of cultural heritage and development of motor skills can be obtained through organized group participation under adult instruction.

Los Peregrinos [Color. 97 min. Sound. 16mm. Inform (1973)]. Anthropologist and historian Jose Torres presents the seventeen-thousand-year history of the Indo-Hispanic people of the Southwest. Begins with the maternal Indian and paternal Spanish lineages and traces the anthropological, historical, and socioeconomic/political aspects of *los peregrinos* (the seekers).

El Pueblo Chicano: The Beginnings [Color. 15 min. Sound. 16mm. Bilingual Education Services, Inc. (1979)]. A comprehensive yet detailed introduction to the history and culture of the Chicano people. Includes descriptions of the pre-Columbian people, the Spanish Colonial period, and the formation of the mestizo culture.

El Pueblo Chicano: The Twentieth Century [Color. 20 min. Sound. 16mm. Bilingual Education Services, Inc. (1978)]. Explains how even though Chicanos have lived in the American Southwest since the sixteenth century and despite positive contributions to the United States during World War II and the Vietnam War, Chicanos still encounter discrimination.

Los Que Curan [Color. 45 min. Sound. 16mm. Independent Film Lab (1978)]. The *curanderos* of the Rio Grande Valley show their magical medicinal art in the treatment of the sick.

La Raza, the Story of Mexican Americans [Color. 38 min. Sound. 16mm. Inform (1971)]. The hopes, dreams, problems, and activities of Chicanos in the United States are presented through interviews with Mexican Americans from a variety of backgrounds.

Reflectiones: Barrio Library Service [Color. 30 min. Sound. U-matic. New Line Cinema]. Points out that few Chicano librarians are working in the public libraries in the Los Angeles area. Describes the programs available to educate and recruit more Chicano librarians.

Requiem 29 [Color. 31 min. Sound. 16mm. David Garcia: TRIC (1971)]. Presents the story of the National Chicano Moratorium on Vietnam (August, 1970) in Los Angeles. Interweaves footage of the mass march and the police brutalilty with the later inquest into the death of Chicano journalist Rubén Salazar, who was killed by police during the demonstration.

Santa Fe [Color. 16 min. Sound. 16mm. National Audio-Visual Center (1954)]. The richness of the southwestern tradition and Spanish and Mexican culture of Santa Fe, New Mexico.

Strangers in Their Own Land [Color. 17 min. Sound. 16mm. ABC (1971)]. Focuses on the story of Alonso Lopez, a teacher with a degree in government who is tried for his participation in a peaceful demonstration that became violent. This film examines the Anglo attitudes that prevent full realization of civil rights for Chicanos.

Strangers in Their Own Land: The Puerto Ricans [Color. 16 min. Sound. 16mm. ABC (1971)]. Examines a family of fifteen in the New York City environment, with the attendant problems of being Puerto Rican in a large U.S. city. Since 1917, when an act of Congress granted citizenship to Puerto Ricans, more than one-third of the entire population has left the island for the mainland.

Talkin' Union [B&W. 58 min. Sound. 16mm. University of Texas (1979)]. Presents the oral history of four Texas women (Mexican American, black, and white) and their union organizing activities in the years 1930 through 1960. Highlights the problems of low pay, with few benefits and poor working conditions, for "women's work."

Tapestry with Rosa Guerrero [Color. 28 min. Sound. 16mm. Lito White (1974)]. Presents the evolution of dance forms and their adaptation into various cultures. Highlights Rosa Guerrero's performance, which stresses music and dance and how they serve as a means of exchanging feelings and thoughts on nationality, religion, and language.

El Teatro Campesino (Farmworkers Theater) [B&W. 61 min. Sound. 16mm. NET (1970)]. Presents a history of El Teatro Campesino, from its beginnings in the fields, where it boosted the morale of Mexican American farmworkers, to its present role as theater committed to broad social change. Shows a group directed by Luis Valdez performing musical numbers, a satirical skit, a puppet show, and an excerpt from a full-length play.

Tejedores [Color. 28 min. Sound. 16mm. Bluesky (1978)]. Documents the art of traditional Hispanic weaving in New Mexico. Historic examples are shown, as well as modern Hispanic weavers illustrating traditional methods and techniques.

Tijerina [B&W. 30 min. Sound. 16mm. University of California Extension Media Center (1968)]. A fiery speech made by the charismatic Mexican American Reies López Tijerina at a public symposium at UCLA in 1968. Tijerina calls for a struggle for justice and equality for Mexican Americans, with changes in economics and for unification against the Anglo power structure.

Los Trabajadores Agricolas de Tejas [Color. 22 min. Sound. 16mm. Texas Farmworkers Union (1978)]. The formation of the Union de Campesinos de Tejas was a result of the conditions of the predominantly Mexican American workers in the lower Rio Grande Valley. These workers suffered the effects of wages below poverty level along with lack of education, medical care, adequate housing, and legislation to protect them. Spanish narration.

Trail North [Color. 28 min. Sound. U-matic. KPBS-TV (1983)]. Presents the work of anthropologist Robert Alvarez in his study of the history of Mexican immigration to the United States. Follows Alvarez and his son as they re-create the journey their familial ancestors made in coming north from Mexico.

The Unwanted [Color. 52 min. Sound. 16mm. KNBC-TV (1977)]. Examines the plight of Mexican workers in California. Shows practices designed to contain illegal immigration, the operations of the United States Border Patrol, and the hardships in Mexico that spur border crossing.

Vayan Volando [Color. 27 min. Sound. 16mm. Armando Valdez; Southwest Network (1975)]. In the mid-1800's, more than 300,000 acres of land were granted for the settlers from San Miguel del Vado. H. H. Mondragon relates the difficulties of the early settlers with real estate companies and the difficulties today with government agencies. Gives a good explanation of the early concepts of open grazing with no fences and how that practice was discontinued when parcels of land were rented to outsiders.

Viva la Causa [Color. 15 min. Sound. 16mm. Kartemquin Films (1974)]. An examination of Mexican mural art in Chicago, Illinois.

FEATURE FILMS

American Me [Color. 125 min. Sound. VHS. Movies Unlimited (1992)]. A realistic account of the rise and fall of the Hispanic leader of an East L.A. gang. Edward James Olmos directs and stars as Santana, the tough crime kingpin who starts his gang while a young man serving a term in Folsom Prison. With William Forsythe, Pepe Serna, and Evelina Fernandez.

Angelo My Love [Color. 90 min. Sound. VHS. Movies Unlimited (1983)]. A look at real-life gypsies in New York City. Angelo is a precocious twelve-year-old who is after an ancient family ring that was stolen. While he is on his adventure, viewers see the colorful world of the gypsies. Robert Duvall wrote and directed.

The Barefoot Contessa [B&W. 128 min. Sound. VHS. Facets (1954)]. Ava Gardner stars as a fiery Latin dancer destined to be a major Hollywood star. Loosely based on the life of Rita Hayworth, this cynical drama uncovers the underbelly of show business and marriage to the upper crust. With Humphrey Bogart, Edmund O'Brien, and Rossano Brazzi.

The Blackboard Jungle [B&W. 101 min. Sound. VHS. Facets (1955)]. Based on the novel by Evan Hunter. Glenn Ford is a teacher trying to survive in the New York Public School system. His class of juvenile delinquents includes Vic Morrow, Sidney Poitier, Jamie Farr, and Paul Mazursky. A serious drama that launched Bill Haley's "Rock Around the Clock."

Body Moves [Color. 98 min. Sound. VHS. Movies Unlimited (1991)]. Rival gangs battle for love and turf, and compete in dance contests. With Diane Granger and Kirk Rivera.

Born in East L.A. [Color. 85 min. Sound. VHS. Movies Unlimited (1987)]. Cheech Marin stars as a Hispanic American who is mistakenly nabbed by immigration officials and sent to Tijuana. Marin wrote and directed.

Bring Me the Head of Geraldo Rivera [Color. 30 min. Sound. VHS. Facets (1989)]. Two shorts shot in super-8mm. by Chicago filmmaker Jim Sekora. A dark comedy that takes aim at the talk show business and its hosts.

Cheech and Chong's Next Movie [Color. 95 min. Sound. VHS. Movies Unlimited (1980)]. Cheech Marin and Tommy Chong wreak havoc in a welfare office, a movie studio, a massage parlor, and outer space.

Cheech and Chong's Nice Dreams [Color. 87 min. Sound. VHS. Movies Unlimited (1981)]. Cheech and Chong discover a new ice cream flavor and take a rocky road to riches. Cheech Marin and Tommy Chong, with Timothy Leary and Pee Wee Herman.

Cheech and Chong's Still Smokin' [Color. 91 min. Sound. VHS. Movies Unlimited (1983)]. The organizers of a Dutch film festival want Burt Reynolds and Dolly Parton as their guests of honor; instead they get Cheech Marin and Tommy Chong.

Cheech and Chong's Up in Smoke [Color. 86 min. Sound. VHS. Movies Unlimited (1978)]. Cheech and Chong's first film, about a spoiled rich kid and a hippie hitchhiker who try to smuggle a van with a body made of marijuana across the Mexican border. Stars Cheech Marin and Tommy Chong.

Colors [Color. 120 min. Sound. VHS. Facets (1988)]. Controversial police story about two partners on an anti-gang patrol in the Los Angeles area. Robert Duvall is the seasoned pro and Sean Penn is the cocky rookie. Actual L.A. gang members played supporting roles. With Maria Conchita Alonso and Trinidad Silva. Directed by Dennis Hopper.

Cuando Viajan las Estrellas [B&W. 108 min. Sound. VHS. Facets (1942)]. When a Hollywood star comes to Mexico to learn flamenco, she falls in love with a genteel *charro* played by Jorge Negrette, a singing cowboy. With Raquel Rojas and Joaquin Pardave. In Spanish.

Death of a Bureaucrat [Color. 87 min. Sound. VHS. Facets (1966)]. From Cuba, this film by Tomas Gutierrez Alea pays homage to the history of film comedy from Bunuel and Vigo, to the satire of Billy Wilder. Spanish with English subtitles.

Far Out Man [Color. 84 min. Sound. VHS. Movies Unlimited (1990)]. Tommy Chong is the perpetually stoned roadie who gets hypnotized and is sent on a whacked-out trek to find his 1960's roots. In this spaced-out farce he comes face-to-face with actress-daughter Rae Dawn Chong.

Kiss of the Spider Woman [Color. 119 min. Sound. VHS. Facets (1985)]. Based on the novel by Manuel Puig. The story of a gay man and a political activist locked together in a South American prison cell. With William Hurt and Sonia Braga.

L.A. Bad [Color. 101 min. Sound. VHS. Movies Unlimited (1987)]. A tough Latino teenage gang member is faced with cancer. With Esai Morales, Chuck Bail, and Carrie Snodgrass.

Last Supper [Color. 101 min. Sound. VHS. Facets (1976)]. A moral tale of a pious slaveholder who decides to improve his soul and instruct his slaves in the glories of Christianity by inviting twelve of them to participate in a reenactment of the Last Supper. Spanish with English subtitles.

Llanito [Color. 50 min. Sound. VHS. Facets (Picture from Films) (1971)]. Story of a group of retarded boys who live on the fringe of society with Indians and Chicanos. Contains strange Christian symbolism.

Magdalena Viraga [Color. 90 min. Sound. VHS. Facets (1986)]. An experimental feature film by Nina Menkes that concerns the inner life of a prostitute who is arrested as a murder suspect. The film uses closeup shots and surreal details.

Mambo [Color. 94 min. Sound. VHS. Facets (1954)]. Story of a beautiful young Venetian woman who resents her drab lot as a factory worker and fosters ambitions to be a great dancer. With Michael Rennie, Silvana Mangano, and Shelley Winters.

Mambo Kings [Color. 104 min. Sound. VHS. Facets (1992)]. A stylized adaptation of Oscar Hijuelos' Pulitzer Prize-winning novel *The Mambo Kings Play Songs of Love* (1989). Centers on the lives of two young immigrant brothers who reach for fame as pioneers of mambo music. With Armand Assante and Antonio Banderas.

Mambo Mouth: John Leguizamo [Color. 60 min. Sound. VHS. Movies Unlimited]. A one-man stage show from Hispanic actor-comic-writer John Leguizamo. Looks at Latino life in the United States.

El Mariachi [Color. 81 min. Sound. VHS. Movies Unlimited (1993)]. Director Robert Rodriguez shot this low-budget action comedy for the Hispanic home video market. The tale of a mariachi singer who finds himself in the middle of a gang rivalry when he is mistaken for a killer. Spanish with English subtitles.

Memories of Underdevelopment [Color. 97 min. Sound. VHS. Facets (1968)]. A Cuban intellectual is too idealistic to leave for Miami but too decadent to fit into the new Cuban society. One of the first Cuban films to be released in the United States. Spanish with English subtitles.

The Milagro Beanfield War [Color. 112 min. Sound. VHS. Facets (1988)]. Set in New Mexico, this story concerns the war between a greedy land developer and a small-time bean farmer. Steeped in the lore of Chicano culture, the film draws on myth and folklore to evoke a regional culture. Directed by Robert Redford.

Rude Awakening [Color. 101 min. Sound. VHS. Movies Unlimited (1989)]. A pair of radicals who fled the United States in the late 1960's uncover a Central Intelligence Agency plot to foment war in Central America. When they return home, they encounter culture shock. Starring Cheech Marin and Eric Roberts.

The Shrimp on the Barbie [Color. 87 min. Sound. VHS. Movies Unlimited (1990)]. Cheech Marin plays an enterprising restaurateur who wants to open the first Mexican eatery in Australia.

Skyline [Color. 96 min. Sound. VHS. Movies Unlimited (1984)]. A comedy that deals with a Spanish photographer who emigrates to New York in the hope of pursuing a career. His plans are threatened when he falls in love and must choose between his two worlds. Spanish and English, with English subtitles.

Stand and Deliver [Color. 105 min. Sound. VHS. Movies Unlimited (1988)]. The true story of Jaime Escalante, a Colombian-born engineer who left the business world to teach the youth of Los Angeles' barrio slums, using unorthodox methods to inspire them. Starring Edward James Olmos.

El Super [Color. 90 min. Sound. VHS. Facets (1979)]. A comedy set in New York, shot by two Cuban exiles. The story of a building superintendent who longs to return to Miami or Cuba, where it does not snow. Spanish with English subtitles.

El Tango en Broadway [B&W. 95 min. Sound. VHS. Facets (1934)]. A rare musical comedy starring the master of the tango, Carlos Gardel. With Trini Ramos, Blanca Vischer, and Vicente Padula. In Spanish without English subtitles.

Things Are Tough All Over [Color. 88 min. Sound. VHS. Movies Unlimited (1982)]. Cheech Marin and Tommy Chong encounter trouble in downtown Las Vegas as they play womanizers who run afoul of the mob and Arab sheiks.

West Side Story [Color. 149 min. Sound. VHS. Movies Unlimited (1961)]. Leonard Bernstein's classic musical based on *Romeo and Juliet*. Lovers Natalie Wood and Richard Beymer are doomed when rival street gangs clash. Directed by Robert Wise and Jerome Robbins.

Organizations

American G.I. Forum
331 Manor Road
Austin, TX 78723
Advocacy group for Latinos, with about twenty thousand members. Various programs target education, business development, veterans' rights, and social issues.

ASPIRA Association
1112 16th Street NW
Suite 340
Washington, DC 20036
Dedicated to Latino dropout prevention and the promotion of leadership skills among Latinos.

Association of Hispanic Arts
173 E. 116th St.
2nd Floor
New York, NY 10029
Promotes Hispanic arts by providing services to nonprofit Hispanic arts organizations.

Central American Resource Center
P.O. Box 2327
Austin, TX 78768
A clearinghouse for information on Central American refugees and U.S. policy. Maintains a library of human rights reports and provides legal services for refugees.

Chicanos por la Causa, Inc.
1112 East Buckeye Rd. #1
Phoenix, AZ 85034
With offices in twenty-three cities, CPLC supports economic development, housing programs, opportunities for leadership, child care, and legalization services.

Comision Femenil Mexicana Nacional, Inc.
2001 Tyler Ave. #204
South El Monte, CA 91733
Promotes involvement of Latinas in social, political, and economic in-

stitutions. Chapters in Arizona, New Mexico, and Texas.

Comite de Festejos de la Independencia Centroamericana
660 S. Bonnie Brae
Los Angeles, CA 90057
Supports civic and cultural projects associated with the Central American community. About ten thousand members.

Committee in Solidarity with Latin American Non-Violent Movements
c/o Joanna Swanger
910 W. 26th Street
Apt. 302
Austin, TX 78705
Supports nonviolent movements in Latin America. Promotes networking among leaders in peace movements and religious and political organizations.

Cuban American Legal Defense and Education Fund
2119 S. Webster St.
Fort Wayne, IN 46804
Advocates nondiscriminatory treatment for Latinos in education, employment, politics, housing, and the legal system.

Descendants of Mexican War Veterans
P.O. Box 830482
Richardson, TX 75083-0482
Members include descendants of and persons interested in the Mexican American War. Maintains a library and provides genealogical research assistance.

Encuentros Encantadores
P.O. Box 133
Montrose, CA 91021
A singles organization for Latinos, with about two thousand members.

Farm Labor Organizing Committee
714½ S. St. Clair St.
Toledo, OH 43609
Seeks to unionize Hispanic migrant farmworkers.

Feministas Unidas
2101 E. Coliseum Blvd.
Ft. Wayne, IN 46805
Members are feminist scholars in Hispanic, Hispanic American, or Latin American studies.

Hispanic Outreach Taskforce
P.O. Box 9124
Whittier, CA 90601
Acts as a network of community resources for better health education and socioeconomic conditions for the Hispanic community.

Hispanic Policy Development Project
36 E. 22nd Street
9th Floor
New York, NY 10010
Promotes public awareness of Hispanic issues, especially in the areas of employment, education, and public policy.

Labor Council for Latin American Advancement
815 16th Street NW
Suite 310
Washington, DC 20006
Representing about forty national and international trade unions, LCLAA seeks to ensure justice, decent living standards, and social dignity for Latinos.

League of United Latin American Citizens
900 E. Karen Street C-215
Las Vegas, NV 89109
Promotes voter registration and political awareness among Latinos in order to gain full social, political,

education, and economic rights. More than 100,000 members.

Mexican American Legal Defense and Educational Fund
634 S. Spring St.
11th Floor
Los Angeles, CA 90014
Protects the civil rights of Hispanics through litigation in the areas of education, employment, immigration, and voting rights. Maintains a law school scholarship program.

Mexican-American Opportunity Foundation
6252 Telegraph Rd.
Commerce, CA 90040
Provides programs in child care, employment, and educational services for Spanish-speaking and other minority Americans.

National Alliance of Spanish-Speaking People for Equality
1701 16th Street NW #601
Washington, DC 20009
A civil rights organization seeking equality for all U.S. Hispanics. Projects focus on education, employment, health, and living conditions.

National Association of Cuban American Women U.S.A., Inc.
2119 S. Webster St.
Fort Wayne, IN 46802
Provides information to Cuban American women and other Spanish-speaking groups regarding opportunities in local, state, and federal agencies.

National Association of Latino Elected and Appointed Officials
3409 Garnet St.
Los Angeles, CA 90023
Leadership network dedicated to the advancement of Hispanic people. This clearinghouse for citizenship information and voting statistics maintains a database of citizenship service providers, His-

panic businesses, and mailing lists of Latino elected officials.

National Council of Hispanic Women
L'Enfant Plaza Station
Washington, DC 20026
Seeks to strengthen the leadership role of Hispanic women and improve social and economic conditions for Hispanics.

National Council of La Raza
810 First St. NE #300
Washington, DC 20002-4205
Serves as a national voice for more than one hundred Hispanic organizations. Maintains a library with statistics and census information.

National Hispanic Council on Aging
2713 Ontario Rd. NW
Washington, DC 20009
Promotes the well-being of the elderly Hispanic community through education and research.

National IMAGE, Inc.
930 W. Seventh Ave.
Suite 117-121
Denver, CO 80204
Works to increase employment opportunities for Latinos and to seek equality with other groups. Provides scholarships to Latinas changing careers or reentering the work force.

National Latina Health Organization
P.O. Box 7567
Oakland, CA 94601
Promotes understanding of health and reproductive issues among Hispanic women through education and bilingual access to health care.

National Latino Communications Center
3171 Los Feliz Blvd.
Suite 201
Los Angeles, CA 90039
Promotes, produces, and distributes

Hispanic-oriented programs on current and cultural affairs.

Neighbor to Neighbor
2601 Mission St.
Suite 400
San Francisco, CA 94110
Seeks to change U.S. policy in Central America from military aid to reconstruction aid.

Office of the Americas
8124 W. 3rd St. #201
Los Angeles, CA 90048-4309
Educates U.S. citizens on Latin American issues. Seeks to end intervention by the United States in Latin American countries. Produces the weekly radio program *Focus on the Americas.*

Operation PUSH (People United to Serve Humanity)
930 E. 50th Street
Chicago, IL 60615
Seeks educational and economic equality for all people. Works with schools to reestablish academic excellence and discipline.

Partners of the Americas
1424 K Street NW
Suite 700
Washington, DC 20005
Links U.S. states with cultural, agricultural, development, and other exchange projects in Latin America and the Caribbean.

Pueblo to People
2105 Sibler Rd.
Suite 101
Houston, TX 77055
Educates U.S. citizens on Latin American issues. Works with community-based cooperatives in Latin America to sell goods and crafts in the United States.

Puerto Rican Legal Defense and Education Fund
99 Hudson St.
14th Floor

New York, NY 10013
Protects and promotes the civil rights of Puerto Ricans and other Latinos through litigation in such areas as education, employment, voting rights, and housing. Also works to increase the number of Latinos in the legal profession.

Republican National Hispanic Assembly
440 First St. NW #414
Washington, DC 20001
Strives to increase the number of Hispanic Republican elected officials at all levels of government.

SER-Jobs for Progress National, Inc.
100 Decker St.
Suite 200
Irving, TX 75062
Organization with offices around the country, dedicated to providing job preparation and training, adult basic education, and counseling.

Spanish Institute
684 Park Ave.
New York, NY 10021
Dedicated to the promotion of the culture, life, and history of Spanish-speaking countries through classes and art programs.

U.S. Hispanic Chamber of Commerce
2000 Massachusetts Ave. NW, #860
Washington, DC 20036-3307
Promotes a positive image for Hispanic businesses and supports their development. Compiles statistics, reports on business achievements, and sponsors competitions and awards.

Serial Publications

The following is a representative, but not comprehensive, list of Chicano/Latino databases, journals, magazines, and newspapers. The short bibliographic citations include title, place of publication, publisher, language, frequency, and founding date. The term "bilingual" refers to English and Spanish. A hyphen and space following the date indicate that the periodical was still being published as of 1994. —*Marisol Zapater-Ferrá*

INDEXES

Chicano Database on CD-ROM. Berkeley, Calif.: Chicano Studies Library Publications Unit, University of California at Berkeley. 1990-   , semiannual.

The Chicano Index. Berkeley, Calif.: Chicano Studies Library Publications Unit, University of California at Berkeley. 1989-   , annual (irregular).

JOURNALS

Agenda: A Journal of Hispanic Issues. Washington, D.C.: National Council of La Raza. English. 1977, semiannual. Merged with the quarterly magazine in 1977 to form a bimonthly journal with the same title.

Alborada. Northridge, Calif.: Amigos de la Cultura Hispanoamericana, California State University, Northridge. Spanish. 1978-   , semiannual.

The Americas Review. Houston, Tex.: University of Houston. Bilingual. 1986, quarterly. Continues *Revista Chicano-Riqueña*.

Atisbos: Journal of Chicano Research. Stanford, Calif.: Chicano Graduate Association, Stanford University. English. 1975?, irregular.

Aztlán: A Journal of Chicano Studies. Los Angeles, Calif.: Chicano Studies Research Center, UCLA. English. 1970-   , semiannual.

Bilingual Research Journal. Washington, D.C.: National Association for Bilingual Education. English. 1992-   , semiannual. Continues *The NABE Journal*.

Bilingual Review/Revista Bilingüe. Tempe, Ariz.: Bilingual Review/ Revista Bilingüe. Bilingual. 1974-   , triannual.

Blue Mesa Review. Albuquerque, N.Mex.: Department of English, University of New Mexico. English. 1989-   , triannual.

Borderlands Journal. Brownsville, Tex.: South Texas Institute of Latin and Mexican American Research, Texas Southmost College. Bilingual. 1980, semiannual. Continues *South Texas Journal of Research and the Humanities*.

CACR Review. Fort Collins, Colo.: Colorado Association for Chicano Research. English. 1982, irregular.

Calmécac. Pico Rivera, Calif.: Calmécac de Aztlán en Los, Inc. Bilingual. 1980, triannual.

Campo Libre: Journal of Chicano Studies. Los Angeles, Calif.: Department of Chicano Studies, California State University. English. 1981, semiannual.

Centro de Estudios Puertorriqueños Bulletin. New York, N.Y.: Centro de Estudios Puertorriqueños, Hunter College, City University of New York. Bilingual. 1987-   , irregular.

Chicano Latino Law Review. Los Angeles, Calif.: School of Law, UCLA. English. 1991-   , quarterly. Continues *Chicano Law Review*.

Chiricú. Bloomington, Ind.: Chicano-Riqueño Studies, Indiana University. Bilingual. 1976-   , irregular.

Chismearte. Los Angeles, Calif.: Los Angeles Latino Writers Association. Bilingual. 1976, quarterly. First published by the Concilio de Arte Popular.

Confluencia. Greeley, Colo.: Department of Hispanic Studies, University of Northern Colorado. Bilingual. 1985-   , semiannual.

Crítica. La Jolla, Calif.: Chicano Studies, University of California, San Diego. Bilingual. 1984, quarterly.

El Cuaderno. Dixon, N.Mex.: Academia de la Nueva Raza. Bilingual. 1971, irregular.

Cuban Studies. Pittsburgh, Pa.: Center for Latin American Studies, University Center for International Studies, University of Pittsburgh. English. 1986-   , annual. Continues *Cuban Studies Newsletter*.

De Colores: Journal of Chicano Expression and Thought. Albuquerque, N.Mex.: Pajarito Publications. Bilingual. 1978, quarterly. Continues *De Colores: Journal of Emerging Raza Philosophies*.

Encuentro Femenil. San Fernando, Calif.: Hijas de Cuauhtémoc. English. 1973, irregular.

Época. Washington, D.C.: National Concilio for Chicano Studies. English. 1970?, irregular.

Ethnic Affairs. Center for Mexican Studies, University of Texas, Austin. English. 1987-   , semiannual.

Fragmentos de Barro = Pieces of Clay. San Diego, Calif.: Chicano Studies Department, San Diego Mesa College. Bilingual. 1976, annual.

Fuego de Aztlán. Berkeley, Calif. Bilingual. 1976/1977, quarterly.

El Grito. Berkeley, Calif.: Quinto Sol Publications. Bilingual. 1967, quarterly.

El Grito del Sol. Berkeley, Calif.: Tonatiuh Quinto Sol International. Bilingual. 1976, quarterly.

The Guadalupe Review. San Antonio, Tex.: The Guadalupe Cultural Arts Center. English. 1991-   , annual.

Harvard Journal of Hispanic Policy. Cambridge, Mass.: Hispanic Student Caucus, John F. Kennedy School of Government, Harvard University. English. 1986/

1987-   , irregular. Previous title *Journal of Hispanic Policy*. Continues *Journal of Hispanic Politics*.

Hispanic Journal of Behavioral Sciences. Newbury Park, Calif.: Sage Publications. English. 1979-   , quarterly.

Hispanic Review of Business. Washington, D.C.: Latin National Publishing Corporation. English. 1983?, 10/year. Continues *Hispanic Business Monthly*.

Imagine. Boston, Mass.: Imagine. Bilingual. 1984-   , irregular.

The Journal of the Association of Mexican American Educators. Turlock, Calif.: Association of Mexican American Educators. Bilingual. 1986/1987, annual.

Journal of Borderlands Studies. Las Cruces, N.Mex.: Department of Economics, New Mexico State University. English. 1986-   , irregular.

The Journal of Contemporary Puerto Rican Thought. Chicago, Ill.: Midwest Institute of Puerto Rican Studies and Culture. English. 1975, triannual. Continues *The Rican*.

Journal of Mexican American History. Santa Barbara, Calif.: Journal of Mexican American History. English. 1970-   , annual (irregular).

Latino Studies Journal. Chicago, Ill.: Center for Latino Research. English. 1990-   , irregular.

Llueve Tlaloc. Tucson, Ariz.: Bilingual Bicultural Program, Pima Community College. Bilingual. 1975-   , irregular.

Lo Sencillo. San Fernando, Calif.: Grupo Poético Literario Los Sencillos. Bilingual. 1976, irregular.

Maize. San Diego, Calif.: Centro Cultural de la Raza. Bilingual. 1977, quarterly. Originally published with subtitle *Cuadernos de Arte y Literatura Xicana*.

Mango. San Jose, Calif.: Mango. Bilingual. 1976/1977, irregular.

Metamorfosis. Seattle, Wash.: Centro de Estudios Chicanos, University of Washington. Bilingual. 1977, semiannual.

Mexican Studies = Estudios Mexicanos. Berkeley, Calif.: UC Mexus/UNAM. Bilingual. 1985-   , semiannual.

New Visions of Aztlán. Riverside, Calif.: Aztlán Cultural Arts Foundation, University of California, Riverside. Bilingual. 1990-   , irregular.

Palabra: Revista de Literatura Chicana. Tempe, Ariz.: Palabra. Spanish. 1979, semiannual.

Puerto del Sol. Las Cruces, N.Mex.: Department of English, New Mexico State University. English. 1960?, semiannual.

The Puerto Rican Journal. Chicago, Ill.: Latino Heritage Press. English, Spanish, and Creole. 1982-   , quarterly.

La Raza Law Journal. Berkeley, Calif.: Boalt Hall School of Law, University of California at Berkeley. 1983-   , biannual.

Revista Mujeres. Santa Cruz, Calif.: Mujeres, University of California, Santa Cruz. Bilingual. 1984, biannual.

Saguaro. Tucson, Ariz.: Mexican American Studies and Research Center, University of Arizona. Bilingual. 1984-   , annual.

Tejidos. Austin, Tex.: Tejidos. Bilingual. 1973/1974, quarterly.

Third Woman. Bloomington, Ind.: Chicano-Riqueño Studies, Indiana University. Bilingual. 1981-   , semiannual.

Xalmán: Alma Chicana de Aztlán. Santa Barbara, Calif.: Xalmán. Bilingual. 1974, irregular.

MAGAZINES

Alma Latina: For the Interest of Latin-American Children. San Antonio, Tex.: N. Aguilar & Sons. Bilingual. 1932, monthly.

Areito. Miami, Fla.: Areito, Inc. Spanish. 1974?-   , irregular.

El Barrio. Detroit, Mich.: Casa de Unidad. Bilingual. 1990-   , irregular.

Barrio Warriors. Los Angeles, Calif.: Gus Frias. English. 1990-   , irregular.

¡Cambio!: Hispanic Bilingual Magazine. Phoenix, Ariz.: L. M. Ortiz & Associates. Bilingual. 1988-   , irregular.

Caminos. Los Angeles, Calif.: Caminos. Bilingual. 1980, monthly.

Caracol. San Antonio, Tex.: Caracol. Bilingual. 1974/1975, monthly.

Comadre. Santa Barbara, Calif.: Comadre. English. 1977, irregular.

Con Safos. Los Angeles, Calif.: Con Safos. Bilingual. 1968, irregular.

Corazón de Aztlán. Los Angeles, Calif.: Corazón de Aztlán. Bilingual. 1981, irregular.

Correspondencia. San Antonio, Tex.: Interchange Woman to Woman. Bilingual. 1987-   , irregular.

Cubatimes. New York, N.Y.: Cuba Resource Center. English. 1980-   , bimonthly.

Firme. San Gabriel, Calif.: Mexican American Ventura in Corporate Organizations. English. 1981, irregular.

Hispanic. Washington, D.C.: Hispanic Publishing Corporation. English. 1988-   , monthly.

Hispanic Business. Santa Barbara, Calif.: Hispanic Business. English. 1979-   , monthly.

Hispanic Engineer. Los Angeles, Calif.: Career Communications Group. English. 1984-   , quarterly.

Hispanic Entrepreneur. New York, N.Y.: Sun. English. 1987-   , irregular.

Hispanic Outlook in Higher Education. Fairfield, N.J.: Hispanic Outlook in Higher Education. English. 1990-   , monthly.

Hispanic Physician. Arcadia, Calif.: California Hispanic American Medical Association. English. 1989- , quarterly.

Hispanic Times. Woodland Hills, Calif.: Hispanic Times Enterprises. English. 1980- , 5/year.

Intercambios Femeniles. Los Angeles, Calif.: National Network of Hispanic Women. English. 1980- , irregular.

Latin Quarter. Los Angeles, Calif.: Latin Quarter. English. 1974, irregular.

Latina. Santa Monica, Calif.: Charisma Enterprises. English. 1982, irregular.

Latino Stuff Review. Miami, Fla.: Latino Stuff Review. Bilingual. 1990- , quarterly.

Lector. Encino, Calif.: Floricanto Press. English. 1982/1983, irregular.

Low Rider. San Jose, Calif.: Park Avenue Design. English. 1977- , monthly.

La Luz. Denver, Colo.: La Luz Publications. English. 1972, monthly.

Magazín. San Antonio, Tex.: Magazín. Bilingual. 1971, monthly.

Más. New York, N.Y.: Univision Publications. Bilingual. 1989?, quarterly.

National Hispanic Journal. Austin, Tex.: National Hispanic Institute. English. 1981, irregular.

Nuestro. New York, N.Y.: Americana Communications. English. 1977, monthly.

Pachucos Modern Chicano Fashions. Stockton, Calif.: Pachuco's Fashion. English. 1990- , irregular.

El Pocho Che. Oakland, Calif.: El Pocho Che. English. 1969, irregular.

Pocho Magazine. Berkeley, Calif.: Pocho Magazine. English. 1992- , irregular.

Q-VO Magazine. San Gabriel, Calif.: Hernández. Bilingual. 1979, irregular.

Raíces. San Jose, Calif.: Editorial Raíces. Spanish. 1990- , irregular.

La Raza. Los Angeles, Calif.: Barrio Communications Project. Bilingual. 1970- , triannual.

La Raza Habla. Las Cruces, N.Mex.: Chicano Affairs Program, New Mexico State University. Bilingual. 1973, irregular.

The Red/Net: The Hispanic Journal of Education, Commentary and Reviews. Encino, Calif.: Floricanto Press. English. 1988?- , quarterly.

Regeneración. Los Angeles, Calif.: Regeneración. English. 1970, bilingual.

Somos. San Bernardino, Calif.: Los Padrinos of Southern California. Bilingual. 1978, irregular.

Temas. New York, N.Y.: Temas Magazine. Spanish. 1974?- , monthly.

Viaztlan. San Antonio, Tex.: Centro Cultural Aztlán. Bilingual. 1983?, irregular.

Vista. Coral Gables, Fla.: Horizons. Bilingual. 1985, weekly.

NEWSPAPERS

¡Adelante Raza! Appleton, Wisc.: La Raza, Inc. Bilingual. 1972?- , monthly.

El Águila. Los Angeles, Calif.: El Águila. Spanish. 1981?, weekly.

El Andar. Santa Cruz, Calif.: Bilingual. 1989- , monthly.

Ave Fénix de Arizona. Glendale, Calif.: Ave Fénix. Spanish. 1989- , biweekly.

El Azote. El Paso, Tex.: Grupo de Caballeros Católicos Amantes de la Verdad. Spanish. 1922, irregular.

Azteca News. Santa Ana, Calif.: Azteca News. Spanish. 1991- , weekly.

¡Basta Ya! Los Siete. Bilingual. 1969, irregular.

El Chicano. Colton, Calif.: Inland Empire Community Newspapers. Bilingual. 1969?, irregular.

Claridad. New York, N.Y.: Betances. Bilingual. 1972, weekly.

Compass. Houston, Tex.: Compass. English. 1967?, irregular.

Dos Mundos. Kansas City, Mo.: Manuel Reyes. Bilingual. 1980?- , biweekly.

Eastside Sun. Los Angeles, Calif.: Eastern Group Publications. 1945- .

El Eco de Virginia. Norfolk, Va.: El Eco de Virginia. Bilingual. 1991- , monthly.

El Eco del Pacífico. San Francisco, Calif.: El Eco del Pacífico. Spanish. 1856, daily.

El Editor. Lubbock, Tex.: Amigo Publications. Bilingual. 1978, weekly.

El Extra. Dallas, Tex.: Futuro Enterprises. Spanish. 1986?- , weekly.

El Gallo. Denver, Colo.: El Gallo News. Bilingual. 1968, monthly.

Hijas de Cuauhtemoc. Long Beach, Calif.: Hijas de Cuauhtemoc. Bilingual. 1971, irregular.

Hispania. Colorado Springs, Colo.: Confe Communications. Bilingual. 1986?- , weekly. Title changed to *Hispania News* in 1993.

Hispanic News. Portland, Oreg.: Hispanic News. Bilingual. 1981?- , irregular.

El Hispano. Albuquerque, N.Mex.: El Hispano. Spanish. 1966- , weekly.

El Hispano. Sacramento, Calif.: Chavez Newspapers. Bilingual. 1969- , weekly. Supersedes *El Hispano-americano*.

Horizontes. San Francisco, Calif.: Juan Pifarre, San Francisco Hispanic Center. Spanish. 1983- , biweekly.

El Informador. Chicago, Ill.: El Informador. Bilingual. 1965?- , weekly.

Latin Times. East Chicago, Ind.: Latin Times. English. 1956, weekly.

El Latino. San Diego, Calif.: Latina Enterprises. Spanish. 1988- .

El Malcriado. Delano, Calif.: Union del Campesino de America. Bilingual. 1964, irregular.

El Mensajero. San Francisco, Calif.: Hispanimedia L. P. Spanish. 1987- , weekly.

El Mexicalo. Bakersfield, Calif.: El Mexicalo. Bilingual. 1979?- , weekly.

El Mundo. Oakland, Calif.: Alameda. Spanish. 1960?- , weekly.

El Mundo. Wenatchee, Wash.: The Wenatchee World. Spanish. 1989- , weekly.

Nuestro Tiempo: Bilingual Section of the Los Angeles Times. Los Angeles, Calif.: Los Angeles Times. Bilingual. 1990?- , monthly.

El Observador. San Jose, Calif.: El Observador. English. 1980- , weekly.

La Oferta Review. San Jose, Calif.: La Oferta Review. Bilingual. 1978?- , weekly.

La Opinión. Los Angeles, Calif.: I. E. Lozano. Spanish. 1926- , daily.

El Pregonero. Washington, D.C.: Carrol. Spanish. 1976?- , weekly.

La Prensa. San Antonio, Tex.: Duran Duran. Bilingual. 1989- , weekly.

La Prensa. San Diego, Calif.: La Prensa. Bilingual. 1977- , weekly.

La Raza. Chicago, Ill.: La Raza Publications. Spanish with some English. 1971?- , weekly.

El Renacimiento. Lansing, Mich.: El Renacimiento. Bilingual. 1970, biweekly.

San Benito News. San Benito, Tex.: News Publishing. English. 1956?- , semiweekly.

Semanario Azteca. Santa Ana, Calif.: Fernando Velo. Spanish. 1980?- , weekly.

Sí Se Puede. Santa Barbara, Calif.: Sí Se Puede. Bilingual. 1974, irregular.

El Sol. Houston, Tex.: El Sol. Bilingual. 1966?- , weekly.

El Sol de Fort Bragg. Fort Bragg, Calif.: North Coast Hispanic Education Foundation. Spanish. 1989- , monthly.

El Tecolote. San Francisco, Calif.: Acción Latina. Bilingual. 1970- , irregular.

El Tenaz. Santa Barbara, Calif.: Teatro Nacional de Aztlán. Bilingual. 1971?, irregular.

La Tribuna de New Jersey & New York. Union City, N.J.: Ruth Molenaar. Spanish. 1988- , biweekly.

La Verdad. Abiquiu, N.Mex.: La Verdad. Spanish. 1844, weekly.

La Verdad. Crystal City, Tex.: La Raza Unida Party. Spanish. 1970?, irregular.

Vida. Oxnard, Calif.: Vida Newspaper. Spanish. 1983?- , weekly.

La Voz Hispana de Colorado. Denver, Colo.: Hispano Publications & Graphics. Bilingual. 1975- , weekly. Continues *El Eco.*

La Voz Libre. Los Angeles, Calif.: La Voz Libre. Spanish. 1981- , Weekly.

¡Ya Mero! Pharr, Tex.: ¡Ya Mero! Spanish. 1969, Irregular.

STUDENT NEWSPAPERS

Adelante. Riverside, Calif.: MECHA, University of California at Riverside. English. 1969, irregular.

Advocate. Sacramento, Calif.: ASUC Student Lobby. English. 1972?, monthly (irregular).

Águila. Stanford, Calif.: MECHA de Stanford. English. 1986?, irregular.

El Aguila. Santa Monica, Calif.: El Águila MECHA, Santa Monica College. English, some Spanish. 1971, semiannual.

El Alacrán. Long Beach, Calif.: MECHA, California State University, Long Beach. Bilingual. 1970, irregular.

Alternative. Santa Barbara, Calif.: Associated Students and Press Council, University of California, Santa Barbara. English. 1976?, weekly.

The Blade. Irvine, Calif.: Students at the University of California, Irvine. English. 1975, monthly (irregular).

Bronce. Oakland, Calif.: Mexican American Student Confederation. Bilingual. 1968, irregular.

Carnalismo. Santa Cruz, Calif.: Carnalismo Publications, Student Activities, UC Santa Cruz. Bilingual. 1977, irregular.

Chicanismo. Stanford, Calif.: Chicano Press, Stanford University. English. 1970?, irregular.

Chicano Student Movement. Los Angeles, Calif.: Chicano Student Movement. English. 1968, monthly.

Chispas. Berkeley, Calif.: MECHA. Bilingual. 1971 or 1972, quarterly.

Daily Aztec. San Diego, Calif.: Associated Students of San Diego State College. English. 1962, daily Tuesday through Friday except summer session. Continues *San Diego Daily Aztec.*

Destinos. Fresno, Calif.: Chicano Journalism Students Association. English. 1990, irregular.

El Diario de la Gente. Boulder, Colo.: United Mexican American Students, University of Colorado. English. 1972, monthly.

Estos Tiempos. Stanford, Calif.: El Centro Chicano, Stanford University. English. 1983?, irregular.

El Estudiante del Pueblo. Santa Clara, Calif.: Frente Estudiantil, University of Santa Clara. Bilingual. 1976, irregular.

Evening Elan. Los Angeles, Calif.: Associated Students, East Los Angeles College, Los Angeles Community College District. English. 1949?, irregular.

The Fifth Sun. Davis, Calif.: Chicano/ Latino Students at UC-Davis. Bilingual. 1992- , irregular.

La Gente de Aztlán. Los Angeles, Calif.: Communications Board of ASUCLA, UCLA. Bilingual. 1986- , 2/quarter during academic year.

Nuestra Cosa. Riverside, Calif.: Chicano Student Programs-35, University of California, Riverside. Bilingual. 1972?, irregular.

Sentimientos. Fresno, Calif.: California State University, Fresno. English. 1978, irregular.

Student Mobilizer. Boston, Mass.: National Student Coalition Against Racism. English. 1975?, irregular.

Voces del Norte. East Lansing, Mich.: Chicano Students for Progressive Action (Chispas), Michigan State University. Bilingual. 1978?, irregular.

Voz Fronteriza. La Jolla, Calif.: Voz Fronteriza, UC San Diego. Bilingual. 1976-   , irregular.

Time Line

The time line that follows lists important historical events in Latino history as well as providing illustrative snapshots of cultural development.

—*Russell M. Magnaghi*

1000-300 B.C.E.	The Olmec civilization of coastal Veracruz-Tabasco, Mexico, is considered to be the first in Mesoamerica.
250-850 C.E.	The Mayan civilization flourishes.
700-900	The Toltecs dominate central Mexico.
711	North African Moors invade Spain and within a few years conquer it.
718-1492	The Christian Reconquest of Spain is conducted.
1325	Tenochtitlán (modern Mexico City), the Aztec capital, is founded.
1492	Christopher Columbus lands in the New World.
1496	Santo Domingo, Dominican Republic, is founded. It is the oldest continuous European settlement in the Americas.
1508	Juan Ponce de León explores Puerto Rico.
1513	Juan Ponce de León visits the coast of Florida.
1514	Diego Velásquez de Cuéllar completes the conquest of Cuba.
1519	Havana, Cuba, is founded.
	Alonzo Álvarez de Pineda discovers and names the Rio Espiritu Santo (Mississippi River).
1519-1521	Hernán Cortés conquers the Aztec Empire, using La Malinche as an interpreter.
1521	Mexico City is founded. It becomes the capital of the viceroyalty of New Spain and later of Mexico.
1522	Gregorio Villalobos introduces cattle from Hispaniola to Mexico and starts the cattle industry on the mainland.
1525	Cuauhtémoc, the last Aztec emperor who refuses to surrender, is captured and killed by the Spanish.
	Esteban Gómez sails along the Atlantic Coast from Newfoundland to Cuba.
1526	Lucas Vázquez de Ayllón attempts to settle the Cape Fear River area of North Carolina.
1528-1536	Álvar Núñez Cabeza de Vaca and three other survivors of an expedition led by Pánfilo de Narváez begin their famous odyssey from Florida through Texas and the Southwest to Culiacán, Mexico.
1539	The Hernán de Soto expedition lands in Florida.
1540	Francisco Vázquez de Coronado leads an expedition that eventually takes him to central Kansas.
1542	Juan Rodríguez Cabrillo explores the coast of Alta California.
1550's	Spanish Basque whalers establish stations on the coast of Labrador.
1553	The University of Mexico, the oldest in the Americas, is founded by royal charter.
1565	St. Augustine, Florida, is founded. It is the first permanent European town in what is now the United States.
1566	Missionary work begins in Guale (modern Georgia).
1571	Jesuit missionary efforts in Virginia come to a bloody end.
1598	Juan de Oñate establishes a colony in New Mexico.

1610	Santa Fe, New Mexico, is founded.
	The epoch work of Gaspar Pérez de Villagrá, *Historia de Nuevo México*, is published. This is an early literary work recounting the founding of New Mexico by Juan de Oñate.
1659	El Paso-Juárez begins as a mission.
1680	The Pueblo Revolt in New Mexico drives out the Spanish.
1692	Diego de Vargas reconquers New Mexico.
1698	Andrés de Arriola founds Pensacola, Florida.
1700	Eusebio Francisco Kino establishes Mission San Xavier del Bac south of modern Tucson, Arizona.
1706	Albuquerque, New Mexico, is founded.
1736	The discovery of Arizonac, a silver mine just south of the Arizona border, attracts hundreds of prospectors and miners.
1769	Gaspar de Portolá and Junípero Serra lead an expedition that begins the settlement of California. Mission San Diego is established as the first mission.
1770	Spanish Franciscan missionaries introduce the first citrus fruits into California.
1774	Juan Pérez is the first Spaniard to sail north of California. He reaches the northern tip of Queen Charlotte Island, British Columbia, and is the first European to encounter the local Indians.
1775	Manuel Butrón is granted land and becomes the first rancher in California.
1776	Juan Bautista de Anza and 240 settlers establish San Francisco.
1778	During the American Revolution, the Spanish attack British positions. Governor Fernando de Leyba of St. Louis aids George Rogers Clark's conquest of the Illinois Country.
1780	Bernardo de Gálvez, governor of Louisiana, successfully captures British-held Mobile.
1781	A Spanish force from St. Louis seizes Fort St. Joseph (modern Niles, Michigan).
	Governor Bernardo de Gálvez takes British Pensacola.
	Los Angeles is founded as a Spanish pueblo.
1785 and 1788	Thomas Jefferson, in a series of letters from Paris, stresses the importance of Spain and the Spanish language in the United States.
1788-1789	Esteban José Martínez establishes a fort and mission at Nootka Sound, Vancouver Island, British Columbia.
1791	A slave revolt in Haiti leads to independence.
1792	Alejandro Malaspina leads a scientific expedition into Alaskan waters. This is the farthest north that Spain reaches.
1794	In the Nootka Convention between Great Britain and Spain, the latter yields sovereignty over the Northwest Coast.
1800	The New Mexican Penitente Brotherhood, a lay Hispanic society organized for penance and mutual aid, flourishes in New Mexico.
	Census data show that there are 20,000 settlers in New Mexico, 4,000 settlers in Texas, and 1,200 settlers in California.
1804	More than 600 Mexican miners are working the Santa Rita copper mine in southern New Mexico.
1806	Gabriel Moraga enters California's San Joaquin Valley.
1810	Miguel Hidalgo y Costilla, with El Grito de Dolores, leads the first revolt against Spain in Mexico.

1818	Hippolyte de Bouchard, sailing under the flag of the "Republic of Buenos Aires," seizes Monterey, California, and destroys property before he and his pirates leave.
1821	Stephen F. Austin is given a land grant in Texas and settles the first Anglo-Americans.
	The Santa Fe Trail opens between New Mexico and Missouri.
1822	California Governor Pablo Sola convenes a junta. He and its members swear allegiance to Agustín Iturbide's government in Mexico.
	Luis Antonio Argüello, a native Californian, is the first popularly chosen governor of California.
1823	President James Monroe presents the Monroe Doctrine.
c. 1823	Mexicans open the New Almadén mercury mines south of San Jose, California.
1824	A Mexican colonization law opens thousands of acres of land in Texas and other areas to settlement.
1828	*Pastorelas* (shepherd's plays) are popular, and *Pastorela en dos actos* is staged at missions in the Southwest.
1830	Mexico closes Texas to emigration from the United States.
1831	Fifty Cubans are working in a Cuban-owned cigar factory in Key West, Florida.
1833	Secularization of the missions of Alta and Baja California begins in earnest.
1834	New Mexico's first newspaper, *Crepúsculo de la Libertad*, is published for a month.
	José María Padrés and José María Hijar lead an expedition that unsuccessfully attempts to settle California's Sonoma Valley.
1836	Texas declares its independence from Mexico.
	Lorenzo de Zavala is elected vice president of the Republic of Texas but resigns in October because of ill health.
	Governor Albino Pérez issues a proclamation on the establishment of a public education system in New Mexico.
	About 180 men, including 9 Tejanos, defend the Alamo for two weeks before it falls to a Mexican army under General Antonio López de Santa Anna.
1840	Mexican-born Francisco García Diego y Moreno is appointed bishop of the new diocese of both Californias.
1842	Francisco López, a rancher at San Feliciano Canyon, discovers the first gold in California and starts a short-lived gold rush.
1845-1854	Some 80,000 Mexican Americans are added to the United States population.
1846	War with Mexico is declared by the U.S. Congress.
	General Andrés Pico inflicts serious losses on General Stephen Kearney's invading army at the Battle of San Pascual, California.
1847	The Treaty of Cahuenga is signed by rebellious Californios in Los Angeles and John C. Frémont.
	The Taos Rebellion in New Mexico leads to the death of Governor Charles Bent and others.
1848	Discovery of gold in California precipitates a rush that attracts hundreds of Mexicans, Chileans, and Peruvians, among thousands of others. Racial tensions are common in the gold fields.
	By the Treaty of Guadalupe Hidalgo, the United States obtains the Southwest.
1849	Of the 48 delegates to the California constitutional convention, 8 are Californios. They obtain passage of an article in the constitution calling for all state laws and regulations to be bilingual.
1850's	U.S. filibusters illegally send arms to Cuban revolutionaries.
1850	A Foreign Miner's Tax is passed, affecting foreign-born and California-born Hispanics.

1851	Congress passes a land act that makes it difficult for native Californians to reclaim their lands.
	Joseph Morehead invades Sonora and Baja California with no effect.
1851-1856	The California Board of Land Commissioners reviews Spanish and Mexican claims.
1852	Raousset de Boulbon, a filibuster, lands 250 men at Guaymas, Sonora, but his actions fail.
1853	By the terms of the Gadsden Purchase, the United States obtains southern Arizona from Mexico in exchange for a future railroad.
	William Walker unsuccessfully invades both Baja California and Sonora.
	José Sadoc Alemany from Catalonia becomes the first archbishop of the new diocese of San Francisco.
1855	*El Clamor Público* is established as the first Spanish-language newspaper in Los Angeles.
	A California anti-vagrancy law is anti-Mexican and becomes known as the "Greaser Law."
	The California legislature negates the constitutional requirement to have laws and regulations appear in both Spanish and English.
1857	The Cart War develops in Texas when Anglo businessmen try to take over the lucrative trade between the coast and San Antonio from Mexicans.
1859	Juan Cortina crosses from Mexico to Brownsville and seizes the town in an attempt to highlight injustices against Mexicans.
1861	When the Civil War breaks out, Santos Benavides of Laredo, Texas, joins the Confederate Army and recruits fellow Chicanos.
1862	The Mexican army defeats French forces at Puebla on May 5. Annual Cinco de Mayo festivities now commemorate that event
	David G. Farragut, of Spanish origin, captures New Orleans and later Mobile.
1866	The United States demands the withdrawal of French forces from Mexico.
1866-1877	The Salt War develops over use of salt mines about one hundred miles east of El Paso.
1867	Antonio Coronel, an educator and civic leader, is elected California state treasurer on the Democratic ticket.
1868	A group of Puerto Ricans start a small but unsuccessful rebellion with El Grito de Lares on September 23. In October, Cubans issue El Grito de Yara, a declaration of independence from Spain.
1869	Cuban bacteriologist Carlos Juan Finlay of the U.S. Academy discovers that yellow fever is transmitted by the mosquito.
1870	David G. Farragut is named the first admiral of the U.S. Navy.
1872	*La Crónica*, a Spanish-language weekly, begins publication in Los Angeles.
1875	Romualdo Pacheco is the first Californio governor of American California, serving for 9 months.
1876	Casimiro Barela is elected to the first Colorado senate; he was reelected often.
1880	Cuban patriot José Martí arrives in New York City, where he will stay for 15 years.
	The federal census shows there are 230,000 people of Mexican descent in the United States.
1883	Hispanic *vaqueros* in the Texas Panhandle successfully lead a cowboy's strike.
	Daniel de León of Columbia University in New York offers the first course in Latin American history.
1884	Elfego Baca becomes an immediate folk hero as a result of a shootout in New Mexico. Later, as a lawyer, he follows an unsuccessful career in politics.

1886	Vicente Martínez Ybor, a Spanish businessman, arrives from Cuba and starts the tobacco industry in Tampa, Florida.
1888	Esteban Ochoa dies. As mayor of Tucson, he was known for establishing the public school system in Arizona.
1889	The first Conference of American States, the forerunner of the Organization of American States, is held in Washington, D.C.
	The White Caps (Las Gorras Blancas), angry at white domination in New Mexico, begin a series of destructive raids against Anglo and Nuevo Mexicano property.
1890	El Partido del Pueblo is formed and fights for the objectives of the White Caps.
1891-1904	The Court of Private Land Claims reviews claims in New Mexico, Arizona, and Colorado.
1891	Creation of the U.S. Forestry Service and subsequent federal regulation of range land within the public domain has a direct impact on Mexican American sheep and cattle raising in northern New Mexico.
1892	Francisco Torres is accused of murdering his employer, and he is lynched by a mob in Santa Ana, California. This is the last of many lynchings in California and Southwestern history.
1893	Charles F. Lummis publishes *Land of Poco Tiempo* and *The Spanish Pioneers*, creating a fantasy heritage of the Spanish in the Southwest. This mythic view angers many Mexican Americans.
1894	La Alianza Hispano-Americana is founded in Tucson. Membership quickly grows across the West.
1897-1906	Miguel A. Otero is the only Hispanic American to serve as territorial governor of New Mexico.
1898	The Spanish-American War is fought. Puerto Rico is ceded to the United States.
1900	The first emigration of Puerto Ricans begins and sees people going to the Hawaiian Islands and New York City.
1902	A Texas state poll tax and other devices disfranchise Tejanos.
	The United States recognizes the independence of Cuba.
	The first Hispanic Catholic parish opens in New York City.
1903	Chicano copper miners in Clifton-Morenci, Arizona, unsuccessfully strike over a reduction in pay.
	More than 1,000 Mexican and Japanese sugar beet workers successfully strike in Ventura, California.
1907	Pedro Jaramillo dies. He was one of the best-known Mexican American folk healers, or *curanderos*, in South Texas.
	Aurelio Espinosa publishes a version of the New Mexican folk drama *Los Comanches*, thus beginning the study of Mexican American folklore.
1908	It is estimated that between 60,000 and 100,000 Mexicans annually enter the United States.
1910	The Mexican Revolution begins. During the years of upheaval, thousands of Mexicans immigrate to the United States.
	Thirty-five out of 100 delegates to the New Mexico constitutional convention are Hispanos.
1911	The Mexican Protective Association, one of the earliest agricultural unions, is founded in Texas.
1912	The Council of Spanish-American Work, an agency of the National Council of Churches, is organized to coordinate missionary work among Hispanics.
1913	A strike and riot by Mexican workers known as the Durst Ranch affair occurs near Wheatland, California. It leads to the establishment of the California Commission on Immigration and Housing.
1914	The first Mexicans begin to arrive in Chicago.

1915	John Lomax publishes several versions of border ballads (*corridos*).
	Liga Protectora Latina, a fraternal and mutual aid society, is established in Arizona.
1916	The Texas Folklore Society begins publication of a series of Mexican American folklore.
	Ezequiel Cabeza de Vaca is elected governor of New Mexico on the Democratic ticket.
1917	The Jones Act gives American citizenship to Puerto Ricans.
	About 120,000 Puerto Ricans register for the U.S. Army. Many see action in World War I.
	Striking miners, mostly Mexicans in Bisbee, Arizona, are deported to Mexico. No court action is taken against the vigilantes.
1918	Octaviano A. Larrazolo is elected governor of New Mexico.
1919	Many Puerto Rican soldiers remain in New York City.
	During a steel strike in the Chicago-Calumet area, many Mexicans are brought in as strikebreakers.
1920	The Michigan, Holland-St. Louis, Columbia, and Continental sugar companies recruit more than 5,000 Mexicans to work in the sugar beet fields of Michigan and Ohio.
1921	The Order of Sons of America is established by Hispanic leaders in San Antonio who seek rights and representation in Texas.
1923	Bethlehem Steel brings 1,000 Mexicans to work in the Pennsylvania steel mills.
	Actor Ramón Novarro appears in his first film, *Prisoner of Zenda*.
1924	The first Mexican Catholic church is established in South Chicago.
	New immigration legislation favors nationals from the Western Hemisphere and leads to increased immigration from Mexico.
	The Border Patrol is established to control illegal immigration.
1925	Mexican workers, many from sugar beet fields, take jobs in the auto plants of Detroit. A Mexican community forms in Detroit.
1926	The Arizona Cotton Growers Association arranges for 2,000 Puerto Rican workers to immigrate.
1927	Historian and educator Carlos E. Castañeda begins his career at the University of Texas.
1928	The Confederation of Mexican Labor Unions (Confederación de Uniones Obreras Mexicanas) is founded.
	Octaviano Larrazolo, formerly governor of New Mexico, is elected to the U.S. Senate.
1928-1929	President-elect Herbert Hoover makes an extended trip to Latin America.
1929	The League of Latin American Citizens combines with the Sons of America and the Knights of America to form the League of United Latin American Citizens in Corpus Christi, Texas.
	The Great Depression begins. Economic conditions and discrimination force thousands of Mexicans and Mexican Americans to move to Mexico during the Depression.
1930	Leo Carrillo begins his motion picture career, later becoming the sidekick of the Cisco Kid.
	Chicanos comprise 75 percent of the workforce of the six major Western railroads.
1931	The radical Cannery and Agricultural Workers Industrial Union is formed in California.
	Massive deportation of Mexicans from California begins.
1930's	Mexican muralist Diego Rivera paints murals in Detroit, San Francisco, and New York and aids unemployed Mexicans in the United States.

1933	The Confederation of Mexican Farm Workers' and Laborers' Unions is created.
	The San Joaquin Cotton Strike breaks out. It is the largest and best organized of a series of strikes.
	The El Monte Berry Strike in California sees Mexican pickers strike for better hours and pay.
1934	The Liga Obrera de Habla Español, a coal miners union composed of Mexicans and Mexican Americans in central New Mexico, is organized.
	A U.S.-Cuban treaty relieves the latter from the onerous terms of the Platt Amendment.
1935	Mexican muralist David Alfaro Siqueiros opens an exposition of paintings in New York City.
	The Congress of Industrial Organizations forms, offering representation to Hispanics who do not have access to craft unions.
1936	Anthony Quinn begins his film career with *The Plainsman*. Later he will promote Mexican American causes.
1938	The Congreso de los Pueblos de Habla Español, an early national Chicano civil rights organization, is founded in Los Angeles.
	The Pecan Shellers' Strike in San Antonio, Texas, sees considerable violence and leads to improvements in working conditions and mechanization of the industry.
1939	After a long career as a *santero* (carver of wooden saints), Patrocinio Barela of New Mexico exhibits his woodcarvings at the New York World's Fair.
1940	Census data show that Mexican Americans are the most rural of the major ethnic groups in the United States.
	Vicki Carr, one of the top female vocalists in the United States, is born in Texas.
1941-1945	During World War II, 400,000 Mexican Americans serve in the U.S. military.
1941	Joan Báez, folksinger and Vietnam War activist, is born.
	The Fair Employment Practices Committee is established in the Office of Production Management by executive order. In the Southwest, more than a third of all complaints come from Mexican Americans.
1942	The Bracero Program is initiated by a U.S.-Mexican executive agreement, allowing short-term contract laborers into the United States.
	One project in Ohio, three in Minnesota, and twenty-one in Michigan focus on instruction of the children of migrant workers.
1943	The governor of Texas authorizes the creation of the Good Neighbor Commission, which works to improve Anglo understanding of Mexican and Mexican American culture.
	The zoot-suit riots break out in Los Angeles, spreading to San Diego, Oakland, and other cities.
1944	Guy Gabaldón, a U.S. Marine, becomes a hero during the battle for Saipan in the South Pacific.
1945	La Union Cívica is created in Saginaw, Michigan, to promote social and cultural activities.
	The Bishops' Committee for the Spanish-Speaking is formed.
1946	Poor working conditions spur bracero workers to walk from Millington, Michigan, to Detroit to protest to the Mexican consul.
	Méndez v. Westminster School District bans separate Chicano schools in California.
1947	President Harry S Truman is the first U.S. president to make an official visit to Mexico.
1947-1949	Famed dancer José Limón achieves artistic success in the United States.

1948	*Delgado v. Bastrop Independent School District* bans separate Chicano schools in Texas.
	A Texas mortician refuses to hold services for serviceman Félix Longoria, who was killed in Luzon, Philippines. Lyndon B. Johnson, a new senator, secures his burial in Arlington National Cemetery. The incident leads to creation of the American G.I. Forum.
	Luis Muñoz Marín becomes the first elected governor of Puerto Rico.
1949	Mariano S. Garriga is appointed as the first Mexican American bishop of Corpus Christi.
	New Mexico passes a fair employment practices act largely in response to the League of United Latin American Citizens' fight against discrimination in that state.
	The Wisconsin Board of Health takes over regulation and certification of all migrant labor camps in the state.
1940's	Catholic dioceses in the Midwest develop ministries among Mexican American workers.
1950	According to census data, there are 2.2 million people of Mexican descent in the United States.
	The American Council of Spanish-Speaking People is founded as an alliance of Mexican Americans in the Southwest. Its goal is to eliminate ethnic discrimination in education and increase Chicano political participation.
	The sugar beet industry recruits Puerto Ricans and flies them to Michigan. The effort is soon discontinued.
	The Protestant National Council of Churches begins its Migrant Ministry in Michigan.
1950's	Immigration from Argentina, Chile, and Uruguay increases. These immigrants closely resemble Western European immigrants to the United States in terms of socioeconomic status and demographics.
1951	The first large migration of Puerto Ricans to New York begins.
1952	The McCarran-Walter Immigration and Nationality Act continues the quota system set up by the immigration acts of 1921 and 1924. It has been used to deport Mexican labor organizers.
	Puerto Rico becomes a commonwealth of the United States.
1954	Operation Wetback cracks down on illegal Mexican immigrants.
1954-1961	Richard Alonzo "Pancho" Gonzales is a top-ranking professional tennis player.
1956	Henry B. González becomes the first Mexican American to be elected to the Texas state senate in 110 years.
1959	Fidel Castro's revolutionary forces seize control of Havana and Cuba. Between that time and 1962, some 155,000 Cubans immigrate to the United States.
	José Antonio Villareal's autobiographical novel *Pocho* is the first Chicano novel published by a major U.S. publishing company and is the forerunner of the Chicano literary renaissance.
1960	More than 750 Dominicans arrive in the United States. Large Dominican American communities will form later in many cities.
	Viva Kennedy clubs are formed to support the presidential ambitions of John F. Kennedy.
1961	Henry B. González is the first Texan of Mexican American background to be elected to Congress.
	Since World War II, some 847,000 Puerto Rican have settled in New York City, Chicago, and Los Angeles.
1961-1969	During the Vietnam War, 19.2 percent (8,016) of all casualties have Spanish surnames.
1961-1978	Thousands of people flee from internal unrest in Central America (38,900 Salvadorans, 35,700 Panamanians, 35,500 Guatemalans, and 28,000 Hondurans) and legally enter the United States.
1962	César Chávez organizes the Farm Workers' Association in Delano, California.

1963	Reies López Tijerina and his followers found the Alianza Federal de los Pueblos Libres/Federal Alliance of Free Towns to implement his ideas concerning Spanish and Mexican land grants in New Mexico.
	A group of five working-class Mexican Americans (Los Cinco) win election to the Crystal City, Texas, city council and end Anglo domination.
	Trini López becomes a successful singer.
	The Treaty of El Chamizal is signed by the United States and Mexico, settling a land dispute.
1964	Everett Álvarez, Jr., a naval aviator, is shot down over North Vietnam and becomes the first American prisoner.
	Leo Grebler, at the University of California, Los Angeles, starts the Mexican American Study Project, a comprehensive socioeconomic study.
	A blueberry strike among Mexican American workers in Grand Ledge, Michigan, is union related.
	Joseph Montoya is the first Mexican American to be elected to the U.S. Senate.
	César Chávez founds the newspaper *El Malcriado* in Delano, California.
	The Venceremos Brigade is established by radical Chicanos who in 1969-1970 go to Cuba to cut cane to demonstrate their solidarity.
1965	The Mexican and U.S. governments create the *maquiladora* system.
	The Association of Mexican American Educators is established in Redwood City, California.
	The Delano Grape Strike begins and permanently alters Chicano consciousness.
	Rodolfo "Corky" Gonzáles founds the Crusade for Justice in Denver, Colorado, to articulate the demands of the Chicano movement.
	El Teatro Campesino is founded by Luis Valdez to augment the work of César Chávez's United Farm Workers movement. It becomes an independent organization.
1965-1973	The Freedom Airlift takes thousands of Cubans to the United States.
1966	Chamizal National Memorial is created in El Paso, Texas, to commemorate the peaceful settlement of a boundary dispute.
	In what came to be known as the Albuquerque Walkout, 50 Chicano leaders leave an Equal Employment Opportunity conference, alleging that the needs of La Raza are not being considered.
	Jesús Salas stages an 80-mile "March on Madison" in Wisconsin to protest working conditions on farms.
	César Chávez merges the National Farm Workers Association with the Agricultural Workers Organizing Committee and forms the United Farm Workers Organizing Committee of the AFL-CIO.
1967	Quinto Sol Publications begins publishing in Berkeley, California.
	The Brown Berets are established in Los Angeles. They disbanded in 1972.
	The Chicano epic poem "Yo soy Joaquin"/"I am Joaquin" is published by Rodolfo "Corky" Gonzáles.
1968	Hemisfair 68 is held in San Antonio, Texas, to promote Hispanic cultural contributions.
	Rodolfo "Corky" Gonzáles and Reies López Tijerina lead a Chicano contingent in the Poor People's March on Washington.
	The Bilingual Education Act requires that students who do not speak English be given instruction in both English and their native language.
	The Mexican American Legal Defense and Education Fund is founded.

1969	Students attending a conference issue *El Plan de Santa Bárbara: A Chicano Plan for Higher Education*, calling for reforms in the educational system.
	The first Chicano college, Colegio Jacinto Treviño, is founded in Mission, Texas.
	The first annual Chicano Youth Liberation conference unites Chicanos and allows them to discuss self-determination.
	Active Mexicanos is founded as a private social club in Seattle, Washington, and provides a wide variety of public services.
	The Cabinet Committee on Opportunities for Spanish Speaking Peoples is created by President Lyndon B. Johnson.
	The Academia de la Nueva Raza, first known as Academia de Aztlán, is established in New Mexico. It helps youngsters rediscover the culture of the barrio.
	The Black Berets, a somewhat nationalistic paramilitary youth group, is formed and develops in California and New Mexico. It acts as the "shock troops" of the Chicano movement.
	La Raza Unida Party gains control of the government and school board of Crystal City, Texas.
	The Chicano Priests' Organization is formed in San Jose, California, to provide ministerial and political support to the Chicano movement.
1970	The U.S. Bureau of the Census estimates that Central and South Americans account for 7 percent of the Hispanic population in the United States. Of the 6 million Mexican Americans, 85 percent are urban dwellers. The 1970 census is the first to specifically identify a "Hispanic" population.
	Persons born in Cuba or of Cuban descent account for 8 percent of the population of Tampa, Florida.
	The AFL-CIO begins a successful drive in Wisconsin, Michigan, Indiana, and Illinois to unionize Mexican American workers.
	César Chávez of the United Farm Workers Organizing Committee signs a pact with a majority of California's Central Valley table-grape growers, ending a five-year grape pickers' strike.
	Immigrants to the United States from South America and their children number more than 350,000.
	Deganawidah-Quetzalcóatl University is incorporated near Davis, California. It is the only Indian-Mexican university in the United States.
	The Comisión Femenil Mexicana Nacional is formed to advance the image of Chicanas.
	World War II hero Guy Gabaldón returns his Navy Cross and Purple Heart in a protest against discrimination against minorities in the United States.
	The Salinas Lettuce Strike begins.
	There are some 27,000 first- and second- generation Colombian Americans living in New York City and about 3,500 foreign-born Colombian Americans in Chicago.
1971	Hispanic nuns form Las Hermanas.
	Romana Acosta Bañuelos is appointed by President Richard Nixon as the first Mexican American treasurer of the United States.
	The novel *The Plum Plum Pickers* by Raymond Barrio is considered to be one of the leading novels of the contemporary Chicano literary renaissance.
	Lee Trevino earns $231,000 and becomes the first golfer to win the U.S., Canadian, and British Opens in a single year.
	Quechua shepherds from Peru emigrate to work on sheep ranches in the American West.

1972	The Puerto Rican Legal Defense and Education Fund is created in New York.
	The Farah strike begins, directed against Farah Manufacturing Company, a clothing manufacturer operating along the Texas-Mexico border.
	The United Farm Workers Organizing Committee becomes a full-fledged AFL-CIO union, changing its name to the United Farm Workers of America.
1973	Francisco S. Álvarez, holder of more than 80 U.S. and foreign patents, is appointed principal scientist at Syntex in Palo Alto, California.
	The Chicano Police Officers Association is established in Albuquerque, New Mexico, to protect civil rights.
	Porfirio Salinas, Jr., a Texas artist, dies. He was known for his Southwestern scenes and was Lyndon Johnson's favorite painter.
	Juan Corona, a labor contractor in California, is found guilty of killing 25 migrant farmworkers. Five years later, the conviction is overturned and a new trial is ordered.
1974	The Equal Educational Opportunity Act changes official policy, as stated in the Bilingual Education Act of 1968, to emphasize use of English in schools, with native languages used only as necessary for the transition to English.
	Robert Sánchez is appointed as the first Mexican American archbishop of Santa Fe, New Mexico.
	The Forum of National Hispanic Organizations, a nonpolitical umbrella organization, is established.
1975	Fuerzas Armadas de Liberación Nacional (FALN) is created by a merger of Puerto Rican groups. Members are involved in bombing incidents.
	Jerry Apodaca, a Democrat, becomes governor of New Mexico, and Raúl Castro becomes governor of Arizona.
	Asociación Nacional Pro Personas Mayores is established.
	The California Agricultural Labor Relations Act, promoted by Governor Jerry Brown, passes. It gives agricultural workers the benefits of the National Labor Relations Act (1935).
1976	The U.S. Bureau of the Census estimates that Central and South Americans from Spanish-speaking nations account for 7 percent of the Hispanic-origin population in the United States.
	Latinos in Texas and Ohio provide presidential candidate Jimmy Carter with votes that help swing those states in his favor; 81 percent of the Hispanic vote is for Carter.
	The Congressional Hispanic Caucus is established to highlight Hispanic contributions.
1977	The Annual Chicano Film Festival in San Antonio draws 7,000 people who view as many as 55 films and videotapes.
	Leonel J. Castillo is appointed as the first Mexican American commissioner of the U.S. Immigration and Naturalization Service.
1978	Polly Baca-Barragán becomes the first Chicana to be elected to the Colorado senate.
1979	President Jimmy Carter appoints Edward Hidalgo as secretary of the Navy.
	A California Chicano federation, the Latino Political Task Force, is formed with a goal of political organization among Latinos.
	Luis Valdez's *Zoot Suit* is the first Chicano play to be performed on Broadway.
	Patrick Flores, a supporter of the Chicano struggle for social justice, is appointed archbishop of San Antonio, Texas.
	The National Association of Spanish Broadcasters and the United States Hispanic Chamber of Commerce are established in Washington, D.C.

1979-1986	Fleeing violence in Guatemala, thousands of Indians immigrate to Florida and the West Coast of the United States.
1980	The Committee in Solidarity with the People of El Salvador (CISPES) forms. It seeks self-determination for Salvadorans and an end to U.S. intervention in El Salvador.
	The U.S. Bureau of the Census reports that there are approximately 9 million Mexican Americans.
	The League of United Latin American Citizens reports a membership of 200,000.
	During the Mariel boatlift, some 140,000 Cubans arrive in Florida.
1980's	During the early part of the decade, between 300,000 and 500,000 Dominicans come to the United States. They represent 10 percent of the population of the Dominican Republic.
	Guatemalan government oppression of the Maya Indians causes thousands to emigrate to the United States.
	Conditions in Sandinista-controlled Nicaragua cause 200,000 people to leave the country; many settle in the United States.
1981	Henry Cisneros becomes the first Mexican American mayor of San Antonio, Texas.
1983	Official estimates show that there are 500,000 Salvadorans in the United States. Los Angeles, with 200,000-300,000 Salvadoran residents, is the second largest Salvadoran city in the world.
1984	Raúl González is the first Tejano elected by popular vote to a statewide office, that of associate justice of the Texas Supreme Court.
1986	The Immigration Reform and Control Act stipulates sanctions against employers who knowingly hire illegal immigrants and offers amnesty to some undocumented residents.
	A report shows that there are 304 county officials, 1,948 municipal officials, and 183 mayors of Mexican descent in the United States.
	Roberto Martínez is the first Latino to be elected governor of Florida since statehood.
1989	President George Bush appoints individuals of Hispanic origin to high-level positions. They include Lauro F. Cavazos, secretary of education; Manuel Luján, secretary of the interior; Antonia Novello, surgeon general; and Catalina Villalpando, treasurer of the United States.
1990	The Western Ranch Association notes that the majority of shepherds on the ranches surveyed are Latinos, including people of Chilean, Ecuadoran, and Mexican descent. Approximately three-quarters were of Peruvian descent.
	The newspaper *Perú* is published in Burlingame, California, to represent the interests of Peruvian immigrants.
	There are more than half a million Latino businesses in the United States, with a majority of them in California.
	Courts order the Immigration and Naturalization Service to reconsider applications for political asylum by 150,000 Central Americans who had been denied fair treatment.
1991	The Senate of Puerto Rico makes Spanish the only official language on the island.
1992	Palo Alto Battlefield National Historic Site is established near Brownsville, Texas, commemorating the first battle of the Mexican American War.
1993	President Bill Clinton appoints Henry Cisneros as secretary of housing and urban development and Federico Peña as secretary of transportation.
1994	The North American Free Trade Agreement goes into effect on January 1.

Bibliography of Literature

Expanding the base of North American literature, Latino literature traces its roots to the first arrival in the United States of Spanish-speaking people. This bibliography is intended for the general public as an introduction to and historical and literary overview of Latino literature. For additional information, readers are especially referred to essays in the *Handbook of Hispanic Culture in the United States: Literature and Art*, edited by Francisco Lomelí (1994). A major database resource is the University of California's *Chicano Database*, prepared by the Chicano Studies Library Publications at the University of California, Berkeley. Important work developing that database was performed by Lillian Castillo-Speed at the University of California, Berkeley, and by Richard Chabrán at the University of California, Los Angeles.

This bibliography is divided into six sections: novels and autobiographies; short stories; poetry; essays; drama; anthologies; and criticism and bibliographies. The last section is intended to list aids to readers of the primary works previously listed and to provide sources of information about authors and their works. Publication information is provided for particular editions of certain works; these are not necessarily the only or earliest editions.

—*César A. González-T. and José F. Salgado*

NOVELS AND AUTOBIOGRAPHIES

Acosta, Oscar Z. *The Autobiography of a Brown Buffalo*. Popular Edition, 1972.

_____. *The Revolt of the Cockroach People*. San Francisco: Straight Arrow, 1973.

Agüeros, Jack. *Dominoes and Other Stories*. Willimantic, Conn.: Curbstone, 1994.

Alegría, Fernando. *The Fun House*. Translated by Stephen Kessler. Houston: Arte Público Press, 1986.

Alire Saez, Benjamin. *Flowers for the Broken: Stories*. Seattle: Broken Moon, 1993.

Alvarado, Arturo Rocha. *Crónica de Aztlán: A Migrant's Tale*. Berkeley, Calif.: Quinto Sol, 1977.

Anaya, Rudolfo A. *The Adventures of Juan Chicaspatas*. Houston: Arte Público Press, 1985.

_____. *Alburquerque*. Albuquerque: University of New Mexico Press, 1992.

_____. *Bless Me, Ultima*. New York: Warner, 1972.

_____. *A Chicano in China*. Albuquerque: University of New Mexico Press, 1986.

_____. *Heart of Aztlán*. Berkeley, Calif.: Justa, 1976.

_____. *The Legend of La Llorona*. Berkeley, Calif.: Quinto Sol, 1984.

_____. *Lord of the Dawn: The Legend of Quetzalcóatl*. Albuquerque: University of New Mexico Press, 1987.

_____. *Tortuga*. Berkeley, Calif.: Justa, 1979.

Anzaldúa, Gloria, ed. *Making Face, Making Soul= Haciendo Caras: Creative and Critical Perspectives by Feminists of Color*. San Francisco: Aunt Lute Foundation Books, 1990.

Arias, Ron. *The Road to Tamazunchale*. Albuquerque, N.Mex.: Pajarito, 1974.

Baca, Jimmy Santiago. *Working in the Dark: Reflections of a Poet of the Barrio*. Santa Fe, N.Mex.: Red Crane, 1992.

Barreto, Lefty (Manuel). *Nobody's Hero*. New York: New American Library, 1977.

Barrio, Raymond. *The Plum Plum Pickers*. Sunnyvale, Calif.: Ventura, 1969.

Benites, Sandra. *A Place Where the Sea Remembers*. Minneapolis: Coffee House, 1993.

Brito, Aristeo. *The Devil in Texas*. Translated by David William Foster. New York: Anchor, 1992.

_____. *El Diablo en Texas*. Tucson: Peregrinos, 1976.

Candelaria, Nash. *Inheritance of Strangers*. Binghamton, N.Y.: Bilingual Press, 1985.

_____. *Leonor Park*. Tempe, Ariz.: Bilingual Press, 1991.

_____. *Memories of the Alhambra*. Palo Alto, Calif.: Cibola, 1977.

_____. *Not by the Sword*. Tempe, Ariz.: Bilingual Press, 1982.

Cano, Daniel. *Pepe Rios*. Houston: Arte Público Press, 1991.

Carralde, Carlos. *Carlos Esparza: A Chicano Chronicle*. San Francisco: R & E Research Associates, 1977.

Casas, Celso A. de. *Pelón Drops Out*. Berkeley, Calif.: Tonatiuh-Quinto Sol, 1979.

Castillo, Ana. *Massacre of the Dreamers*. Albuquerque: University of New Mexico Press, 1993.

_____. *The Mixquiahuala Letters*. Binghamton, N.Y.: Bilingual Press, 1992.

_____. *Sapogonia*. Tempe, Ariz.: Bilingual Press, 1990.

_____. *So Far from God: A Novel*. New York: Norton, 1993.

Chávez, Denise. *Face of an Angel*. Houston: Arte Público Press, 1990.

_____. *The Last of the Menu Girls*. Houston: Arte Público Press, 1986.

Cintrón, N. Humberto. *Frankie Christo*. New York: Taino, 1970.

Cisneros, Sandra. *The House on Mango Street*. Houston: Arte Público Press, 1983.

Corpi, Lucha. *Delia's Song*. Houston: Arte Público Press, 1989.

_____. *Eulogy for a Brown Angel: A Mystery Novel*. Houston: Arte Público Press, 1992.

Cota-Cárdenas, Margarita. *Puppet: A Chicano Novella*. Austin, Tex.: Relámpago, 1985.

Cruz, Nicky, and Jamie Buckingham. *Run, Baby, Run*. Plainfield, N.J.: Logos, 1968.

Cruz Martínez, Alejandro. *The Woman Who Outshone the Sun: The Legend of Lucía Centeno/La mujer que brillaba mas aún que el sol: La leyenda de Lucía Centeno*. San Francisco: Children's Books, 1991.

Delgado, Abelardo. *Letters to Louise*. Berkeley, Calif.: Tonatiuh-Quinto Sol, 1982.

Durán, Mike. *Don't Split on My Corner*. Houston: Arte Público Press, 1991.

Elizondo, Sergio D. *Muerte en una Estrella*. Mexico City: Tinta Negra, 1984.

_____. *Suruma*. El Paso, Tex.: Dos Pasos, 1990.

Espada, Martín. *Rebellion Is the Circle of a Lover's Hands*. Willimantic, Conn.: Curbstone, 1990.

Esteves, Sandra María. *Bluestown Mockingbird Mambo*. Houston: Arte Público Press, 1990.

Fernández, Carole. *Sleep of the Innocents*. Houston: Arte Público Press, 1991.

Fernández, Roberta. *Intaglio: A Novel in Six Stories*. Houston: Arte Público Press, 1990.

Fernández, Roberto. *La montaña rusa*. Houston: Arte Público Press, 1985.

_____. *Raining Backwards*. Houston: Arte Público Press, 1988.

Galarza, Ernesto. *Barrio Boy*. Notre Dame, Ind.: University of Notre Dame Press, 1971.

García, Lionel G. *Hardscrub*. Houston: Arte Público Press, 1990.

_____. *I Hear the Cow Bells Ringing: Growing Up in South Texas*. Houston: Arte Público Press, 1994.

_____. *Leaving Home*. Houston: Arte Público Press, 1985.

_____. *A Shroud in the Family*. Houston: Arte Público Press, 1987.

_____. *To a Widow with Children*. Houston: Arte Público Press, 1994.

González, Celedonio. *Los cuatro embajadores*. Miami: Ediciones Universal, 1973.

_____. *Los Primos*. Miami: Ediciones Universal, 1971.

González, Genaro. *Only Sons*. Houston: Arte Público Press, 1991.

_____. *Rainbow's End*. Houston: Arte Público Press, 1988.

Gonzales-Berry, Erlinda. *Paletitas de guayaba*. Albuquerque, N.Mex.: Academia/El Norte, 1991.

Hernández, Irene Beltrán. *Across the Great River*. Houston: Arte Público Press, 1990.

Hernández Cruz, Victor. *Rhythm, Content, and Flavor*. Houston: Arte Público Press, 1989.

Hijuelos, Oscar. *The Mambo Kings Play Songs of Love*. New York: Farrar Strauss & Giroux, 1989.

_____. *Our House in the Last World*. New York: Washington Square, 1983.

Hinojosa, Rolando. *Los Amigos de Becky*. Houston: Arte Público Press, 1990.

_____. *Becky and Her Friends*. Houston: Arte Público Press, 1989.

_____. *Claros Varones de Belken/Fair Gentlemen of Belken County*. Translated by Julia Cruz. Tempe, Ariz.: Bilingual Press, 1986.

_____. *Dear Rafe*. Houston: Arte Público Press, 1985.

_____. *Estampas del Valle y Otras Obras*. Berkeley, Calif.: Quinto Sol, 1973.

_____. *Generaciones y Semblanzas*. Berkeley, Calif.: Justa, 1977.

_____. *Klail*. Houston: Arte Público Press, 1986.

_____. *Klail y sus Alrededores*. Havana: Casa de las Américas, 1976.

_____. *Mi Querido Rafe*. Houston: Arte Público Press, 1981.

_____. *Partners in Crime: A Rafe Buenrostro Mystery*. Houston: Arte Público Press, 1985.

_____. *Rites and Witnesses*. Houston: Arte Público Press, 1982.

_____. *This Migrant Earth*. Houston: Arte Público Press, 1987.

_____. *Useless Servants*. Houston: Arte Público Press, 1993.

_____. *The Valley*. Tempe, Ariz.: Bilingual Press, 1983.

Islas, Arturo. *Migrant Souls*. New York: Morrow, 1990.

_____. *The Rain God*. Palo Alto, Calif.: Alexandrian, 1984.

Labarthe, Pedro Juan. *The Son of Two Nations: The Private Life of a Columbia Student*. New York: Carranza, 1931.

Levine, Barry B., ed. *Benny López: A Picaresque Tale of Emigration and Return*. New York: Basic Books, 1980.

Limón, Graciela. *In Search of Bernabé*. Houston: Arte Público Press, 1993.

_____. *The Memories of Ana Calderón*. Houston: Arte Público Press, 1994.

López, Arcadia. *Barrio Teacher*. Houston: Arte Público Press, 1994.

López-Medina, Sylvia. *Cantora: A Novel*. Albuquerque: University of New Mexico Press, 1992.

Manrique, Manuel. *Island in Harlem*. New York: Day, 1966.

Martínez, Eliud. *The Dream of Santa María de las Piedras*. Translated by David William Foster. Tempe, Ariz.: Bilingual Press, 1989.

_____. *Peregrinos de Aztlán*. Tucson: Peregrinos, 1974.

_____. *Pilgrims in Aztlán*. Translated by David William Foster. Tempe, Ariz.: Bilingual Press, 1992.

_____. *Voice-Haunted Journey*. Tempe, Ariz.: Bilingual Press, 1990.

Mohr, Nicholasa. *Nilda*. Houston: Arte Público Press, 1986.

Montes Huidobro, Matías. *Desterrados al fuego*. Mexico City: Fondo de Cultura Económica, 1975.

Moraga, Cherríe. *Loving in the War Years: Lo que nunca pasó por sus labios*. Boston: South End, 1983.

Morales, Alejandro. *The Brick People*. Houston: Arte Público Press, 1988.

_____. *Caras viejas y vino nuevo*. Mexico City: Joaquín Mortiz, 1975.

_____. *Death of an Anglo*. Tempe, Ariz.: Bilingual Press, 1988.

_____. *Old Faces and New Wine*. San Diego: Maize, 1981.

_____. *The Rag Doll Plagues*. Houston: Arte Público Press, 1992.

_____. *Reto en el paraíso*. Ypsilanti, Mich.: Bilingual Press, 1983.

_____. *La verdad sin voz*. Mexico City: Joaquín Mortiz, 1979.

Muñoz, Elías Miguel. *Crazy Love*. Houston: Arte Público Press, 1988.

_____. *Greatest Performance*. Houston: Arte Público Press, 1991.

Nava, Michael. *The Hidden Law*. New York: HarperCollins, 1992.

Navarro, J. L. *Blue Day on Main Street*. Berkeley, Calif.: Quinto Sol, 1973.

Nelson, Eugene, ed. *Pablo Cruz and the American Dream: The Experiences of an Undocumented Immigrant from Mexico*. Salt Lake City: Peregrine Smith, 1975.

Niggli, Josefina. *Mexican Village*. Chapel Hill: University of North Carolina Press, 1945.

Novás Calvo, Lino. *Maneras de contar*. New York: Las Américas, 1970.

Ornelas, Berta. *Come Down from the Mound*. Phoenix: Midter, 1975.

Ortega, Adolfo. *Calo Tapestry*. Berkeley, Calif.: Justa, 1977.

Ortiz Cofer, Judith. *Line of the Sun*. Athens: University of Georgia Press, 1989.

Ortiz Taylor, Sheila. *Spring Forward/Fall Back*. Tallahassee, Fla.: Naiad, 1985.

Otero, Miguel, A. *My Life on the Frontier 1865-1882*. 2 vols. Albuquerque: University of New Mexico Press, 1987.

Paredes, Américo. *George Washington Gómez: A Mexicotexan Novel*. Houston: Arte Público Press, 1990.

Pérez, Ramón T. *Diary of an Undocumented Immigrant*. Houston: Arte Público Press, 1991.

Pietri, Pedro. *Lost in the Museum of Natural History/Perdido en el Museo de Historia Natural*. Río Piedras, Puerto Rico: Huracán, 1981.

Piñeda, Cecile. *Face*. New York: Viking, 1985.

_____. *Frieze*. New York: Viking, 1986.

Piñero, Miguel. *La Bodega Sold Dreams*. Houston: Arte Público Press, 1980.

Ponce, Mary Helen. *Taking Control*. Houston: Arte Público Press, 1994.

_____. *The Wedding*. Houston: Arte Público Press, 1990.

Portillo Trambley, Estela. *Trini*. Binghamton, N.Y.: Bilingual Press, 1986.

Prieto, Jorge. *Elsewere in a Parallel Universe*. Introduction by Domitri Mihalas. Urbana, Ill.: Red Herring, 1992.

_____. *Manhattan Memories*. Barstow, Calif.: Esoterica, 1989.

_____. *The Quarterback Who Almost Wasn't*. Houston: Arte Público Press, 1994.

_____. *The Twenty-four Hour Wake*. Urbana, Ill.: Red Herring, 1989.

Quinn, Anthony. *The Original Sin*. Boston: Little, 1972.

Quintana Rank, Katherine. *Portrait of Doña Elena*. Berkeley, Calif.: Tonatiuh-Quinto Sol, 1982.

Ramos, Manuel. *The Ballad of Rocky Ruiz*. St. Martin's Press, 1993.

Rechy, John. *Bodies and Souls*. New York: Carroll & Graf, 1983.

_____. *City of Night*. New York: Ballantine, 1963.

_____. *The Miraculous Day of Amalia Gómez*. New York: Little, Brown, 1991.

_____. *Rushes*. New York: Grove, 1979.

_____. *This Day's Death*. New York: Grove, 1969.

_____. *The Vampires*. New York: Grove, 1971.

Rico, Armando B. *Three Coffins for Niño Lencho*. Berkeley, Calif.: Tonatiuh International, 1984.

Ríos, Isabela. *Victumm*. Venture: Diana-Etna, 1976.

Rivera, Edward. *Family Installments: Memories of Growing Up Hispanic*. Harmondsworth, England: Penguin, 1983.

Rivera, Oswaldo. *Fire and Rain*. New York: Four Windows, Eight Walls, 1990.

Rivera, Tomás. *This Migrant Earth*. Edited by Rolando Hinojosa. Houston: Arte Público Press, 1987.

_____. *. . . y no se lo tragó la tierra. . ./And the Earth Did Not Part*. Translated by Evangelina Vigil. Houston: Arte Público Press, 1987.

Rocha Alvarado, Arturo. *Crónica de Aztlán: A Migrant's Tale*. Berkeley, Calif.: Quinto Sol, 1977.

Rodríguez, Alfredo. *Estas Tierras*. El Paso, Tex.: Dos Pasos Ediciones, 1987.

Rodríguez, Joe. *Oddsplayer*. Houston: Arte Público Press, 1989.

Rodríguez, Rafael. *The Gypsy Wagon*. Los Angeles: Aztlán, 1974.

Rodríguez, Richard. *Days of Obligation: An Argument with My Mexican Father*. New York: Viking, 1992.

———. *Hunger of Memory: The Education of Richard Rodríguez, an Autobiography*. Boston: Godine, 1982.

Romero, Orlando. *Nambe—Year One*. Berkeley, Calif.: Tonatiuh International, 1976.

Ruiz, Richard. *The Hungry American*. Bend, Oreg.: Maverick, 1978.

Ruiz, Ronald. *Happy Birthday Jesús*. Houston: Arte Público Press, 1994.

Salas, Floyd. *Buffalo Nickel: A Memoir*. Houston: Arte Público Press, 1992.

———. *Lay My Body on the Line*. Berkeley, Calif.: Y'Bird, 1978.

———. *Tattoo the Wicked Cross*. New York: Grove, 1967.

———. *What Now My Love*. Houston: Arte Público Press, 1994.

Sánchez, Thomas. *Zoot Suit Murders: A Novel*. New York: Dutton, 1978.

Sauvageau, Juan. *A pesar del río/In Spite of the River*. Kingsville, Tex.: Twin Palms, 1977.

Soto, Gary. *Lesser Evils: Ten Quartets*. Houston: Arte Público Press, 1987.

Suáres, Vigil. *Latin Jazz*. New York: Morrow, 1988.

Thomas, Piri. *Down These Mean Streets*. New York: Alfred A. Knopf, 1967.

———. *Savior, Savior Hold My Hand*. New York: Doubleday, 1972.

———. *Seven Long Times*. New York: Mentor, 1975.

Torres, Edwin. *Carlito's Way*. New York: Saturday Review, 1975.

Torres, Omar. *Al partir*. Houston: Arte Público Press, 1986.

———. *Apenas un bolero*. Houston: Arte Público Press, 1981.

———. *Fallen Angels Sing*. Houston: Arte Público Press, 1991.

Torres-Metzgar, Joseph V. *Below the Summit*. Berkeley, Calif.: Tonatiuh International, 1976.

Unipierre, Luz María. *En el país de las maravillas*. Bloomington, Ind.: Third Women, 1985.

Vallbona, Rima de. *Mundo, demonio, y mujer*. Houston: Arte Público Press, 1991.

Vásquez, Richard. *Chicano*. New York: Doubleday, 1970.

Vega, Bernardo. *Memórias de Bernardo Vega*. Río Piedras, Puerto Rico: Huracán, 1977.

Vega, Ed. *The Comeback*. Houston: Arte Público Press, 1985.

———. *Mendoza's Dreams*. Houston: Arte Público Press, 1987.

Velásquez, Gloria. *Juanita Fights the School Board*. Houston: Arte Público Press, 1994.

Villarreal, José Antonio. *Clemente Chacón*. Binghamton, N.Y.: Bilingual Press, 1984.

———. *The Fifth Horseman*. New York: Doubleday, 1974.

———. *Pocho*. New York: Anchor, 1959.

Villaseñor, Victor. *Macho!* New York: Bantam, 1973.

———. *Rain of Gold*. Houston: Arte Público Press, 1991.

Viramontes, Helena María. *The Moths and Other Stories*. Houston: Arte Público Press, 1985.

———. *Naked Ladies*. Houston: Arte Público Press, 1992.

———. *The Ultraviolet Sky*. Tempe, Ariz.: Bilingual Press, 1988.

SHORT STORIES

Acosta Torres, José. *Cachito Mío*. Berkeley, Calif.: Quinto Sol, 1973.

Aguilar, Ricardo, Armando Armengol, and Oscar U. Somoza, eds. *Palabra Nueva: Cuentos Chicanos*. El Paso: Texas Western, University of Texas at El Paso, 1984.

Alarcón, Justo S. *Chulifeas fronteras*. Albuquerque, N.Mex.: Pajarito, 1981.

Alurista and Xelina Rojas-Urista, eds. *Southwest Tales: A Contemporary Collection*. Colorado Springs, Colo.: Maize, 1986.

Alvarez, Julia. *How the García Girls Lost Their Accents*. Chapel Hill, N.C.: Algonquin Books of Chapel Hill, 1991.

Anaya, Rudolfo A. *The Farolitos of Christmas: A New Mexico Christmas Story*. Santa Fe: New Mexico Magazine, 1987.

———. *The Silence of the Llano*. Berkeley, Calif.: Tonatiuh-Quinto Sol, 1982.

Anaya, Rudolfo A., and José Griego y Maestas. *Cuentos: Tales from the Hispanic Southwest*. Santa Fe: Museum of New Mexico Press, 1980.

Anaya, Rudolfo A., and Antonio Márquez, eds. *Cuentos Chicanos: A Short Story Anthology*. Rev. ed. Albuquerque: University of New Mexico Press, 1984.

Avila, Alfred. *Mexican Ghost Tales of the Southwest*. Houston: Arte Público Press, 1994.

Bruce-Novoa, Juan, comp. *Antología Retrospectiva del cuento Chicano*. Mexico City: Consejo Nacional de Población, 1988.

Burciaga, José Antonio. *Weedee Peepo*. Edinburg, Tex.: Pan American University, 1988.

Candelaria, Nash. *The Day the Cisco Kid Shot John Wayne*. Tempe, Ariz.: Bilingual Press, 1988.

Castillo, Rafael. *Distant Journeys*. Tempe, Ariz.: Bilingual Press, 1991.

Chavez, Denise. *The Last of the Menu Girls*. Houston: Arte Público Press, 1987.

———. *Woman Hollering Creek*. New York: Random House, 1991.

Chávez, Fray Angélico. *The Short Stories of Fray Angélico Chávez*. Edited by Genaro M. Padilla. Albuquerque: University of New Mexico Press, 1987.

Colón, Jesus. *A Puerto Rican in New York and Other Sketches*. New York: Mainstream, 1961.

Cruz, Nicky. *The Lonely Now*. Plainfield: Logos, 1971.

Elizondo, Sergio. *Rosa, la Flauta*. Berkeley, Calif.: Justa, 1980.

Elizondo, Sergio, Armando Armengol, and Ricardo Aguilar, eds. *Palabra Nueva: Cuentos Chicanos II*. El Paso, Tex.: Dos Pasos, 1986.

Espinosa, Herberto. *Viendo morir a Teresa y otros relatos*. San Diego: Maize, 1983.

Garza, Beatriz de la. *The Candy Vendor's Boy and Other Stories*. Houston: Arte Público Press, 1994.

Gómez, Alma, et al., eds. *Cuentos: Stories by Latinas*. New York: Kitchen Table, 1983.

González, Genaro. *Only Sons*. Houston: Arte Público Press, 1991.

González, Ray, ed. *Mirrors Beneath the Earth: Short Fiction by Chicano Writers*. Willimantic, Conn.: Curbstone, 1992.

Griep-Ruíz, Leo. *Daily in All the Small*. Colorado Springs, Colo.: Maize, 1984.

Keller, Gary D. *Zapata Rose in 1992 and Other Tales*. Tempe, Ariz.: Bilingual Press, 1992.

Martínez, Max. *Adventures of the Chicano Kid and Other Stories*. Houston: Arte Público Press, 1994.

———. *A Red Bikini Dream*. Houston: Arte Público Press, 1990.

Martínez-Herro, Hugo. *The Last Laugh and Other Stories*. Houston: Arte Público Press, 1994.

Méndez, Miguel. *Cuentos para niños traviesos*. Berkeley, Calif.: Justa, 1979.

———. *De la vida y del folclore de la frontera*. Tucson: University of Arizona Press, 1986.

———. *Tata casehua y otros cuentos*. Berkeley, Calif.: Justa, 1980.

Mohr, Nicholasa. *El Bronx Remembered*. Houston: Arte Público Press, 1986.

———. *In Nueva York*. Houston: Arte Público Press, 1988.

———. *Rituals of Survival: A Woman's Portfolio*. Houston: Arte Público Press, 1986.

Morales, Aurora Levins, and Rosario Morales. *Getting Home Alive*. Houston: Arte Público Press, 1986.

Murgía, Alejandro. *Southern Front*. Tempe, Ariz.: Bilingual Press, 1990.

Navarro, J. L. *Blue Day on Main Street*. Berkeley, Calif.: Quinto Sol, 1973.

Ortiz Cofer, Judith. *Silent Dancing: A Partial Remembrance of a Puerto Rican Childhood*. Houston: Arte Público Press, 1990.

Paredes, Américo. *The Hammon and the Beans and Other Stories*. Houston: Arte Público Press, 1994.

Ponce, Mary Helen. *Taking Control*. Houston: Arte Público Press, 1987.

Portillo Trambley, Estella. *Rain of Scorpions and Other Stories*. Tempe, Ariz.: Bilingual Press, 1993.

Preciado Martín, Patricia. *Days of Plenty, Days of Want*. Tempe, Ariz.: Bilingual Press, 1988.

Ríos, Alberto. *The Iguana Killer: Twelve Stories of the Heart*. New York: A Blue Moon and Confluence, 1984.

Ríos, Isabela. *Victuum*. Ventura: Diana-Etna, 1976.

Rivera, Tomás. *The Harvest: Short Stories by Tomás Rivera*. Houston: Arte Público Press, 1990.

Rodríguez, Abraham, Jr. *Ashes to Ashes*. Houston: Arte Público Press, 1989.

Rodríguez, Leonardo. *They Have to Be Puerto Ricans*. Chicago: Puerto Rican Parade Committee, 1988.

Sagel, Jim. *Más Que No Love It: Cuentos/Short Stories*. Albuquerque, N.Mex.: West End, 1992.

Sánchez, Rosaura, ed. *Requisa treinta y dos*. San Diego: Chicano Studies Program, University of California at San Diego, 1979.

Sánchez, Saul. *Hay plesha lichans tu di flac*. Berkeley, Calif.: Justa, 1977.

Silva, Beverly. *The Cat and Other Stories*. Tempe, Ariz.: Bilingual Press, 1986.

Somosa, Oscar U., ed. *Nueva Narrativa Chicana*. Mexico City: Diógenes, 1983.

Soto, Gary. *Baseball in April and Other Stories*. Houston: Arte Público Press, 1990.

———. *Living up the Street*. San Francisco: Strawberry Hill, 1985.

———. *Small Faces*. Houston: Arte Público Press, 1986.

Thomas, Piri. *Stories from El Barrio*. New York: Alfred A. Knopf, 1978.

Topete, Eutimio, and Jerry Gonzales. *Recordar es vivir*. Berkeley, Calif.: Justa, 1978.

Ulibarrí, Sabine R. *El Cóndor and Other Stories*. Houston: Arte Público Press, 1990.

———. *Governor Glu Glu and Other Stories*. Tempe, Ariz.: Bilingual Press, 1988.

———. *Mi abuela fumaba puros y otros cuentos de Tierra Amarilla/My Grandma Smoked Cigars and Other Stories of Tierra Amarilla*. Berkeley, Calif.: Quinto Sol, 1977.

———. *Primeros Encuentros/First Encounters*. Ypsilanti, Mich.: Bilingual Press, 1982.

———. *Tierra Amarilla: Stories of New Mexico*. Albuquerque: University of New Mexico Press, 1971.

Ulica, Jorge, and Juan Rodríguez. *Crónicas diabólicas*. San Diego: Maize, 1982.

Vega, Ed. *Casualty Reports*. Houston: Arte Público Press, 1991.

Villanueva, Alma Luz. *La Llorona/Weeping Woman*. Houston: Arte Público Press, 1993.

Villaseñor, Victor. *Walking Star*. Houston: Arte Público Press, 1994.

POETRY

Aguilar, Ricardo, Armando Armengol, and Sergio D. Elizondo, eds. *Palabra Nueva: Poesía Chicana*. El Paso: Texas Western, 1985.

Alarcón, Francisco X. *Body in Flames/ Cuerpo en Llamas*. San Francisco: Chronicle, 1990.

Alurista. *A'nque*. San Diego: Maize, 1979.

_____. *Floricanto en Aztlán*. Los Angeles: Chicano Studies Center, University of California, Los Angeles, 1971.

_____. *Nationchild Plumaroja*. San Diego: Centro Cultural de la Raza, 1972.

_____. *Return: Poems Collected and New*. Ypsilanti, Mich.: Bilingual Press, 1982.

_____. *Spik in Glyph?* Houston: Arte Público Press, 1981.

_____. *Timespace Huracán*. Albuquerque, N.Mex.: Pajarito, 1976.

_____. *Tremble Purple*. Oakland: Unity Publications, 1987.

_____, et al., eds. *Literatura Fronteriza: Antología del Primer Festival San Diego-Tijuana, Mayo 1981*. San Diego: Maize, 1982.

Alvarado de Ricord, Elsie, Lucha Corpi, and Concha Michel. *Fireflight: Three Latin American Poets*. n.p.: Oyez/West Coast Print Center, n.d.

Arguelles, Iván. *What Are They Doing to My Animal?* Houston: Arte Público Press, 1985.

Baca, Jimmy Santiago. *Immigrants in Our Own Land*. Baton Rouge: Louisiana State University Press, 1979.

_____. *Martín and Meditations on the South Valley*. New York: New Directions, 1987.

_____. *What's Happening*. Willimantic, Conn.: Curbstone, 1982.

Bornstein-Somoza, Miriam. *Bajo Cubierta*. Tucson: Scorpion, 1976.

Bruce-Novoa, Juan. *Chicano Poetry: A Response to Chaos*. Austin: University of Texas Press, 1982.

_____. *Inocencia Perversa/Perverse Innocence*. Phoenix: Baleen, 1977.

Burciaga, José Antonio. *Drink Cultura Refrescante*. San Jose, Calif.: Mango, 1979.

_____. *Restless Serpents*. Menlo Park, Calif.: Diseños Literarios, 1976.

_____. *Undocumented Love/Amor Indocumentado*. San Jose: Chusma House, 1992.

Candelaria, Cordelia. *Chicano Poetry: A Critical Introduction*. Westport, Conn.: Greenwood, 1986.

_____. *Ojo de la Cueva*. Colorado Springs, Colo.: Maize, 1984.

Castellano, Olivia. *Blue Horse of Madness*. Sacramento, Calif.: Crystal Clear, 1983.

_____. *Spaces That Time Missed*. Sacramento, Calif.: Crystal Clear, 1986.

Castillo, Ana. *My Father Was a Toltec*. Novato, Calif.: West End, 1988.

_____. *Women Are Not Roses*. Houston: Arte Público Press, 1984.

Cervantes, Lorna Dee. *Emplumada*. Pittsburgh: University of Pittsburgh, 1981.

_____. *From the Cables of Genocide: Poems on Love and Hunger*. Houston: Arte Público Press, 1991.

Chávez, Fray Angélico. *Selected Poems: With an Apologia*. Santa Fe, N.Mex.: Press of the Territorian, 1969.

Cisneros, Sandra. *My Wicked Wicked Ways*. Houston: Arte Público Press, 1987.

Corpi, Lucha. *Palabras de Mediodia/Noon Words*. Translated by Catherine Rodríguez-Nieto. Oakland: Fuego de Aztlán, 1980.

_____. *Variaciones sobre una tempestad/Variations on a Storm*. Berkeley, Calif.: Third Woman, 1990.

Daydí-Tolson, Santiago, ed. *Five Poets of Aztlán*. Binghamton, N.Y.: Bilingual Press, 1985.

Delgado, Abelardo. *Chicano: Twenty-five Pieces of a Chicano Mind*. El Paso, Tex.: Barrio, 1970.

Elizondo, Sergio D. *Libro para vatos y chavalas chicanas (A Book for Chicano Guys and Gals)*. Translated by Edmundo García Girón. Berkeley, Calif.: Justa, 1977.

_____. *Perros y Antiperros: Una Epica Chicana*. Translated by Gustavo Segade. Berkeley, Calif.: Quinto Sol, 1972.

Empringham, Toni, ed. *Fiesta in Aztlán: Anthology of Chicano Poetry*. Santa Barbara, Calif.: Capra, 1982.

Gaspar de Alba, Alicia, María Herrera-Sobek, and Demetria Martínez. *Three Times a Woman*. Tempe, Ariz.: Bilingual Press, 1989.

Gonzáles, Rudolfo. *I Am Joaquín*. New York: Bantam, 1972.

González, César A., and Luis Urrea. *Fragmentos de Barro: The First Seven Years*. San Diego: Toltecas en Aztlán (Centro Cultural de la Raza), 1987.

_____. *Fragmentos de Barro: Pieces of Clay VIII*. San Diego: Mesa College, Movimiento Estudiantil Chicano de Aztlán, Chicano Studies, 1991.

González, Rafael Jesus. *El hacedor de juegos/The Maker of Games*. San Francisco: Casa Editorial, 1977.

González, Ray. *Twilights and Chants*. Golden, Colo.: James Andrews, 1987.

González-T., César A. *Unwinding the Silence*. La Jolla, Calif.: Lalo, 1987.

Herrera, Juan Felipe. *Exiles of Desire*. Fresno, Calif.: Lalo, 1983.

Herrera, Juan Felipe, Alurista, and Gloria Amalia, eds. *Rebosos of Love: We Have Woven Sudor de Pueblos on Our Back*. San Diego: Toltecas en Aztlán, 1974.

Hinojosa, Rolando. *Korean Love Songs*. Berkeley, Calif.: Justa, 1978.

Hoyos, Angela de. *Arise Chicano and Other Poems*. Bloomington, Ind.: Backstage Books, 1975.

_____. *Chicano Poems for the Barrio*. San Antonio, Tex.: M & A Editions, 1977.

_____. *Selected Poems/Selecciones*. Houston: Arte Público Press, 1989.

_____. *Woman, Woman*. Houston: Arte Público Press, 1985.

Limón, José E. *Mexican Ballads, Chicano Poems: History and Influence in Mexican-Americans Social Poetry*. Berkeley: University of California Press, 1992.

López Dzur, Carlos A. *La Casa*. Santa Ana, Calif.: n.p., 1988.

Luera, Yolanda. *Solitaria J*. San Diego, Calif.: Lalo, 1986.

Medina, Rubén. *Amor de lejos . . . Fools' Love*. Translated by Jennifer Sternbach with Robert Jones. Houston: Arte Público Press, 1986.

Mora, Pat. *Borders*. Houston: Arte Público Press, 1986.

_____. *Chants*. Houston: Arte Público Press, 1984.

Padilla, Ernesto. *Cigarro Lucky Strike*. San Diego: Lalo, 1986.

Paredes, Américo. *Between Two Worlds*. Houston: Arte Público Press, 1991.

Quiñonez, Naomi. *Sueño de colibrí: Hummingbird Dream*. Los Angeles: West End, 1985.

Quintana, Leroy. *Hijo del Pueblo: New Mexico Poems*. Las Cruces, N.Mex.: Puerto del Sol, 1976.

_____. *Interrogations*. Chevy Chase, Md.: Burning Cities, 1990.

_____. *Sangre*. Las Cruces, N.Mex.: Prima Aqua, 1981.

_____. *The Story of Home*. Tempe, Ariz.: Bilingual Press, 1993.

Robles, Margarita Luna. *Triptych: Dreams, Lust, and Other Performances*. Santa Monica, Calif.: Lalo, 1992.

Rodríguez, Luis J. *The Concrete River*. Willimantic, Conn.: Curbstone, 1991.

Romero, Leo. *Agua Negra*. Boise, Idaho: Ahsahta, 1981.

_____. *Celso*. Houston: Arte Público Press, 1985.

Romero, Lin. *Happy Songs Bleeding Hearts*. San Diego: Toltecas en Aztlán (Centro Cultural de la Raza), 1974.

Salinas, Luis Omar. *Crazy Gypsy*. Fresno, Calif.: Orígenes, 1970.

_____. *Darkness Under the Trees/Walking Behind the Spanish*. Berkeley: Chicano Studies Library Publications, University of California, 1982.

_____. *The Sadness of Days: Selected and New Poems*. Houston: Arte Público Press, 1987.

Salinas, Raul R. *Un Trip Through the Mind Jail y Otras Excursions*. San Francisco: Pocho-Che, 1980.

Sánchez, Ricardo. *Brown Bear Honey Madness: Alaskan Cruising Poems*. Austin, Tex.: Slough, 1981.

_____. *Canto y grito mi liberación*. Garden City, N.Y.: Anchor, 1973.

_____. *Eagle-Visioned/Feathered Adobes*. El Paso, Tex.: Cinco Puntos, 1990.

_____. *Hechizospells: Poetry/Stories/Vignettes/Articles/Notes on the Human Condition of Chicanos & Pícaros, Words & Hopes Within Soulmind*. Creative Series No. 4. Los Angeles: Chicano Studies Center, University of California, Los Angeles, 1976.

_____. *Selected Poems*. Houston: Arte Público Press, 1984.

Santana, Francisco. *Triste Alegría: Poems*. Tempe, Ariz.: Bilingual Press, 1991.

Soto, Gary. *Black Hair*. Pittsburgh: University of Pittsburgh Press, 1985.

_____. *Elements of San Joaquín*. Pittsburgh: University of Pittsburgh Press, 1977.

_____. *Home Course in Religion*. San Francisco: Chronicle, 1991.

_____. *The Tales of Sunlight*. Pittsburgh: University of Pittsburgh Press, 1978.

_____. *Who Will Know Us?* San Francisco: Chronicle, 1990.

Tafolla, Carmen. *Curandera*. La Jolla, Calif.: Lalo, 1987.

_____. *Sonnets to Human Beings and Other Selected Works by Carmen Tafolla*. A Lalo Critical Edition: Chicano Literature Series. Santa Monica, Calif.: Lalo, 1992.

Urrea, Luis. *The Fever of Being*. Albuquerque, N.Mex.: West End, 1994.

Vigil, Evangelina. *Thirty An' Seen a Lot*. Houston: Arte Público Press, 1985.

Vigil-Piñon, Evangelina. *The Computer Is Down*. Houston: Arte Público Press, 1987.

Villanueva, Alma. *Bloodroot*. Austin, Tex.: Place of Herons, 1982.

_____. *Life Span*. Austin, Tex.: Place of Herons, 1985.

Villanueva, Tino. *Chronicle of My Worst Years/Crónica de mis años peores*. Evanston, Ill.: Northwestern University Press, 1994.

_____. *Crónica de mis años peores*. La Jolla, Calif.: Lalo, 1987.

_____. *Hay otra voz*. New York: Editorial Mensaje, 1972.

_____. *Scene from the Movie Giant*. Willimantic, Conn.: Curbstone, 1994.

_____. *Shaking Off the Dark*. Houston: Arte Público Press, 1984.

Zamora, Bernice. *Restless Serpents*. Menlo Park, Calif.: Diseños Literarios, 1976.

ESSAYS

Anaya, Rudolfo A., and Francisco Lomelí, eds. *Aztlán: Essays on the Chicano Homeland.* Albuquerque: University of New Mexico Press, 1989.

Baca, Jimmy Santiago. *Working in the Dark: Reflections of a Poet of the Barrio.* Santa Fe: Red Crane, 1992.

Bruce-Novoa, Juan. *Retrospace: Collected Essays on Chicano Literature.* Houston: Arte Público Press, 1990.

Burciaga, Jose. *Drink Cultura.* Santa Barbara, Calif.: Capra, 1993.

Castillo, Ana. *Massacre of the Dreamers: Reflections on Mexican-Indian Women in the United States Five Hundred Years After the Conquest.* Albuquerque: University of New Mexico Press, 1993.

Gonzales-Berry, Erlinda, ed. *Pasó Por Aquí: Critical Essays on the New Mexican Literary Tradition, 1542-1988.* Albuquerque: University of New Mexico Press, 1989.

González, Lawrence. *El Vago.* Santa Barbara, Calif.: Capra, 1976.

Hernández, Guillermo R. *Chicano Satire: A Study in Literary Culture.* Austin: University of Texas Press, 1991.

Hinojosa-Smith, Rolando R. *Rites and Witnesses.* Houston: Arte Público Press, 1982.

Laviera, Tato. *Mainstream Ethics.* Houston: Arte Público Press, 1988.

Martín, Patricia Preciado. *Songs My Mother Sang: An Oral History of Mexican-American Women.* Tucson: University of Arizona Press, 1992.

Martínez, Al. *Ashes in the Rain: Selected Essays.* Berkeley, Calif.: Tonatiuh, 1989.

Missions in Conflict: Essays on U.S.-Mexican Relations and Chicano Culture. Tübingen, Germany: Gunter Narr Verlag, 1986.

Saldivar, José David, ed. *The Rolando Hinojosa Reader: Essays Historical and Critical.* Houston: Arte Público Press, 1985.

Sommers, Joseph, and Tomás Ybarra-Frausto, eds. *Modern Chicano Writers: A Collection of Critical Essays.* Englewood Cliffs, N.J.: Prentice-Hall, 1979.

Urrea, Luis Alberto. *Across the Wire: Life and Hard Times on the Mexican Border.* New York: Anchor, 1993.

DRAMA

Acosta, Iván. *Un cubiche en la luna.* Houston: Arte Público Press, 1989.

_____. *El Super.* Miami: Ediciones Universal, 1982.

Chávez, Denise, and Lida Macías Feyder, comps. and eds. *Shattering the Myth: Plays by Hispanic Women.* Houston: Arte Público Press, 1992.

Chicanos and Film: Essays on Chicano Representation and Resistance. New York: Garland, 1992.

Contemporary Chicano Theatre. Edited by Roberto J. Garza. Notre Dame, Ind.: University of Notre Dame Press, 1976.

Fornes, María Irene. *Plays.* New York: PAJ, 1986.

_____. *Promenade and Other Plays.* New York: PAJ, 1987.

Fregoso, Rosa Linda. *The Bronze Screen: Chicana and Chicano Film Culture.* Minneapolis: University of Minnesota Press, 1993.

Hernández, Alfonso. *The False Advent of Mary's Child and Other Plays.* Berkeley, Calif.: Justa, 1979.

Huerta, Jorge A. *Chicano Theater-Themes and Forms.* Ypsilanti, Mich.: Bilingual Press, 1982.

_____. *Necessary Theater: Six Plays About the Chicano Experience.* Houston: Arte Público Press, 1990.

Kanellos, Nicolás, ed. *A History of Hispanic Theatre in the United States: Origins to 1940.* Houston: Arte Público Press, 1990.

_____. *Mexican-American Theatre: Legacy and Reality.* Pittsburgh: Latin American Literary Review, 1987.

_____. *Mexican American Theatre: Then and Now.* Houston: Arte Público Press, 1983.

León, Neftalí de. *Five Plays.* Denver: Totinem Publications, 1972.

Moraga, Cherrie. *Giving Up the Ghost: Teatro in Two Acts.* Los Angeles: West End, 1986.

Morton, Carlos. *The Many Deaths of Danny Rosales and Other Plays.* Houston: Arte Público Press, 1983.

Noriega, Chon A., ed. *Chicanos and Film: Representation and Resistance.* Minneapolis: University of Minnesota Press, 1992.

Osbourne, M. Elizabeth, ed. *On New Ground: Contemporary Hispanic-American Plays.* New York: Theatre Communications Group, 1987.

Piñero, Miguel. *Outrageous and Other One-Act Plays.* Houston: Arte Público Press, 1986.

_____. *Short Eyes.* Houston: Arte Público Press, 1988.

_____. *The Sun Always Shines for the Cool.* Houston: Arte Público Press, 1984.

Portillo Trambly, Estela. *"The Day of the Swallows,"* El Espejo. Berkeley, Calif.: Quinto Sol, 1972.

_____. *Sor Juana and Other Plays.* Ypsilanti, Mich.: Bilingual Press, 1983.

Prida, Dolores, *Beautiful Señoritas and Other Plays.* Edited by Judith Wess. Houston: Arte Público Press, 1991.

Valdez, Luis. *Actos: El Teatro Campesino.* San Juan Bautista, Calif.: Cucaracha, 1971.

_____. *Luis Valdez—Early Works: Actos, Bernabé, and Pensamiento Serpentino.* Houston: Arte Público Press, 1990.

_____. *Zoot Suit and Other Plays.* Houston: Arte Público Press, 1992.

ANTHOLOGIES

Alarcón, Norma, Ana Castillo, and Cherríe Moraga, eds. *Third Woman: The Sexuality of Latinas.* Berkeley, Calif.: Third Woman Press, 1989.

Albi, F. E., and Jesus Nieto, comps. *Sighs and Songs of Aztlán: New Anthology of Chicano Literature.* Bakersfield, Calif.: Universal, 1975.

Alurista, et al., eds. *Festival de Flor y Canto: An Anthology of Chicano Literature.* Los Angeles: University of Southern California Press, 1976.

Anaya, Rudolfo, ed. *Blue Mesa Review.* Albuquerque: University of New Mexico Press, 1993.

_____. *Voces: An Anthology of Nuevo Mexicano Writers.* Albuquerque, N.Mex.: El Norte, 1987.

Anaya, Rudolfo, and Francisco Lomelí, eds. *Aztlán: Essays on the Chicano Homeland.* Albuquerque: University of New Mexico Press, 1989.

Anaya, Rudolfo, and Antonio Márquez, eds. *Cuentos Chicanos: A Short, Story Anthology.* Rev. ed. Albuquerque: New America, University of New Mexico, 1980.

Anaya, Rudolfo, and Simón J. Ortiz, eds. *Ceremony of Brotherhood: 1680-1980.* Albuquerque, N.Mex.: Academia, 1981.

Anzaldúa, Gloria. *Borderlands: The New Mestiza=La Frontera.* San Francisco: Spinsters/Aunt Lute, 1987.

Boza, María del Carmen, Beverly Siliva, and Carmen Valle, eds. *Nosotras: Latina Literature Today.* Binghamton, N.Y.: Bilingual Press, 1986.

Broadsides: Literature of the United States Hispanos. Tempe, Ariz.: Bilingual Review, 1990.

Burunat, Silvia, and Ofelia García, eds. *Veinte años de literatura cubanoamericana.* Tempe, Ariz.: Bilingual Review Press, 1988.

Calderón, Hector, and José David Saldívar. *Criticism in the Borderlands: Studies in Chicano Literature, Culture, and Ideology.* Durham, N.C.: Duke University Press, 1991.

Campa, Arthur. *Treasure of the Sangre de Cristo: Tales and Traditions of the Spanish Southwest.* Norman: University of Oklahoma Press, 1963.

Cortina, Rodolfo J. *Cuban American Theater.* Houston: Arte Público Press, 1990.

Fernández, José B., and Nasario García, ed. *Nuevos horizontes: Cuentos Chicanos, Puertorriqueños y Cubanos.* Lexington, Mass.: D. C. Heath, 1982.

Fernández, Roberta, ed. *In Other Words: Literature by Latinas of the United States.* Houston: Arte Público Press, 1994.

Festival San Diego-Tijuana. *Literatura fronteriza: Antología del primer festival San Diego-Tijuana, Mayo 1981.* San Diego: Maize, 1982.

Flor y Canto IV and V: An Anthology of Chicano Literature from the Festivals Held in Albuquerque, New Mexico, 1977 and Tempe, Arizona, 1978. Albuquerque, N.Mex.: Pajarito, 1980.

Gómez, Alma, Cherríe Moraga, and Mariana Romo-Carmona, eds. *Cuentos: Stories by Latinas.* Binghamton, N.Y.: Bilingual Review Press, 1983.

González, Ray, ed. *After Aztlán: Latino Poets of the Nineties.* Boston: Godine, 1992.

González-Cruz, Luis F., and Francesca M. Colechía. *Cuban Theater in the United States: A Critical Anthology.* Tempe, Ariz.: Bilingual Review Press, 1992.

Grupo Areíto. *Contra viento y marea.* Havana: Casa de las Américas, 1978.

Hernández Miyares, Julio, ed. *Narradores Cubanos de hoy.* Miami: Editorial Universal, 1975.

Hospital, Carolina, ed. *Cuban American Writers: Los Atrevidos.* Princeton, N.J.: Ediciones Ellas/Linden Lane, 1988.

Huerta, Jorge, and Nicolás Kanellos, eds. *Nuevos Pasos: Chicano and Puerto Rican Drama.* Houston: Arte Público Press, 1989.

Jiménez, Francisco, ed. *Mosaico de la Vida: Prosa Chicana, Cubana, y Puertorriqueña.* New York: Harcourt, 1981.

Kanellos, Nicolás. *A Decade of Hispanic Literature: An Anniversary Anthology.* Houston: Arte Público Press, 1982.

_____. *Short Fiction by Hispanic Writers of the United States.* Houston: Arte Público Press, 1991.

Keller, Gary D., and Francisco Jiménez, eds. *Hispanics in the United States: An Anthology of Creative Literature.* 2 vols. Ypsilanti, Mich.: Bilingual Review Press, 1980 and 1982.

Ludwig, Ed, and James Santibáñez, eds. *The Chicanos: Mexican American Voices.* Baltimore: Penguin, 1971.

Moraga, Cherríe, and Gloria Anzaldúa. *This Bridge Called My Back: Writings by Radical Women of Color.* Watertown, Mass.: Persephone, 1981.

Morton, Carlos. *Johnny Tenorio and Other Plays.* Houston: Arte Público Press, 1992.

Olivares, Julián, ed. *Cuentos Hispanos de los Estados Unidos.* Houston: Arte Público Press, 1991.

Ortego, Philip D. *We Are Chicanos: An Anthology of Mexican-American Literature.* New York: Washington Square, 1973.

Padilla, Ernesto, ed. *Sonnets to Human Beings and Other Poems and Stories by Carmen Tafolla.* A Lalo Critical Edition: Chicano Literature Series. Santa Monica, Calif.: Lalo, 1992.

Poey, Delia, and Virgil Suarez, eds. *Iguana Dreams: New Latino Fiction.* New York: HarperPerennial, 1993.

Rebolledo, Tey Diana, Erlinda Gonzales-Berry, and Teresa Márquez, eds. *Las Mujeres Hablan: An Anthology of Nuevo Mexicana Writers.* Albuquerque, N.Mex.: El Norte, 1988.

Rebolledo, Tey Diana, and Eliana S. Ribero, eds. *Infinite Divisions.* Tucson: University of Arizona Press, 1993.

Rivera, Tomás. *Tomás Rivera: The Complete Works*. Edited by Julián Olivares. Houston: Arte Público Press, 1992.

Romano-V., Octavio Ignacio, ed. *El Espejo-The Mirror: Selected Mexican-American Literature*. Berkeley, Calif.: Quinto Sol, 1969.

Salinas, Luis Omar, and Lillian Faderman, comps. *From the Barrio: A Chicano Anthology*. San Francisco: Canfield, 1973.

Shular, Antonia Castañeda, Tomás Ybarra-Frausto, and Joseph Sommers, comps. *Literatura Chicana: Texto y Contexto—Chicano Literature: Text and Context*. Englewood Cliffs, N.J.: Prentice-Hall, 1972.

Silén, Iván, ed. *Los paraguas amarillos: Los poetas Latinos en Nueva York*. Hanover, N.H.: Ediciones del Norte, 1983.

Simmer, Edward, ed. *The Chicano: From Caricature to Self-Portrait*. New York: New American, 1971.

Suáres, Vigil. *Welcome to the Oasis and Other Stories*. Houston: Arte Público Press, 1991.

Tatum, Charles M., ed. *Mexican-American Literature*. San Diego: Harcourt Brace Jovanovich, 1990.

_____. *New Chicana/Chicano Writing: 1*. Tucson: University of Arizona Press, 1992.

Trujillo, Charley, ed. *Soldados: Chicanos in Viet Nam*. San Jose, Calif.: Chusma, 1990.

Ulibarrí, Sabine R. *The Best of Sabine R. Ulibarrí*. Albuquerque: University of New Mexico Press, 1993.

Valdez, Luis, and Stanley Steiner, comps. *Aztlán: Anthology of Mexican American Literature*. New York: Alfred A. Knopf, 1972.

Vento, Arnold C., et al., eds. *Festival Flor y Canto II: An Anthology of Chicano Literature*. Albuquerque, N.Mex.: Pajarito, 1979.

Vigil-Piñón, Evangelina, ed. *Woman of Her Word: Hispanic Women Write*. Houston: Arte Público Press, 1983.

Villanueva, Tino, ed. *Chicanos: Antología histórica y literaria*. Mexico City: Fondo de Cultura Económica, 1980.

Voices from the Rio Grande: Selections from the First Rio Grande Writers Conference. Albuquerque, N.Mex.: Rio Grande Writers Association, 1976.

CRITICISM AND BIBLIOGRAPHIES

Bruce-Novoa, Juan. *Chicano Authors: Inquiry by Interview*. Austin: University of Texas Press, 1980.

_____. *La literatura Chicana a través de sus autores*. Mexico City: Siglo Veintiuno, 1983.

Bruce-Novoa, Juan, and José Guillermo Saavedra, eds. *Antología Retrospectiva del Cuento Chicano*. Mexico City: Consejo Nacional de Población, 1988.

Castillo-Speed, Lillian. *The Chicano Studies Index*. Berkeley: Chicano Studies Library, University of California, 1992.

Chabrán, Angie, and Rosalinda Fregoso, eds. *Chicana/o Cultural Representations: Reframing Critical Discourses*. Special issue of *Cultural Studies*, no. 3 (1990).

Chabrán, Richard. *Tools for Latino Research*. Chicano Studies Library Publication Series 14. Los Angeles: University of California.

Chicana Creativity and Criticism: Charting New Frontiers in American Literature. Houston: Arte Público Press, 1988.

Eger, Ernestina N. *A Bibliography of Criticism of Contemporary Chicano Literature*. Berkeley: Chicano Studies Library, University of California, 1982.

Fabre, Genvieve, ed. *European Perspectives on Hispanic Literature of the United States*. Houston: Arte Público Press, 1988.

González-T., César A., ed. *Rudolfo A. Anaya: Focus on Criticism*. La Jolla, Calif.: Lalo, 1990.

Güereña, Salvador, and Raquel Quiroz González. *Luis Leal: A Bibliography with Interpretative and Critical Essays*. Berkeley: Chicano Studies Library, University of California, 1988.

Gutiérrez, David, and Robert G. Trujillo, comps. *The Chicano Public Catalog: A Collection Guide for Public Libraries*. Berkeley, Calif.: Floricanto, 1987.

Hernández, Guillermo. *Chicano Satire: A Study in Literary Culture*. Austin: University of Texas Press, 1991.

Hernández y Gutiérrez, Manuel de Jesús. *El colonialismo interno en la narrativa Chicana*. Tempe, Ariz.: Bilingual Press, 1992.

Herrera-Sobek, María, ed. *Beyond Stereotypes: The Critical Analysis of Chicana Literature*. Binghamton, N.Y.: Bilingual Press, 1985.

_____. *The Mexican Corrido: A Feminist Analysis*. Bloomington: Indiana University Press, 1992.

_____. *Reconstructing a Chicano/a Literary Heritage*. Tucson: University of Arizona Press, 1993.

Horno Delgado, Asunción, ed. *Breaking Boundaries: Latina Writing and Critical Readings*. Amherst: University of Massachusetts Press, 1988.

Jiménez, Francisco, ed. *The Identification and Analysis of Chicano Literature*. New York: Bilingual Press, 1979.

Kanellos, Nicolás, ed. *Biographical Dictionary of Hispanic Literature in the United States: The Literature of Puerto Ricans, Cuban Americans, and Other Hispanic Writers*. New York: Greenwood, 1989.

Keller, Gary D., ed. *Chicano Cinema: Research, Reviews, and Resources*. New York: Bilingual Press, 1985.

Lattin, Vernon E., ed. *Contemporary Chicano Fiction: A Critical Survey*. Binghamton, N.Y.: Bilingual Press, 1986.

Lattin, Vernon E., Rolando Hinojosa, and Gary D. Keller, eds. *Tomás Rivera 1935-1984: The Man and His Work*. Tempe, Ariz.: Bilingual Review, 1988.

Leal, Luis. *Aztlán y México: Perfiles literarios e históricos*. Binghamton, N.Y.: Bilingual Press, 1985.

Leal, Luis, et al., eds. *A Decade of Chicano Literature (1970-1979): Critical Essays and Bibliography*. Santa Barbara, Calif.: Editorial La Causa, 1982.

Lomelí, Francisco. *Chicano Writers*. Detroit: Gale Research, 1992.

_____, ed. *Handbook of Hispanic Cultures in the United States: Literature and Art*. Houston: Arte Público Press, 1994.

Lomelí, Francisco, and Julio A. Martínez, eds. *Chicano Literature: A Reader's Encyclopedia*. Westport, Conn.: Greenwood, 1984.

Lomelí, Francisco, and Carl Shirley, eds. *Dictionary of Literary Biography*. Vol. 82. *Chicano Writers: First Series*. Detroit: Gale Research, 1989.

_____. *Dictionary of Literary Biography*. Vol. 122. *Chicano Writers: Second Series*. Detroit: Gale Research, 1992.

Lomelí, Francisco, and Donaldo W. Urioste, eds. *Chicano Perspective in Literature: A Critical and Annotated Bibliography*. Albuquerque, N.Mex.: Pajarito, 1976.

Maciel, David. *Mexico, a Selected Bibliography of Sources for Chicano Studies*. Los Angeles: University of California Press, 1975.

Martínez, Julio A., and Francisco A. Lomelí, eds. *Chicano Literature: A Reference Guide*. Westport, Conn.: Greenwood, 1985.

Méndez-M., Miguel. *De la vida del folclore de la frontera*. Tucson: Mexican-American Studies and Research Center, University of Arizona, 1986.

Olivares, Julián, ed. *International Studies in Honor of Tomás Rivera*. Houston: Arte Público Press, 1986.

Ramos, Luis Arturo. *Angela de Hoyos: A Critical Look: Lo Heroico y lo Antiheroico en su Poesia*. Albuquerque, N.Mex.: Pajarito, 1979.

Rodríguez del Pino, Salvador. *La novela Chicana escrita en Español: Cinco autores comprometidos*. Ypsilanti, Mich.: Bilingual Review, 1982.

Ryan, Bryan, ed. *Hispanic Writers: Selection of Sketches*. Detroit: Gale Research, 1991.

Saldivar, Ramón. *Chicano Narrative: The Dialectics of Difference*. Madison: University of Wisconsin Press, 1990.

Sánchez, Marta Ester. *Contemporary Chicana Poetry: A Critical Approach to an Emerging Literature*. Berkeley: University of California Press, 1985.

Schon, Isabel. *A Hispanic Heritage, Series III: A Guide to Juvenile Books About Hispanic People and Cultures*. Metuchen, N.J.: Scarecrow Press, 1988.

Somoza, Oscar U. *Narrativa Chicana contemporanea: Principios fundamentales*. Mexico City: Signos, 1983.

Tatum, Charles. *La literatura Chicana*. Translated by Víctor Manuel Velarde. Mexico City: Secretaría de Educación Pública, 1986.

_____. *A Selected and Annotated Bibliography of Chicano Studies*. Manhattan, Kans.: Society of Spanish and American Studies, 1976.

Trujillo, Roberto G., and Andrés Rodríguez. *Literatura Chicana: Creative and Critical Writings Through 1984*. Oakland, Calif.: Floricanto, 1985.

Bibliography of Reference Works

The following bibliography, although highly select, attempts to provide broad coverage across the various Latino subgroups and across topic areas. It reflects the fact that, at present, there is much more published material available on Chicanos than on other groups. Puerto Ricans and Cubans also receive significant attention. The bibliography focuses on recent works and on those that have been identified as important in their fields. Some of the works, particularly directories of various sorts, are updated periodically; only one citation is given for these. Works known to undergo periodic updating, such as bibliographies, sometimes appear with the date of first publication followed by a hyphen.

The bibliography presents major reference works first, followed by works categorized by topic. Some works could have been included in any one of several sections; they are presented where they were thought to be most useful. Because of the organization of this bibliography, users are encouraged to skim through the primary and secondary headings to find those sections of most interest and usefulness. —*Richard Chabrán*

GENERAL REFERENCE WORKS AND BIBLIOGRAPHY

Bibliography
Herrera, Diane. *Puerto Ricans and Other Minority Groups in the Continental United States: An Annotated Bibliography*. Detroit: B. Ethridge—Books, 1979.

MacCorkle, Lyn. *Cubans in the United States: A Bibliography for Research in the Social Sciences, 1960-1983*. Westport, Conn.: Greenwood Press, 1984.

Trujillo, Roberto. *The Chicano Public Catalog: A Collection Guide for Public Libraries*. Berkeley, Calif.: Floricanto Press, 1987.

Valk, Barbara. *Borderline: A Bibliography of the United States-Mexico Borderlands*. Los Angeles: Latin American Center, 1988.

Vivo, Paquita. *The Puerto Ricans: An Annotated Bibliography*. New York: Bowker, 1973.

Biography
Fowlie-Flores, Fay. *Index to Puerto Rican Collective Biography*. New York: Greenwood Press, 1987.

Maldonado, Adal Alberto. *Mango Mambo: Portraits*. San Juan: Marrozzini/Illustres, 1988.

Meier, Matt S. *Mexican American Biographies: A Historical Dictionary, 1836-1987*. New York: Greenwood Press, 1988.

Notable Hispanic American Women. Detroit: Gale Research, 1993.

Who's Who Among Hispanic Americans. Detroit: Gale Research, 1991.

Woods, Richard Donovan. *Mexican Autobiography/La Autobiografia Mexicana*. New York: Greenwood Press, 1988.

Dictionaries
Cobos, Ruben. *A Dictionary of New Mexico and Southern Colorado Spanish*. Santa Fe: Museum of New Mexico, 1983.

Galvan, Roberto A. *El Diccionario del Español Chicano: The Dictionary of Chicano Spanish*. Rev. ed. Silver Spring, Md.: Institute of Modern Languages, 1977.

Padilla, Francisco. *Bilingual Dictionary of Anglicismos, Barbarismos, Pachuquismos, y Otras Locuciones en el Barrio: Bilingual Dictionary of Anglicisms, Barbarisms, Pachuquisms, and Other Locutions in the Barrio*. Denver, Colo.: Author, 1980.

Polkinhorn, Harry, Alfredo Velasco, and Malcolm Lambert. *El libro de Calo*: Rev. ed. Berkeley, Calif.: Floricanto Press, 1986.

Santamaria, Francisco Javier. *Diccionario de mejicanismos, razonado; comprobado con citas de autoridades, comparado con el de americanismos y con los vocabularios provinciales de los mas distinguidos diccionaristas hispanoamericanos*. Mejico: Porrua, 1959.

Vasquez, Librado Keno. *Regional Dictionary of Chicano Slang*. Austin, Tex.: Jenkins, 1975.

Directories
Gonzales, Sylvia. *Hispanic American Voluntary Organizations*. Westport, Conn.: Greenwood Press, 1985.

Hispanic Human Service Directory. 2d ed. New York: R. Amalbert, 1989.

National Association of Latino Elected and Appointed Officials. *National Roster of Hispanic Elected Officials*. Washington, D.C.: NALEO Education Fund, 1993.

Schorr, Alan Edward. *Hispanic Resource Directory*. Juneau, Alaska: Denali Press, 1992.

Smith, Darren L., ed. *Hispanic Americans Information Directory*. Detroit: Gale Research, 1990.

Veciana-Suarez, Ana. *Hispanic Media, USA: A Narrative Guide to Print and Electronic News Media in the United States*. Washington, D.C.: The Media Institute, 1987.

Encyclopedias/Sourcebooks
CUNY Centro de Estudios Puertorriqueños. *Sources for*

the Study of Puerto Rican Migration, 1879-1930. New York: Author, 1982.

Kanellos, Nicolás, ed. *The Hispanic-American Almanac: A Reference Work on Hispanics in the United States*. Detroit: Gale Research, 1993.

Kanellos, Nicolás, and Claudio Esteva-Fabregat, eds. *Handbook of Hispanic Cultures in the United States*. 4 vols. Houston: Arte Público Press, 1994.

Meier, Matt, and Feliciano Rivera. *Dictionary of Mexican American History*. Westport, Conn.: Greenwood Press, 1981.

Stoddard, Ellwyn R., et al. *Borderlands Sourcebook: A Guide to the Literature on Northern Mexico and the American Southwest*. Norman: University of Oklahoma Press, 1983.

Thermstrom, Stephan, et al. *Harvard Encyclopedia of American Ethnic Groups*. Cambridge, Mass.: The Belknap Press of Harvard University Press, 1980.

Guides to Literature

Garcia-Ayvens, Francisco, et al. *Quien Sabe?: A Preliminary List of Chicano Reference Material*. Los Angeles: Chicano Studies Research Center, 1981.

Martinez, Julio. *Mexican Americans: An Annotated Bibliography of Bibliographies*. Saratoga: R&E, 1984.

Robinson, Barbara J. *The Mexican American: A Critical Guide to Research Aid*. Greenwich, Conn.: JAI Press, 1980.

Indexes

Bibliographic Guide to Latin American Studies. Boston: G. K. Hall, 1978.

Castillo-Speed, Lillian, Richard Chabran, and Francisco Garcia-Ayvens, eds. *The Chicano Index: A Comprehensive Subject, Author, and Title Index to Chicano Materials*. Berkeley, Calif.: Chicano Studies Library, 1989.

_____, eds. *Chicano Periodical Index*. Berkeley, Calif.: Chicano Studies Library, 1981-1988.

Chicano Database on CD-ROM. Berkeley, Calif.: Chicano Studies Library Publications Unit, University of California at Berkeley, 1990.

Comite de Mexico y Aztlan. *News Monitoring Service*. Oakland, Calif.: COMEXAZ, 1972-1980.

CUNY Centro de Estudios Puertorriqueños. *Index to Articles in the New York Times Relating to Puerto Rico and Puerto Ricans Between 1899 and 1930*. New York: Author, 1981.

_____. *Preliminary Guide to Articles in La Prensa Relating to Puerto Ricans in New York City Between 1922 and 1929*. New York: Author, 1981.

_____. *Preliminary Guide to Articles in Puerto Rican Newspapers Relating to Puerto Rican Migration Between 1900 and 1929*. New York: Author, 1981.

Garcia-Ayvens, Francisco. *Chicano Anthology Index: A Comprehensive Author, Title, and Subject Index to Chicano Anthologies, 1965-1987*. Berkeley, Calif.: Chicano Studies Library, 1990.

_____. *Chicanos in These Times: A Cumulative Subject Index to Articles About Chicanos in the Los Angeles Times*. Santa Fe Springs, N.Mex.: ATM Information Services, 1985- .

Library of Congress. Hispanic Division. *Handbook of Latin American Studies*. Austin: University of Texas Press, 1935- .

Valk, Barbara, ed. *Hispanic American Periodical Index (HAPI)*. Los Angeles: Latin American Studies Center, 1977- .

Serial Directories

Cobos, Anna Maria, et al. *Magazines for Libraries*. New York: Bowker, 1992.

State Historical Society of Wisconsin. Library. *Hispanic Americans in the United States: A Union List of Periodicals and Newspapers Held by the Library of the State Historical Society of Wisconsin and the Libraries of the University of Wisconsin-Madison*. Madison: Author, 1979.

Varona, Esperanza Bravo de. *Cuban Exile Periodicals at the University of Miami Library: An Annotated Bibliography*. Madison, Wisc.: Secretariat, Seminar on the Acquisition of Latin American Library Materials, Memorial Library, University of Wisconsin—Madison, 1987.

HISTORY

General

Acuña, Rodolfo. *Occupied America: A History of Chicanos*. 3d ed. New York: Harper & Row, 1988.

Altamirano, Teofilo. *Los que se fueron: peruanos en Estados Unidos*. Lima, Peru: Pontificia Universidad Catolica del Peru, Fondo Editorial, 1990.

Camarillo, Albert. *Latinos in the United States: A Historical Bibliography*. Santa Barbara, Calif.: ABC-Clio, 1986.

_____. *Mexican Americans in Urban Society: A Selected Bibliography*. Berkeley, Calif.: Floricanto Press, 1986.

Garcia, Mario T. *Mexican Americans: Leadership, Ideology, and Identity, 1930-1960*. New Haven, Conn.: Yale University Press, 1989.

Gomez-Quinones, Juan. *Chicano Politics: Reality and Promise, 1940-1990*. Albuquerque: University of New Mexico Press, 1990.

_____. *Roots of Chicano Politics, 1600-1940*. Albuquerque: University of New Mexico Press, 1994.

Griswold del Castillo, Richard, and Manuel Hidalgo, eds. *Chicano Social and Political History in the Nineteenth Century*. Encino, Calif.: Floricanto Press, 1992.

Lopez, Adalberto, ed. *The Puerto Ricans, Their History, Culture, and Society.* Cambridge, Mass.: Schenkman, 1980.

McWilliams, Carey. *North from Mexico: The Spanish-Speaking People of the United States.* Rev. ed., updated by Matt S. Meier. New York: Greenwood Press, 1990.

Meier, Matt S. *Bibliography of Mexican American History.* Westport, Conn.: Greenwood Press, 1984.

Meier, Matt S., and Feliciano Rivera. *Mexican Americans, American Mexicans: From Conquistadors to Chicanos.* Rev. ed. New York: Hill and Wang, 1993.

Novas, Himilce. *Everything You Need to Know About Latino History.* New York: Plume, 1994.

Poyo, Gerald Eugene. *With All, and for the Good of All: The Emergence of Popular Nationalism in the Cuban Communities of the United States, 1848-1898.* Durham, N.C.: Duke University Press, 1989.

Samora, Julian, and Patricia Vandel Simon. *A History of the Mexican-American People.* Rev. ed. Notre Dame, Ind.: University of Notre Dame Press, 1993.

Tutorow, Norman E. *The Mexican-American War: An Annotated Bibliography.* Westport, Conn.: Greenwood Press, 1981.

History-Arizona

Officer, James E. *Hispanic Arizona, 1536-1856.* Tucson: University of Arizona Press, 1987.

Sheridan, Thomas E. *Los Tucsonenses: The Mexican Community in Tucson, 1854-1941.* Tucson: University of Arizona Press, 1986.

History-California

Camarillo, Albert. *Chicanos in a Changing Society: From Mexican Pueblos to American Barrios in Santa Barbara and Southern California, 1848-1930.* Cambridge, Mass.: Harvard University Press, 1979.

_____. *Chicanos in California: A History of Mexican Americans in California.* San Francisco: Boyd & Fraser, 1984.

Griswold del Castillo, Richard. *The Los Angeles Barrio, 1850-1890: A Social History.* Berkeley: University of California Press, 1979.

Monroy, Douglas. *Thrown Among Strangers: The Making of Mexican Culture in Frontier California.* Berkeley: University of California Press, 1990.

Pitt, Leonard. *The Decline of the Californios: A Social History of the Spanish-Speaking Californians, 1846-1890.* Berkeley: University of California Press, 1971.

Rios-Bustamante, Antonio Jose, and Pedro Castillo. *An Illustrated History of Mexican Los Angeles, 1781-1985.* Los Angeles: University of California, Chicano Studies Research Center Publications, 1986.

Romo, Ricardo. *East Los Angeles: History of a Barrio.* Austin: University of Texas Press, 1983.

Sanchez, George J. *Becoming Mexican American: Ethnicity, Culture, and Identity in Chicano Los Angeles, 1900-1945.* New York: Oxford University Press, 1993.

History-Colorado

De Onis, Jose, ed. *The Hispanic Contribution to the State of Colorado.* Boulder, Colo.: Westview Press, 1976.

Deutsch, Sarah. *No Separate Refuge: Culture, Class, and Gender on an Anglo-Hispanic Frontier in the American Southwest, 1880-1940.* New York: Oxford University Press, 1987.

History-Florida

Balseiro, Jose Agustin, ed. *Presencia hispanica en la Florida: Ayer y hoy, 1513-1976.* Miami, Fla.: Ediciones Universal, 1976.

Mormino, Gary Ross, and George E. Pozzetta. *The Immigrant World of Ybor City: Italians and Their Latin Neighbors in Tampa, 1885-1985.* Urbana: University of Illinois Press, 1987.

History-Midwest

Lane, James B., and Edward J. Escobar, eds. *Forging a Community: The Latino Experience in Northwest Indiana, 1919-1975.* Chicago: Cattails Press, 1987.

Padilla, Felix M. *Puerto Rican Chicago.* Notre Dame, Ind.: University of Notre Dame Press, 1987.

Valdes, Dennis Nodin. *Al Norte: Agricultural Workers in the Great Lakes Region, 1917-1970.* Austin: University of Texas Press, 1991.

History-New Mexico

Gutierrez, Ramon A. *When Jesus Came, the Corn Mothers Went Away: Marriage, Sexuality, and Power in New Mexico, 1500-1846.* Stanford, Calif.: Stanford University Press, 1991.

History-New Spain

Barnes, Thomas C., Thomas H. Naylor, and Charles W. Polzer. *Northern New Spain: A Research Guide.* Tucson: University of Arizona Press, 1981.

Beers, Henry P. *Spanish and Mexican Records of the American Southwest: A Bibliographical Guide to Archive and Manuscript Sources.* Tucson: University of Arizona Press, 1979.

Weber, David J. *The Mexican Frontier, 1821-1846: The American Southwest Under Mexico.* Albuquerque: University of New Mexico Press, 1982.

_____. *The Spanish Frontier in North America.* New Haven, Conn.: Yale University Press, 1992.

History-New York

Sanchez Korrol, Virginia. *From Colonia to Community: The History of Puerto Ricans in New York City, 1917-1948.* Westport, Conn.: Greenwood Press, 1983.

Vega, Bernardo. *Memoirs of Bernardo Vega: A Contribution to the History of the Puerto Rican Community in New York*. Edited by Cesar Andreu Iglesias; translated by Juan Flores. New York: Monthly Review Press, 1984.

History-Texas

De Leon, Arnoldo. *The Tejano Community, 1836-1900*. Albuquerque: University of New Mexico Press, 1982.
_____. *They Called Them Greasers: Anglo Attitudes Toward Mexicans in Texas, 1821-1900*. Austin: University of Texas Press, 1983.

Garcia, Mario T. *Desert Immigrants: The Mexicans of El Paso, 1880-1920*. New Haven, Conn.: Yale University Press, 1981.

Garcia, Richard A. *Rise of the Mexican American Middle Class: San Antonio, 1929-1941*. College Station: Texas A&M University Press, 1991.

Montejano, David. *Anglos and Mexicans in the Making of Texas, 1836-1986*. Austin: University of Texas Press, 1987.

Zamora, Emilio. *The World of the Mexican Worker in Texas*. College Station: Texas A&M University Press, 1993.

HUMANITIES

Art

Beardsley, John, and Jane Livingston. *Hispanic Art in the United States*. New York: Museum of Fine Art, 1987.

The Decade Show: Frameworks of Identity in the 1980s. New York: Museum of Contemporary Hispanic Art, 1990.

Giffords, Gloria Fraser. *Mexican Folk Retablos: Masterpieces on Tin*. Tucson: University of Arizona Press, 1974.

Goldman, Shifra, and Tomas Ybarra Frausto. *Arte Chicano: A Comprehensive Annotated Bibliography of Chicano Art, 1965-1981*. Berkeley, Calif.: Chicano Studies Library, 1985.

Griswold del Castillo, Richard, Teresa McKenna, and Yvonne Yarbro-Bejarano. *Chicano Art: Resistance and Affirmation, 1965-1985*. Los Angeles: Wight Art Gallery, University of California, Los Angeles, 1991.

Latin American Spirit: Art and Artists in the United States, 1920-1970. Bronx, N.Y.: Bronx Museum of the Arts, 1988.

Quirarte, Jacinto, ed. *Chicano Art History: A Book of Selected Readings*. San Antonio: Research Center for the Arts and Humanities, University of Texas at San Antonio, 1984.
_____, ed. *The Hispanic American Aesthetic: Origins, Manifestations, and Significance*. San Antonio: Research Center for the Arts and Humanities, University of Texas at San Antonio, 1983.

_____. *Mexican American Artists*. Austin: University of Texas Press, 1973.

Romotsky, Jerry, and Sally R. Romotsky. *Los Angeles Barrio Calligraphy*. Los Angeles: Dawson's Book Shop, 1976.

Sperling Cockcroft, Eva, and Holly Barnet-Sanchez. *Signs from the Heart: California Chicano Murals*. Venice, Calif.: Social and Public Art Resource Center, 1993.

Film

Fregoso, Rosa Linda. *The Bronze Screen: Chicana and Chicano Film Culture*. Minneapolis: University of Minnesota Press, 1993.

Hadley-Garcia, George. *Hispanic Hollywood: The Latins in Motion Pictures*. New York: Carol Publishing, 1990.

Keller, Gary D., ed. *Chicano Cinema: Research, Reviews, and Resources*. Binghamton, N.Y.: Bilingual Review/Press, 1985.

Maciel, David. *El Norte: The U.S.-Mexican Border in Contemporary Cinema*. San Diego, Calif.: Institute for Regional Studies of the Californias, San Diego State University, 1990.

Noriega, Chon A., ed. *Chicanos and Film: Representation and Resistance*. Minneapolis: University of Minnesota Press, 1992.

Language

Alvarez, Celia, et al. *Speech and Ways of Speaking in a Bilingual Puerto Rican Community: Final Report to the National Institute of Education*. New York: Language Policy Task Force, Center for Puerto Rican Studies, Hunter College, City University of New York, 1984.

Amastae, Jon, and Lucia Elias-Olivares, eds. *Spanish in the United States: Sociolinguistic Aspects*. Cambridge, Mass.: Cambridge University Press, 1982.

Duran, Richard P., ed. *Latino Language and Communicative Behavior*. Norwood, N.J.: Ablex, 1981.

Fishman, Joshua A., et al. *Bilingualism in the Barrio*. 2d ed. Bloomington: Indiana University, 1975.

Penalosa, Fernando. *Chicano Sociolinguistics, a Brief Introduction*. Rowley, Mass.: Newbury House, 1980.

Teschner, Richard V., et al. *Spanish and English of United States Hispanos: A Critical Annotated Linguistics Bibliography*. Arlington, Va.: Center for Applied Linguistics, 1975.

Literature

Calderon, Hector, and Jose David Saldivar. *Criticism in the Borderlands: Studies in Chicano Literature, Culture, and Ideology*. Durham, N.C.: Duke University Press, 1991.

Candelaria, Cordelia. *Chicano Poetry: A Critical Introduction*. Westport, Conn.: Greenwood Press, 1986.

Cortina, Rodolfo J., and Alberto Moncada, eds. *Hispanos en los Estados Unidos*. Madrid: Ediciones de Cultura Hispanica, 1988.

Eger, Ernestina. *A Bibliography of Criticism of Contemporary Chicano Literature*. Berkeley, Calif.: Chicano Studies Library Publications, 1982.

Fernandez Olmos, Margarite. *Sobre la literatura puertorriqueña de aqui y de alla: Aproximaciones feministas*. Santo Domingo, Dominican Republic: Editora Alfa & Omega, 1989.

Foster, David William. *Puerto Rican Literature: A Bibliography of Secondary Sources*. Westport, Conn.: Greenwood Press, 1982.

Gonzales-Berry, Erlinda, ed. *Paso por Aqui: Critical Essays on the New Mexican Literary Tradition, 1542-1988*. Albuquerque: University of New Mexico Press, 1989.

Gutierrez, Ramon, and Genaro Padilla, eds. *Recovering the U.S. Hispanic Literary Heritage*. Houston: Arte Público Press, 1993.

Hernandez, Guillermo. *Chicano Satire: A Study in Literary Culture*. Austin: University of Texas Press, 1991.

Herrera-Sobek, Maria, ed. *Beyond Stereotypes: The Critical Analysis of Chicana Literature*. Binghamton, N.Y.: Bilingual Press, 1985.

_____. *The Bracero Experience: Elitelore Versus Folklore*. Los Angeles: UCLA Latin American Center Publications, University of California, 1979.

_____, ed. *Reconstructing a Chicano/a Literary Heritage: Hispanic Colonial Literature of the Southwest*. Tucson: University of Arizona Press, 1993.

Herrera-Sobek, Maria, and Helena Maria Viramontes, eds. *Chicana Creativity and Criticism: Charting New Frontiers in American Literature*. Houston, Tex.: Arte Público Press, 1988.

Hill, Marnesba, and Harold B. Schleifer. *Puerto Rican Authors: A Biobibliographical Handbook/Autores Puertorriqueños: Una Guia Biobibliografia*. Metuchen, N.J.: Scarecrow Press, 1974.

Horno-Delgado, Asuncion, et al., eds. *Breaking Boundaries: Latina Writing and Critical Readings*. Amherst: University of Massachusetts Press, 1989.

Kanellos, Nicolás, ed. *Biographical Dictionary of Hispanic Literature in the United States: The Literature of Puerto Ricans, Cuban Americans, and Other Hispanic Writers*. New York: Greenwood Press, 1989.

Lattin, Vernon E., ed. *Contemporary Chicano Fiction: A Critical Survey*. Binghamton, N.Y.: Bilingual Press/Editorial Bilingüe, 1986.

Leal, Luis. *Aztlan y Mexico: perfiles literarios e historicos*. Binghamton, N.Y.: Editorial Bilingüe, 1985.

Limon, Jose Eduardo. *Mexican Ballads, Chicano Poems: History and Influence in Mexican-American Social Poetry*. Berkeley: University of California Press, 1992.

Lomeli, Francisco A., and Carl R. Shirley, eds. *Chicano Writers: First Series*. Detroit: Gale Research, 1989.

_____, eds. *Chicano writers: Second Series*. Detroit: Gale Research, 1992.

Lopez-Adorno, Pedro, ed. *Papiros de Babel: antologia de la poesia puertorriqueña en Nueva York*. Rio Piedras, Puerto Rico: Editorial de la Universidad de Puerto Rico, 1991.

Maratos, Daniel C., and Marnesba D. Hill. *Escritores de la Diaspora Cubana: Manual Biobibliografica = Cuban Exile Writers: a Biobibliographic Handbook*. Metuchen, N.J.: Scarecrow Press, 1986.

Martinez, Julio, and Francisco Lomeli. *Chicano Literature: A Reference Guide*. Westport, Conn.: Greenwood Press, 1985.

Marting, Diane E. *Women Writers of Spanish America: An Annotated Bio-Bibliographical Guide*. New York: Greenwood Press, 1987.

Mohr, Eugene V. *The Nuyorican Experience: Literature of the Puerto Rican Minority*. Westport, Conn.: Greenwood Press, 1982.

Ryan, Bryan, ed. *Hispanic Writers: A Selection of Sketches from Contemporary Authors*. Detroit: Gale Research, 1991.

Saldivar, Ramon. *Chicano Narrative: The Dialectics of Difference*. Madison: University of Wisconsin Press, 1990.

Sanchez, Marta Ester. *Contemporary Chicana Poetry: A Critical Approach to an Emerging Literature*. Berkeley: University of California Press, 1985.

Sanchez-Boudy, Jose. *Historia de la literatura cubana en el exilio*. Miami: Ediciones Universal, 1975.

Shirley, Carl R., and Paula W. Shirley. *Understanding Chicano Literature*. Columbia: University of South Carolina Press, 1988.

Sommers, Joseph, and Tomas Ybarra-Frausto, eds. *Modern Chicano Writers: A Collection of Critical Essays*. Englewood Cliffs, N.J.: Prentice-Hall, 1979.

Zimmerman, Marc. *U.S. Latino Literature: An Essay and Annotated Bibliography*. Chicago: MARCH/Abrazo Press, 1992.

Media

Greenberg, Bradley S., et al. *Mexican Americans and the Mass Media*. Norwood, N.J.: Ablex, 1983.

Valdez, Armando, ed. *Telecommunications and Latinos: An Assessment of Issues and Opportunities: Proceedings of the Conference on Telecommunications and Latinos*. Stanford, Calif.: Stanford Center for Chicano Research, 1985.

Music

Amira, John. *The Music of Santeria: Traditional Rhythms of the Bata Drums*. Crown Point, Ind.: White Cliffs Media, 1992.

Arana, Federico. *Yo, mariachi*. Mexico: J. Mortiz, 1991.

Boggs, Vernon. *Salsiology: Afro-Cuban Music and the Evolution of Salsa in New York City.* New York: Greenwood Press, 1992.

Gerard, Charley. *Salsa!: The Rhythm of Latin Music.* Crown Point, Ind.: White Cliffs Media, 1989.

Herrera-Sobek, Maria. *The Mexican Corrido: A Feminist Analysis.* Bloomington: Indiana University Press, 1990.

_____. *Northward Bound: The Mexican Immigrant Experience in Ballad and Song.* Bloomington: Indiana University Press, 1993.

Loza, Steven Joseph. *Barrio Rhythm: Mexican American Music in Los Angeles.* Urbana: University of Illinois Press, 1993.

Manuel, Peter, ed. *Essays on Cuban Music: North American and Cuban Perspectives.* Lanham, Md.: University Press of America, 1991.

Mauleon, Rebeca. *Salsa Guidebook: For Piano and Ensemble.* Petaluma, Calif.: Sher Music, 1993.

Mendheim, Beverly. *Ritchie Valens: The First Latino Rocker.* Tempe, Ariz.: Bilingual Press/Editorial Bilingüe, 1987.

Orovio, Helio. *Diccionario de la musica cubana: Biografico y tecnico.* Ciudad de la Habana, Cuba: Editorial Letras Cubanas, 1981.

Paredes, Americo, ed. *A Texas-Mexican Cancionero: Folksongs of the Lower Border.* Urbana: University of Illinois Press, 1976.

_____. *"With His Pistol in His Hand": A Border Ballad and Its Hero.* Austin: University of Texas Press, 1958.

Pena, Manuel H. *The Texas-Mexican Conjunto: History of a Working-Class Music.* Austin: University of Texas Press, 1985.

Robb, John Donald. *Hispanic Folk Music of New Mexico and the Southwest: A Self-Portrait of a People.* Norman: University of Oklahoma Press, 1980.

Roberts, John S. *The Latin Tinge: The Impact of Latin American Music on the United States.* New York: Oxford University Press, 1979.

Simmons, Merle Edwin. *The Mexican Corrido as a Source for Interpretive Study of Modern Mexico, 1870-1950.* New York: Kraus Reprint, 1969.

Photography

Fusco, Paul. *La Causa: The California Grape Boycott.* New York: Collier, 1970.

Hall, Douglas Kent. *The Border on the Line.* New York: Abbeville Press, 1988.

Martin, Patricia Preciado. *Images and Conversations: Mexican Americans Recall a Southwestern Past.* Tucson: University of Arizona Press, 1983.

Martinez, Elizabeth, ed. *500 Años del Pueblo Chicano/ 500 Years of Chicano History in Pictures.* Albuquerque, N.Mex.: Southwest Organizing Project, 1991.

Rebolledo, Tey Diana, ed. *Nuestras Mujeres: Hispanas of New Mexico: Their Images and Their Lives, 1582-1992.* Albuquerque, N.Mex.: El Norte Publications/ Academia, 1992.

Young Lords Party. *Palante: Young Lords Party.* Photos by Michael Abramson, text by the Young Lords Party and Michael Abramson. New York: McGraw-Hill, 1971.

Theater

Huerta, Jorge A. *Chicano Theater: Themes and Forms.* Ypsilanti, Mich.: Bilingual Press, 1982.

Kanellos, Nicolás, ed. *Hispanic Theatre in the United States.* Houston, Tex.: Arte Público Press, 1984.

_____. *A History of Hispanic Theatre in the United States: Origins to 1940.* Austin: University of Texas Press, 1990.

RELIGION

Arroyo, Antonio M. Stevens, ed. *Prophets Denied Honor: An Anthology on the Hispano Church of the United States.* Maryknoll, N.Y.: Orbis, 1980.

Brackenridge, R. Douglas. *Iglesia Presbiteriana: A History of Presbyterians and Mexican Americans in the Southwest.* San Antonio, Tex.: Trinity University Press, 1974.

Elizondo, Virgil. *Galilean Journey: The Mexican-American Promise.* Maryknoll, N.Y.: Orbis, 1983.

Gonzalez-Wippler, Migene. *The Santeria Experience: A Journey into the Miraculous.* Rev. ed. St. Paul, Minn.: Llewellyn, 1992.

Guerrero, Andres Gonzales. *A Chicano Theology.* Maryknoll, N.Y.: Orbis, 1987.

Isasi-Diaz, Ada Maria. *Hispanic Women Prophetic Voice in the Church: Toward a Hispanic Women's Liberation Theology.* San Francisco: Harper & Row, 1988.

McNally, Michael J. *Catholicism in South Florida, 1868-1968.* Gainesville: University Presses of Florida, 1982.

Mosqueda, Lawrence J. *Chicanos, Catholicism, and Political Ideology.* Lanham, Md.: University Press of America, 1986.

Murphy, Joseph M. *Santeria: An African Religion in America.* Boston: Beacon Press, 1988.

Perez y Mena, Andres Isidoro. *Speaking with the Dead: Development of Afro-Latin Religion Among Puerto Ricans in the United States: A Study into the Interpenetration of Civilizations in the New World.* New York: AMS Press, 1991.

Romero, C. Gilbert. *Hispanic Devotional Piety: Tracing the Biblical Roots.* Maryknoll, N.Y.: Orbis, 1991.

Sandoval, Moises. *On the Move: A History of the Hispanic Church in the United States.* Maryknoll, N.Y.: Orbis, 1990.

Weigle, Marta. *Brothers of Light, Brothers of Blood: The Penitentes of the Southwest.* Santa Fe, N.Mex.: Ancient City Press, 1989.

SOCIAL SCIENCES

Customs and Folklore

Brown, Lorin W., et al. *Hispano Folklife of New Mexico: The Lorin W. Brown Federal Writers' Project Manuscripts.* Albuquerque: University of New Mexico Press, 1978.

Campa, Arthur L. *Hispanic Culture in the Southwest.* Norman: University of Oklahoma Press, 1979.

Espinosa, Aurelio Macedonio, ed. *The Folklore of Spain in the American Southwest: Traditional Spanish Folk Literature in Northern New Mexico and Southern Colorado.* Norman: University of Oklahoma Press, 1985.

Espinosa, Carmen Gertrudis. *Shawls, Crinolines, Filigree: The Dress and Adornment of the Women of New Mexico, 1739 to 1900.* El Paso: Texas Western Press, 1970.

Glazer, Mark. *A Dictionary of Mexican American Proverbs.* New York: Garland, 1987.

Graham, Joe S., ed. *Hecho en Tejas: Texas-Mexican Folk Arts and Crafts.* Denton: University of North Texas Press, 1991.

————. *Hispanic American Material Culture: An Annotated Directory of Collections, Sites, Archives, and Festivals in the United States.* New York: Greenwood Press, 1989.

Heisley, Michael. *An Annotated Bibliography of Chicano Folklore from the Southwestern United States.* Los Angeles: Center for the Study of Comparative Folklore and Mythology, UCLA, 1977.

Paredes, Americo. *Folklore and Culture on the Texas-Mexican Border.* Austin: CMAS Books, Center for Mexican American Studies, University of Texas at Austin, 1993.

Rael, Juan Bautista. *Cuentos Espanoles de Colorado y Nuevo Mexico = Spanish Folk Tales from Colorado and New Mexico: Spanish Language Originals with English Summaries.* Rev. ed. Santa Fe: Museum of New Mexico Press, 1977.

Robe, Stanley Linn. *Index of Mexican Folktales, Including Narrative Texts from Mexico, Central America, and the Hispanic United States.* Berkeley: University of California Press, 1973.

Sandoval, Ruben. *Games, Games, Games/Juegos, Juegos, Juegos: Chicano Children at Play: Games and Rhymes.* Garden City, N.Y.: Doubleday, 1977.

Weigle, Marta, ed. *Hispanic Arts and Ethnohistory in the Southwest: New Papers Inspired by the Work of E. Boyd.* Santa Fe, N.Mex.: Ancient City Press, 1983.

————, et al. *The Lore of New Mexico.* Albuquerque: University of New Mexico Press, 1988.

West, John O. *Mexican-American Folklore: Legends, Songs, Festivals, Proverbs, Crafts, Tales of Saints, of Revolutionaries, and More.* Little Rock, Ark.: August House, 1988.

Education

Benitez, Mario A. *The Education of the Mexican American: A Selected Bibliography.* Rosslyn, Va.: National Clearinghouse for Bilingual Education, 1979.

Cafferty, Pastora San Juan. *The Politics of Language: The Dilemma of Bilingual Education for Puerto Ricans.* Boulder, Colo.: Westview Press, 1981.

Cordasco, Francesco. *The Puerto Rican Community and Its Children on the Mainland: A Source Book for Teachers, Social Workers, and Other Professionals.* Metuchen, N.J.: Scarecrow Press, 1972.

Delgado, Gilbert L., ed. *The Hispanic Deaf: Issues and Challenges for Bilingual Special Education.* Washington, D.C.: Gallaudet College Press, 1984.

Duran, Richard P. *Hispanics' Education and Background: Predictors of College Achievement.* New York: College Entrance Examination Board, 1983.

Mackey, William Francis. *Bilingual Schools for a Bicultural Community: Miami's Adaptation to the Cuban Refugees.* Rowley, Mass.: Newbury House, 1977.

Olivas, Michael A., ed. *Latino College Students.* New York: Teachers College Press, 1986.

Padilla, Amado, Halford H. Fairchild, and Concepcion M. Valadez, eds. *Bilingual Education: Issues and Strategies.* Newbury Park, Calif.: Sage Publications, 1990.

Padilla, Raymond V., ed. *Bilingual Education Technology.* Ypsilanti: Department of Foreign Languages and Bilingual Studies, Eastern Michigan University, 1981.

————, ed. *Ethnoperspectives in Bilingual Education Research: Bilingual Education and Public Policy in the United States.* Ypsilanti: Department of Foreign Languages and Bilingual Studies, Eastern Michigan University, 1979.

————, ed. *Theory, Technology, and Public Policy on Bilingual Education.* Rosslyn, Va.: National Clearinghouse for Bilingual Education, 1983.

Padilla, Raymond V., and Alfredo H. Benavides, eds. *Critical Perspectives on Bilingual Education Research.* Tempe, Ariz.: Bilingual Press/Editorial Bilingüe, 1992.

Padilla, Raymond V., and Eugene E. Garcia, eds. *Advances in Bilingual Education Research.* Tucson: University of Arizona Press, 1985.

Rivera, Ralph, and Sonia Nieto, eds. *The Education of Latino Students in Massachusetts.* Boston: Mauricio Gaston Institute for Latino Community Development and Public Policy, University of Massachusetts, 1993.

Walsh, Catherine E. *Pedagogy and the Struggle for Voice: Issues of Language, Power, and Schooling for Puerto Ricans.* New York: Bergin & Garvey, 1991.

Ethnography

Chavez, Leo R. *Shadowed Lives: Undocumented Immigrants in American Society*. Fort Worth, Tex.: Harcourt Brace Jovanovich College Publishers, 1992.

Davis, Marilyn P. *Mexican Voices/ American Dreams: An Oral History of Mexican Immigration to the United States*. New York: H. Holt, 1990.

Foley, Douglas E. *Learning Capitalist Culture: Deep in the Heart of Tejas*. Philadelphia: University of Pennsylvania Press, 1990.

Kutsche, Paul. *Canones, Values, Crisis, and Survival in a Northern New Mexico Village*. Albuquerque: University of New Mexico Press, 1981.

Lamphere, Louise, et al. *Sunbelt Working Mothers: Reconciling Family and Factory*. Ithaca, N.Y.: Cornell University Press, 1993.

Moore, Joan, and Raquel Pinderhughes, eds. *In the Barrios: Latinos and the Underclass Debate*. New York: Russell Sage Foundation, 1993.

Shorris, Earl. *Latinos: A Biography of the People*. New York: W. W. Norton, 1992.

Health and Mental Health

Becerra, Rosina M., and Milton Greenblatt. *Hispanics Seek Health Care: A Study of 1,088 Veterans of Three War Eras*. Lanham, Md.: University Press of America, 1983.

Becerra, Rosina M., Marvin Karno, and Javier I. Escobar, eds. *Mental Health and Hispanic Americans: Clinical Perspectives*. New York: Grune & Stratton, 1982.

Furino, Antonio, ed. *Health Policy and the Hispanic*. Boulder, Colo.: Westview Press, 1992.

Hernandez, Carrol A. , Marsha J. Haug, and Nathaniel N. Wagner, comps. *Chicanos: Social and Psychological Perspectives*. 2d ed. Saint Louis, Mo.: Mosby, 1976.

Lamberty, Gontran, and Cynthia Garcia Coll. *Puerto Rican Women and Children*. New York: Plenum Press, 1994.

Martinez, Joe L., Jr., and Richard H. Mendoza. *Chicano Psychology*. 2d ed. Orlando, Fla.: Academic Press, 1984.

Maxwell, Bruce, and Michael Jacobson. *Marketing Disease to Hispanics: The Selling of Alcohol, Tobacco, and Junk Foods*. Washington, D.C.: Center for Science in the Public Interest, 1989.

Newton, Frank, Esteban L. Olmedo, and Amado M. Padilla. *Hispanic Mental Health: A Research Guide*. Berkeley: University of California Press, 1982.

Padilla, Eligio R., and Amado M. Padilla, eds. *Transcultural Psychiatry: An Hispanic Perspective*. Los Angeles: Spanish Speaking Mental Health Research Center, 1977.

Perrone, Bobette, H. Henrietta Stockel, and Victoria Krueger. *Medicine Women, Curanderas, and Women Doctors*. Norman: University of Oklahoma Press, 1989.

Ramirez, Manuel. *Psychology of the Americas: Mestizo Perspectives on Personality and Mental Health*. New York: Pergamon Press, 1983.

U.S. Department of Health and Human Services. *Hispanic Health Issues. Report of the Secretary's Task Force on Black and Minority Health*. Washington, D.C.: Author, 1986.

Zambrana, Ruth E., ed. *Work, Family, and Health: Latina Women in Transition*. Bronx, N.Y.: Hispanic Research Center, Fordham University, 1982.

Labor

Borjas, George J., and Marta Tienda, eds. *Hispanics in the U.S. Economy*. Orlando, Fla.: Academic Press, 1985.

Daniel, Cletus E. *Bitter Harvest: A History of California Farmworkers, 1870-1941*. Ithaca, N.Y.: Cornell University Press, 1981.

Fernandez-Kelly, Maria Patricia. *For We Are Sold, I and My People: Women and Industry in Mexico's Frontier*. Albany: State University of New York Press, 1983.

Jenkins, J. Craig. *The Politics of Insurgency: The Farm Worker Movement in the 1960s*. New York: Columbia University Press, 1985.

Kiser, George C., and Martha Woody Kiser, eds. *Mexican Workers in the United States: Historical and Political Perspectives*. Albuquerque: University of New Mexico Press, 1979.

Knouse, Stephen B., Paul Rosenfeld, and Amy Culbertson, eds. *Hispanics in the Workplace*. Newbury Park, Calif.: Sage Publications, 1992.

Morales, Rebecca, and Frank Bonilla, eds. *Latinos in a Changing U.S. Economy: Comparative Perspectives on Growing Inequality*. Newbury Park, Calif.: Sage Publications, 1993.

Prieto, Yolanda. *Women, Work, and Change: The Case of Cuban Women in the U.S.* Erie: Northwestern Pennsylvania Institute for Latin American Studies, 1979.

Romero, Mary. *Maid in the U.S.A.* New York: Routledge, 1992.

Ruiz, Vicki. *Cannery Women, Cannery Lives: Mexican Women, Unionization, and the California Food Processing Industry, 1930-1950*. Albuquerque: University of New Mexico Press, 1987.

Taylor, Paul Schuster. *Mexican Labor in the United States*. New York: Arno Press, 1970.

Zavella, Patricia. *Women's Work and Chicano Families: Cannery Workers of the Santa Clara Valley*. Ithaca, N.Y.: Cornell University Press, 1987.

Politics

De la Garza, Rodolfo O., et al., eds. *Latino Voices: Mexican, Puerto Rican, and Cuban Perspectives on American Politics*. Boulder, Colo.: Westview Press, 1992.

De la Garza, Rodolfo O., Martha Menchaca, and Louis DeSipio, eds. *Barrio Ballots: Latino Politics in the 1990 Elections*. Boulder, Colo.: Westview Press, 1994.

Estades, Rosa. *Patterns of Political Participation of Puerto Ricans in New York City*. Rio Piedras: Editorial Universitaria, Universidad de Puerto Rico, 1978.

Fernandez, Ronald. *Los Macheteros: The Wells Fargo Robbery and the Violent Struggle for Puerto Rican Independence*. New York: Prentice-Hall, 1987.

Garcia, F. Chris, ed. *Latinos and the Political System*. Notre Dame, Ind.: University of Notre Dame Press, 1988.

_____, et al., comps. *Latinos and Politics: A Selected Research Bibliography*. Austin: Center for Mexican American Studies, University of Texas, 1991.

Griswold del Castillo, Richard. *The Treaty of Guadalupe Hidalgo: A Legacy of Conflict*. Norman: University of Oklahoma Press, 1990.

Hardy-Fanta, Carol. *Latina Politics, Latino Politics: Gender, Culture, and Political Participation in Boston*. Philadelphia, Pa.: Temple University Press, 1993.

Hero, Rodney E. *Latinos and the U.S. Political System: Two-Tiered Pluralism*. Philadelphia, Pa.: Temple University Press, 1992.

Jennings, James. *Puerto Rican Politics in New York City*. Washington, D.C.: University Press of America, 1977.

Jennings, James, and Monte Rivera, eds. *Puerto Rican Politics in Urban America*. Westport, Conn.: Greenwood Press, 1984.

Moncada, Alberto, and Juan Olivas. *Los hispanos en la politica norteamericana*. Madrid: Instituto de Cooperacion Iberoamericana, 1989.

Munoz, Carlos. *Youth, Identity, Power: The Chicano Movement*. New York: Verso, 1989.

Ribes Tovar, Federico. *Lolita Lebron, la prisionera*. New York: Plus Ultra Educational Publishers, 1974.

Skerry, Peter. *Mexican Americans: The Ambivalent Minority*. New York: Free Press, 1993.

Suarez, Manuel. *Requiem on Cerro Maravilla: The Police Murders in Puerto Rico and the U.S. Government Coverup*. Maplewood, N.J.: Waterfront Press, 1987.

Villarreal, Roberto E., and Norma G. Hernandez, eds. *Latinos and Political Coalitions: Political Empowerment for the 1990s*. New York: Greenwood Press, 1991.

Villarreal, Roberto E., Norma G. Hernandez, and Howard D. Neighbor, eds. *Latino Empowerment: Progress, Problems, and Prospects*. New York: Greenwood Press, 1988.

Sociology

Acosta-Belen, Edna, and Barbara R. Sjostrom, eds. *The Hispanic Experience in the United States: Contemporary Issues and Perspectives*. New York: Praeger, 1988.

Blea, Irene I. *Towards a Chicano Social Science*. New York: Praeger, 1988.

Boone, Margaret S. *Capital Cubans: Refugee Adaptation in Washington, D.C.* New York: AMS Press, 1989.

Boswell, Thomas D. *The Cuban-American Experience: Culture, Images, and Perspectives*. Totowa, N.J.: Rowman & Allanheld, 1984.

Chenault, Lawrence Royce. *The Puerto Rican Migrant in New York City*. New York: Columbia University Press, 1938.

Connor, Walker. *Mexican-Americans in Comparative Perspective*. Washington, D.C.: Urban Institute Press, 1985.

Cortes, Carlos E., ed. *Cuban Exiles in the United States*. New York: Arno Press, 1980.

_____, ed. *The Cuban Experience in the United States*. New York: Arno Press, 1980.

De la Garza, Rodolfo O., et al. *The Mexican American Experience: An Interdisciplinary Anthology*. Austin: University of Texas Press, 1985.

Grebler, Leo, et al. *The Mexican-American People: The Nation's Second Largest Minority*. New York: Free Press, 1970.

Greneir, Guillermo, and Alex Stepick III. *Miami Now!: Immigration, Ethnicity, and Social Change*. Gainesville: University Press of Florida, 1992.

Hayes-Bautista, David E. *The Burden of Support: Young Latinos in an Aging Society*. Stanford, Calif.: Stanford University Press, 1988.

_____, et al. *No Longer a Minority: Latinos and Social Policy in California*. Los Angeles: UCLA Chicano Studies Research Center, 1992.

Hurtado, Aida, et al. *Redefining California: Latino Social Engagement in a Multicultural Society*. Los Angeles: UCLA Chicano Studies Research Center, 1992.

Jorge, Antonio, Jaime Suchlicki, and Adolfo Leyva de Varona. *Cuban Exiles in Florida: Their Presence and Contributions*. Coral Gables, Fla.: University of Miami, North-South Center Publications for the Research Institute for Cuban Studies, 1991.

Melendez, Edwin, and Edgardo Melendez, eds. *Colonial Dilemma: Critical Perspectives on Contemporary Puerto Rico*. Boston: South End Press, 1993.

Mirande, Alfredo. *The Chicano Experience: An Alternative Perspective*. Notre Dame, Ind.: University of Notre Dame Press, 1985.

Moore, Joan W., and Harry Pachon. *Hispanics in the United States*. Englewood Cliffs, N.J.: Prentice-Hall, 1985.

Morales, Julio. *Puerto Rican Poverty and Migration: We Just Had to Try Elsewhere*. New York: Praeger, 1986.

Padilla, Elena. *Up from Puerto Rico*. New York: Columbia University Press, 1958.

Pastora, San Juan Cafferty, and William C. McCready, eds. *Hispanics in the United States: A New Social Agenda*. New Brunswick, N.J.: Transaction, 1985.

Rodriguez, Clara E. *Puerto Ricans: Born in the U.S.A.* Boulder, Colo.: Westview Press, 1991.

Rodriguez, Clara E., Virginia Sanchez Korrol, and Jose Oscar Alers, eds. *The Puerto Rican Struggle: Essays on Survival in the U.S.* New York: Puerto Rican Migration Research Consortium, 1980.

Rodriguez de Laguna, Asela, ed. *Images and Identities: The Puerto Rican in Two World Contexts.* New Brunswick, N.J.: Transaction, 1987.

Rogg, Eleanor Meyer, and Rosemary Santana Cooney. *Adaptation and Adjustment of Cubans, West New York, New Jersey.* Bronx, N.Y.: Hispanic Research Center, Fordham University, 1980.

Rogler, Lloyd Henry. *Migrant in the City: The Life of a Puerto Rican Action Group.* Maplewood, N.J.: Waterfront Press, 1984.

Rosenberg, Terry Jean. *Residence, Employment, and Mobility of Puerto Ricans in New York City.* Chicago: University of Chicago, Department of Geography, 1974.

Sutton, Constance R., and Elsa M. Chaney, eds. *Caribbean Life in New York City: Sociocultural Dimensions.* New York Center for Migration Studies, 1987.

United States. Commission on Civil Rights. *Puerto Ricans in the Continental United States: An Uncertain Future: A Report of the United States Commission on Civil Rights.* Washington, D.C.: Author, 1976.

Valdez, Armando, Albert Camarillo, and Tomas Almaguer, eds. *The State of Chicano Research on Family, Labor, and Migration: Proceedings of the First Stanford Symposium on Chicano Research and Public Policy.* Stanford, Calif.: Stanford Center for Chicano Research, 1983.

Wagenheim, Kal. *A Survey of Puerto Ricans on the U.S. Mainland in the 1970s.* New York: Praeger, 1975.

SOCIAL ISSUES

The Border

Bustamante, Jorge A., Clark W. Reynolds, and Raul A. Hinojosa Ojeda. *U.S.-Mexico Relations: Labor Market Interdependence.* Stanford, Calif.: Stanford University Press, 1992.

Ganster, Paul, and Hartmut Walter, eds. *Environmental Hazards and Bioresource Management in the United States-Mexico Borderlands.* Los Angeles: UCLA Latin American Center Publications, University of California, Los Angeles, 1990.

Hansen, Niles M. *The Border Economy: Regional Development in the Southwest.* Austin: University of Texas Press, 1981.

Ross, Stanley R., ed. *Views Across the Border: The United States and Mexico.* Albuquerque: University of New Mexico Press, 1978.

Families

Griswold del Castillo, Richard. *La Familia: Chicano Families in the Urban Southwest, 1848 to the Present.* Notre Dame, Ind.: University of Notre Dame Press, 1984.

Navarro, Jose D. *The Family and Child Abuse in a Latino Community: A Study.* [S.l.], J. W., Gaterman & Associates, 1981.

Sotomayor, Marta, ed. *Empowering Hispanic Families: A Critical Issue for the '90s.* Milwaukee, Wisc.: Family Service America, 1991.

Gangs

Harris, Mary G. *Cholas: Latino Girls and Gangs.* New York: AMS Press, 1988.

Jankowski, Martin Sanchez. *Islands in the Street: Gangs and American Urban Society.* Berkeley: University of California Press, 1991.

Moore, Joan W., et al. *Homeboys: Gangs, Drugs, and Prison in the Barrios of Los Angeles.* Philadelphia, Pa.: Temple University Press, 1978.

Padilla, Felix M. *The Gang as an American Enterprise.* New Brunswick, N.J.: Rutgers University Press, 1992.

Rodriguez, Luis J. *Always Running: La Vida Loca, Gang Days in L.A.* Willimantic, Conn.: Curbstone Press, 1993.

Vigil, James Diego, et al. *Barrio Gangs: Street Life and Identity in Southern California.* Austin: University of Texas Press, 1988.

Identity

Anaya, Rudolfo A., and Francisco A. Lomeli, eds. *Aztlan: Essays on the Chicano Homeland.* Albuquerque, N.Mex.: University of New Mexico Press, 1991.

Arteaga, Alfred. *An Other Tongue: Nation and Ethnicity in the Linguistic Borderlands.* Durham, N.C.: Duke University Press, 1994.

Bernal, Martha E., and Phyllis C. Martinelli, eds. *Mexican American Identity.* Encino, Calif.: Floricanto Press, 1993.

Flores, Juan. *Divided Borders: Essays on Puerto Rican Identity.* Houston, Tex.: Arte Público Press, 1993.

Keefe, Susan E., et al. *Chicano Ethnicity.* Albuquerque: University of New Mexico Press, 1987.

Padilla, Amado M., ed. *Acculturation: Theory, Models, and Some New Findings.* Boulder, Colo.: Westview Press, 1980.

Padilla, Felix M. *Latino Ethnic Consciousness: The Case of Mexican Americans and Puerto Ricans in Chicago.* Notre Dame, Ind.: University of Notre Dame Press, 1985.

Immigration/Migration

Cardoso, Lawrence A. *Mexican Emigration to the United States, 1897-1931: Socio-Economic Patterns.* Tucson: University of Arizona Press, 1980.

Center for Puerto Rican Studies. History Task Force. *Labor Migration Under Capitalism: The Puerto Rican Experience.* New York: Monthly Review Press, 1979.

Corwin, Arthur F., ed. *Immigrants—and Immigrants: Perspectives on Mexican Labor Migration to the United States.* Westport, Conn.: Greenwood Press, 1978.

Fitzpatrick, Joseph P. *Puerto Rican Americans: The Meaning of Migration to the Mainland.* 2d ed. Englewood Cliffs, N.J.: Prentice-Hall, 1987.

Garcia, Juan Ramon. *Operation Wetback: The Mass Deportation of Mexican Undocumented Workers in 1954.* Westport, Conn.: Greenwood Press, 1980.

Georges, Eugenia. *The Making of a Transnational Community: Migration, Development, and Cultural Change in the Dominican Republic.* New York: Columbia University Press, 1990.

Grasmuck, Sherri, and Patricia R. Pessar. *Between Two Islands: Dominican International Migration.* Berkeley: University of California Press, 1991.

Hoffman, Abraham. *Unwanted Mexican Americans in the Great Depression: Repatriation Pressures, 1929-1939.* Tucson: University of Arizona Press, 1974.

Hondagneu-Sotelo, Pierrette. *Gendered Transitions: Mexican Experiences of Immigration.* Berkeley: University of California Press, 1994.

McCoy, Clyde B., and Diana H. Gonzalez. *Cuban Immigration and Immigrants in Florida and the United States: Implications for Immigration Policy.* Gainesville: Bureau of Economic and Business Research, University of Florida, 1985.

Maldonado-Denis, Manuel. *The Emigration Dialectic: Puerto Rico and the U.S.A.* New York: International Publishers, 1980.

Portes, Alejandro, and Robert L. Bach. *Latin Journey: Cuban and Mexican Immigrants in the United States.* Berkeley: University of California Press, 1985.

Powers, Mary G., and John J. Mocisco, Jr. *Los Puertorriqueños en Nueva York: Un analisis de su participacion laboral y experiencia migratoria, 1970.* San Juan, Puerto Rico: Centro de Investigaciones Sociales-UPR, 1982.

Intermarriage

Fitzpatrick, Joseph P., and Douglas T. Gurak. *Hispanic Intermarriage in New York City, 1975.* Bronx, N.Y.: Hispanic Research Center, Fordham University, 1979.

Murguia, Edward. *Chicano Intermarriage: A Theoretical and Empirical Study.* San Antonio, Tex.: Trinity University Press, 1982.

Older People

Applewhite, Steven R., ed. *Hispanic Elderly in Transition: Theory, Research, Policy, and Practice.* New York: Greenwood Press, 1988.

Becerra, Rosina M., et al. *The Hispanic Elderly: A Research Reference Guide.* Lanham, Md.: University Press of America, 1984.

Markides, Kyriakos S., et al. *Older Mexican Americans: A Study in an Urban Barrio.* Austin: Center for Mexican American Studies, University of Texas at Austin, 1983.

Torres-Gil, Fernando, ed. *Hispanics in an Aging Society.* New York: Carnegie Corporation of New York, 1986.

Social Services

Rodriguez, Orlando. *Hispanics and Human Services: Help-Seeking in the Inner City.* Bronx, N.Y.: Hispanic Research Center, Fordham University, 1987.

Substance Abuse

Bullington, Bruce. *Heroin Use in the Barrio.* Lexington, Mass.: Lexington Books, 1977.

Gilbert, Jean, ed. *Alcohol Consumption Among Mexicans and Mexican Americans: A Binational Perspective.* Los Angeles: Spanish Speaking Mental Health Center, University of California, 1988.

Glick, Ronald, and Joan Moore, eds. *Drugs in Hispanic Communities.* New Brunswick, N.J.: Rutgers University Press, 1990.

Youth

Ambert, Alba N., and Maria D. Alvarez, eds. *Puerto Rican Children on the Mainland: Interdisciplinary Perspectives.* New York: Garland, 1992.

Canino, Ian A., et al. *The Puerto Rican Child in New York City: Stress and Mental Health.* Bronx, N.Y.: Hispanic Research Center, Fordham University, 1980.

Garcia, Eugene E., ed. *The Mexican-American Child: Language, Cognition, and Social Development.* Tempe: Center for Bilingual Education, Arizona State University, 1983.

Hernandez, Jose. *Puerto Rican Youth Employment.* Maplewood, N.J.: Waterfront Press, 1983.

Jankowski, Martin Sanchez. *City Bound: Urban Life and Political Attitudes Among Chicano Youth.* Albuquerque: University of New Mexico Press, 1986.

Santos, Richard. *Hispanic Youth: Emerging Workers.* New York: Praeger, 1985.

STATISTICS/DEMOGRAPHY

Bean, Frank D., et al. *Mexican American Fertility Patterns.* Austin: University of Texas Press, 1985.

Bean, Frank D., and Marta Tienda. *The Hispanic Population of the United States.* New York: Russell Sage Foundation, 1987.

The Hispanic Almanac. 2d ed. New York: Hispanic Policy Development Project, 1990.

Hispanic Databook of U.S. Cities and Counties. Milpitas, Calif.: Toucan Valley Publications, 1994.

Jaffe, Abram J., Ruth M. Cullen, and Thomas D. Boswell. *The Changing Demography of Spanish Americans.* New York: Academic Press, 1980.

Lorey, David E. *United States-Mexico Border Statistics Since 1900*. Los Angeles: UCLA Latin American Center Publications, UCLA Program on Mexico, University of California, Los Angeles, 1990.

Reddy, Marlita A., ed. *Statistical Record of Hispanic Americans*. Detroit: Gale Research, 1993.

Schick, Frank L., and Renee Schick, eds. *Statistical Handbook on U.S. Hispanics*. Phoenix, Ariz.: Oryx Press, 1991.

U.S. Bureau of the Census. *Persons of Hispanic Origin in the United States. 1990*. Washington, D.C.: U.S. Dept. of Commerce, Economics and Statistics Administration, Bureau of the Census, 1993.

THEORY

Anzaldúa, Gloria. *Borderlands: The New Mestiza=La Frontera*. San Francisco: Spinsters/Aunt Lute, 1987.

_____. *Making Face, Making Soul = Haciendo Caras: Creative and Critical Perspectives by Feminists of Color*. San Francisco: Aunt Lute Foundation Books, 1990.

Barrera, Mario. *Beyond Aztlan: Ethnic Autonomy in Comparative Perspective*. New York: Praeger, 1988.

_____. *Race and Class in the Southwest: A Theory of Racial Inequality*. Notre Dame, Ind.: University of Notre Dame Press, 1979.

Rosaldo, Renato. *Culture and Truth: The Remaking of Social Analysis*. Boston: Beacon Press, 1993.

Sanchez, Rosaura. *Chicano Discourse: Socio-Historic Perspectives*. 2d ed. Houston: Arte Público Press, 1994.

WOMEN

Acosta-Belen, Edna, ed. *The Puerto Rican Woman: Perspectives on Culture, History, and Society*. New York: Praeger, 1986.

Alarcon, Norma, et al., eds. *Chicana Critical Issues*. Berkeley, Calif.: Third Woman Press, 1993.

Baca Zinn, Maxine, and Bonnie Thornton Dill, eds. *Women of Color in U.S. Society*. Philadelphia, Pa.: Temple University Press, 1994.

Blea, Irene I. *La Chicana and the Intersection of Race, Class, and Gender*. New York: Praeger, 1992.

Castillo-Speed, Lillian. *Chicana Studies Index: Twenty Years of Gender Research, 1971-1991*. Berkeley, Calif.: Chicano Studies Library Publications, 1992.

Cordova, Teresa, et al., eds. *Chicana Voices: Intersections of Class, Race, and Gender*. Colorado Springs, Colo.: National Association for Chicano Studies, 1990.

De la Torre, Adela, and Beatriz M. Pesquera, eds. *Building with Our Hands: New Directions in Chicana Studies*. Berkeley: University of California Press, 1993.

Del Castillo, Adelaida R., ed. *Between Borders: Essays on Mexicana/Chicana History*. Encino, Calif.: Floricanto Press, 1990.

Knaster, Meri. *Women in Spanish America: An Annotated Bibliography from Pre-Conquest to Contemporary Times*. Boston: G. K. Hall, 1977.

Martin, Patricia Preciado. *Songs My Mother Sang to Me: An Oral History of Mexican American Women*. Tucson: University of Arizona Press, 1992.

National Women's History Project. *Las Mujeres: Mexican American/Chicana Women*. Windsor, Calif.: National Women's History Project, 1991.

Padilla, Felix M., and Lourdes Santiago. *Outside the Wall: A Puerto Rican Woman's Struggle*. New Brunswick, N.J.: Rutgers University Press, 1993.

Timberlake, Andrea, et al. *Women of Color and Southern Women: A Bibliography of Social Science Research, 1975 to 1988*. Memphis: Center for the Research on Women, 1988.

Trujillo, Carla, ed. *Chicana Lesbians: The Girls Our Mothers Warned Us About*. Berkeley, Calif.: Third Woman Press, 1991.

Entries by Latino Subgroup or Region of Origin

THE CARIBBEAN

Achiote
Alou family
Alvarez, Julia
Andujar, Joaquín
Babalâo
Bell, George
Caribbean native communities
Caribs
Carty, Rico
Cedeño, César
Dominican Americans
Dominican Republic
Española, La (Hispaniola)
Fernandez, Tony
Foodways, Dominican
Franco, Julio
Garifuna
Geronimo, Cesar
González, José Luis
Guerrero, Pedro
Haitian Americans
Haitian boat people
Lechón
Marichal, Juan
Mofonguitos
Montez, María
Mota, Manny
Music and musicians, Caribbean
Peña, Tony
Santo Domingo emigration
Vodun

CENTRAL AMERICA

American Baptist Churches in the United States v. Thornburgh
Arguello, Alexis
Aztec civilization
Aztlán
Baeza, Braulio
Belizean Americans
Blades, Rubén
Bruca-Novoa, Juan D.
Carew, Rod
Carrera, Barbara
Central American Refugee Center
Chang-Díaz, Franklin Ramón
Chilam Balam, Books of
Cíbola

Comal
Committee in Solidarity with the People of El Salvador
Costa Rican Americans
Dance, Central and South American
Duran, Roberto
Folklore, Central American
Foodways, Central American
Garifuna
Guatemalan Americans
Honduran Americans
Literature, pre-Columbian
Manioc
Martinez, Dennis
Mayan civilization
Mesoamerican native communities
Moreno, Luisa
Mount Pleasant riots
Music and musicians, Central American
North American Indians
Ogilvie, Ben
Olmecs
Pérez-Méndez, Victor
Pincay, Laffit, Jr.
Popol Vuh
Quelite
Quetzalcóatl
Religion, Mesoamerican
Repartimiento system
Rescate, El
Salvadoran Americans
Sanctuary movement
Sarape
Velasquez, Jorge Luis, Jr.
Zambos

CUBA

Afro-Cubans
Alfonso, Carlos
Algaze, Mario
Alonso, Maria Conchita
Arenas, Reinaldo
Arnaz, Desi, Sr.
Art, Cuban American
Azaceta, Luis Cruz
Azpiazú, Don
Balseros
Barrera, Lazaro Sosa

Bay of Pigs invasion
Bencomo, Mario
Bolero
Bongos
Boza, Juan
Bujones, Fernando
Cabrera, Lydia
Calle Ocho
Calle Ocho Open House—Carnaval Miami
Campaneris, Bert
Canseco, José
Capablanca, José Raúl
Castro, Fidel
Catalá, Rafael
Centro Español, West Tampa
Cha-cha
Cigar manufacturing
Conga
Conjunto
Cruz, Celia
Cuba
Cuba, Joe
Cuban American Foundation
Cuban American Legal Defense and Education Fund
Cuban American National Foundation
Cuban Americans
Cuban immigration
Cuban Missile Crisis
Cuban Refugee Program
Cuban Revolution
Cuban War of Independence
Danzón
Dihigo, Martin
D'Rivera, Paquito
Estefan, Gloria
Estrada Palma, Tomás
Falero, Emilio
Fernández, Agustín
Fernández, Joseph A.
Fernández, Roberto
Florit, Eugenio
Folklore, Cuban
Foodways, Cuban American
Freedom Airlift
Fusco, Coco
García, Cristina

Escalona, Beatriz
Esparza, Moctezuma Díaz
Espinosa, Paul
Esquivel, Laura
Estrada, Leobardo
Fábregas, Virginia
Fajita
Family life—Spanish borderlands
Farah Strike
Farolito
Favela, Ricardo
Félix, María
Fender, Freddy
Fernández, Manuel José "Manny"
Fernandez, Rudy
Festival of the Flowers
Fiesta de los Remedios
Fiesta de San Juan de los Lagos
Fiesta of Our Lady of Guadalupe
Flauta
Flores, Patricio Fernández
Flores, Tom
Flores Magón, Ricardo
Flores Salinas, Juan
Folklore, Mexican American
Foodways, Mexican American
Foreign Miners' Tax Law
Four, Los
Freighters, Mexican
Fresquez, Carlos
Frijoles refritos
Fuentes, Carlos
Fuentes, Juan R.
Fur trade
Furniture
Gabacho
Gadsden Purchase
Galarza, Ernesto
Gallinas de la tierra
Gallup incident
Gálvez, Daniel
Gamboa, Diane
Gamboa, Harry, Jr.
Gamio, Manuel
Gandert, Miguel Adrian
García, Gus C.
García, Héctor Pérez
Garcia, Jerome John "Jerry"
García, Rupert
García Diego y Moreno, Francisco
Garriga, Mariano Simon
Garza, Catarino
Garza, Reynaldo
Gaston, Cito
Gomes, Lloyd H.

Gómez-Peña, Guillermo
Gómez-Quiñones, Juan
Gonsalves, Paul
Gonzales, Pancho
Gonzáles, Rodolfo "Corky"
González, Adalberto Elías
González, Genaro
González, Henry Barbosa
González, Myrtle
González, Pedro J.
González, Ray
González Parsons, Lucía
Gorras Blancas
Gran Círculo de Obreros de México
Gran Liga Mexicanista de
    Beneficiencia y Protección, La
Grape boycotts
Grito de Dolores, El
Gronk
Guacamole
Gutiérrez, José Ángel
Gutierrez, Sidney
Guzmán, Ralph C.
Guzmán Aguilera, Antonio
H-2 provision
Hacendado
Hacienda system
Hanigan trials
Harrison, Gloria Macías
Hernández, Antonia
Hernández, Ester
Hernandez, Keith
Herrera, Efren
Herrera, Juan Felipe
Herrera, Miguel
Herrera-Sobek, María
Hidalgo y Costilla, Miguel
Hinojosa, Rolando
Holidays and festivals, Mexican
    American
Huapango
Huerta, Dolores Fernández
Huerta, Jorge
Huesero
Huevos rancheros
Illegals, Los
Inter-Agency Committee on
    Mexican American Affairs
Islas, Arturo, Jr.
Jalapeño
Jarabe tapatío
Jaramillo, Cleofas Martinez
Jaramillo, Mari-Luci
Jaramillo, Pedro
Jarocho

Jiménez, Leonardo "Flaco"
Jiménez, Luis Alfonso, Jr.
Jordan, Steve
Jornaleros
Jurado, Katy
Kahlo, Frida
Kapp, Joseph Robert
Kerr, Louise Año Nuevo
Kid Frost
King Ranch
Kino, Eusebio Francisco
Kit Carson National Forest takeover
Land Act of 1851
Land tenure issues
L'Archeveque, Sostenes
Latin Breed
Lazaro, Ladislas
Leal, Luis
Legal system, Spanish/Mexican
    colonial
Liga Obrera de Habla Español
Limón, José Arcadio
Lincoln County War
Literatura chicanesca
Literature, Mexican American
Little Joe and the Latinaires
Llorona, La
Lobos, Los
Lomas Garza, Carmen
Lomelí, Francisco
Lopez, Aurelio
López, Ignacio
López, José Dolores
Lopez, Nancy
López, Trinidad "Trini"
López, Yolanda
López del Castillo, Gerardo
Low riders and low riding
Loyalist
Lozano, Ignacio Eugenio, Sr.
Lucas, María Elena
Luján, Gilbert Sánchez
Luján, Manuel, Jr.
McLish, Rachel Livia Elizondo
Madrugadores, Los
Malinche, La
Manuel, Herschel Thurman
Maquiladoras
Maravilla
March to Austin
March to Sacramento
Mares, Michael Allen
Mariachi
Mariachi Los Camperos de Nati
    Cano

Venegas, Daniel
Verdugo, Elena
Villa, Francisco "Pancho"
Villagrá, Gaspar Pérez de
Villalongín, Carlos
Villalpando, Catalina Vasquez
Villanueva, Daniel "Danny"
Villanueva, Tino
Villarreal, José Antonio
Villarreal family
Villaseñor, Victor Edmundo
Viramontes, Helena María
Wetback
Ximenes, Vicente Treviño
Yañez, Agustín
Zambrano, Sergio
Zapata, Carmen
Zapata, Emiliano
Zavala, Lorenzo de
Zavella, Patricia

PUERTO RICO
Acosta-Belén, Edna
Albizu, Olga
Albizu Campos, Pedro
Alcapurrias
Algarín, Miguel
Alomar family
Armiño, Franca de
Art, Puerto Rican
Arzola, Marina
Asopao
Ataque
Bacalaitos
Badillo, Herman
Baldorioty de Castro, Román
Barbosa, José Celso
Barretto, Ray
Bendito
Betances, Ramón Emeterio
Bithorn, Hiram
Bomba
Bonilla, Frank
Boricua
Borinquen
Bracetti, Mariana
Burgos, Julia de
Campeche, José
Cancel Miranda, Rafael
Capetillo, Luisa
Carrero, Jaime
Cepeda, Orlando
Clemente, Roberto
Collazo, Oscar
Colón, Jesús

Colón, Miriam
Colón, William Anthony "Willie"
Concepción de Gracia, Gilberto
Constitutional Convention of Puerto
    Rico
Cordero, Ángel Tomás, Jr.
Cotto-Thorner, Guillermo
Cruz, Nicky
Cruz, Victor Hernández
Danza
De Diego, José
Díaz, Justino
Díaz Valcárcel, Emilio
Elizondo, Hector
Escobar, Sixto
Esteves, Sandra María
Evelina Lopez Antonetty Puerto
    Rican Research Collection
Falcon, Angelo
Federación Libre de los
    Trabajadores
Feliciano, José Monserrate
Fernandez, Carole Fragoza
Fernández, Joseph A.
Fernández, Ricardo
Ferre, Luis A.
Ferre, Maurice Antonio
Ferré, Rosario
Ferrer, Fernando
Ferrer, José Vicente
Fiesta de San Juan
Figueroa Cordero, Andrés
Figueroa family
Fitzpatrick, Joseph
Flores, Juan
Folklore, Puerto Rican
Fomento
Foodways, Puerto Rican
Foraker Act
Fuerzas Armadas de Liberación
    Nacional
García, Roberto
García-Ramis, Magali
García Rivera, Oscar
González, José Luis
González-Irizarry, Aníbal
Grito de Lares, El
Habichuelas
Harlem riots
Hermandades
Hernández, Guillermo "Willie"
Hernández, Juano
Hidalgo, Hilda
Holidays and festivals, Puerto Rican
Homar, Lorenzo

Hostos y Bonilla, Eugenio María de
Institute for Puerto Rican Policy
Jíbaro
Jones Act
Jones-Costigan Act
Jueyes
Julia, Raúl
Kanellos, Nicolás
Labarthe, Pedro Juan
Laguerre, Enrique A.
Laviera, Jesús Abraham "Tato"
Lebrón Soto, Lolita
Literature, Puerto Rican
Llorens Torres, Luis
Luis, Juan
Maldonado-Denis, Manuel
Mari Brás, Juan
Marqués, René
Martorell, Antonio
Matos Paoli, Francisco
Mauricio Gaston Institute for Latino
    Community Development and
    Public Policy
Meléndez, Edwin
Menudo
Millan, Felix
Mohr, Nicholasa
Morales, Esai
Morales, Noro
Moreno, Rita
Movimiento Pro Independencia
Muñoz Marín, Luis
Muñoz Rivera, Luis
National Conference of Puerto
    Rican Women
National Congress for Puerto Rican
    Rights
National Puerto Rican Coalition
National Puerto Rican Forum
Novello, Antonia Coello
Nuyorican Poets' Café
Nuyoricans
Oller, Francisco
O'Neill, Gonzalo
Operation Bootstrap
Ortiz, Carlos
Ortiz, Vilma
Ortiz Cofer, Judith
Osorio, Carlos
Palés Matos, Luis
Palmieri, Carlos Manuel "Charlie"
Pantoja, Antonia
Paoli family
Partido Autonomista
Partido Estadista Republicano

Fiestas patrias
Filipinos
Filmmaking and filmmakers
Filmography (appendix)
Flamenco
Flan
Florida
Folk arts and crafts
Folk medicine
Forty-eighters
Fourteenth Amendment
Gachupín
Galleries and museums
Games and toys
Gandules
Gangs and gang activity
Garbanzo
Garza v. County of Los Angeles,
    California Board of Supervisors
Gazpacho
Gender roles
Gentrification
Gerrymandering
Gold and silver rushes, Colorado
Gold rush, California
Golf
Good Neighbor Policy
Graffiti
Graham v. Richardson
Grassroots organizations
Greaser
Great Society programs
Green card
Gringo
Guadalupe, Virgin of
Guava
Guineos
Güiro
Guitarrista
Hawaii
Health and illness
Health care policy
Herbal medicine
Hermanas, Las
Hernández v. New York
Hernández v. Texas
Higher education
Hispanic
Hispanic Academy of Media Arts
    and Sciences
Hispanic American Festival
Hispanic Health and Nutrition
    Examination Survey
Hispanic Heritage Awards
Hispanic Heritage Festival

Hispanic Heritage Month
Hispanic Music Association
Hispanic National Bar Association
Hispanic Policy Development
    Project
Hispanic Radio Network
Hispanic Walk of Fame
Hispanics in Public Radio
Homestead Act
Horchata
Houston, Texas
Huelga
Hypertension
Illegal alien
Illegitimacy
Immigration Act of 1917
Immigration Act of 1924
Immigration Act of 1990
Immigration and Nationality Act of
    1952
Immigration and Nationality Act of
    1965
Immigration and Naturalization
    Service
Immigration legislation, U.S.
Immigration Reform and Control
    Act of 1986
Imperialism
Income and wage levels
Indígenas
Industrial Areas Foundation
Industrial Workers of the World
Infant mortality
Intelligence testing
Inter-American Music Festival
Intermarriage
Internal colonialism
International Ladies' Garment
    Workers' Union
Jai alai
Jews
Journalism
Justice for Janitors
Kachinas
Kansas
Labor force, Latinas in the
Labor force, Latinos in the
Labor-Management Relations Act
Labor unionism
Ladino
Language bias, history of
Laredo, Texas
Latin jazz
Latin rock
Latina writers

Latinas, history and issues of
Latino National Political Survey
Latino World Festival
Latinos
Latins Anonymous
Lau v. Nichols
Law enforcement and the Latino
    community
League of United Latin American
    Citizens
League of United Latin American
    Citizens v. Pasadena Independent
    School District
Liberation theology
Libraries and archives
Life cycle customs
Liga Femenil
Liga Protectora Latina
Literacy and illiteracy
Literary history and criticism
Literature, American, Latinos in
Los Angeles, California
Los Angeles riots
Louisiana
Ludlow Massacre
Machismo
Maize
Manifest Destiny
Mano
Maracas
Marianismo
Marimba
Marketing and advertising
Masa
Matachines
Matthews v. Díaz
Medicine, pre-Columbian
Medrano v. Allee
Melting pot theory
Méndez v. Westminster School
    District
Mental health
Merienda
Mestizaje
Mestizo
Metate
Miami, Florida
Midwest
Midwest Voter Registration
    Education Project
Migra
Migrant education
Migrant Health Act
Migrant labor
Military participation

Entries by Subject

LITERATURE AND THE MEDIA

Cortés, Hernán
Cortina, Juan
Cuban Missile Crisis
Cuban Revolution
Cuban War of Independence
Fuerzas Armadas de Liberación
  Nacional
Gálvez, Bernardo de
Garza, Catarino
Gomes, Lloyd H.
Grito de Dolores, El
Grito de Lares, El
Grito de Yara, El
Guevara, Che
L'Archeveque, Sostenes
León, Alonso de
Loyalist
Martí, José
Mexican American War
Mexican Revolution
Mexican War for Independence
Military participation
Pershing Expedition
Plan de San Diego
Popé's Revolt
Salcedo, Manuel María de
San Jacinto, Battle of
San Pascual, Battle of
Santa Fe Expedition
Selective Service Act of 1917
Sixty-fifth Infantry Regiment
Soldaderas, Las
Spanish-American War
Spanish Conquest
Taos Rebellion
Texas Rangers
Texas Revolt
Ugarte y Loyola, Jacobo
Vargas, Diego
Velázquez, Loreta Janeta
Villa, Francisco "Pancho"
Villarreal family

MUSIC. *See* PERFORMING AND VISUAL ARTS; CUSTOMS AND TRADITIONS

ORGANIZATIONS
Agricultural unions
Alianza Hispano-Americana
Alliance for Progress
American G.I. Forum
Asociación Nacional Pro Personas
  Mayores
Bilingual Foundation for the Arts

Bishop's Committee for the
  Spanish-Speaking Peoples
Brown Berets
Catholic Youth Organization
Católicos por la Raza
Central American Refugee Center
Centro Asturiano
Centro de Acción Autónoma-
  Hermandad General de
  Trabajadores
Centro de la Raza
Centro Español, West Tampa
Coalition for Humane Immigrant
  Rights of Los Angeles
Comisión Femenil Mexicana
  Nacional
Committee in Solidarity with the
  People of El Salvador
Communities Organized for Public
  Service
Community Service Organization
Congressional Hispanic Caucus
Cuban American Foundation
East Los Angeles Community
  Union, The
Farm Labor Organizing Committee
Federación Libre de los Trabajadores
Fomento
Gran Liga Mexicanista de
  Beneficiencia y Protección, La
Grassroots organizations
Hermanas, Las
Hermandades
Hispanic Academy of Media Arts
  and Sciences
Hispanic National Bar Association
Hispanic Policy Development
  Project
Immigration and Naturalization
  Service
Industrial Areas Foundation
Institute for Puerto Rican Policy
International Ladies' Garment
  Workers' Union
Justice for Janitors
League of United Latin American
  Citizens
Liga Femenil
Liga Obrera de Habla Español
Liga Protectora Latina
Mexican-American
  Anti-Defamation Committee
Mexican American Bar Association
Mexican American Legal Defense
  and Education Fund

Mexican American Movement
Mexican American Political
  Association
Mexican American Unity Council
Mexican American Women's
  National Association
Mexican American Youth
  Organization
Midwest Voter Registration
  Education Project
Mothers of East L.A.
Movimiento Estudiantil Chicano de
  Aztlán
Movimiento Pro Independencia
Mujeres Activas en Letras y Cambio
  Social
Mutualistas
National Agricultural Workers Union
National Alliance of Spanish-
  Speaking People for Equality
National Association of
  Cuban-American Women
National Association of Hispanic
  Journalists
National Association of Hispanic
  Publications
National Association of Latino
  Elected and Appointed Officials
National Chicano Health
  Organization
National Coalition of Hispanic
  Health and Human Services
  Organizations (appendix)
National Conference of Puerto
  Rican Women
National Congress for Puerto Rican
  Rights
National Council of Hispanic
  Women
National Council of La Raza
National Farm Labor Union
National Farm Workers Association
National Hispanic Media Coalition
National Puerto Rican Coalition
National Puerto Rican Forum
Nosotros
Organizations (appendix)
Partido Autonomista
Partido Estadista Republicano
Partido Independentista
  Puertorriqueño
Partido Liberal Mexicano
Partido Nacionalista de Puerto Rico
Partido Popular Democratico
Partido Revolucionario Cubano

Partido Revolucionario Institucional
Political Association of Spanish
   Speaking Organizations
Political organizations
Porto Rican Brotherhood of America
Puerto Rican Association for
   Community Affairs
Puerto Rican Bar Association
Puerto Rican Community
   Development Project
Puerto Rican Legal Defense and
   Education Fund
Raza Unida Party, La
Republican National Hispanic
   Assembly of the United States
Rescate, El
Select Commission on Immigration
   and Refugee Policy
Sociedad Progresista Mexicana
Society of Hispanic Professional
   Engineers
Sons of America
Southwest Voter Registration
   Education Project
Spanish American League Against
   Discrimination
Spanish-Speaking People's
   Division, Office of
   Inter-American Affairs
Spanish Speaking Unity Council
Texas Good Neighbor Commission
Texas Rangers
Unión Patriótica Benéfica Mexicana
   Independiente
United Mexican American Students
Volunteers in Service to America
Young Lords

PERFORMING AND VISUAL
ARTS

Aceves, José
Acosta, Manuel Gregorio
Aguilera-Hellweg, Max
Alacranes Mojados, Los
Albizu, Olga
Alfonso, Carlos
Algaze, Mario
Alicia, Juana
Alienz, The
Almeida, Laurindo
Alonso, Maria Conchita
Alurista
Alvarez, Cecilia Concepción
Annual Awards in the Hispanic Arts
Aragón, José Rafael

Architecture and architects
Areito
Armendáriz, Pedro
Armiño, Franca de
Arnaz, Desi, Sr.
Arriola, Gustavo Montaño
Art, Cuban American
Art, Latin American
Art, Mexican American
Art, Puerto Rican
Art, Spanish American
ASCO
Astol, Lalo
Ávalos, David
Azaceta, Luis Cruz
Azpiazú, Don
Baca, Judith F.
Báez, Joan Chandos
Barbieri, Leandro J. "Gato"
Barela, Patrocinio
Barraza, Santa
Barretto, Ray
Barrio, Raymond
Beltrán, Lola
Bencomo, Mario
Bilingual Foundation for the Arts
Blades, Rubén
Bolero
Bomba
Bongos
Bossa nova
Botero, Fernando
Boza, Juan
Buitron, Robert
Bujones, Fernando
Burciaga, José Antonio
Campeche, José
Campusano, Jesús "Chuy"
Canción
Cantinflas
Carpas
Carr, Vikki
Carrasco, Barbara
Carrera, Barbara
Carrillo, Eduardo
Carrillo, Leo
Casas, Melesio, II
Castanets
Cervántez, Yreina
Cha-cha
Charango
Chávez, Eduardo Arcenio
Chicano, El
Chicano Film Festival
Chicano Park

Cid, Armando
Cisneros, Evelyn
Colón, Miriam
Colón, William Anthony "Willie"
Comedia
Con safos
Conga
Conjunto
Contradanza
Córdova, Arturo de
Corridos
Cortéz, Ricardo
Cruz, Celia
Cuatro
Cuba, Joe
Cugat, Xavier
Cumbia
Dance, Central and South American
Dance, Mexican American
Dance, Spanish
Daniels, Bebe
Danza
Danza de los viejitos
Décima
Del Rio, Dolores
Desiga, Daniel
De Soto, Rosana
Devil dance
Díaz, Justino
Dr. Loco's Rockin' Jalapeño Band
Domingo, Placido
Don Francisco
D'Rivera, Paquito
Duardo, Richard
Elizondo, Hector
Enriquez, Gaspar
Enriquez, Rene
Escalona, Beatriz
Esparza, Moctezuma Díaz
Espinosa, Paul
Estefan, Gloria
Fábregas, Virginia
Falero, Emilio
Fandango
Favela, Ricardo
Feliciano, José Monserrate
Félix, María
Fender, Freddy
Fernández, Agustín
Fernández, Royes
Fernandez, Rudy
Ferrer, José Vicente
Figueroa family
Filmmaking and filmmakers
Filmography (appendix)

Pastorius, Jaco
Paternosto, César Pedro
Patlán, Raymond M.
Pelli, Cesar
Peña, Amado Maurilio, Jr.
Peña, Elizabeth
Perez, Pedro
Pérez, Ruby Nelda
Photography
Piazzola, Astor
Piñero, Miguel
Ponce de León, Michael
Porter, Liliana
Poster art
Pottery and ceramics
Pous, Arquímides
Pozo y Gonzáles, Luciano "Chano"
Prado, Pérez
Prinze, Freddie
Puente, Tito
Puerto Rican Dance Theatre
Puerto Rican Traveling Theater
Purim, Flora
Quena
Quesada, Eugenio
Quinn, Anthony
Quiñones, Wanda Maria
Quirarte, Jacinto
Ramírez, Joel Tito
Ranchera music
Raya, Marcos
Religious art
Renaldo, Duncan
Revista
Rivera, Chita
Rivera, Diego
Rivera, Geraldo
Rivera, Graciela
Riverón, Enrique
Roche Rabell, Arnaldo
Rodríguez, Arsenio
Rodríguez, Beatriz
Rodriguez, Patricia
Rodríguez, Paul
Rodríguez, Peter
Roland, Gilbert
Romance
Romero, César
Romero, Frank
Ronstadt, Linda Marie
Rosario, Hector
Rubalcaba, Gonzalo
Ruíz, Caribe
Salinas, Baruj
Salinas, Porfirio, Jr.

Samba
San Juan, Olga
Sanchez, Ildefonso "Poncho"
Sanromá, Jesús María
Santamaría, Ramón "Mongo"
Santana, Carlos
Santos and santo art
Sculpture and sculptors
Secada, Jon
Selena
Serra, Richard
Serrano, Andrés
Sheen family
Sheila E.
Sierra, Paul Alberto
Sierra, Rubén
Siqueiros, David Alfaro
Smits, Jimmy
Solís, Gloria
Son
Sori, Susana
Soto, Jorge
Sunny and the Sunliners
Tacla, Jorge
Tamayo, Rufino
Tango
Tanguma, Leo
Tapia, Luis
Teatro Campesino
Teatro de la Esperanza
Teatro Nacional de Aztlán
Tejano Conjunto Festival
Tejano Music Awards
Texas Folklife Festival
Texas Tornados
Theater and drama, Cuban American
Theater and drama, Latin American
Theater and drama, Mexican
    American
Theater and drama, Puerto Rican
Tigres del Norte, Los
Timbales
Tiple
Tirado, Romualdo
Tizol, Juan
Tjader, Cal
Treviño, Jesús Salvador
Trio Borinquen
Trio los Panchos
Trova
Trujillo Herrera, Rafael
Tucson International Mariachi
    Conference
Urueta, Cordelia
Vacunao

Valadez, John
Valdez, Luis Miguel
Valens, Ritchie
Valse
Vando Rodriguez, Erasmo
Varo, Remedios
Vega, Salvador
Velázquez, Juan Ramon
Velez, Eddie
Velez, Lupe
Verdugo, Elena
Villalongín, Carlos
Welch, Raquel
Zambrano, Sergio
Zampoña
Zapata, Carmen
Zarzuela

POLITICS AND GOVERNMENT
Adams-Onís Treaty
Affirmative action
Aguilar, Robert Peter
Alatorre, Richard
Albizu Campos, Pedro
Allen v. State Board of Elections
Alvarado, Juan Bautista
Anarco-syndicalism
Anaya, Toney
Apodaca, Jerry
Armijo, Manuel
Avila, Joaquín
Ayuntamiento
Baca-Barragán, Polly
Badillo, Herman
Baldorioty de Castro, Román
Bandini de Couts, Ysidora
Bañuelos, Romana Acosta
Barbosa, José Celso
Barela, Casimiro
Bay of Pigs invasion
Becerra, Xavier
Benavides, Santos
Betances, Ramón Emeterio
Bonilla, Rubén "Tony"
Bracetti, Mariana
Cabello, Domingo
Cabeza de Baca family
Cabinet Committee on
    Opportunities for Spanish
    Speaking People
Cacique
California
Cancel Miranda, Rafael
Castillo, Leonel Javier
Castro, Fidel

Telles, Raymond L., Jr.
Texas Revolt
Tolan Committee hearings
Torres, Art
Torres, Esteban Edward
Torres-Gil, Fernando
Trist, Nicholas
Urueta, Cordelia
Valdés, Jorge E.
Vallejo family
Vasconcelos, José
Velez, Ramón S.
Villa, Francisco "Pancho"
Villalpando, Catalina Vasquez
Visitador
Viva Kennedy clubs
Volunteers in Service to America
Voting rights
Voting Rights Act of 1965
Voting Rights Act of 1970
Voting Rights Acts of 1975 and 1982
White House Conference on
   Hispanic Affairs
Women's suffrage
Works Progress Administration
Ximenes, Vicente Treviño
Young Lords
Zavala, Lorenzo de

PREJUDICE, DISCRIMINATION, ASSIMILATION, AND INTERGROUP RELATIONS

Abejeños
Acculturation versus assimilation
Affirmative action
Agringado
Albuquerque Walkout
Americanization programs
Anglo
Antivagrancy Act
Baca, Elfego
Biculturalism
Black Legend
Bolillo
Border region and culture
Brown Scare
Busing
California
Californios
Cholo
Cisneros v. Corpus Christi Independent School District
Colonia
Cortez, Gregorio

Criminal justice system
Cultural conflict
Cultural democracy
Cultural exchange
Cultural nationalism
Cultural pluralism
Delgado v. Bastrop Independent School District
Discrimination, bigotry, and
   prejudice against Latinos
English language acquisition
English-only controversy
Ethnic identity
Foreign Miners' Tax Law
Gabacho
Gachupín
Gente de razón
Good Neighbor Policy
Gorras Blancas
Gran Liga Mexicanista de
   Beneficiencia y Protección, La
Greaser
Gringo
Harlem riots
Intermarriage
Internal colonialism
Language bias, history of
L'Archeveque, Sostenes
Law enforcement and the Latino
   community
Melting pot theory
Mexican-American
   Anti-Defamation Committee
Minority group status of Latinos
Multicultural education
Multiculturalism
Murieta, Joaquín
Pan Americanism
Pocho
Police brutality
Puerto Rican nationalism
Racism
Raza, La
Rumford Act
Salt War
Segovia, Josefa
Segregation, desegregation, and
   integration
Skin color
Slavery
Sleepy Lagoon case
Social bandits
Spanish American League Against
   Discrimination
Stereotypes of Latinas

Stereotypes of Latinos
Tío Taco
Vendido
Wetback

RADIO. *See* **LITERATURE AND THE MEDIA**

REGIONS OF ORIGIN
Archaeology
Argentinean Americans
Aztec civilization
Aztlán
Belizean Americans
Boricua
Borinquen
Brazilian Americans
Caribbean native communities
Cuba
Cuban War of Independence
Dieciséis de Septiembre
Dominican Republic
El Paso, Texas, and Ciudad Juárez,
   Mexico
Jarocho
Mayan civilization
Mesoamerican native communities
Mexican War for Independence
Mexico
Mythical biography
Olmecs
Pimería Alta
Puerto Rico
Puerto Rico—status debate
Sonora
South American native communities
Spain
Tenochtitlán
Teotihuacán
Tijuana, Mexico

RELIGION AND RELIGIOUS ISSUES
Alabado
Altars, home
Argüello, Concepción
Babalâo
Bandini de Couts, Ysidora
Bishop's Committee for the
   Spanish-Speaking Peoples
Botánicas
Brujo
Bultos
Camino Real, El
Carnaval

Chicano movement
Chicano Youth Liberation
  Conference
Comisión Femenil Mexicana
  Nacional
Communities Organized for Public
  Service
Community Service Organization
Con safos
Crusade for Justice
Cuban Revolution
Delano Grape Strike
Dieciséis de Septiembre
East Los Angeles riot
Favela, Ricardo
Feminism and the women's
  movement
Figueroa Cordero, Andrés
Flores Magón, Ricardo
Flores Salinas, Juan
Fuerzas Armadas de Liberación
  Nacional
Gallup incident
Gangs and gang activity
Garza, Catarino
Gaston, Mauricio
Gentrification
Gerrymandering
Gonzáles, Rodolfo "Corky"
González, Pedro J.
González Parsons, Lucía
Gorras Blancas
Graffiti
Great Society programs
Grito de Dolores, El
Grito de Lares, El
Grito de Yara, El
Guevara, Che
Gutiérrez, José Ángel
Hidalgo, Hilda
Hidalgo y Costilla, Miguel
Kit Carson National Forest takeover
Latinas, history and issues of
Lebrón Soto, Lolita
Liberation theology
Los Angeles riots
March to Austin
March to Sacramento
Martí, José
Melville, Margarita Bradford
Mendoza, Hope
Mexican Revolution
Morín, Raul R.
Mothers of East L.A.
Mount Pleasant riots

Movimiento Estudiantil Chicano de
  Aztlán
Multiculturalism
National Chicano Moratorium on
  Vietnam
New Mexico Rebellion
Olivares, Luis
Padres Asociados por Derechos
  Religiosos, Educativos, y Sociales
Plan Espiritual de Aztlán, El
Political activism
Ruiz Belvis, Segundo
Sanctuary movement
Sinarquista movement
Social bandits
Socialism
Student movement
Tagging and taggers
Tecatos
Tierra Amarilla
Tijerina, Reies López
Tortilla Curtain Incident
United Mexican American Students
United Neighborhoods Organization
Vando Rodriguez, Erasmo
Vásquez, Tiburcio
Velásquez, William
Villarreal family
Viva Kennedy clubs
Vivó, Paquita
Zapata, Emiliano

SPORTS
Alomar family
Alou family
Andujar, Joaquín
Aparicio, Luis Ernesto
Arguello, Alexis
Avila, Bobby
Baeza, Braulio
Barrera, Lazaro Sosa
Baseball
Bell, George
Bithorn, Hiram
Boxing
Bueno, María Ester Audion
Campaneris, Bert
Canseco, José
Capablanca, José Raúl
Carbajal, Michael
Carew, Rod
Carrera de Gallos
Carty, Rico
Casals, Rosemary
Cedeño, César

Cepeda, Orlando
Chacón, Bobby
Charreada
Charro
Chávez, Julio César
Clemente, Roberto
Concepción, Dave
Cordero, Ángel Tomás, Jr.
De la Hoya, Oscar
Dihigo, Martin
Duran, Roberto
Escobar, Sixto
Fernández, Manuel José "Manny"
Fernandez, Tony
Flores, Tom
Franco, Julio
Galarraga, Andres
Gaston, Cito
Geronimo, Cesar
Golf
Gomez, Lefty
Gomez, Preston
Gonzales, Pancho
Guerrero, Pedro
Hernández, Guillermo "Willie"
Hernandez, Keith
Herrera, Efren
Jai alai
Kapp, Joseph Robert
Lopez, Alfonso Ramon
Lopez, Aurelio
Lopez, Nancy
Luque, Dolf
McLish, Rachel Livia Elizondo
Marichal, Juan
Martinez, Dennis
Mendez, José
Millan, Felix
Minoso, Minnie
Morales, Pedro Pablo, Jr.
Mota, Manny
Muñoz, Michael Anthony
Ogilvie, Ben
Oliva, Tony
Olmedo, Alejandro "Alex"
Ortiz, Carlos
Ortiz, Manuel
Palomino, Carlos
Pascual, Camilo Alberto
Pelé
Peña, Tony
Perez, Tony
Pincay, Laffit, Jr.
Plunkett, Jim
Ramírez, Raul Carlos

THE
LATINO
ENCYCLOPEDIA

INDEX

Page numbers in italics refer to photographs.